Dance Discourses

Dance Discourses collects together original writings from an international community of renowned dance scholars who engage different theoretical perspectives and methodologies to establish a framework for the study of dance. There are contributions from:

- Inge Baxmann
- Ramsay Burt
- Thomas F. DeFrantz
- Susan Leigh Foster
- Susanne Franco
- Mark Franko
- Isabelle Ginot
- Andrée Grau
- Laure Guilbert
- Yvonne Hardt
- Nathalie Lecomte
- Susan Manning
- Hélène Marquié
- Marina Nordera
- Linda J. Tomko

The book is divided into three sections, each structured around a keyword and key topic in current dance scholarship. The essays cover genres such as modern and contemporary dance, *ballet d'action* and *ballet de cour*, and themes such as politics, gender and identity. This invaluable collection will appeal to scholars and students interested in exploring new directions for dance research.

Susanne Franco teaches dance history at the University IUAV of Venice, Italy.

Marina Nordera is Professor and Chair of the Dance Department at Nice University, France.

Dance Discourses

Keywords in dance research

Edited by
Susanne Franco and
Marina Nordera

In conjunction with the Centre national de la danse

LONDON AND NEW YORK

First published 2007
by Routledge
2 Park Square, Milton Park, Abingdon, Oxon OX14 4RN

Simultaneously published in the USA and Canada
by Routledge
270 Madison Ave, New York, NY 10016

Routledge is an imprint of the Taylor & Francis Group, an informa business

Essays by Inge Baxmann, Susanne Franco, Isabelle Ginot, Andrée Grau, Laure Guilbert, Nathalie Lecomte, Hélène Marquié and Marina Nordera have been translated by Marlene Klein

Typeset in Baskerville by
Florence Production Ltd, Stoodleigh, Devon
Printed and bound in Great Britain by
MPG Books Ltd, Bodmin

British Library Cataloguing in Publication Data
A catalogue record for this book is available from the British Library

Library of Congress Cataloging in Publication Data
Discorsi della danza. English
Dance discourses: keywords for dance research/edited by Susanne Franco and Marina Nordera in conjunction with the Centre National de la Danse.
p. cm.
Includes bibliographical references and index.
1. Dance – Research – Methodology. I. Franco, Susanne, 1969– II. Nordera, Marina. III. Centre national de la danse (France) IV. Title.
GV1589.D5716 2007
792.8072–dc22 2007006631

ISBN10: 0–415–42308–2 (hbk)
ISBN10: 0–415–42309–0 (pbk)

ISBN13: 978–0–415–42308–3 (hbk)
ISBN13: 978–0–415–42309–0 (pbk)

Contents

Illustrations

Figures

Tables

Notes on contributors

Inge Baxmann is Professor in the Department of Theater Sciences at the University of Leipzig. Her publications include *Die Feste der Französischen Revolution. Inszenierung von Gesellschaft als Natur* (Weinheim, Basel: Beltz, 1989); *Mythos Gemeinschaft: Körper und Tanzkulturen in der Moderne* (Munich: Wilhelm Fink Verlag, 2000); with Franz Anton Cramer, *Deutungsräume. Bewegungswissen als kulturelles Archiv der Moderne* (Munich: K-Kieser, 2005); and with Claire Rousier and Patrizia Veroli, *Les Archives Internationales de la Danse* (Pantin: Centre national de la danse, 2006).

Ramsay Burt is Professor at De Montfort University (UK). He is the author of *The Male Dancer: Bodies, Spectacle, Sexualities* (London and New York: Routledge, 1995); *Alien Bodies: Representations of Modernity, "Race," and Gender in Early Modern Dance* (London and New York: Routledge, 1998); and *Judson Dance Theater: Performative Traces* (London and New York: Routledge, 2006).

Thomas F. DeFrantz teaches at the University of Stanford and is Associate Professor at the Massachusetts Institute of Technology. He has also taught the history of dance program at the Alvin Ailey School for many years. He is the editor of *Dancing Many Drums: Excavations in African American Dance* (Madison, WI: University of Wisconsin Press, 2002) and the author of *Dancing Revelations: Alvin Ailey's Embodiment of African American Culture* (Oxford University Press, 2003).

Susan Leigh Foster is Professor in the Department of World Arts and Cultures at the University of California, Los Angeles. She is the author of *Reading Dancing: Bodies and Subject in Contemporary American Dance* (Berkeley, CA: University of California Press, 1986); *Choreography and Narrative: Ballet's Staging of Story and Desire* (Bloomington, IN: Indiana University Press, 1996); and *Dances that Describe Themselves: The Improvised*

Choreography of Richard Bull (Middletown, CT: Wesleyan University Press, 2002). She is the editor of *Choreographing History* (Bloomington, IN: Indiana University Press, 1995) and *Corporealities: Dancing, Knowledge, Culture and Power* (London and New York: Routledge, 1996).

Susanne Franco teaches dance history at University IUAV of Venice, Faculty of Arts and Design and has taught at the Institut d'études théâtrales of the University La Sorbonne Nouvelle Paris III and at the Dance Department of Nice University. She has edited, with Marina Nordera, *I discorsi della danza. Parole chiave per una metodologia della ricerca* (Turin: UTET Libreria, 2005), and more recently *Ausdruckstanz. Il corpo, la danza e la critica*, no. 78, special issue of *Biblioteca Teatrale* (Rome: Bulzoni, 2006). She is the author of *Martha Graham* (Palermo: L'Epos, 2003) and editor of the series *Dance For Word/Dance Forward: Interviste sulla coreografia contemporanea* (Palermo: L'Epos), the first volume of which is her *Frédéric Flamand* (2004). She has been a board member of AIRDanza (Italian Association for Research in Dance) from 2001 to 2004.

Mark Franko is Professor in the Theater Arts Department at the University of California, Santa Cruz. He is the author of *The Dancing Body in Renaissance Choreography* (Birmingham: Summa, 1986); *Dance as Text: Ideologies of the Baroque Body* (Cambridge: Cambridge University Press, 1993); *Dancing Modernism/Performing Politics* (Bloomington, IN: Indiana University Press, 1995); *The Work of Dance: Labor, Movement and Identity in the 1930s* (Middletown, CT: Wesleyan University Press, 2002); *Excursion for Miracles: Paul Sanasardo, Donya Feuer, and Studio for Dance 1955–1964* (Middletown, CT: Wesleyan University Press, 2005). He has also edited, in collaboration with Annette Richards, *Acting on the Past: Historical Performance Across the Disciplines* (Middletown, CT: Wesleyan University Press, 2000) and more recentely *Ritual and Event: Interdisciplinary Perspectives* (London and New York: Routledge, 2007).

Isabelle Ginot is Professor at the Department of Dance at the University of Paris VIII and is a Feldenkrais practitioner. Her primary interest lies in analyzing works of contemporary dance. She is the author of *Dominique Bagouet, un labyrinthe dansé* (Pantin: Centre national de la danse, 1999) and, in collaboration with Marcelle Michel, *La danse au XXème siècle* (Paris: Bordas, 1995; Larousse, 1998/2002).

Andrée Grau teaches at the University of Roehampton in Surrey (UK), where she directs the dance programs. She has published *Eyewitness*

Dance (London: Dorling Kindersley, 1998), translated into French as *Le monde de la danse* (Paris: Gallimard, 1998), and co-edited, with Stephanie Jordan, *Following Sir Fred's Steps: Ashton's Legacy* (London: Dance Books, 1996) and *Europe Dancing: Perspectives on Theatre Dance and Cultural Identity* (London and New York: Routledge, 2000); and with Georgiana Wierre-Gore, *Anthropologie de la danse* (Pantin: Centre national de la danse, 2005).

Laure Guilbert is head of publications at the Paris Opéra. She has taught at the Department of Performing Arts at the University of Metz and at Paris III, and has also completed various research projects for the Cité de la musique and Centre national de la danse. She is the author of *Danser avec le IIIème Reich: les danseurs modernes sous le nazisme* (Complexe: Bruxelles, 2000).

Yvonne Hardt works at the Institute of Theater Sciences of the Freie Universtität in Berlin, where she is collaborating on creating a new dance studies program. She is the author of *Politische Körper: Ausdruckstanz, Choreographien des Protests und die Arbeiterkulturbewegung in der Weimarer Republik* (Münster: LIT Verlag, 2004) and *Sasha Waltz*, part of the series *Dance For Word/Dance Forward: Interviste sulla coreografia contemporanea* (Palermo: L'Epos, 2007). She has edited, with Kirsten Maar, *Tanz – Metropole – Provinz*, special issue of *Jahrbuch der Gesellschaft für Tanzforschung*, vol. 17, Münster: Lit, 2007.

Nathalie Lecomte is an independent researcher and teacher. She acted as an advisor for the *Dictionnaire de la musique en France aux XVIIème et XVIIIème siècles* (Paris: Fayard, 1992) and the *Dictionnaire de la danse* (Paris: Larousse-Bordas, 1999), for which she also edited various entries. She has edited, in collaboration with Laura Naudeix and Jean-Noël Laurenti, *Traité historique de la danse (1754)* by Cahusac (Pantin: Centre national de la danse, 2004) and prepares, with Jerôme de la Gorce, the publication of *La troupe de l'Académie Royale de Musique à Paris (1699–1733) d'après les distributions des livrets*.

Susan Manning is Professor in the Department of English, Theatre and Performance Studies at Northwestern University. She is the author of *Ecstasy and the Demon: Feminism and Nationalism in the Dances of Mary Wigman* (Berkeley, CA: University of California Press, 1993); *Ecstasy and the Demon: The Dances of Mary Wigman* (Minneapolis, MN: University of Minnesota Press, 2nd edn, 2006); and *Modern Dance, Negro Dance: Race in Motion* (Minneapolis, MN: University of Minnesota Press, 2004). She has been the President of the Society of Dance History Scholars.

Hélène Marquié has a Ph.D. in Aesthetics and she has the *Aggregation* in biology. She works on the representations and constructions of social relationships regarding sex, gender and sexuality, and has taught at the Dance Departement of Nice University. She published: "Occuper l'espace, inventer l'espace . . . les espaces de la danse ont-ils un genre?, Les femmes et l'espace," in *Résonances*, no. 7, 2003; *Imaginaires et corps: perspectives et enjeux des recherches sur le genre et recherches féministes en danse*, in *Le genre comme catégorie d'analyse – Sociologie, histoire, littérature*, edited by D. Fougeyrollas-Schwebel, C. Planté, M. Riot-Sarcey and C. Zaidman (Paris: L'Harmattan, 2003).

Marina Nordera is Professor and Chair of the Dance Department and member of the RITM research center at Nice University (France). She has taught early dance and performed early dance (*Il ballarino, Ris et danceries, Fêtes Galantes, L'éventail*). She has been the curator of the exhibition and editor of the catalogue of *La construction de la féminité dans la danse*, held at the Centre national de la danse (2004–5); she edited, with Susanne Franco, *I discorsi della danza. Parole chiave per una metodologia della ricerca* (Turin: UTET Libreria, 2005), and, with Simone Beta, Luciano: *La danza* (Venice: Marsilio, 1992). She has contributed to several collected volumes. She has been president of AIRDanza (Italian Association for Research in Dance) and is currently working on a book on dance and gender in Early Modern Italy (Palermo: L'Epos, forthcoming).

Linda J. Tomko is Associate Professor at the University of California, Riverside. Former president of the Society of Dance History Scholars, she currently directs the collection "Dance and Music" published by Pendragon. She is the author of *Dancing Class: Gender, Ethnicity and Social Divides in American Dance, 1890–1920* (Bloomington, IN: Indiana University Press, 1999).

Acknowledgments

Most of the texts collected in this volume were first presented at the international symposium "Les discours de la danse. Mots-clefs pour une méthodologie de la recherche" held at the Palais des Festivals et des Congrès in Cannes (November 29–December 1 2003) and of which the scientific board was composed of Susanne Franco, Marina Nordera and Claire Rousier. The event was promoted and organized by the Centre national de la danse, the RITM (Centre de recherches sur l'analyse et l'interprétation des textes en musique et dans les arts du spectacle), the Dance Department at Nice University and Adem 06 (Délégation départementale à la musique et à la danse).

We thank Claire Rousier (Director of the Département du développement de la culture chorégraphique) and Michel Sala (General Director) at the Centre national de la danse for granting the rights of the essays by Inge Baxmann, Ramsay Burt, Thomas F. DeFrantz, Susan Leigh Foster, Andrée Grau, Laure Guilbert, Nathalie Lecomte, Susan Manning, and Linda Tomko. We are also grateful to Mark Franko, Isabelle Ginot, Yvonne Hardt and Hélène Marquié who gave permission for us to reproduce their essays for this publication.

The friendliness and enthusiasm of the authors during the preparation of the volume have supported us and proved the existence of a community of scholars willing to cooperate and join forces to make work pleasant and stimulating.

We would particularly like to thank Richard Carlin for the initial support given to this project and Minh Ha Duong and Sue Leaper for their very professional help in bringing it to conclusion. For their advice, suggestions and rereadings we also thank: Stefano Chinellato, Jean Louis Leleu, Lizbeth Langston, and Luisa Passerini. To Patrizia Veroli and Shaul Bassi all our gratitude is not enough for what they did for this project.

Finally, a personal note. The book would not have seen light without the frank intellectual dialogue and the ironic, at times hilarious, way in which we "supervised" each other through several hundred emails, phone calls and chats that have fortified an already profound friendship.

Introduction

Susanne Franco and Marina Nordera

Dance discourses

The development of dance studies has been paralleled by an emerging need to pause and reflect upon the theoretical and methodological premises of dance research and upon the actual limits of the discipline itself. This volume proposes to take another step in the process begun by an international community of scholars engaged in formulating discourses on the making of a discipline. Michel Foucault has written that disciplines are defined as a sort of:

> anonymous system, freely available to whoever wishes, or whoever is able to make use of them, without there being any question of their meaning and their validity being derived from whoever happened to invent them. [. . .] For a discipline to exist, there must be the possibility of formulating – and of doing so ad infinitum – fresh proposition. But there is more, and there is more, probably, in order that there may be less. A discipline is not the sum total of all the truths that may be uttered concerning something; it is not even the total of all that may be accepted, by virtue of some principle of coherence and systematization [. . .] Disciplines constitute a system of control in the production of discourse, fixing its limits through the action of an identity taking the form of a permanent reactivation of the rules.[1]

This book is designed to accompany the formulation and reformulation of discourses and their placement in an appropriate theoretical framework. It has been structured to encourage the discussion of theories and methods through comparison and dialogue, by throwing into play the various perspectives, approaches, and guidelines applicable to research in general and the individual studies in particular.

Toward a research methodology

The epistemological revolution provoked by the advance of critical theory has had a decisive impact on dance research. The exclusively or predominantly aesthetic, historical, philological (when not merely anecdotal) analyses that characterized much prior research have given way to studies privileging the ways in which dance works as an art and/or a social practice, its ideological charge, and its theoretical assumptions. Postmodernism and poststructuralism (and within them deconstruction, feminist and gender studies, postcolonial, philosophical and psychoanalytical criticism, and so forth) created space for subjects such as the body (and not only the dancing body), which had rarely been the subject of academic studies. This was accompanied by a general crisis in traditional disciplinary areas, a contamination of methodological tools, and the questioning of the artist's and the scholar's subjectivity.

Critical theory revealed how traditional disciplines had always presented their subject as eternal and absolute. Once disciplinary boundaries had crumbled in the recognition of their arbitrariness the idea took root that every cultural object had to be studied as a sign to be decoded in relation to a broader spectrum of codes and conventions, leading to the opening of the transdisciplinary field of cultural studies.

Last but not least, critical theory introduced a new language, which has made conversing with traditional disciplinary areas and older generations of scholars difficult. A drastic terminological shift and the adoption of a theoretical jargon seen as self-referential and overriding its subject matter caused great perplexity. Scholars who had been trained within the broad scope of cultural studies found it exciting and stimulating to bring in theoretical concepts and methodological instruments from other disciplinary contexts and apply them to the "subject of dance." Other visions, on the contrary, emphasized the need to find methods and instruments of analysis within dance itself. The former perceived an interdisciplinary approach as a preliminary and unavoidable condition, while the latter saw it as a sort of colonization of a terrain, still considered marginal and thus constitutionally fragile, endowed with its own laws and "original" identity that only a gaze from within could make known.

Opening new prospects

The question we have asked ourselves in our daily work becomes paramount here. Is it possible to think of these apparently contradictory approaches as complementary or reciprocally useful? In other words, can the means that characterize a specific methodology find a place in an interdisciplinary project without losing value? And might they, on the contrary, nurture the goal of never ceasing to ask new questions about dance and its history, an aim all dance scholars share?

The tension between often antithetical positions led us to take into account the factors that condition the respective ways of thinking and of doing research.

Coming back to Foucault, to what degree does the development of a discipline and the discourses it implies have to reckon with the restrictive and constrictive function implicit in its own definition? In the way that, as Susan Foster points out, the "reconstruction of historical bodies, one that presents them as political, aesthetic, and also consummately physical entities [. . .] might impact on the very structuring of knowledge as it is constituted in a given discipline."[2] To what extent does an interdisciplinary perspective protect us from the risks of disciplinary conditioning? In this respect Randy Martin's suggestion that dance studies be seen as an "emergent field of knowledge"[3] – not as a set of empirical inquiries focused on dance but as an interdisciplinary project applicable to dance as well as other cultural practices – appears particularly convincing.

Other questions are posed by the relationships between research methods and their subjects. What does a given methodology reveal about its subject? What does it conceal? What does it overlook? How can we measure the difference between what is brought to light by research done with a specific methodology and the phenomenology of the subject under study? And then, how are we to structure the relationship with the traces bodies leave in history, if, alongside Foucault, we postulate that a source becomes a source in the moment in which historians name it as such? How can we grasp the nature of the subjective gesture a researcher makes in choosing a source? How can we recognize the potential for any document, subject, event, or individual to become a source?

The research presented in this volume seems to be moving toward the idea that every methodology is one of many possible choices if it is considered the result of a dynamic and reciprocal relationship between the subject and the field of research. The issues that emerge illustrate how dance studies are continually re-written, and how the discipline and the process of knowledge demands incessantly renewed methodological proposals.

Keywords, fields, and topics

This book is organized in three sections, each of which focuses on a keyword: "Politics," "Feminine/Masculine," "Identities." The keywords were selected on the basis of the frequency with which they appear in recent studies both inside and outside of the discipline, on the basis of the quantity and quality of the studies that have been conducted in each of the fields of inquiry they suggest and circumscribe, and, last but not least, on the basis of their relevance to our research. Each section includes five essays: a "state-of-the-art," which aims at presenting and discussing the major research that has already been done in each field of study; three "case studies," which present different approaches to a precise and circumscribed topic; and an essay on "prospects," which sums up the major issues raised in the preceding essays and identifies new directions of research. Once this structure was conceived, we asked each of the authors to formulate their ideas according to their own theoretical and methodological positions. We tried to avoid imposing restrictive definitions on the keywords so as to remain open to as many approaches as possible.

The keyword "Politics" opens a wide field of investigation that ranges from the relationships of the dancers with political and cultural institutions, to the communication, performance, and reception of a dance work, to the ways in which dance connects with the individual, the collective, society, the state, and power. It also embraces the construction and transmission of the political and social imaginary of bodies in motion, the relationship between dance and historical trauma, and, shifting the attention from the subject of research to the researcher's subjectivity, the processes of interpretation and of historical theorization and contextualization.

"Feminine/Masculine" is a terminological articulation that makes it possible to introduce the category of gender without naming it. This choice is determined by the limited spread of the word "gender" outside of the English speaking contexts. The field of investigation includes the forms of representation and imaginary that gender comports as well as the stereotypes it has established, the systems of relations it organizes, and the acts of conservation, resistance, and subversion it produces.

"Identities" are considered in the plural so as to emphasize the ambiguity or multi-valence of a category that simultaneously unites (shared identity) and separates (individual identity and multiple identities). Interest is focused on the body as a primary identitarian, subjective, and social sign, on the anthropology of representation and vision, on the stratification and fragmentation of body techniques, on the memory of the dancer's body, on the creative process, and, finally, on identification.

For each of these areas we selected a topic that was to serve as a focal point for consideration and discussion, so as to promote an investigation and exchange of ideas and to emphasize theoretical and methodological issues. The topic of the first section, *Ausdruckstanz* (dance of expression), has been widely explored over the past twenty years. As a result this area of research is full of stimulating ideas and potential but, given the difficulty of accessing German sources, has always been limited to "specialists among specialists." The accessibility of these studies to a wider, more heterogeneous audience remains a pressing issue.

The second section is centered around eighteenth-century theatrical dance, a topic that has hitherto been treated only in a fragmentary and sporadic way. Further investigation would make it possible to measure ourselves against a distant era that was so consequential for dance history because of its theoretical and artistic productions and innovations.

The topic of the third section is the hardest to bring into focus. We are still immersed in the thick of it, and the debates are often quite heated, misleading, polemic, or contradictory. "Contemporary dance" does not imply an easily labeled genre or phenomenon. It refers, instead, to that which is innovative or original in current artistic activity. As such, it is in direct dialogue with what is happening in the social and political sphere and, consequently, subject to unstable critical and public reception.

Essays and intersections

The three sections of this book are not to be taken as self-contained units. Independent echoes and guidelines weave throughout the various texts, demonstrating the interdisciplinary nature of their theoretical premises and methodological approaches. The issues that bring the authors together continue to intersect, creating crossroads and other possible readings. Here are a few.

The texts by Mark Franko, Laure Guilbert, and Susan Foster put their authors' subjectivities into play. Franko's essay challenges the very premises of the relationship between dance and the political by asking a tough round of questions. He elaborates the notion of "states of exception" to come to an understanding of how politically alert methodologies can reveal more about dance than dance itself is perhaps "willing" to.

Moving from another perspective, Guilbert's essay pivots around the case of the intellectual and modern dance critic Fritz Böhme, considered within the larger framework of the relationship between dance and Nazi ideology. She constructs a narrative of the history about how her research began and unfolded, about the methods she used, about the archives that nourished her work, about the problems she encountered, and about the conclusions she reached. In doing so, she gives form to the political dynamics of the relationship between the memory of dance and the writing of its history, a subject Susanne Franco further develops in her "prospects," tying it back to the issue of the definition of the topic itself and of the tradition and translation of dance practices. Like Guilbert,

Foster makes the various steps of her study manifest, sharing them with the reader in the form of a ballet libretto. In her analysis of the narrative structure of Jean Georges Noverre's *Didon et Enée*, she brings self-reflection together with feminist and postcolonial theoretical – methodological perspectives, focusing on how the gender and ethnic identities described interpenetrate and reinforce each other reciprocally, thereby constructing a convincing interpretation of otherness tightly bound to the political and commercial programs of late-eighteenth-century France.

The tools of postcolonial criticism and those of feminist theory are re-proposed in the essay by Thomas F. DeFrantz, who questions how the conception of "beauty as an action" is put into play in two works by the African-American choreographer Donald Byrd. DeFrantz concludes that these choreographies perceive beauty as a specific function of black American performance practice or, rather, as a progressive act that has material consequences for both the performers and the audience. The project is simultaneously identitarian and political.

The idea that dance may be conceived as a means of implementing a political project provides the basis for the two essays written respectively by Yvonne Hardt and Inge Baxmann. Hardt analyzes the figure and work of Jean Weidt, demonstrating how *Ausdruckstanz* was used for political ends, not only by National Socialism but also by the left-wing movements of the Weimar Republic, which identified this new dance practice as a means of cultural "elevation" among workers. Baxmann studies how the notions of femininity and masculinity take form in the republican *fêtes* of post-revolutionary France, in relation to the two key concepts of "nature" and "history" specific to these historical and cultural circumstances. In this case, the reassignment of well-defined and codified gender roles was intended to guarantee the new social order against the crisis of difference provoked by the Revolution, which had opened the way to excessive social mobility. The staging of bodies clearly marked by gender was seen as an attempt to impede this sort of degeneration.

The essay by the anthropologist Andrée Grau considers the relationship between dance, identity (conceived as dynamic and fluid), and identification processes in the postcolonial world bringing to light the way in which these forces interact in whoever practices or observes a certain genre of dance. These issues are also central to the essay by Susan Manning, who explores a crucial passage in the transmission of modern dance by the German dancers who had trained in the core of *Ausdruckstanz* and, between 1920 and 1960, immigrated to the United States to escape Hitler's regime or in search of artistic and economic opportunities. Studying the 1930s and, in particular, the careers of Hanya Holm and Eugene von Grona makes it possible to understand how the German dancers who had come into contact with a different sort of cultural politics and nationalism made a profound mark on the future development of modern and postmodern dance in America.

Another transversal path is found in the essays dealing with the reconstruction and embodiment of dance based on original sources. Linda Tomko examines the importance of this in her investigation of Feminine/Masculine in studies on eighteenth-century theatrical dance, placing emphasis on the need for a re-contextualization of bodies and styles that aims at going beyond the prevalently taxonomic trend of eighteenth-century dance sources. Nathalie Lecomte's systematic study of the cast lists in the librettos from the works staged between 1700 and 1725 at the Paris Opéra urges the need for comparative analyses and for the reconstruction of the choreographic scores attributed to those dancers who are named in sources but remain virtually unknown. Tomko's sketch of gender studies is completed by Marina Nordera, who goes on to note the importance of reconstruction in future dance research, emphasizing the need for constant interaction between theoretical studies and staged works. If one follows Foster and Franko in considering choreography as theory, paying attention to the actual material of dance – body, movement, and the system of codes in which they take on meaning – becomes crucial in understanding both the dance phenomenon itself and the culture of an era. The problem is by nature epistemological.

In this respect, Isabelle Ginot's overview of the section on "Identities" invites us to refocus the way in which we look at works, at their instability, and at the choice of the analytical methods that establish or explode meaning by reading in it different and at times contradictory aspects over time. For Ginot the question of identity crystallizes a theoretical issue that crosses the entire field of dance studies: the status of the gesture, of what is alive, and of perception in a given culture.

The approach of the second section is also adopted by Hélène Marquié, who deconstructs the discourses on gender identity and sexuality claimed by the French choreographer Alain Buffard in *Dispositif 3.1*, an apparatus that includes a choreographic work and all of the discourses intended to guide its reception. Her study focuses on the discrepancy – and quite often the contradiction – between the performance and the discursive apparatus, a discrepancy that reveals both the ideologies that trouble the spaces of dance and the subversive weight of the works. Subversion is also of interest to Ramsay Burt, who analyzes the cases of two contemporary choreographers for whom identity is the central theme: the British Lea Anderson and the German Felix Ruckert. Both adopt strategies that aim to disrupt and disturb normalizing discourses and processes so as to create new spaces for resistant or alternative identities. Burt draws on the theoretical premises of Maurice Merleau-Ponty and Jacques Lacan, and, in part, on iconographic analyses, like those of Hardt and Baxmann, even if applied to completely different topics and subjects.

We hope that the varied approaches presented here will open new areas of interest for research and help establish a framework for the study of dance (and its discourses), understood not only as the history of bodily practices and ways of dancing, but also as the history of the way in which dancing itself has been questioned in the production of knowledge and has become both a "subject" and a "tool" of reflection.

Notes

1 M. Foucault, 'The Discourse on Language', trans. R. Swyer, in *The Archaeology of Knowledge and the Discourse on Language*, trans. A.M. Sheridan Smith, New York: Pantheon Books, 1972, pp. 222–4 (orig. edn *L'ordre du discours*, Paris: Gallimard, 1971).

2 S.L. Foster, 'Choreographing History', in S.L. Foster (ed.), *Choreographing History*, Bloomington, IN: Indiana University Press, 1995, p. 16.

3 R. Martin, 'For Dance Studies', in R. Martin, *Critical Moves. Dance Studies in Theory and Politics*, Durham, NC and London: Duke University Press, 1998, p. 183.

Part I

Keyword: **POLITICS**

Topic: ***AUSDRUCKSTANZ***

1 Dance and the political

States of exception

Mark Franko

My first idea was to compare *Ausdruckstanz* (dance of expression) literature to work in other fields on the theorization of fascist aesthetics.[1] This would establish a critical framework for the vexed question of the fascistization of German modern dance. As the research of Susan Manning, Marion Kant, and Laure Guilbert has made patently evident, *Ausdruckstanz* begs the question of dance and politics because of the easy and massive accommodation of German modern dance to the cultural policies of the Third Reich.[2] The history of *Ausdruckstanz* has long been veiled, but the original research of these scholars persuades us to reconsider dance modernism from the political perspective. An early twentieth-century avant-garde art movement and an authoritarian state apparatus encounter each other at a moment crucial in the development of each; something new is being created, both artistically and politically that reveals contradictory forces and tendencies at work. Only once these dance scholars lifted the veil and rewrote history could we begin to perceive dance in the full light of the political. They have inaugurated an area of inquiry that requires further work. But, any serious critical development of dance study methodology must also be tested against their re-evaluation of *Ausdruckstanz*.

Yet, I can understand why it is better I do not discuss *Ausdruckstanz* here. My areas of specialization are the French baroque and North American modernism. When the conference organizers asked me to widen the scope of my presentation I wrote the following abstract:

> In what historical and aesthetic circumstances does it become justifiable and necessary to speak of dance as political? Of what kind of politics are we speaking in such cases – what kind of power? Above all, what sort of relationship can be established between dance and the political such that politically alert methodologies can reveal more about dance than dance itself is perhaps “willing” to reveal? Is the

> politics of dance necessarily mute? Or, is it possible for a (any) politics to control dance – to manipulate its meaning? Does dance have a "political unconscious"?

No sooner had I written this abstract than it became very hard to write the paper. I became tangled in the phenomenal presence of dance, the politics of the relation between dancer, choreographer, and institution, and so-called real-world politics: the political sphere itself. The best approach was, I decided, to try to answer one by one my own questions.

In what historical and aesthetic circumstances does it become justifiable and necessary to speak of dance as political?

It is justifiable and necessary to speak of dance as political in circumstances that are *conjunctural*; that is, in circumstances where forms of movement and socio-political life take shape simultaneously if apparently independently. Dance frequently attains heightened cultural visibility at such moments, which makes it productive to examine within the terms of our problematic. Dance can also intervene in political considerations in a proto-conjunctural context. Rather than being quintessentially visible because culturally central, it may in such cases be highly marginal and invisible. Since the seventeenth century dance has served to fashion and project images of monarchy, national identity, gendered identity, racialized identity, and ritualized identity. But, in most of these areas it has also demonstrated the ability to stand apart, acting as a critical theory of society. It goes without saying that I would consider both functions as political.

With the development of modern dance in Germany and North America earlier in the twentieth century, the body in motion became a choreographic touchstone of national identity. Choreographers sought themes and subject matter that celebrated national identity in terms of physical types and qualities of energy and resolve, all of which were construed to have racial overtones. In the 1930s and 1940s dance entered the field of ideological conflict between capitalism, fascism, and communism in America and Western Europe.[3] The growth and development of the nation state and its attendant ideologies has determined the semiotics of the relationship between dance and politics until at least the end of World War II. For Sally Banes, even the most experimental choreographic production of the sixties took place under the ideological aegis of democracy, bringing the experiments of Judson Church Dance Theater thirty years later into line with a certain ideology of American identity.[4] More recently, this semiotic relation of dance to the modern nation state has become relevant to postcolonial identities in international situations.[5]

In the case of artists who achieve iconic national status, the impact of national consciousness on the creative process can be tracked at the level of strategic artistic and publicity-related decisions. It is possible that the artist's situation becomes one of intentional cooperation, or of the more or less willing co-optation of the dancer/choreographer by a bureaucratic state apparatus. Manning's work on Mary Wigman opened up this area of inquiry, and indeed this very kind of inquiry. Whether we call it appropriation, accommodation, or collaboration, the artist's politics are frequently compounded by the situation of the woman artist in the twentieth century who both manipulated her own image and suffered its manipulation by forces beyond her control. For example, the price paid by Martha Graham in the late thirties and early forties for her national celebrity was a discourse transforming her artistic profile. She was prominent enough to appear in an editorial cartoon next to Mussolini and Hitler in 1942. The image is of Graham looking religiously at a piece of fabric. "Strange Talisman," the legend reads. "Dancer Martha Graham always carries with her a bit of 500-year old cloth from the dress of a medieval Italian saint."[6] Graham may be side by side with men who are world leaders, but she is presented as out of touch with the modern world, and as superstitious. Even as a counterweight to Hitler and Mussolini, Graham is presented under the auspices of what Toril Moi has identified apropos of the critical reception of Simone de Beauvoir as "the personality topos." "The implication," specifies Moi, "is that whatever a woman says, or writes, or thinks, is less important and less interesting than what she is."[7] Since her *Frontier* (1935) and *American Document* (1938) Graham took it upon herself to personify American identity. A Nazi radio broadcast acknowledged this, and proposed that Germany was masculine and the United States feminine. Therefore, the American media feminized Graham throughout the early 1940s in the name of a masculinized national identity. My point is that for Graham, different and contradictory motives impinged on a structurally confined cultural space, which was her own space of cultural action. The possibilities this space represents can be both enabling and distorting for personal and aesthetic identity. I would consider the political as very precisely the entanglement of these different forces and motives that partake of the personal, the artistic, and the institutional. Politics are not located directly "in" dance, but in the way dance manages to occupy (cultural) space.

Given this state of affairs, I find continued resistance to the idea of dance and the political perplexing. Mark Morris is one highly visible choreographer (at least in the United States) who publicly denounces the validity of a connection between dance and the political.[8] His denial surely has something to do with the politics required to undergird his own canonical reputation as a choreographer. The canon determines whose work is seen and survives over time: the modernist canon requires that dance be a-political to qualify as great art that is worthy of entrance into the canon.[9] I believe that politics is as closely and substantially connected to dance in the real world as dance itself is connected to ritual in anthropology. Dance, however, does not operate directly in the political sphere, and thus dance is not strictly speaking political. As against Morris, there actually is no "is" in the presumed equation between dance and the political; to say that dance is not political is not to say much. An adequate Dance Studies should therefore constantly return to the complex interactions between dance and the political designated as political in a variety of ways. It is reflection on this variety or diversity of relationships that has true methodological value for dance research.

If dance is not political strictly speaking, then what is it? I would answer that dance is ideological, and it carries inevitable political effects for this reason.[10] Ideologies are the persuasive kinesthetic and visual means by which individual identities are called or hailed to larger group formations. If, conversely, dance is anti-ideological, then it is deconstructive in the sense that it practices a critical self-reflexivity. The self-reflexivity that can be said to characterize some postmodern dance since the 1960s can be explained in political terms as a rejection of ideology's hold on dance. "Dance can only be subversive," writes Janet Wolff, "when it questions and exposes the construction of the body in culture."[11] However we characterize the great divide between modernism and the postmodern that separates the world of contemporary movement research from the compromises of an earlier period, formal shifts can be accounted for in ideological terms.

On a micro-historical level, dance may perform protest, a direct and local way of upsetting a power balance.[12] What the body itself, when given pride of place, can be thought to oppose also lends definition to how dance makes the political flare up. The dancer's body, as Dominique Dupuy has said, can be "intolerable," "a provocation," and "a living blasphemy."[13] Somewhere between these poles of ideological suasion, deconstruction, and protest we can pinpoint resistance. Resistance is a trope within which movement and representation are ambiguously articulated. This is because dance can absorb and retain the effects of political power as well as resist the very effects it appears to incorporate within the same gesture. This is what makes dance a potent political form of expression: it can encode norms as well as deviation from the norms in structures of parody, irony, and pastiche that appear and disappear quickly, often leaving no trace.

Here, we could refer to appropriative restagings and the debates over political intent they give rise to. For example, Pina Bausch's rewriting of

Vaslav Nijinsky's *Rite of Spring* recasts the seminal ballet story as a battle of the sexes much more explicitly than does the original. This raised, at least for the American public, the question of Bausch's gender politics.[14] When Matthew Bourne restaged *Swan Lake* for a cast of male swans, the way in which dance can represent sexual orientation takes on a new dimension. In these and similar cases, it is the presence of a work from the past that acts as a foil for a heightening of the unrealized political possibilities in the original.

The dancing body has rhetorical, persuasive, and deconstructive force in the social field of the audience, which is a variant of the public sphere. Public controversies are not necessary for a danced politics. The way in which dance alters public space by occupying it is full of political innuendos, as is any unprecedented use of public space for the circulation of bodies. Dance can exert ideological power without emblematizing it. Thoinot Arbeau called dance "a mute rhetoric."[15] If ideology is a persuasive and therefore fundamentally rhetorical appeal to the mind and the senses, choreography is its potent means of captation. But choreography can also effectively undo or counter such rhetorics. The notion of *détournement* as Situationists theorized it in the 1960s with its procedures of quotation and citation, have been particularly relevant to dance and the political in the last decades of the twentieth century. Distancing from the cultural constructions of the body has proceeded not just through a questioning of the body per se, but through the questioning of lexicons and syntaxes that have effected such constructions in dance. Thus, we could note that Morris's cross-dressed roles in *Dido and Aeneas* (1989) play with the sex/gender construct. But they also evoke baroque and modernist vocabularies, which themselves encoded this construct in particular historical ways, and come to do it yet again in *Dido and Aeneas* with different inflections. The sex/gender politics in which this dance engages is also therefore engaged with a politics of dance history expressed in, by, and through choreography.

The tools with which to unpack this persuasiveness or this dissuasion vary according to historical period. One can talk of spectacle in the baroque and one can appropriate John Martin's terminology of metakinesis in the 1920s and 1930s. It is important methodologically, in my view, both to think *with*, but not *within*, the models of the historical period under scrutiny, and also to develop those models in the direction of relevant terms for contemporary analysis. To understand the mechanisms of power in baroque spectacle, for example, one examines the relation of court ballets to narrative, the role of text, image and movement in their construction, the historical circumstances of their production, the dance techniques, musical techniques, and choreographic genres, etc. Here one comes across notions of the intermediate, of *gli affetti*, of military culture and aristocratic culture, etc.[16] But one should also engage with the extensive theorization of the baroque since the 1920s, a theorization relaying that historical period to our present. This would include a rethinking of sovereignty both politically and aesthetically (Walter Benjamin, Carl Schmitt), of the baroque in relation to the postmodern (Guy Debord, Mario Perniola), of baroque aesthetics in the contemporary context (Heinrich Wölfflin, Severo Sarduy), and of baroque political thought (Ernst Kantorowicz, Giorgio Agamben). The manner in which the historical models can be brought into dialogue with the subsequent theoretical crystallizations illuminates the relation of dance to critical studies. Dance Studies is fundamentally interdisciplinary in the way it conjugates specific knowledge of structured movement systems and choreographic protocols as well as performance styles with the critical approaches to power and representation that would otherwise remain relatively disembodied.

Of what kind of politics are we speaking? What kind of power?

When we speak of dance and politics, we speak of the power of dance to make and unmake identities. Because dance molds the body and its ways of moving, it cannot help but propose models of subjectivity in either an affirmative or a negative sense. Sound, costume, staging, plot, and text influence to various degrees such models. When we speak of dance and the political, we also infer the politics of interpretation. Which critics or theorists have provided influential, indeed canonical, interpretations that have shaped our apprehension of what we see? What are the presuppositions of such influential texts – even if they appear as ephemera – and what other writings have been suppressed or gone unnoticed? What ideological credence has been bestowed on the "great" critic, and with what ideological consequences for the art of dance? The history of dance and politics can often be read and deconstructed in the encounters between performance and the print discourse that marks its passage with a discursive afterlife.

But politics can also be internal to dance. William Forsythe has recently identified the connection between dance and politics in the relation between dancer and choreographer in that the choreographer curates the dancer's autonomy. Forsythe spoke recently of ballet – like computer language – as an art of command. But countering this quality, he proposed choreography as an enabling practice that can promote the dancer's autonomy.[17] For Forsythe, the dancer–choreographer relation is where dance meets the political. From this vision of the dancer–choreographer relationship emerges a political potential that also becomes visible in performance. One can say by extension that in dance we read the relation of dancer to choreographer as a political relation.

In the sixties, small dance companies in New York were something like the micro-groups with which Fredric Jameson characterized the decade.[18] Our understanding of choreography – specifically of how it gets done – extends to the small social groups enabling choreographic practice. In this way, by examining dance's social conditions of possibility, we have already moved beyond strictly formal considerations. The evocation of everyday movement and improvisation seems inevitable at this level. Systems of technical training or protocols for non-technical training have been instrumental in the fostering of communitarian identities. Accounts of such communities and how they support practice require ethnographic approaches. Mass dance in the thirties played a role in the creation of Communist Party culture (known as movement culture). In *The Work of Dance* I have tried to extend our understanding of the impact of dance on the (mass) spectator to the relationship between choreographic procedures and the administrative entities responsible for group movement in social life. This would be the first step in the description of a choreo-politics, following the sense in which Michel Foucault has spoken of a bio-politics. Manning has discussed the relationship between leader and group in Wigman's company during the 1920s. These and similar analyses presuppose a continuum between what happens offstage and onstage, an important presupposition of any methodology that wishes to highlight the confluence of dance and the political.[19]

Power also encompasses cultural policy and the ways in which dance fulfills the role of public art. This is the case of commissions – frequently governmental commissions and grants that have existed in the United States since the 1930s through the Works Projects Administration (WPA), the Eisenhower Fund, and the National Endowment for the Arts (NEA). We see that the lack of any critical awareness of ideology in the political sphere today goes hand in hand with the dismissal of performance as cultural diplomacy. While dance was exported across the world by the United States during the Cold War as a tool of foreign policy, today dance – like all the arts – plays little or no role in international relations.[20]

In authoritarian societies, such commissions aim to institute a totalized environment through which architecture and interior design, media and gesture become relays in a cultural *mode d'emploi* of body, space, and movement. In democratic societies, public interpretation of publicly commissioned or sited work can have volatile effects frequently leading to the manipulation of the public sphere.[21] This was certainly the case with the controversies over certain artists funded by the National Endowment for the Arts in the 1980s, which led to the downsizing of that agency.

Cultural policy defines itself with respect to emergent identities that are construed as offensive to the public, and thus dance becomes by definition public art. In situations such as these, the political class appears radically estranged from the artist class, and the deepest animosity emerges between the agents of political bureaucracy and those who labor in the studio. It has mostly been the case of late that the political class also mobilizes the public against the artist class. This has much to do with what Michael Brenson has called "the political banishment of the artist's body" and of their "living histories."[22]

We are speaking of cultural politics, and therefore of cultural power. Although we are constantly reminded that dance has no power, the move to squelch it once it stands forth in an unorthodox manner is often immediate. The possibility for a cultural politics to manifest itself in/as dance presupposes the political feasibility of its performance in the face of cultural policy. Exceptional moments are those in which dance has escaped censure. Here we speak of dance in relation to events and eventfulness.

This was also the context of the seminar on dance and politics that took place under the auspices of Le Mas de la Danse and the Centre national de la danse at Vincennes in 2001. The publication *Danse et politique* documents those presentations and debates.[23] The seminar was organized around the concept of the political as linked to events, notably the bombing of the Cathedral of Reims, the October revolution, the stock market crash of 1929, and the bombing of Hiroshima. Topics were resumed under the rubrics of dance and state power, dance and work, the collective body as body politic and/or national body, and the notion of historical trauma.

I would like to call attention to a methodological debate that emerges from the Vincennes discussions. What I shall call formalism and contextualism for lack of better terms appears to divide the interpretive community of the seminar.[24] Those who favor movement analysis over all other critical methods are formalist in a disciplinary sense. For the formalist sensibility critical theory is imported from outside the discipline. It is of the nature of the strictest disciplinary conception of Dance Studies therefore to diminish the interpretive importance of context. I am pointing out a tension over issues of disciplinarity in Dance Studies, but I hope this will not be misunderstood as an attempt to foster an opposition between two methodological tendencies; we need both, but they should be better integrated.[25] Historians seem to be taken for contextualists even though not all are enamored of critical theory. From the perspective of this debate, Dance Studies is either a new and self-sufficient discipline (the formalist model) or a parasitic trans-discipline (the contextualist model). History without critical theory can of course just be considered a supplement to movement analysis, and in this sense a subset of history.

The issues raised in this debate are largely methodological, but they also have interpretive consequences. The formalist model seeks descriptive and theoretical tools that account for the dance experience in the most unmediated manner possible (for example, movement analysis) whereas the contextualist model takes dance as an extension or distillation of social practices – a symbolic action – and thus conceptualizes dance as to some degree mediated. To be an unmediated discourse of dance is to function as closely to dance as possible as a discursive and experimental complement to movement research and contemporary performance. The historically, culturally, and institutionally determined conditions in which this movement research crucially takes place – the historical conditions of its possibility – are displaced in the name of dance's immediacy. What seems to characterize the formalist persuasion in Dance Studies is a brand of antihistorical impulse. This is a consequence of phenomenology that implies an eternal present. This idea can, in my opinion, lead to a narrow definition of the contemporary, one that is both anti-social and anti-historical; and for this very reason, actually anti-contemporary. André Lepecki writes:

> An art that needs living bodies to exist is projected, as a research object, to an intangible past. It is as if one needed the veil of death in order to face the essence of dance. (Or is this veil a symptom that something unbearable may lie at the core of dance?)[26]

What do we have to fear from confronting ghosts, or from engaging with layers of seeing and meaning that complexify dance's presence rather than associate it with the figure of truth: the body unveiled? Lepecki's question can be turned against itself. What is unbearable in the past? Cannot the "intangible past" be thought of in terms of Foucauldian genealogies? What does it mean to pry apart the terms dance and the past? This is a strategy whose effect would be to foreclose quotation and citationality, both of which always presuppose a previous discourse, and therefore a previous inscription. Toward the end of her masterly study of German modern dance and its relationship to the Nazi era, Guilbert invites aestheticians to grapple with that archival inscription in movement terms. But, does not Guilbert's book itself count as dance history?[27] And if so, then cannot dance history be actually intra-disciplinary? Must the social and political entailments of dance, the history of movements within the dance community, and of the sensibility to movement itself, be rigorously segregated within Dance Studies? The methodological challenge we face is to articulate awareness of the traffic between bodies and ideologies acquired by virtue of all that has happened both in dance and in Dance Studies with the close analysis of how dancing itself actually works.[28]

What sort of relationship can be established between dance and the political such that politically alert methodologies can reveal more about dance than dance itself is perhaps "willing" to reveal? Is the politics of dance necessarily mute? Or, is it possible for a (any) politics to control dance – to manipulate its meaning?

In order for a methodology of danced politics or political dance to exist, there must be a general theory of the political in dance. Certainly, such a theory would directly concern the three methodological areas proposed in this conference: politics, gender, and identities. Yet, politics – my assigned area here today – is the term closest to the "political sphere" properly speaking. So what is the "political sphere" and when or where did dance enter it?

The history of dance can be useful to us here. Western theater dance begins in the political sphere. The seventeenth-century Theater State is so named because in it the real operations of theater have direct political significance. It is an historical commonplace that court ballets, particularly in France, mirror the diplomatic maneuvers and ideological aims of the monarchy. At the center of these early-modern media exercising control over the territory of early national states, is the king's body itself: a privileged site of interaction between dance and power.

Jürgen Habermas proposes that "representative publicness" preceded the existence of a public sphere: "This *publicness* (or *publicity*) *of representation* was not constituted as a social realm, that is, as a public sphere; rather, it was something like a status attribute."[29] It is the effect of public self-display as epitomized in court ballet to distinguish power from the private and hence to function as a status attribute against the public sphere. Public self-display in a prestige economy was embedded in dance aesthetics influenced by traditions of courtly social dance. We can hypothesize, following Habermas, that courtly social dance and its adaptations to court ballets were, despite their class restrictions, fundamentally *public* acts. There was no place for privacy within them.

Representative publicity has the effect of "subjecting" the onlooker – that is, of bestowing upon the onlooker his or her subjectivity, which is cognate with subjugation. "Public authority was consolidated into a palpable object confronting those who were merely subject to it and who at first were only negatively defined by it."[30] Foucault similarly envisages the direct exercise of monarchical authority in the political sphere as a form of subjugation.[31] Dance is an attractive site at which to test such a theory since it is far removed from punitive violence and yet the most characterized by public display of the sovereign person.

In *Dance as Text* I asked whether the late sixteenth- and early seventeenth-century monarch, rather than being the sole agent of political power, was not actually a protagonist of ritualized political struggle.[32] Here, the context of theater is more than just a platform for display, but also a social process. The importance of the burlesque ballets between 1620 and 1636 was their emergence as a form of symbolic political negotiation carried out between feudal rivals and sovereign authority. I claimed that the burlesque was not an embarrassment to people of good taste, but an innovative use of movement in dialogue with the absolutist entailments of ballet spectacle. Within the carnivalesque reversals of the burlesque genre, a key figure of which was the androgyne, a power struggle with class dimensions took on performative dimensions.[33] The figure of the androgyne was subversive in this context because it could imply the dynamic inversion of power relationships between king and nobility.

Royal cross-dressing further complexifies this picture, as well as the notion of representative publicness itself. The cross-dressed king unsettled the patriarchal basis of hyper-masculine iconography in relation to royal power. It signaled a choice, in my interpretation, to move beyond representations of power toward evocations of force. "Sovereign is he," wrote political theorist Schmitt in 1922, "who decides on the exception."[34] The exception is the suspension of the juridico-political order, but in ballet it marks the suspension of consecrated relations between representation and power. If power is force in mourning, as Louis Marin put it, then force brought out of mourning is the most transgressive of power's resources.[35] The king's sexual indeterminacy in ballets where he plays the androgyne are also directly linked to problems of succession for which mourning and melancholy are the symptoms. Similarly, but at a different level, some of the king's cross-dressed roles are anti-normative figures of force that imply the exception implicit in sovereignty.[36] Thus, the king's performance of anti-normative roles is both an assertion of legitimacy and a threat of legitimacy's suspension. In both cases power is performed in unorthodox, because non-representational, terms. Dance history contains insights not just into the relation of dance to political power, but also into dance and the politics of representation. It is precisely at the level of the politics of representation that we touch upon the question of how dance history is to be represented.

What allows a danced event to emerge on the horizon of historicality or narrativity? Any serious discussion of the exception challenges the canon itself. Challenging the canonical exclusivity of dance history obliges us to invoke forgotten or suppressed alternatives – culturally, aesthetically, and politically. If, as Hayden White claims, the possibility of historical narrative is founded on law, legality, and legitimacy, then the effect of Dance Studies on dance history is to destabilize the subject of history itself.[37]

Interdisciplinary, intertextual, and ethnographic, Dance Studies may be unsettling to a dance world that functions on the basis of canonical representations and historical narrative. Canonical works are often made to appear politically neutral because of their aesthetic excellence. Comparison of canonical and non-canonical figures, however, can reveal the political alternatives contained within canonical works.[38] If we are to seriously explore dance and the political as an historical relation, we too must decide on the exception. Seventeenth-century court ballet is exemplary in this respect because certain works reveal something not revealed to be knowledge anywhere else: the representation of the exception. Because the notion of the exception is encoded in that of sovereignty, the key word, I believe, is not representative publicness, but sovereignty, with all it entails of the relationship between power, force, and the exceptional.

The context of these remarks is to situate the relation of dance to the political sphere. If dance sits squarely within the political sphere in the seventeenth century, this is not subsequently the case. For Habermas, the public sphere develops as a bourgeois phenomenon in the wake of representative publicness. The public sphere is formed of "private individuals who came together to form a public."[39] The public sphere is the domain of property owners and family members who elaborate a notion of their own subjectivity in public through fiction and letter writing. Most interesting for us is that that very subjectivity becomes dependent for its elaboration on the presence of an audience:

> The diary became a letter addressed to the sender, and the first-person narrative became a conversation with one's self addressed to another person [. . .]. Subjectivity, as the innermost core of the private, was already oriented to an audience (*Publikum*).[40]

This eighteenth- and nineteenth-century development of a public sphere that could engage in rational dialogue with power shifted away from the literary to the choreographic and performative. How and why modernity invested in the trope of motion is beyond the scope of this paper. But I ask you to consider here the revolution of Isadora Duncan as an instance of the dancer discovering and elaborating her subjectivity in/as the public sphere. It is possible that with Duncan, dance enters the public sphere.

Elsewhere I have written:

> Duncan's subjectivity was unstably positioned on a threshold between privacy and publicity because her dance was an act of public display unveiling hidden nature as prior to or intrinsically outside society,

> from elsewhere by definition. Although opposed to the separation of these spheres, Duncan also relied on their segregation to dramatize her opposition. In this sense she took performance where she found it as a public act for a private self.[41]

The dialectic in Duncan's work between privacy and publicity is what makes her choreography foundational for a Habermassian concept of the public sphere in dance. It is the appearance of the body before an audience in the elaboration of its private subjectivity which enables dance to enter the public sphere and thereby obtain political relevancy at that point in history.

Catastrophic events of the twentieth century cannot be accounted for or responded to in adequate corporeal and choreographic terms with the notions of sovereignty and public sphere.[42] What these events point to in different ways is "historical trauma." In *Dance Pathologies* Felicia McCarren points out connections to trauma from Romantic Ballet (*Giselle*) to the early female soloist of historical modern dance (Loïe Fuller). In this context trauma is diagnosed as hysteria, and its iconography is contained in the photographs of Charcot's Salpetrière clinic.[43] McCarren's analysis is based on the figure of the pathological, and more particularly, of hysteria.[44] Hysteria, although having lost its scientific validity, persists as a general term for the changing manifestations of trauma whose violence breaks the limits of the self or of the body.[45] The relation between the unconscious and the body is forged in the historical crucible of hysteria, which stands at the origin of Freudian psychoanalysis. Parts of the body become fragmented and dispersed as parts of a scene, as is frequently the case in the *Tanztheater* of Pina Bausch.[46] It seems that we touch here upon a psychoanalytic dimension of dance that Dance Studies has left relatively untouched. This problematic also opens onto memory and how the body remembers. Trauma also occasions the blotting out of memory. Dance Studies should be alert to how the body forgets.

If we explore the issues of dance and the political with reference to the tropes of sovereignty, public sphere, and trauma they need not necessarily be ordered in any historical sequence nor do they necessitate the correlation of dance and event in any cause-effect sense. To the contrary, they are present in dance today as elements of the genealogy of the political. Perhaps they constitute a first step toward a general theory of the political in dance from which further methodological developments can be derived. It should be added that methodology is not limited to the operations our sources allow us to perform, but extends to the theoretical grids we can set up and the sorts of questions these grids enable us to ask.

Does dance have a "political unconscious"?

Rather than divide Dance Studies between mediated historiographic and immediate descriptive schools, I propose the historico-critical practice of writing and choreography I have practiced to illustrate other possibilities. For example, I have asked by means of choreography whether some baroque dance could deal with subjugation as an effect of representative publicness rather than only with the embodiment of representative publicness itself. In other terms, I have attempted to conjugate trauma with sovereignty.

Le marbre tremble was premiered at the Toulon Art Museum in the photography exhibit "Le corps/la galère: noir et blanc," curated by François Soulages in 1986. It was developed in conjunction with Ernestine Rubin's photographs of Pierre Puget's caryatids in Toulon, themselves modeled after galley slaves in the Marseilles harbor.[47] *La galère* is the galley ship set into motion by slave labor, but also the bodily suffering of that labor (*la galère* is slang for suffering in modern French). The patterns and gestures of the dance dialogue with the dissolving montage of photographed statues. Photographs of the caryatids were projected onto the performer's body, as well as onto a screen behind him. The costume, designed to evoke the disappearance of the caryatid/slave's lower body into a stone block, was made of a material that also acted as screen capturing the projected photographic image.

Not unlike my scholarly attempt in *Dance as Text* to rehabilitate the burlesque as an artistically viable because politically motivated choreographic act, *Le marbre tremble* inverted the conventional "subject" of seventeenth-century baroque dance. This subject becomes the subject of the *reception* of representative publicness rather than of its projection. Through this juxtaposition of research and choreographic methodologies the political exists within the folds of dance (to borrow Deleuze's term) – within the folds of history, movement, and iconography; and in the choreography of the fold itself. *Le marbre tremble* was a spatialized and temporalized mode of thinking in which the dance reflected self-consciously on the history of its own relation to politics. It fragments that history in the multiplicitous figures of its past engagements with form. An internal history of dance, one that favors the integrity and self-sufficiency of dance without essentializing its presence, constitutes the political context.

I would like to suggest that the representation of political reality itself is what allows us to understand aesthetics precisely as historical insight. Power cannot function outside of the representational field, and representation, along with its crises, is an aesthetic matter.[48] This is why I believe not only that dance and politics have much to do with one another, but also that a theory of dance and the political need not necessarily resolve itself into action or be crassly propagandistic. Although politics may appear to be a "hard" word, the insights associated with it can be subtle and pervasive.

The intertwining of research and writing with choreography and performance is for me also a political move, one in which dance accedes to the discourse of its own interpretation. This double practice obviates the rejection of history in the name of a more direct engagement with dance. Dance, when conscious of its own politics, stands in the most unmediated or immediate relation to itself. The very awareness of the political history carried by the body enables us to think the relation between dance and the political choreographically, and therefore within the logic of movement and its performance. The choreographic relationship between dance and the political becomes critical in relation to its own history. Methodologies of dance and the political could be construed in this context as intra-disciplinary. This is the only viable compromise position in the methodological split of Dance Studies itself.

Notes

I wish to thank Janet Wolff, Isabelle Ginot, and Susanne Franco for their helpful suggestions on earlier drafts of this essay.

1 A sampling of analyses of cultural fascism and/or of fascist aesthetics might include E.G. Carlston, *Thinking Fascism: Sapphic Modernism and Fascist Modernity*, Stanford, CA: Stanford University Press, 1998; S. Falasca-Zamponi, *Fascist Spectacle: The Aesthetics of Power in Mussolini's Italy*, Berkeley, CA: University of California Press, 1997; A. Yaeger Kaplan, *Reproductions of Banality: Fascism, Literature, and French Intellectual Life*, Minneapolis, MN: University of Minnesota Press, 1986; V.M. Patraka, *Spectacular Suffering: Theater, Fascism, and the Holocaust*, Bloomington, IN: Indiana University Press, 1999; J.T. Schnapp, *Staging Fascism: 18BL and the Theater of the Masses for Masses*, Stanford, CA: Stanford University Press, 1996; B. Spackman, *Fascist Virilities: Rhetoric, Ideology, and Social Fantasy in Italy*, Minneapolis, MN: University of Minnesota Press, 1996; and the anthology J. T. Schnapp, B. Spackmann (eds), *Fascism and Culture*, monografic issue of *Stanford Italian Review*, 1990, vol. VIII, nos. 1–2.

2 Susan Manning has written of Wigman's "accommodation with fascist aesthetics" instead of a fascist appropriation of her work in her *Ecstasy and the Demon: Feminism and Nationalism in the Dances of Mary Wigman*, Berkeley, CA: University of California Press, 1993, p. 45 (2nd edn *Ecstasy and the Demon*: *The Dances of Mary Wigman*, Minneapolis, MN: University of Minnesota Press, 2006). See also L. Karina, M. Kant, *Hitler's Dancers: German Modern Dance and the Third Reich*, trans. J. Steinberg, New York and Oxford: Berghahn Books, 2003 (orig. edn *Tanz unterm Hakenkreuz*, Berlin: Henschel, 1996); and L. Guilbert, *Danser avec le IIIème Reich. Les danseurs modernes sous le nazisme*, Brussels: Complexe, 2000.

3 See M. Franko, 'L'utopie antifasciste: *American Document* de Martha Graham', in C. Rousier (ed.), *Être ensemble. Figures de la communauté en danse depuis le XXème siècle*, Pantin: Centre national de la danse, 2003, pp. 283–306.
4 S. Banes, *Greenwich Village 1963. Avant-Garde Performance and the Effervescent Body*, Durham, NC: Duke University Press, 1994.
5 See M. Savigliano, *Tango. The Political Economy of Passion*, Boulder, CO: Westview Press, 1995.
6 E. Cox, 'Private Lives', *Seattle Washington Times*, 16 August 1942, n.p.
7 T. Moi, *Feminist Theory and Simone de Beauvoir*, Oxford: Blackwell, 1990, p. 27. The cartoon also spoofs Mussolini and Hitler for pretending to be that which they are not, or pretending not to be that which they are: Mussolini poses for photographers standing on a table to increase his stature and Hitler submits to nose surgery.
8 At the *On Dance* series at Barnard College, New York City (October 11, 2004) Morris made the claim that the only political choreography ever made was Graham's *Deep Song*, and he encouraged the undergraduate dance students to read and take seriously Arlene Croce's critique of Bill T. Jones's *Still/Here*, which she had called victim art and wrote about without seeing.
9 See M. Franko, 'Period Plots and Canonical Stages in Modern Dance', in C. Gitelman, R. Martin (eds), *The Returns of Alwin Nikolais: Bodies, Boundaries, and the Dance Canon*, Middletown, CT: Wesleyan University Press, 2007, pp. 170–87.
10 I have developed the terms of this claim relative to North American dance of the 1930s in M. Franko, *The Work of Dance: Labor, Movement, and Identity in the 1930s*, Middletown, CT: Wesleyan University Press, 2002.
11 See J. Wolff, 'Reinstating Corporeality: Feminism and Body Politics', in J. Desmond (ed.), *Meaning in Motion: New Cultural Studies of Dance*, Durham, NC: Duke University Press, 1996, pp. 81–99.
12 See S.L. Foster, 'Choreographies of Protest', *Theatre Journal*, 2003, vol. 55, no. 3 (*Dance: A Special Issue*), pp. 395–412.
13 D. Dupuy, 'Ouvertures', in F. Pouillade (ed.), *Danse et politique. Démarche artistique et contexte historique*, Pantin: Centre national de la danse, 2003, p. 15.
14 See A. Daly, 'The Thrill of a Lynch Mob or the Rage of a Woman?', in *Critical Gestures. Writings on Dance and Culture*, Middletown, CT: Wesleyan University Press, 2002, pp. 6–18.
15 See my analysis of this phrase from his *Orchésographie* (1588) in M. Franko, *The Dancing Body in Renaissance Choreography (c. 1416–1589)*, Birmingham: Summa Publications, 1986.
16 See K. Van Orden, *Music, Discipline, and Arms in Early Modern France*, Chicago, IL: University of Chicago Press, 2005.
17 W. Forsythe, public forum at the "Bamdialogue," Brooklin Academy of Music, New York City, October 2, 2003.
18 F. Jameson, 'Periodizing the Sixties', in S. Aronowitz, F. Jameson, S. Sayres, A. Stephanson (eds), *The Sixties Without Apology*, Minneapolis, MN: University of Minnesota Press, 1984, pp. 178–209.
19 Here, the concept of the parergon can be useful. See my 'Dance and Figurability', in S. de Belder (ed.), *The Salt of the Earth: On Dance, Politics, and Reality*, Brussels: Flemish Theater Institute, 2001, pp. 33–57.
20 See N. Prevots, *Dance for Export: Cultural Diplomacy and the Cold War*, Middletown, CT: Wesleyan University Press, 1998.

21 "When . . . guardians of public space refer their power to a source of social unity outside the social, they attempt to occupy – in the sense of filling up, taking possession of, taking possession by filling up – the locus of power that in a democratic society is an empty place." R. Deutsche, 'Agoraphobia', in R. Deutsche, *Evictions: Art and Spatial Politics*, Cambridge, MA: The MIT Press, 1996, p. 275.

22 M. Brenson, *Visionaries and Outcasts. The NEA, Congress, and the Place of the Visual Artist in America*, New York: the New Press, 2001, p. 104.

23 F. Pouillaude (ed.), *Danse et politique*. Along with the conference that followed on dance and figures of community (September 2002) whose results have been published by the Centre national de la danse as *Être ensemble*, it is the precursor to the present volume. These events, when taken together, constitute the first sustained international discussion on dance and politics.

24 The qualities of formalism are not those of abstraction but of formal description. Hayden White uses these terms slightly differently in 'Formalist and Contextualist Strategies in Historical Explanation', in H. White, *Figural Realism. Studies in the Mimesis Effect*, Baltimore, MD and London: The Johns Hopkins University Press, 1999, pp. 43–65.

25 Any analysis that privileges aesthetics to the detriment of context risks reading dance in an a-historical way; one that, most pertinently for my theme, misses the sociological ramifications of aesthetics. This is not by any means to dismiss phenomenological analysis – especially not the French variety that I consider to be the best that there is in this field – but rather to weigh methodological tendencies in the balance of interpretive results. All dances *embody* their own historical context; one cannot separate context from embodiment. Analysis of the conditions of production and reception also serve to historicize different embodiments of a dance.

26 A. Lepecki, 'Rethinking Words: A Field Trip in Dance Criticism', *Contact Quarterly*, 1994, vol. 19, no. 2, p. 23. Although the context of Lepecki's remarks is not fully articulated in this article, he conjoins the challenges of Dance Studies with a rethinking of dance criticism.

27 'A movement history remains to be written in the light of my conclusions . . . But for it to take place there would have to be a veritable exchange between aesthetics and the other disciplines of the human sciences.' See L. Guilbert, *Danser avec le IIIème Reich*, pp. 399 and 403.

28 Dominique Dupuy has underlined the importance of "The relationship between politics and the matter of dance," in 'Ouvertures', in *Danse et politique*, pp. 15–16.

29 J. Habermas, *The Structural Transformation of the Public Sphere. An Inquiry into a Category of Bourgeois Society*, trans. T. Burger, Cambridge, MA: The MIT Press, 1994, p. 7.

30 Habermas, *Structural Transformation*, p. 18.

31 See M. Foucault, *Discipline and Punish. The Birth of the Prison*, trans. A. M. Sheridan, New York: Vintage Books, 1979 (orig. edn *Surveiller et punir. Naissance de la prison*, Paris: Gallimard, 1975), especially the chapters: 'The Body of the Condemned' and 'The Spectacle of the Scaffold'.

32 M. Franko, *Dance as Text: Ideologies of the Baroque Body*, Cambridge: Cambridge University Press, 1993. Margaret M. McGowan laid the groundwork for this approach to dance history in *L'art du ballet de cour en France (1581–1643)*, Paris: C.N.R.S., 1978. *Dance as Text* aimed to extend McGowan's relationship

between statecraft, political conjuncture, and state-sponsored court ballet into choreographic aesthetics.

33 "The 'society of orders' did not exist as a system, but only as one aspect of a distinctive early modern form of a society of classes." See W. Beik, *Absolutism and Society in Seventeenth-Century France. State Power and Provincial Authority in Languedoc*, Cambridge: Cambridge University Press, 1985, p. 335.

34 C. Schmitt, *Political Theology: Four Chapters on the Concept of Sovereignty*, trans. G. Schwab, Cambridge, MA: The MIT Press, 1985, p. 5.

35 L. Marin, *Portrait of the King*, trans. M.M. Houle, Minneapolis, MN: University of Minnesota Press, 1988 (orig. edn *Le portrait du roi*, Paris: Minuit, 1981).

36 See M. Franko, 'The King Cross-Dressed: Power and Force in Royal Ballets', in S. Melzer, K. Norberg (eds), *From the Royal to the Republican Body: Incorporating the Political in Seventeenth- and Eighteenth-Century France*, Berkeley, CA: University of California Press, 1998, pp. 64–84.

37 See H. White, 'The Value of Narrativity in the Representation of Reality', in *The Content of the Form. Narrative Discourse and Historical Representation*, Baltimore, MD and London: Johns Hopkins University Press, 1987, pp. 1–25.

38 This was the approach I took in *Dancing Modernism/Performing Politics* where I compared Duncan to Valentine de Saint-Point, Graham to the left-wing dancers of the thirties, and Cunningham to Douglas Dunn.

39 Habermas, *Structural Transformation*, p. 56.

40 Ibid., p. 49.

41 Franko, *Dancing Modernism/Performing Politics*, pp. 2–3. See also further discussion pp. 14–24.

42 See M. Franko (ed.), *Ritual and Event: Interdisciplinary Perspectives*, London and New York: Routledge, 2007.

43 See G. Didi-Huberman, *Invention de l'hystérie. Charcot et l'iconographie photographique de la Salpetrière*, Paris: Macula, 1982.

44 F. McCarren, *Dance Pathologies. Performance, Poetics, Medicine*, Stanford, CA: Stanford University Press, 1998.

45 See C. Rabant, 'Le "trauma" et les névroses de guerre', in *Danse et politique*, pp. 47–51.

46 See M. Franko, 'Bausch and the Symptom', in G. Brandstetter, G. Klein (eds), *Tanzscripte*, Bielefeld: Transcript Verlag, 2007, pp. 234–64.

47 See M. Franko, 'Pour un nouveau statut du Baroque en chorégraphie: l'effet Puget', in *Image du corps et corps vivant*, conference proceedings, Toulon: École des Beaux Arts, 1988, pp. 87–90.

48 In this paragraph I am indebted to the thoughts of F.R. Ankersmit in *Aesthetic Politics. Political Philosophy Beyond Fact and Value*, Stanford, CA: Stanford University Press, 1996.

2 Fritz Böhme (1881–1952)

Archeology of an ideologue

Laure Guilbert

> I recall that no one in Germany could dance without Fritz Böhme.
> (Karl Silex in *Heidelberger Tagesblatt*, September 1, 1949)[1]

In his book *Tanzkunst* (The Art of Dance), published in 1926, the dance writer Fritz Böhme recounted the impact of Mary Wigman's first appearance on the Berlin stage in October 1919:

> They were the first works born of trance that were not an imitation of theatrical ecstasy. Here, a person imparted a rhythm growing out of the body. Movement, which until now had been considered a beautiful, gracious and proportionate form, shifted to a completely different space. It was no longer an image or a sculpture in movement but a gesture radiating strength [. . .]. The body had rediscovered its own rhythm.[2]

This is how Böhme described the irruption of modernity in dance: an art freed from academic models, independent in its expressive forms, attentive to subjectivity. He confirmed the advent of the new sensorial perception of the body foretold by Nietzsche and the expressionist painters. Böhme was caught in the ardor of this nascent modernity and, from the end of the war on, ran ceaselessly from one theater to another, chronicling a generation of artists impassioned by the invention of a *neuer Tanz* (new dance), called also *Ausdruckstanz* (dance of expression). He wrote for the daily and specialized press, authored well-received essays, lectured, and founded literary and artistic associations, devoting himself body and soul to the modern revolution of dance.

When he died in 1952, Böhme left behind an image of a pioneer and expert that was only one aspect of who he really was. While doing research for my Ph.D. dissertation in the early 1990s,[3] I had the chance to discover another much more complicated side of his life-journey: that of a man who had put his talent in service of the Third Reich and who had dedicated himself to an unprecedented effort to re-write the history and social function of dance.

How could this poet of choreographic modernity, this defender of an ethics of the free body become a Nazi intellectual? And how could this enigma be approached, today, in a Europe marked by the Shoah? Exhuming the ghosts of Nazism from history's oubliettes is not mere chance nor is it an easy task, especially with the intent of contributing to a new field of academic study. It seemed useful therefore to clarify the archeology of this discovery about "the Böhme case."

1989–90; Paris. Getting ready for the trip

In 1989 the professors at the Institut d'Études Politiques in Paris urged us to open our research to multi-disciplinary study and to construct new subjects on the basis of unpublished corpuses. The field of cultural history was growing in France, and I truly enjoyed the seminars I took on committed intellectuals and artists. Karin Waehner, a student of Wigman, had just introduced me to modern dance and told me about the Wigman archives that had recently been deposited at the Akademie der Künste in Berlin. The East was in the air. The frontiers of this other faceless Europe, in the shadow of which my generation had grown up, were finally open.

I knew German and I immediately threw myself into a biographical project. From the early 1980s on, the commemoration of Rudolf von Laban's and Mary Wigman's birth centennials had given modern dance high visibility in Europe. The work of Hedwig Müller and Susan Manning, and the magazine *Tanzdrama,* were widely diffused in Germany and in the United States, but little that was similar existed in France, where what was passed off as dance research was barely visible in the social sciences and humanities. The dance department at the University of Paris VIII, where I picked up my first theoretical baggage, was just getting on its feet. I was in the middle of a desert . . . How to evoke, through an artist's biography and work, dance history understood as a cultural history of representations of the bodies and of sensibilities? One possibility was to conduct an investigation of the Nazi period, an epoch that was still virgin ground and during which censorship, or so they told me, had reigned over the modern avant-garde. The only alternative that remained was to throw myself into an empirical study that relied on the tools of history, sociology, anthropology, and aesthetics.

1990–1; Berlin, Leipzig. First steps toward the East

During my stay in Berlin, I discovered the vertigo of crossing, day after day, from one side of the wall to the other: the long checkpoint lines, the urban opulence of the West, and the wounded buildings of the East. For the first time in fifty years, the entire German cultural patrimony was accessible to researchers. I plunged into the Wigman archives and burrowed through the Staatsbibliothek (national library) in Leipzig and in Berlin looking for published dance sources. The mere abundance of works and magazines from the 1920s evidenced the explosion of bodily practices. Böhme immediately stood out as a remarkable figure. From 1919 on, he had written for *Deutsche Allgemeine Zeitung*, mouthpiece of the conservative industrialist Hugo Stinnes, covering the daily dance column and taking an interest in literature, education, and later on film. His articles covered the gamut of current events in *künstlerischer Tanz*[4] (art dance), ranging from new productions to repertoires, from trends to traditions, from young talent to international stars. His objective style never revealed affinities or friendships, and his professionalism contributed to the emergence of a new generation of critics, evidenced by the founding of the first specialized magazines, *Der Tanz* and *Schrifttanz*. He also wrote and published at least seven books, all of which were widely acclaimed.[5]

Böhme read and was captivated by Laban's first artistic testament, *Die Welt des Tänzers* (The Dancer's World, 1920). From then on, he paid particular attention to Laban's research on the laws of movement and space, which, in his opinion, represented a fundamental revolution in the West that would bring about a new conception of dance as an art and a philosophy of life:

> Laban cannot be imitated, or approached through technique or practice. He is the bearer of an Idea [. . .], the eternal Idea of the living man, in movement. His word is an appeal to contribute to the renewal of the idea of the dancer as an influential force in human culture.[6]

Aware of the possible mystical interpretations this vision could evoke, Böhme insisted on the choreographer's artistic aims:

> In ancient times Laban would have been a priest and a sovereign [. . .]. Today he is the inventor of the new art of dance and choreography, and transmits this energy to man, not through his personal influence, but through a knowledge that goes beyond the self.[7]

Looking ahead, Böhme attempted to read the future signs of this revolution in the trends of the present. Toward the mid-1920s, he became interested in the emergence of group dance and movement choirs, and attempted to analyze their modes of composition and improvisation in light of the contemporary sociological debates on collective stakes. It was then that he began to militate in favor of the secularization of these new practices in Weimar society. He actively defended the recognition of Laban's notation system and the professionalization of the milieu. As a member of the organizing committees of the dance conferences in Magdeburg (1927), Essen (1928), and Munich (1930), his lectures were well-received and his suggestions respected in the decisions that were made.

Böhme was also, however, a proponent of an artistic avant-garde that saw dance history from a point of view inspired by a romantic conception of nature and a cyclical vision of history. For him, dance was not a virtuous form but the expression of "Being" envisioned as a totality of body, soul, and spirit. If he was enthusiastic about the new methods of physical education that emerged at the beginning of the century, it was because they proposed a sensorial apprehension of movement founded on the great rhythmic principles of nature ("tension and release, balance and torsion"). These methods opened dancers to a new interiority that allowed them to renew their creative horizons.

While the forms of modern dance may have been new, its roots were not. Its inventiveness was tied to a golden age of movement, a mythical age in which dance had expressed a bond with the divine. "Hardly anyone imagines that these dances concealed a realm that had been overshadowed in Europe for centuries," wrote Böhme regarding Wigman. In reality, this vision rests on a critique of classical tradition and on the Spenglerian idea that history passes through cycles of grandeur and decadence.[8] Böhme took up on the contemporary discussion of ballet's "decadence," but went on to criticize the thought that presided over this tradition. For him the Cartesian duality of body and soul had killed the expressive space of dance in western theatrical tradition. The modernity he defended was the fruit of the emancipation from the civilizing process, which had made the body an object rather than a way of being in the world. His view of the avant-garde was veiled by nostalgia for a lost world. More than just an expressionist fashion, the new dance was an art of self-expression that drew the premises of its renewal from German romanticism.

I began to discover German criticism of the Enlightenment, a form of cultural pessimism that was quite different from the progressive philosophy I had grown up with in France. I read works by the historians Martin Green, Georg Lachmann Mosse, Fritz Stern, and Michaël Löwy on the generation of "anti-capitalist romanticism" born at the turn of the nineteenth and twentieth centuries in reaction to the excesses of the rational utopia of progress embodied in the industrialization and urbanization of central Europe. Rejecting the disenchantment of the world, this generation was tempted by models of pre-capitalist thought co-inhabited by reactionary and utopian concepts. This current had many ramifications and would nourish socialist ideologies, libertarian Judaism, and national mysticism. Böhme is representative of this intelligentsia, but his dream of "the dancing man" does not always make reference to a political project. Its poles of interest do not bring him toward Erwin Piscator's political theater or the conservative circles promoting academicism in art. His position in the late 1920s seems to be more that of a man who was somewhat deeply absorbed in the flourishing of an art.

I kept on reading at the Staatsbibliothek in Leipzig, where I fell upon some rare publications that had eluded the "ruins of war." In August 1933 Böhme wrote an article for *Kontakt. Körper-Arbeit-Leistung*, a magazine that provided professional information in the milieu of body culture. In it he examined the traditions of China's Chou dynasty, which, by national decree, was to institute "cultural administrators" or "superintendents of ancestry" responsible for overseeing "the transformation of shamanic ecstatic dance into a form of cultish dance with regulated and established rules." This "principle of educating the people" was to find its basis in the "recognition of racial belonging," and the lesson Böhme drew from this example for the present left me dumbfounded. By now German dancers were to individuate the source of dance movement "in the rhythm of their blood, in the breath of their race, in the harmony and in the equilibrium of their people."[9] Hitler came to power in January 1933. Was Böhme expecting the new regime to impose its own "directors of movement"?

In the last pages of *Kontakt*, a note indicates that Böhme had been named head of an office responsible for the development of folk dance under the auspices of the *Reichsbund für Volkstum und Heimat* (Reich League for Folklore and Homeland). Around the same time, he set forth a program in the magazine *Die Musik*. Evoking the creation of the *Verband deutscher Tanzkreise* (Association of German dance circles) in 1927 (over which he had presided from 1931), he underscored the need to "regenerate" artistic dance on the model of folklore "beginning from the elements of movement theory and of regional and national forms and sensibilities."[10] He proposed that the term *Volkstanz* be defined as "dance of the people" and made into a generic definition for all the choreographic practices in Germany.[11] Even if apparently not well-known under Weimar, Böhme's engagement in the movement of traditional dance throws new light on his past interest for collective dance practices. Hadn't he already dreamt of an art that might carry traditional dance's values of social cohesion? In his eyes, Hitler's revolution would represent the right context for favoring this transition from the ecstatic and individualist trends of expressive dance toward a Germanic and communitarian art of the future.

Hitler's rise to power seems to have provoked a revision of Böhme's position. He abandoned his efforts on behalf of the professionalization of art in favor of its submission to certain categories of political thought and turned to an ethnocentric approach backed by racist theories of bodily practices. Whatever did not result from racial and "organic" concepts of the body was guilty "of intellectualism, rationalism and international confusion," all of which were perils capable of destroying the "chain of transmission of German heredity."[12] This is how Böhme justified the recourse to censorship. He systematized his ballet criticism, maintaining that the Germans had to reject any "foreign interference" of this "instrumental technique," which could be used – at most – for training but never as an "expressive style."[13] All the same, he reserved an important place for expressive dance in the framework of a political interpretation. He followed closely the German dance festival of 1934, the regime's first choreographic festival, in which practically all of the modern dancers of Weimar performed.

The project of the Nazi dignitaries sought the emergence of a spontaneous art of the masses, and the model with which Böhme responded was half-folkloric and half-modern. The way in which he "fell into line" is original in two ways, as it refers both to Alfred Rosenberg's reactionary measures of censorship and to Joseph Goebbels's policy of encouraging national modernism. Could the economic and political context at the end of the Weimar Republic and the institutional impasse with which the dance conferences of the late 1920s closed be at the origin of this evolution? Or, on the contrary, did Böhme's intellectual path mask more ancient secret affinities? In any case, Nazism seems to play a role in accelerating his aspirations. Böhme was convinced that the Third Reich opened a new cycle of history tied to the roots of German culture and that dance was the direct testimony and beneficiary of this: "When we dance our dance, the dance of the German people, our invisible ancestors advance with us by the billions."[14]

What stakes were hidden behind this ambitious process of politicization? I read Philippe Lacoue-Labarthe and Jean-Luc Nancy's *Le mythe nazi*,[15] an essay in which the philosophers stress the importance of the artistic mimesis in the building of national identity from Greek antiquity on. A country that had long been fragmented, Germany had been most strongly influenced by its already constituted neighboring states. But the imitation had only functioned to the second degree, leaving the question of national identity unresolved. In the nineteenth century, the romantics, and then

Nietzsche, re-appropriated another Greece, no longer the Apollonian Greece of the Enlightenment but its primitive Dionysian counterpart. The rediscovery of this savage antiquity opened the way for the total work of art, a new form of the appropriation of *Kultur* conceived on the model of fusion. The universe of Böhme's thought seemed to be shaped entirely by this cultural debate. Doesn't his tenacity in re-reading dance history by the standards of his aesthetic emancipation and in guaranteeing this art a place in German public space actually read as identitarian research? In the same way in which Richard Wagner made his vision of opera a new symbol of the common destiny of the German nation, Böhme wanted to find a presence in dance that would allow the Germans to construct a new self-image. His adhesion to Nazism corresponds to this logic.

Böhme's stupifying path led me back to the many individuals who had worked in or around dance: artists, educators, intellectuals, and cultural intermediaries. What had happened to them? The magazine *Kunst der Nation*, which supported Gobbels' action at the Propaganda Ministry (1933–5), attests the absence of aesthetic censorship in artistic dance. Only the minority of Jewish, communist, and socialist dancers and critics had gone into exile. Böhme's path was bound, above all, to a collective history that has to be reconstructed around its discourses, networks, practices, and events. I looked for works that investigated the history of the arts under twentieth-century authoritarian and totalitarian regimes. There were works on film, literature, painting, and theater, but, as far as I know, dance – other than Inge Baxmann's research on Germany and Elisabeth Souritz's on Soviet Russia – seemed to have been forgotten. As the days went on, it appeared more and more essential for me to understand the dark years of Nazism. My project on Wigman's biography evolved progressively toward the portrait of a generation confronted with modernity.

1992; Florence, Cologne, Leipzig. A descent in time

In the meantime I had been accepted at the European University Institute in Florence to continue my dissertation. Eastern Europe was in full transformation. The Soviet Union no longer existed. The German Democratic Republic and the Federal Republic of Germany had been reunited and the urban landscape of new *Länder* had undergone a striking facelift. Had the post-war period been definitively buried? No, because for the first time after forty-five years, a new conflict, between the countries of the ex-Yugoslavia, was once again at our doorstep.

A brief sojourn at the Tanzarchiv in Cologne allowed me to glean some biographical information. But the archives deposited around the mid-1980s by Böhme's widow, Elisabeth, turned out to be disappointing: at her request, access to certain correspondence from the 1930s was denied. A curriculum edited by the archivists informed me that the writer had been born in Berlin on May 10, 1881 to a Protestant father who was a pharmacist. Böhme studied at the University of Berlin, taking courses in the philosophy of history with Kurt Breysig, who was known for his "philosophy of totality." He began working in 1912 as an archivist at the *Gesellschaft für Erziehung und Schulgeschichte* (Society of the History of the Education and the School) and, in 1913, published the complete works of the regional poet Theodor Storm. Rejected from the army for a hearing problem, he went to Warsaw in 1916, where he was hired as a journalist by *Deutscher Warschauer Zeitung*. When he returned to Berlin, he worked at the *Deutsche Allgemeine Zeitung* for ten years. In 1926 he founded the *Gesellschaft Berliner Tanzkritiker* (Association of Berlin Dance Critics) and in 1928 he received a research fellowship to write a *Geschichte des Europäischen Tanznotation* (A History of European Dance Notation). His curriculum for the next two decades is surprisingly concise. It rapidly mentions that, in April 1933, Böhme became member of the National Socialist Party and the *Kampfbund für Deutsche Kultur* (Fighting League for German Culture). He then taught and worked as an archivist at the *Deutsche Meisterwerkstätten für Tanz* (German Master Workshops), and even his denazification trial, which lasted through October 1949, is mentioned briefly. In this period following the war, he published under various pseudonyms; afterwards he began using his own name again and, until his death, he taught, wrote, and reviewed performances in Berlin.

The Tanzarchiv in Leipzig conserves a second Böhme collection, it too donated by his widow.[16] Complete and without restrictions, it contains correspondence, publications, unpublished manuscripts, and a collection of the magazine, *Deutsche Tanz-Zeitschrift*, the mouthpiece for information on artistic dance under the *Reichstheaterkammer* (Reich Theater Chamber), which was published from 1936 until the end of the war and apparently cannot be found elsewhere.

I paused for a while on an unpublished manuscript, *Die letzten Individualisten* (The Last Individualists) by Böhme dated 1926–7, in which he confessed his secret vision of the future in a startling way. The writer gave homage to the "last individualists" – Goethe, Fichte, and Nietzsche – who, aware of the world to come, had been the last to launch an appeal to "raise the forces of isolated people in one great force." Influenced by the German tradition of *Bildung* (education), Böhme defined this future community as an "organism of learned figures." "The group is a religious phenomenon," he clarified. Its realization would require the containment of several "dangers" including: intellectualism ("life is extinguished where intellectualism reigns"), democracy (which provokes a "disruption of the consideration of self"), and collectivism (which produces only "norm, indifference, exterior order and schematism"). These dangers risked provoking "a glaciation, an extinction of the German man, of the European man." Böhme wanted to oppose to that "a collectivism bearing meaning, rooted in nature and in life" and animated by enlightened *Führer* (guides). The sorcerers and priests of primitive times provided the first role models, but, in contemporary times, this mission was to be entrusted to the artist.

These political conceptions do not come across in his public lectures, but one can discern a mystical evolution in his book *Entsiegelung der Geheimnisse* (The Revelation of Secrets, 1928). Influenced by Taoist philosophy, it proposes a metaphysical reflection on movement and its symbols, and concludes with the evocation of a theocratic Third Reich. A real political change was delineated in 1930, when Wigman and the poet Albert Talhoff were in Munich preparing *Totenmal* (Monument to the Dead), a performance of total theater in memory of the dead of World War I conceived as, as the subtitle suggests, a "dramatic choral vision for word, dance, and light" (*dramatisch-chorische Vision für Wort, Tanz und Licht*). This work, which associated soloist roles to a script inspired by movement choirs, awoke the need for renewed fusion in a post-war society wounded by the loss of millions of men. Wigman embodied the charismatic role of a female Christ figure entrusted with mediating between the chorus of dead soldiers and that of the surviving women. Though pacifist in tone, the work was supported by a circle of men of culture who, on this occasion, expressed their longing for a national theater. Böhme was part of this group and published several articles revealing his nostalgia. *Totenmal* gave him his first opportunity to openly express his faith in dance as "a road toward the new culture and community of the people."[17] The model of the dance revolution Böhme intended to coincide with Hitler's revolution in 1933, it seems, had already been in place in 1930: an art bound to vibrant forces of the community and of the artists elected to guide the masses.

These are the ideas Böhme applied to the Reich League for Folklore and Homeland. He was convinced that providing local leaders with specific political training would favor the birth of the new art. His dream of a Third Reich conceived as an assembly of elect figures came to clash, however, with reality. Hitler's conservative revolution ended, and authoritarian adhesion to the National Socialist Party was imposed on the 3,000 members of the Association of German dance circles. Böhme thought it would only be necessary for those in charge to join and, in 1934, he resigned from his responsibilities. His withdrawal from the world of folklore did not, however, make him part of the resistance. He drew closer to the artistic milieu and worked on organizing the international dance festival of the Olympic Games under the leadership of the *Deutsche Tanzbühne* (German

Theater Scene), an organization Laban had directed since 1934 inside the Reich Theater Chamber. Böhme wanted to call to an end the notion that "German dance had only had a modest role in the general history of dance" and published several articles that revealed his ambition of establishing the foundations of a "Germanic dance history."[18] In reality, he did not aspire to "call" the history of dance "to order," but to integrate it into the Nazi *Weltanschauung*. His portrait of the typical Nazi dancer, the new "creator of culture" who was to favor the adhesion of the people to the myth of its race reads as follows:

> He must be educated like his companions, as a political soldier of Hitler [. . .]. Only then might he be able to have an influence on stage as a folkish model [. . .]. He must know that movement transforms not only the dancer but the spectator as well, and that a residue of magic and shamanism always doze in the visionary art of dance [. . .]. The soloist must never let chaos and destruction come through in front of the public.[19]

I looked through some photographs, I consulted rare films, and I questioned myself on the link between these texts, choreographic practices, and their traces. An immense field had opened to historians and aestheticians. But, to me, it seemed impossible to imagine the existence of a "Nazi dance." Certain images are so graphic, their lines so contemporary. Was my own gaze as a spectator, and my attachment to the idea of the subjective experience of art and the irreducibility of the individual, deformed? All the same, little by little, I learned to piece these images together with their landscape and to read them as historical documents. They became superimposed by other images, those of production circuits and backstage maneuvering, and of the mass fusion in the rallies of the regime that attempted to force destiny by molding bodies. For the Germans of that age, participating physically in the vibrant beauty of the communitarian experience was a way of reaching a form of transcendence, a new collective imaginary founded on the social contract of the masses' identification with its leader. The emotions that emanated from these rallies acted like a drug to mask their violence. Éric Michaud explains that the aesthetic goal of Nazi ideology is to forge the Idea – the race – into the form of the Aryan Man and that the dream of this eventuality permitted the Nazis to give ideology a function analogous to that of art.[20] Collective beauty is the Trojan horse of the Nazi instrumentalization of the arts. Böhme's texts are the voice, the photographs the eye. Both, texts and photographs, have the value of legitimating power.

As fascinating as they are, however, the collections at the Tanzarchiv in Leipzig furnish little information on the context of Böhme's work in the 1930s. I still did not have a single administrative document that attested to his relationships with the institutions of the Third Reich.

1993–4; Tel Aviv, Potsdam, Berlin. On the ruins of the Propaganda Ministry

At the beginning of summer 1993, I spent a long time in Israel gathering the testimonies of dance exiles. Many of them, pioneers of a not so well known but very creative period of modern dance, had settled in Palestine in the 1930s. It is difficult for them to speak about the pain of leaving Germany and Austria and about the indifference shown by most of the leaders of the field that remained. The German–Jewish laceration is still very moving and remains a tight node.

When I returned to Berlin, I investigated the collection at the Bundesarchiv (Federal archive) of Potsdam, where I discovered that the registers of the Propaganda Ministry had been conserved under the control of the Soviet army until a short time prior to then. It was there that I met the musicologist and historian Marion Kant,[21] with whom I would exchange a great deal and who was already working with Lilian Karina – a former dancer in exile – on what turned out to be an archeological goldmine: an enormous package of documents that was still intact and had been left untouched for almost half a century. The Bundesarchiv of Berlin-Zehlendorf, formerly the Berlin Document Center, under the control of American authorities, conserves the dossier of the members of the *Reichskulturkammer* (Reich Culture Chamber) and some of the denazification trial records. These archives describe the day-to-day choreographic politics of the Third Reich and reveal, in particular, the role of dance artists in the 1930s and 1940s. The discovery was formidable for the historian, but terrible for the admirer of Terpischore.

I learned a great deal more about Böhme. In November 1933, at the eve of the inauguration of the Reich Culture Chamber, he wrote a letter to Goebbels asking him to create a Chamber devoted to the "art of movement and dance" and the preservation of "the authenticity of German expression." Goebbels was wrapped up in other power conflicts and the request went unanswered but, between 1934 and 1936, the dance professions were integrated into the Reich Theater Chamber. In May 1936 Laban invited Böhme to teach dance history at the German Master Workshops, the new national academy for training dance teachers founded in the core of the German Dance Theater. Böhme accepted and taught two to four hours of lessons a week right up to the end of the war. He also became the chief editor of *Deutsche Tanz-Zeitschrift* (the dance magazine of the Reich Theater Chamber, distributed in 1,800 copies) and, from February 1937 on, worked as the academy's librarian and archivist (a job for which he received special funding and at which he was assisted by the Nazi dance theoretician Gustav Fischer-Klamt). Böhme had an ideal work situation until early March 1943 when English bombing completely destroyed the academy. Böhme's last manuscript, *Geschichte des deutschen Tanzes* (History of German Dance), went up in flames. In the years that followed, he traveled throughout occupied Europe at the expense of the Propaganda Ministry to recompose his obliterated life-work. At the beginning of 1944, at Goebbels's command, he was given the task of moving the academy to the Sudety. The students and the Böhme family settled not far from Karlsbad, in the castle of Seeberg, which had been expressly requisitioned for this purpose. Böhme took over the school's operation and management until it closed in October 1944. On the written exams in June 1944, he posed the following question: "What is the relationship between political history and the history of dance?"

At the official celebration of Böhme's sixtieth birthday held at the Reich Theater Chamber in 1941, his colleagues presented him as the "most important historian of the art of dance" and as an "idealist" who had never been tempted to "transmit his knowledge as doctrine"[22] (Figure 1). Böhme's "doctrine" had no doubt become so "normal" as to be unrecognizable as such. Isn't this how Hannah Arendt defines the phenomenon of the "banalization of evil"?

For days on end I leafed through letters on yellowed paper, feeling under my fingertips the embossed swastikas, following with my finger, word by word, the "language of the Third Reich" so well described by Victor Klemperer.[23] Its "Heil Hitler," its authoritarian terms, its anti-Semitic injunctions: the actual materiality of these archives was not without effect on me. Collecting information, putting things together, ordering, patiently questioning, reconstructing layer after layer, undoing and then re-doing. I was often seized with horror. This down-to-earth work in the dust of the archives is needed to mature. It allowed me to comprehend, in a concrete way, the overturning of European society between the two world wars. My vision of "Weimar the modern" in a struggle against reaction dissipated like a mirage, and my secret hope of seeing dance as a bulwark against inhumanity vanished like an infantile dream. An ethic nonetheless emerged: the responsible awareness of being at the same time a free traveler and a European, heir to this transnational history.

I also discovered some photographs of Böhme. I went through these strangely familiar images quickly, but his ghost surfaced again in an annual questionnaire of the National Socialist Party, where handwritten crosses

Figure 1 Drawing by Harald Kreutzberg for the sixtieth birthday of Fritz Böhme celebrated at the Deutsche Tanzschule Berlin, June 1941. The drawing was presented with the signatures of Rosalia Chladek, Jutta Klamt, Lizzie Maudrick, Aurell von Milloss, Lola Rogge, Max Terpis, Lotte Wernicke, and Mary Wigman, in B. Prilipp, A. Jürgens, J. Günther, *Fritz Böhme zum 60. Geburtstage*, Berlin: Werner & co, 1941. Bundesarchiv Potsdam, Fund R. 55, Propaganda Ministry, Theater Section. Permission kindly granted by Bundesarchiv Potsdam.

ticked off the list of the garments of his uniform. From this document I also learned he had a son, Adalbert, from his first marriage to the sister of the dancer Hertha Feist, and two daughters, Barbara and Jutta, from his second marriage to Elisabeth Schubert. Adalbert had died at the front. Barbara would study at the national academy where her father worked. Böhme was a man like any other.

1995; Potsdam, Cologne, Berlin. Layers of a legend

During my last trip to the Bundesarchiv in Potsdam, I found a letter dated April 1943 in which Böhme requested authorization from the *Reichsliteraturkammer* (Reich Literature Chamber) to publish Goethe's *Elective Affinities*. Was this perhaps a cultural gesture with which I can identify? No. Böhme's Goethe will never be mine, as it was in the name of his Goethe that – like so many others – he threw himself into a crusade with no return against *Zivilisation* (civilization) and arrived at the inconceivable: thinking of one dance that rejected the other, imagining a body that found its source in the destruction of the "Jewish anti-body."

The thinker Mircea Eliade, whose reactionary positions are well known, reminds us nonetheless that even the most barbarian acts and the most aberrant behavior have their divine models.[24]

The contradiction between culture and barbarism raised by the philosopher George Steiner in his essay *In Bluebeard's Castle*[25] is only apparent. Nazi Europe was a vast factory of the "Aryan Man" with its specialized laboratories, those that rejected the impure and those that produced the pure. The concentration camps and the dance halls were part of the same process aimed at inventing the Germanic race. Is it possible to believe that Böhme kept a distance from the morbid productions of the regime? Is it possible to believe that dance escaped this black hole of humanity? I still feel uncomfortable when I hear someone say that the presence of modern dancers under this reactionary regime was a quid pro quo – as if modern dance were an abstraction similar to itself everywhere; as if its works, as genial as they may be, could extract it from time; as if the bodies that had incarnated it had not known the urgency and the limits of their time. Does writing the history of this art's development in all of its diversity, beauty, and harshness go against other conceptions of dance history? Can today's artistic wealth bear this heredity? One has to find the right tone.

I was deeply moved, in 1995, when Jacques Chirac recognized the responsibility of the French state in the deportation of the Jews under Vichy. This act was supported by the efforts of certain historians working against a trend of revisionist history. At about the same time, in Cologne, I consulted another bundle of papers at the origin of Böhme's posthumous legend: the post-war correspondence between Böhme and his friend, the gymnast Carl Diem, secretary-general of the German Committee of the Olympic Games in 1936. In a letter dated February 1949, Böhme asked Diem to write a declaration for his denazification trial – something Diem hastened to do – as Böhme confided in him: "I joined the National Socialist Party to save folk dance from destruction. I worked under Hitler exactly as I had since 1918, concerning myself with issues of dance alone." Many ex-Nazis – men of letters and artists – supported him during his trial. Böhme's legend is rooted in this collective adjustment of memory.[26]

Shortly after, and not without curiosity and anxiety, I visited Elisabeth Böhme in her home in Berlin. Minute, with vivacious blue eyes, she was approaching 100 with freshness. Her husband's life was distant, but she acknowledged emotionally that her youth had been "an intense era." She told me about her "Wednesday evenings," the literary salon of the early 1930s, in which many figures hailing from all sorts of backgrounds had participated. She painted a portrait of her husband as a poet in his free time[27] and as an a-political researcher, passionate about knowledge and education. She justified his efforts in the party repeating word for word the content of his post-war letters – a great escape from guilt.

After his denazification, Böhme did research for the new Akademie der Künste in East Berlin. By that time, two of his studies had been translated into Russian and he was known for his mastery of folklore. He adapted his mythic construction to meet the needs of the moment. In 1996, the Tanzarchiv and University of Leipzig printed Böhme's previously unpublished manuscript on Laban. The biographical introduction presents the choreographer almost as if he had been a victim of the regime, as someone who had been ruined by the loss of his archives and whose political engagement had only been sporadic. The collections at the Bundesarchiv are not cited and the ideological texts are not analyzed.[28] Legend has infiltrated research as well.

I was quite fortunate to have benefited from the structures of the European University Institute in Florence in assembling this corpus of documents. A great deal of silence still subsists around Böhme's life and work that no one will probably be able to probe. But this is also lucky. Memory is not built by obsessing on what is remembered, but on the awareness of the contemporaneity of history. This is the only way the "Böhme case" can reach other shores: those of a cultural history of dance that is also a history of bodies and ideas in our societies.

Notes

1 K. Silex had been an editor-in-chief of the daily newspaper *Deutsche Allgemeine Zeitung.*
2 F. Böhme, *Tanzkunst*, Dessau: Dünnhaupt, 1926. Except where otherwise indicated, the quotations that follow are all taken from this work.
3 L. Guilbert, *Danses macabres. La danse moderne en Allemagne dans l'entre-deux-guerres*, Ph.D. dissertation, European University Institute of Florence, 1991–6, published as *Danser avec le IIIe Reich. Les danseurs modernes sous le nazisme*, Brussels: Complexe, 2000.
4 This is one of the many definitions of modern dance in use at the time: the term promoted a concept that was opposed to the principles of classical ballet and stage dance known in the early twentieth century, and was used in contrast to "artistic" or "concert dance" [eds].
5 He was the author of the following volumes: *Der neue Tanz*, Bielefeld: Velhagen und Klasing, 1925; *Der Tanz der Zukunft*, Munich: Delphin, 1926; *Entsiegelung der Geheimnisse. Zeichen der Seele. Zur Metaphysik der Bewegung*, Berlin: Kinetischer Verlag, 1928. He also edited: O. Desmond, *Rhythmographik*, Leipzig: Breitkopf und Härtel, 1919; *Die Tänzerin Hilde Strinz. Ein Buch des Gedankes*, Berlin: Kinetischer Verlag, 1928; and, with C. Moreck, *Der Tanz in der Kunst*, Stuttgart: Heilbronn, 1924.
6 F. Böhme, 'Laban tänzerischer Nachwuchs', *Schrifttanz*, December, 1929, p. 66.
7 Ibid., p. 67.
8 O. Spengler, *The decline of the West*, trans. C.F. Atkinson, New York: A.A. Knopf, 1926 (orig. ed. *Der Untergang des Abendlandes*, Munich: C.H. Beck Verlag, 1918).
9 F. Böhme, 'Wachsen und Gestalten', *Kontakt. Körper-Arbeit-Leistung*, 1933, August, p. 38.
10 F. Böhme, 'Entwicklung und Aufgaben der deutschen Volkstanzbestrebungen', *Die Musik*, 1933, August, p. 827.
11 F. Böhme, 'Deutscher Tanz und Volkstanz', in *Deutsche Tanzfestspiele 1934*, R. von Laban (ed.), Dresden: Carl Reissner Verlag, 1934, p. 38.
12 F. Böhme, 'Von der Überlieferung', *Körperrhythmus und Tanz*, 1935, May, pp. 4–11.
13 F. Böhme, 'Le ballet est-il allemand?', *Les Archives Internationales de la Danse*, 1934, July, pp. 104–5.
14 F. Böhme, 'Ewiger, deutscher Tanz! Ansprache auf dem Niedersächsischen Heimatfest in Hannover 1933', in *Neue deutsche Tänze*, Leipzig and Berlin: Teubner (Reichsbund für Volkstum und Heimat), 1934, p. 6.
15 P. Lacoue-Labarthe, J.-L. Nancy, *Le mythe nazi*, La Tour d'Aigues: Éditions de l'aube, 1991.
16 Elisabeth Böhme kept up a long correspondence with Kurt Petermann, head archivist and director of the Tanzarchiv in Leipzig, and his wife.
17 F. Böhme, 'Tanz als Weg zur neuer Kultur und Volksgemeinschatft', *Deutsche Frauenkultur und Frauenkleidung*, 1930, no. 5, pp. 130–1.
18 F. Böhme, 'Der Tanz der germanischen Frühzeit', in R. Cunz, G. Fisher-Klamt (eds), *Jahrbuch deutscher Tanz*, Berlin: Dorn, 1937, pp. 29–53.
19 F. Böhme, 'Die Aufgabe des Tänzers der Gegenwart', *Deutsche Tanz-Zeitschrift*, 1936, June, pp. 30–3.
20 É. Michaud, *Une construction de l'éternité. L'image et le temps du national-socialisme*, Paris: Gallimard, 1996.

21 See L. Karina, M. Kant, *Hitler's Dancers: German Modern Dance and the Third Reich*, trans. J. Steinberg, New York and Oxford: Berghahn Books, 2003 (orig. edn *Tanz unterm Hakenkreuz*, Berlin: Henschel, 1996).

22 A. Jürgens, *Fritz Böhme*, in *Fritz Böhme zum 60. Geburtstage*, Berlin: Werner & Co, 1941, p. 4.

23 V. Klemperer, *The Language of the Third Reich: LTI, Lingua Tertii Imperii. A philologist's Notebook*, trans. M. Brady, London and New Brunswick, NJ: Athlone Press, 2000 (orig. edn *LTI: Notizbuch eines Philologen*, Berlin: Aufbau-Verlag, 1947).

24 M. Eliade, *The Sacred and the Profane. The Nature of Religion*, trans. W.R. Trask, New York: Harcourt, Brace, 1959, p. 78 (orig. edn *Das Heilige und das Profane*, Reinbek: Rowohlt, 1957).

25 G. Steiner, *In Bluebeard's Castle*, New Haven, CT and London: Yale University Press, 1971.

26 See also L. Guilbert, 'Aurel Milloss e Fritz Böhme. Storia di un'amicizia', in S. Franco (ed.), *Ausdruckstanz. Il corpo, la danza e la critica*, monographic issue of *Biblioteca teatrale*, 2006, no. 78, pp. 185–225.

27 F. Böhme, *Augewählte Gedichte*, Berlin: Julius Beltz, 1931.

28 F. Böhme, *Rudolf von Laban und die Entstehung des modernen Tanzdramas*, C. Jeschke, M. Dafova (eds), Berlin: Hentrich, 1996.

3 *Ausdruckstanz* across the Atlantic

Susan Manning

Truda Kaschmann, a student of Rudolf von Laban and Mary Wigman during the 1920s, immigrated to the United States in 1933. She spent the next six summers at Bennington, where she integrated what she learned from Martha Graham, Louis Horst, and other American moderns with the improvisational working methods she had acquired studying *Ausdruckstanz* in Germany. Meanwhile, she established herself as a leading teacher of modern dance in Hartford, Connecticut, where she introduced generations of students to modern dance, including the young Alvin Nikolais. Once John Martin asked her: "Truda, when are you finally going to stop improvising?" "Never," she replied, "that's the only way I know how to dance!" Recounting their exchange decades later, she laughed as she recalled Martin's perplexed, admonishing question.[1]

This anecdote points toward the complex transformations of *Ausdruckstanz* across the Atlantic. From the late 1920s to the late 1930s, legions of dancers intermingled the improvisational methods developed by Laban, Wigman, and their many followers in Germany with the modern dance vocabularies emerging in the United States. Like Kaschmann, many of these dancers were immigrants; others were American dancers who traveled to Germany to study the new techniques in their country of origin. Yet whatever the nationality of the dancers who crossed the Atlantic, they encountered a dance world in the US where improvisational methods were not a given, in contrast to Germany during the 1920s, where *Ausdruckstanz* flourished.[2] As Kaschmann's exchange with Martin demonstrates, critical arbiters for modern dance in the US considered improvisation somewhat suspect, not rigorous enough to compete with ballet as a high-art form and perhaps too close for comfort to jazz dance and music. Nonetheless, the improvisational methods of *Ausdruckstanz* powerfully impacted American modern dance during its formative decade, supporting the mass outreach of leftist dance, the Popular Front choreography of modern dancers, and the emerging movement of Negro dance, as African-American concert dance was called during this period.

As American modern dance consolidated over the 1940s and 1950s, Martin's prejudice against improvisation took hold and marginalized the methods of *Ausdruckstanz* or, more accurately, the Americanized versions of *Ausdruckstanz*. During the decades immediately following the Second World War, codified movement techniques developed by Graham, Katherine Dunham, and José Limón dominated modern dance training in New York City. Meanwhile, the war had stopped dancers from criss-crossing the Atlantic, and although dancers resumed the two-way traffic after the war, German-trained dancers did not regain the influence they exerted before the war. Since many German-trained dancers taught in the rapidly expanding dance programs in US colleges and universities, their improvisational methods became more associated with dance education than with choreographic innovation. When improvisation reemerged during the 1960s as a significant resource for dance-making, it had myriad sources beyond the Americanized methods of *Ausdruckstanz*. As Susan Foster has argued, the varieties of improvisation that emerged during the 1960s had roots in diverse sources, notably Africanist performance practices and Asian philosophies.[3]

Tracing the impact of *Ausdruckstanz* on American modern dance from the late 1920s through the late 1930s amplifies two stories that are not yet fully written. The first is the story of improvisation in American modern dance, which critics and scholars generally date from the 1960s. On the contrary, I will argue, improvisational methods entered American modern dance during the 1930s, then became marginalized during the 1940s and 1950s before reemerging during the 1960s. The second story is of the diaspora of dancers trained in *Ausdruckstanz*. For German-trained dancers migrated to France, Great Britain, Poland, Czechoslovakia, Sweden, Italy, Argentina, Chile, Paraguay, Australia, Japan, India, and Israel, as well as to the United States. Thus this case study composes only one chapter of a much larger tale of cross-cultural circulation.[4]

While the Weimar Republic saw the flourishing of a self-consciously modern dance movement, the American Jazz Age saw only the first stirrings of a comparable movement. In the 1930s the situation reversed: while the German modern dance movement floundered in its entanglement with National Socialism, the American modern dance movement came into its own. In 1927 a contemporary theater magazine surveyed the American dance scene and, without mentioning Graham's first independent concert presented the previous year, catalogued the profusion of dance forms in New York:

> The East River Block Party, featuring folk dancers in native costume accompanied by a fiddler or a hand-organ; a hundred ballrooms and

> cabarets with their dress clothes specialists; the acrobatic and eccentric dancers – white and black – of vaudeville and revue; the choruses – Tiller Girls, Gertrude Hoffman girls, and the ballet of Albertina Rasch – enlivening the summer shows and rehearsing, through the long summer days, new routines for autumn openings; Dalcroze Eurhythmics and its variants; aesthetic and interpretive dancing of a dozen kinds.[5]

In this overview, European innovations – the Tiller Girls, Dalcroze Eurhythmics – intermingled with the broad range of genres and styles composing the American dance scene in the late 1920s.

Thus, when the first German-trained dancers arrived in the United States, the press considered them only one novelty among others. Eugene Von Grona, a student of Wigman and of Jutta Klamt, came to New York in 1925. His 1927 work *Spirit of Labor*, described as "a human-spirit-caught-in-the-machine solo with fierce pumping, hauling, and hammering movements performed to the accompaniment of steam whistles and thudding machinery," was included on bills at the Roxy Theater, New York's well-known vaudeville house.[6] Ronny Johansson, a soloist in Central Europe who had studied with Heinrich Kröller, also arrived in 1925. In addition to presenting her own concerts, she taught and performed with Denishawn and with Elsa Findlay, a Hellerau graduate who had emigrated earlier.

At this time only a few American dancers and critics realized that Germany supported a modern dance movement without parallel elsewhere. Horst had heard about Wigman's dancing in the early 1920s, when working as an accompanist for Denishawn. In 1925 he left the company, first to study in Vienna and then to collaborate with his lover who had left two years earlier – Graham. Under Horst's artistic tutelage, Graham adopted methods similar to Wigman's for resolving the music–dance relationship.[7] Martin, engaged by the *New York Times* as its first full-time dance critic in 1927, traveled to Germany to report on the Third Dancers Congress in 1930, and his advocacy of modern dance echoed the writings of his German peers. Edwin Denby, the dance critics' critic, spent a number of years in Germany during the 1920s: a graduate of Hellerau, Denby performed with Cläre Eckstein's dance ensemble in Darmstadt and at the 1930 Dancers Congress that Martin reviewed. As Denby later recalled his experiences within the collective of dancers, "if Wigman was bad, we were depressed for a week."[8]

Thus at least a few observers were prepared for the 1928 arrival of Harald Kreutzberg and Yvonne Georgi on their first of several tours. Their performances sparked the curiosity of the dance world at large about

Ausdruckstanz, and their overwhelmingly positive reception reflected an undercurrent of interest in the new possibilities of modern dance. By the time Wigman arrived two years later on the first of three transatlantic tours, this underlying interest had swelled into a well-publicized preoccupation. Dancers and critics engaged in vigorous debate about the relative merits of German and American dance and about the relevance of German models for American developments. Some, like Lincoln Kirstein who three years later invited George Balanchine to New York, denied that German dance had any value for American dancers.[9] Others, like Ted Shawn who had performed at the same Dancers Congress where Denby appeared, prophesized the coming "brotherhood" of German and American dance.[10] Still others, like Doris Humphrey who had left Denishawn two years earlier in order to work independently, warned that Americans could not imitate German dance but should focus on the development of their own forms.[11] The American dance world responded to Wigman's tours as an inspiration and competitive spur.

From the time of Wigman's tours, the two-way traffic over the Atlantic picked up speed. In 1930 Margarethe Wallmann, director of the Wigman School in Berlin, was invited to teach and lecture at Denishawn; Louise Kloepper was the first American to graduate from the main Wigman School in Dresden; and Lora Deja was the first German-born graduate of the school to accept a full-time teaching position in the US, at the Cornish School in Seattle, a center for progressive education in the arts. Hanya Holm, a long-time member of Wigman's company and a teacher at the Dresden school, estimated that of the students who took the 1931 summer course in Dresden, half were Americans. That fall, under the sponsorship of Sol Hurok, the manager of Wigman's American tours, Holm opened a branch of the Wigman School in New York. Two years later she was invited to teach at the Bennington Summer School of the Dance.

Almost as soon as Holm landed in New York, her responsiveness to the movement environment – a faculty cultivated by Wigman training – led her to adapt her approach to her new surroundings. She retained the emphasis on spatial awareness and improvisation as primary tools for the dancer, but she codified her approach to a greater extent than Wigman had done. This represented, on the one hand, the almost inevitable systematization that occurs when a follower attempts to transmit the teaching of a master and, on the other hand, an accommodation to the practice of leading American modern dancers such as Graham and Humphrey, who aimed to articulate identifiable movement techniques. However, Holm never evolved a set vocabulary based on a single movement principle, as did Graham and Humphrey. Rather, she developed a distinctive technique based on the students' improvisational encounter with space.

Other dancers trained by Wigman and Laban – Erika Thimey, Jan Veen, Kaschmann, Steffi Nossen, Fé Alf, Tina Flade – arrived soon after Holm did, and each in her own way furthered the integration of German and American modern dance.

As American modern dance came into its own, critical attitudes toward German modern dance decidedly changed. Critics noted that the German dancers who appeared on tour did not impress the audience in the way they once had. In attempting to explain the "unsatisfying quality" of Kreutzberg's performances in 1935, Martin attributed the changed response to the growing sophistication of an audience that had come to expect the "seriousness of purpose and depth of emotional perception" of the new American dance.[12] At around the same time Henry Gilfond, reviewer for *Dance Observer*, was more blunt about what he saw happening:

> Yvonne Georgi in [her recent] solo recital [. . .] was not the profoundly moving Georgi we had last seen with Kreutzberg; and for that matter Harald Kreutzberg in his last concerts demonstrated no considerable development of the brilliant technician we had occasion to see with Georgi. Something has happened to the dancers from across the Atlantic [. . .]. From [. . .] reports of the nature of the work of these generally acclaimed masters of the dance, and from the nature of their acquiescence to the brutalization of all the arts in their homeland, we may draw the quite simple conclusion that unlike the dance in America, the dance in Germany is fast becoming (if it has not already become) a matter of little positive significance. Dealing with trivialities, theatrical (not dramatic), its substance is so thoroughly escapist that there is no relation at all to the present scene or audience.[13]

Here Gilfond refers to reports of the collaboration of Wigman and many colleagues, including Georgi and Kreutzberg, with the National Socialists.

These reports were first circulated by leftist dancers, who felt the most betrayed precisely because they had relied so heavily on the improvisational methods of *Ausdruckstanz* (Figure 2). In fact, the New York branch of the Mary Wigman School was the incubator for the New Dance Group, founded in 1932 by students at the school – Miriam Blecher, Fanya Geltman, Nadia Chilkovsky, Becky Lee, Grace Wylie, and Edna Ocko. Charging ten cents for a three-hour class that included one hour of technique, one hour of improvisation, and one hour of political discussion, the New Dance Group recruited students among workers associated with the International Ladies Garment Workers Union. The most committed students then joined their teachers in creating agitprop works

Figure 2 The New Dance Group, *c.* 1933. Permission kindly granted by Jerome Robbins Dance Division, New York Public Library for the Performing Arts, Astor, Lenox and Tilden Foundations.

to perform at Communist party rallies, union meetings, and benefit concerts. Their collectively composed repertory included *Satires,* with subsections titled "Parasite," "Charity," and "Jingoisms – traffic, politicians, peace conferences"; *Strike,* with subsections titled "Uprisings," "Hunger," and "War Trilogy – breadlines, war, on the barricades"; and *Van der Lubbe's Head,* a masked dance set to a poem by Alfred Hayes that commemorated a Communist martyr. One of the original founders of the New Dance Group, Edna Ocko soon became the most important critical advocate of leftist dance, taking a role similar to that played by Martin in relation to the Bennington choreographers.[14]

In response to the leftist dancers' accusations of Wigman's Nazi affiliation, Holm changed the name of her school. As she recounted decades later:

> I was not representing any faction, certainly not. I was interested in the dance. Period. [When Hitler came to power] people who were on top of the Communist party came and said I should make a statement that Wigman had nothing to do with the Hitler government

> though she was living over there. Well, she was left alone, and I said I'd make no statement because that might cost her head [. . .]. All right if you boycott. And they boycotted. They threw stones in the window. At the same time I wrote Wigman and I said, listen, the situation is not easy. It would be easier for me if I would use my own name and not affiliate with the Wigman School, and she said fine.[15]

In November 1936 the New York Wigman School officially became the Hanya Holm Studio, and the following summer Holm premiered *Trend* at Bennington. Many critics consider *Trend* Holm's artistic masterpiece. Interestingly, despite Holm's denial of explicit political interests decades later, the choreography of her 1937 work (Figure 3) reveals an embodied politics that aligns with the Popular Front, the attempt by the US Communist Party to make common cause with socialists and liberals in the mid-1930s. Like dances by the "New Dance Group," *Trend* pointed toward the ills of a capitalist society – mechanized labor, a decadent leisure class, the addiction of money. But like other dances that embodied the spirit of the Popular Front, notably Graham's *Chronicle* and Helen Tamiris's *How Long, Brethren?*, Holm's *Trend* generalized its social critique beyond Communist doctrine. *Trend* also paid homage to Wigman's group works from the 1920s, notably *Szenen aus einem Tanzdrama* (Scenes from a Dance Drama).

Performed to music by Wallingford Riegger and Edgar Varese, *Trend* opened with two group sections collectively titled "Mask Motions": the first, "Our Daily Bread," represented the regimented routine of industrialized life, while the second, "Satiety," represented the ennui of the leisured class. Five "Episodes" followed, each danced by a soloist in counterpoint to the group. Their cumulative effect depicted an ever more decadent society: "The Effete" concerned the false god of aestheticism, "Lucre Lunacy" the false god of money, "From Heaven, Ltd." the fanaticism of religious revivalism, "Lest We Remember" the seduction of drug addiction, and "'he,' the great" the seduction of political cultism. Here Holm clearly intended a reference to Hitler. Next came "Cataclysm," which showed the destruction of the decadent society. The closing sections at last introduced an affirmative note: Holm, making her only appearance, united two disparate groups in "The Gates are Desolate," and their harmonious interplay carried through "Resurgence" and "Assurance."[16]

Like Wigman's *Scenes from a Dance Drama*, *Trend* progressed through the disintegration and reintegration of a social group. But Holm did not function as a leader whose charismatic presence unified the group, as Wigman characteristically did. Rather she functioned as a mediator who ushered in, according to the program note, the "recognition of the common purposes of men and the conscious unity of life."[17] The ending representation

Figure 3 Hanya Holm and Group, *Trend* (1937). Permission kindly granted by Jerome Robbins Dance Division, The New York Public Library for the Performing Arts, Astor, Lenox and Tilden Foundations.

of utopia as the dynamic interplay of individuals echoed the ending of Humphrey's *New Dance* trilogy, which had premiered at Bennington over the course of the preceding two summers. Transforming its German and American antecedents, *Trend* integrated leftist critique and liberal humanism.

Appearing in the chorus of *Trend* was Florence Warwick, a dance instructor from Spelman College, a historically black women's college in Atlanta, who was studying at Bennington for her third summer. The following summer, when Warwick was one of two students enrolled in a special choreography program, her presence created a minor scandal, according to another student enrolled at Bennington, since "she was a 'passing' black dancer . . . and there was a lot of difficulty over this."[18] Did Holm realize that Warwick was a light-skinned African-American when she cast her in *Trend*? It is impossible to know, but her presence in Holm's masterpiece both reinforces and potentially troubles the whiteness of modern dance as it was practiced at Bennington.

By "whiteness" I mean the performance convention whereby bodies in motion exercise the privilege of representing the culturally unmarked body, the universal or the individual body, rather than the culturally marked body, the body that bears the burden of representing a social or ethnic collective. As a performance convention at mid-century whiteness always assumed its corollary, blackness, bodies in motion marked by the African diaspora in the New World. Although related to dancers' offstage identities, whiteness and blackness did not necessarily reduce to performers' skin tones. Rather, whiteness and blackness became perceptual constructs onstage, ways for linking physical bodies and theatrical meanings, ways for reading bodies in motion.

In the US academy "whiteness" emerged as a critical concept in the humanities around 1990. As the changing demographics of the US increasingly revealed the fiction of the black–white binary imposed on a multiracial reality, artists and intellectuals participated in what one scholar has termed "interrogating 'whiteness,' complicating 'blackness.'"[19] Thus only over the last decade have dance scholars recognized how often "high art" in the US context implicitly became "white art." As Isadora Duncan, Ruth St Denis, Ted Shawn, and others developed the new "art of the dance" after the turn of the century, they aligned their practice with the emergent category of "high art," implicitly and explicitly countering the "low art" and "black art" of ragtime and early jazz. This association between high art, white art, and modern dance continued well into the century and created significant barriers for the development of African-American concert dance, or Negro dance, as the practice was called from 1930 to 1970.

The barriers took a distinctive form during the 1930s, as white critics scripted a critical catch-22 for African-American dancers: on the one hand, if African-American choreographers followed Eurocentric models, critics considered them "derivative" rather than "original" artists; on the other hand, if African-American choreographers foregrounded Africanist elements, critics considered them "natural performers" rather than "creative artists." Interestingly, two dancers with German training – Alison Burroughs, the first African-American graduate of Hellerau, and Von Grona, one of the first German dancers to emigrate to the United States – deployed the improvisational basis of German *Technik* to circumnavigate this critical catch-22. In this way eurhythmics and *Ausdruckstanz* influenced the development of African-American concert dance.

Member of a distinguished family of Harlem intellectuals and artists, Burroughs used her Dalcroze training to ground her dance career, as did so many other graduates from the school. In 1930 Burroughs appeared with Edith Segal in the first version of *Black and White*, the interracial duet that became the most widely performed work of leftist dance after it was recast for two men. In 1937 Burroughs collaborated with Edna Guy to present the Negro Dance Evening, an event that historians herald as a milestone in the development of African-American concert dance. In 1940 Burroughs co-founded the Affiliated Schools for Dance and Theater in Harlem to train the next generation of black concert dancers.[20]

After his arrival in 1925, Von Grona participated in the fledgling modern dance scene for a few years before finding more remunerative employment at the Roxy Theater and Radio City Music Hall. Like many New Yorkers, he was drawn to the nightlife in Harlem, but he considered "dance-hall jazz and African rituals [. . .] limited dance forms [. . .] [that] have provided no outlet for the deeper and more intellectual resources of the race."[21] So he placed an ad in the *Amsterdam News*, one of two weekly papers published in Harlem, offering free or low-cost dance training, and from the 150 aspiring dancers who showed up, he chose a group of twenty-five. The group trained and rehearsed three evenings a week for three years before making their debut as the American Negro Ballet (Figure 4). Opening at the Lafayette Theater on November 21, 1937, the American Negro Ballet drew an audience that "included a great number of the more preeminent members of society of both races in the city," according to the *Amsterdam News*.[22]

Figure 4 Eugene Von Grona's American Negro Ballet, *c.* 1937. Permission kindly granted by Jerome Robbins Dance Division, New York Public Library for the Performing Arts, Astor, Lenox and Tilden Foundations.

The program opened with James P. Johnson conducting his new composition "Symphonie Harlem" for the premiere performance of the New York Negro Symphony Orchestra. (Johnson was a composer of serious music who was not related to James Weldon Johnson.) Then Wen Talbert took over the baton and conducted the remainder of the first half of the program: *Children of the Earth*, set to music by Reginald Forsythe; *Air*, set to Bach's "Air for a G String"; and *Southern Episode*, a "simple tale [. . .] [told] in a jazz idiom [. . .] of a revival meeting, a jade who lures a husband from his wife, and the lament of the betrayed," set to Duke Ellington's "Sunday Morning" and W.C. Handy's "St. Louis Woman."[23] James Weldon Johnson, who had retired as executive secretary of the National Association for the Advancement of Colored People (NAACP) several years earlier, spoke during the intermission, and the *Amsterdam News* paraphrased his "brief address":

> [Johnson] praised highly the work of Von Grona in organizing the ballet and pointed out the important step in the progress of the Negro achieved by its formation. Dwelling also on the contribution the Negro had made to the dance, Mr. Johnson cited the occasion as an epoch making event.[24]

The second half of the program was danced to a recording of Stravinsky's *Firebird* in which Lavinia Williams and John Edwards took leading roles. Although widely reviewed in the New York and national press, the American Negro Ballet did not survive more than another season. Nor did Holm's *Trend* remain in the repertory after two more performances in New York in fall 1937. *Trend* was too expensive to mount again, but it also was too much of its Popular Front moment. During the years of the Second World War, an interrelated set of social and artistic changes drew Holm and many other modern dancers away from social commentary and emboldened black choreographers to create works of social protest, racial uplift, and the African diaspora. During the war years Katherine Dunham established black authorship as fundamental to black self-representation. After the American Negro Ballet disbanded, many of its dancers went on to work with other choreographers, most notably, Lavinia Williams, who became a leading member of Dunham's company. After 1940 Von Grona's commitment to create a repertory for black dancers no longer made sense, and the German-born artist returned to the commercial theater, no longer as a dancer and choreographer but rather as an actor and director.

The two-way traffic over the Atlantic came to a standstill during the Second World War, but resumed afterward. Year after year American students went to the Wigman School in Berlin or the Folkwang School in

Essen to explore alternatives to the training available at home. And German students of *Ausdruckstanz* continued to emigrate: Pola Nirenska, Margaret Dietz, Isa Partsch-Bergsohn, Til Thiele, Helmut Gottschild, Anneliese Mertz. All these dancers contributed to the ongoing development of American modern dance. Yet none achieved an impact comparable to the German-trained dancers from the 1930s, for the simple reason that they arrived when American modern dance had become relatively established and no longer looked outside itself for affirmation.

During the 1960s modern dance experienced a rebellion from within, and many of the rebels discovered or, perhaps more accurately, rediscovered improvisation as an important resource for dance-making. Recently David Gere, Ann Cooper Albright, Foster, and Sally Banes have undertaken the formidable and admirable task of writing a history of improvisation in US dance. In so doing they have elevated choreographers such as Anna Halprin, Steve Paxton, and Dianne McIntrye over earlier choreographers "from Mary Wigman to Martha Graham," who "systematically rejected the idea of performing improvisationally on the public stage," even while using improvisation as a rehearsal technique. In so doing, to quote David Gere, the earlier generation asserted "the importance of improvisation as a primary (read: primal) means of unearthing the subterranean geographies of the self."[25] Gere's broad distinction between the earlier and later generations holds true. Yet how could the later choreographers have developed improvisation as a means for choreographing performance onstage without the earlier choreographers having explored improvisation within the studio?

In this new history, improvisation emerges in the 1960s from a combustion of the energies of black nationalism and the counterculture with the embrace of Africanist and Asian precepts and practices. The new history does not take into account the improvisational methods of *Ausdruckstanz* that entered American modern dance in the decade before the Second World War, perhaps rightly so, given the pressures on German-trained dancers to integrate their approach with the codified movement techniques of their contemporaries. As the opening anecdote demonstrates, Martin did not value improvisational approaches to modern dance. Yet, as Kaschmann's response to Martin's rebuke demonstrates, German-trained dancers persisted in practicing improvisational methods learned in Dresden, Berlin, and Hamburg. Surely the Americanized versions of these methods influenced the reappearance of improvisation in the 1960s. Routes for transmission include Nikolais, who first studied with Kaschmann before working with Holm; the New Dance Group, which transmuted from a leftist collective to a multifaceted center for modern dance training during the 1940s and 1950s; and the teaching of Louise Kloepper at the

University of Wisconsin, Anneliese Mertz at Washington University, and innumerable other German-trained dancers at colleges and universities. At Howard University Erika Thimey continued Von Grona's and Burrough's training of black dancers in the tradition of *Ausdruckstanz*.

My point here is not to bemoan the historiographic ellipsis of *Ausdruckstanz* across the Atlantic. Rather, my point is to call for an intercultural historiography of twentieth-century theatrical dance. Too often, we write that history according to national and/or generic boundaries. Hence we produce *Modern Dance, Negro Dance: Race in Motion*, a study of modern dance and African-American concert dance in the United States, or *Krokodil im Schwanensee: Tanz in Deutschland seit 1945,* a study of ballet and modern dance on the stages of postwar Germany. The history of *Ausdruckstanz* in its entirety demands more, for the improvisational methods developed in Germany during the 1920s and 1930s traveled far and wide. Not only to the United States, but also to Japan, where they arguably underlay the emergence of Butoh, and to Israel, where they initiated the development of a distinctly national artistic culture, to name only a few destinations. Cross-cultural influences work in a myriad of directions, creating hybrids and fusions that we have barely begun to fathom.

Notes

My thanks to Susanne Franco, Marina Nordera, and Claire Rousier for their comments on an earlier version of this essay. Thanks as well to Rebecca Katz, who provided research assistance in New York City.

1 Kaschmann received her diploma from the Laban School in Hamburg in 1924 and joined Yvonne Georgi's dance ensemble at the Hanover Opera in 1926. From 1924 until 1933 she "spent many weeks, whenever I got a chance, at the Dresden or Berlin [Wigman] Schools." After she settled in Hartford, Kaschmann taught at the Hartford College for Women and the Hartford Conservatory of Music and Dance. "Wigman Centennial Day Questionnaire," Society of Dance History Scholars, February 17, 1986, author's collection. Kaschmann recollected Martin's remark in a subsequent interview.

2 *Ausdruckstanz* actually emerged as a term in the postwar period to describe the dance movement variously called *Tanzkunst* (dance art), *der moderne Tanz* (modern dance), *der neue künstlerische Tanz* (the new artistic dance), *Kunst-Tanz* (art dance), and *der moderne künstlerische Tanz* (modern artistic dance), among other terms, from the 1920s through the Second World War. In my book *Ecstasy and the Demon: Feminism and Nationalism in the Dances of Mary Wigman*, Berkeley, CA: University of California Press, 1993, p. 7 (2nd edn *Ecstasy and the Demon*: *The Dances of Mary Wigman*, Minneapolis, MN: University of Minnesota Press, 2006) I retained the postwar usage to refer to the choreographic and pedagogical methods associated with "the movement led by Wigman and Laban and practiced by their many followers in Germany . . . a loose alliance of dancers

who worked outside pre-existent institutions and created their own networks around private studios and concert performances." As Franco has pointed out, this definition of *Ausdruckstanz* excludes a broad range of related performance practices across Europe. Following Franco's lead, this essay points toward a cross-cultural definition of *Ausdruckstanz*. For a description of the improvisational methods employed by *Ausdruckstanz*, see Manning, *Ecstasy and the Demon*, pp. 52–6 and 89–96.

3 S.L. Foster, *Dances That Describe Themselves: The Improvised Choreography of Richard Bull*, Middletown, CT: Wesleyan University Press, 2002, pp. 24–68.

4 Patricia Stöckemann makes a first attempt at a comprehensive account of 'Emigranten und ihre Zufluchtsorte', *Tanzdrama*, 1998, no. 42, pp. 19–27.

5 'The Great World Theater', *Theater Arts Monthly*, 1927, vol. 11, August, p. 565.

6 J. Ross Acocella, 'Van Grona and his First American Negro Ballet', *Dance Magazine*, 1982, March, p. 23. Acocella reviewed a concert in which Van Grona (having anglicized the spelling of his family name during the Second World War) appeared and reconstructed several of his dances, including *Spirit of Labor*.

7 Fluent in German, Horst translated writings by Laban and Wigman during his days with Denishawn. When he returned from his European sojourn, he brought photographs of Wigman for Graham. In addition to working with Graham, he accompanied other dancers, including German immigrants and visitors Ronny Johansson, Margarethe Wallman, Harald Kreutzberg, and Yvonne Georgi. He also wrote about Kreutzberg's and Georgi's distinctive use of music in terms that paralleled his contemporary comments on Graham's use of music. J. Soares, *Louis Horst: Musician in a Dancer's World*, Durham, NC: Duke University Press, 1992, *passim*.

8 E. Denby, *Dance Writings*, New York: Alfred Knopf, 1986, p. 17.

9 L. Kirstein, 'Dance Chronicle', *Hound & Horn*, 1931, vol. 4, pp. 574–6.

10 T. Shawn, 'Germany's Contribution to the Art of the Dance', *Foreword*, 1930, vol. 18, p. 5.

11 'What Dancers Think About the German Dance', *Dance Magazine*, 1931, May, p. 15.

12 J. Martin, 'The Dance: Kreutzberg', *New York Times*, March 31, 1935, sec. 10, p. 9.

13 H. Gilfond, 'Review: Yvonne Georgi', *Dance Observer*, 1936, vol. 3, January, pp. 4–5.

14 See E. Graff, *Stepping Left: Dance and Politics in New York City, 1928–1942*, Durham, NC: Duke University Press, 1997, which provides the first comprehensive account of leftist dance in the United States.

15 Marcia Siegel interview with Holm, 'Mary Wigman, 1886–1973: A Tribute', *Dance Magazine*, 1973, November, p. 80.

16 H. Holm, A. Lauterer, H. Kerr, 'Trend', *Magazine of Art*, 1938, vol. 31, March, 137, pp. 142–5 and 184. S.A. Kriegsman, *Modern Dance in America: The Bennington Years*, Boston, MA: G.K. Hall, 1981, pp. 161–73.

17 Program reproduced, ibid., p. 171.

18 Reminiscences of Faith Reyher Jackson (1979), on p. 45 in the Columbia University Oral History Research Office Collection. The following discussion derives from the larger argument of my book *Modern Dance, Negro Dance: Race in Motion*, Minneapolis, MN: University of Minnesota Press, 2004.

19 S. Fisher Fishkin, 'Interrogating "Whiteness", Complicating "Blackness": Remapping American Culture', *American Quarterly*, 1995, vol. 47, September, pp. 428–66.

20 Manning, *Modern Dance, Negro Dance*, pp. 70–3 and 93–101.
21 Program, American Negro Ballet, November 21, 1937, Lafayette Theater, Jerome Robbins Dance Division, New York Public Library for the Performing Arts.
22 S.C. Bourne, 'Capacity Crowd Acclaims Ballet', *Amsterdam News*, 27 November 1937, p. 19.
23 Program, American Negro Ballet. Bourne, 'Capacity Crowd Acclaims Ballet'; 'SRO Sign Hung Out at Harlem Ballet Debut', *Afro-American*, November 27, 1937, p. 11. 'Negro Ballet Has Performance', *New York Sun* November 22, 1937, Von Grona clipping file, Jerome Robbins Dance Division, New York Public Library for the Performing Arts.
24 Bourne, 'Capacity Crowd Acclaims Ballet'.
25 D. Gere, 'Introduction', in D. Gere, A. Cooper Albright (eds), *Taken by Surprise: A Dance Improvisation Reader*, Middletown, CT: Wesleyan University Press, 2003, pp. xiii–xiv. Included in the anthology is the essay: S. Banes, 'Spontaneous Combustion: Notes on Dance Improvisation from the Sixties to the Nineties', pp. 77–85.

4 *Ausdruckstanz* on the left and the work of Jean Weidt

Yvonne Hardt

Examining the work of the dancer and choreographer Jean (Hans)[1] Weidt brings into question the multiple layers of political meaning that can be ascribed to the modern dance form that developed in Germany in the early twentieth century. As Susan Manning's essay[2] in this section demonstrates, *Ausdruckstanz* (dance of expression) could take on several political meanings once transplanted to the US and practiced in different historical contexts. The same heterogeneous political connotations can also be noted about the German modern dance scene in the Weimar Republic. With this essay, I would like to suggest that there is another way of linking politics and dance in the Weimar Republic that may be considered alongside the growing tendency to perceive the political orientation and ideological subtexts of this dance form as linked to notions of national socialism.[3] Exposing rigorously this relationship of the modern dance scene to national socialism is understandable in light of the vehement denial of political involvement that had, until recently, prevailed. While it is important to note these ideological ties to the political right existed, it is also significant to acknowledge that some dancers maintained a very open and explicit affiliation to the political left. Little research has been done on this to date. Though my essay focuses primarily on Weidt, I hope to arouse more general interest in the history of these left-wing dancers in Germany and to help challenge a linear and causal interpretation of history that sees the development of body culture in the Weimar Republic solely as a predecessor to that of national socialism.[4] The importance of the idea of the ideal *Gemeinschaft* (community), elements of irrationality, and the belief in the natural body, which are often linked with national socialist ideology, had a wide range of signification and were used in the Weimar Republic simultaneously by nationalists, socialists, and *Lebensreformer* (life reformers).[5] As such, I am more interested in asking why, at a certain moment in time, it was possible to envision the potential of the body, of dance, and of community with radically different political meanings? How did dancers position themselves within this spectrum of possible political interpretations of *Ausdruckstanz* and was this reflected in their movements and their choreographies?

Because these questions open an immense field of research, I will focus primarily on the explicit political relationships between dance and politics, without losing sight of the more implicit political connotations. In speaking of an explicit political realm of dance, I do not want to rely on an older more exclusive definition of the political as tied to institutions, parties, etc. But, given the dominant belief that dancers actually saw themselves as a-political, it seems quite interesting to ask after their party involvement and their political self-understanding. I am interested, moreover, in those dancers who not only openly expressed political interests but who sought to express them through their dancing. Weidt is an example of this sort of political dancer.

Though Weidt appears as one of the few political dancers in dance histories as the so called *der rote Tänzer* (the red dancer) he is usually seen as an exception to and somewhat at the edge of what is considered *Ausdruckstanz*. Emphasizing the political engagement in his work has been the main focus while his artistic work has not been thoroughly investigated.[6] By doing this, I will suggest that in Weidt's case, *Ausdruckstanz* and politics were linked on many interacting levels. First, by means of a short biographical contextualization, I would like to show that Weidt belonged to a larger group of politically active dancers and socialists interested in dance and that his thoughts on dance and politics can be tied to *Kultursozialismus* (a cultural interpretation of socialism). Second, by looking at how the body and body work are understood in the case of Weidt and in the context of the *Kultursozialisten* (cultural socialists), it is possible to explain why the left was so interested in the modern dance form and how this form could be perceived as a useful way of "culturally uplifting" the working class. Last but not least, and this is the main point of my essay, I want to demonstrate that, aesthetically, Weidt's choreographic work clearly belonged to the *Ausdruckstanz* tradition. My thesis is that the aesthetics of this modern dance form, with its emotionally charged movements and the clear-cut spatial and rhythmical structures of its movement, were ideally suited to staging the worker's body and political issues. *Ausdruckstanz* could be used for political purposes and was quite often interpreted in that way.

In speaking of political dances and in looking for the representational and symbolic elements of this art, I am not in any way suggesting that this is the only possible reading or that it can be simply understood on this representational level. Quite on the contrary, it is important to show how movement and movement images are historically, socially, and culturally shaped and, in consequence, can take on quite different meanings outside of their original context or even within different groups of spectators and how dances can never be properly translated into a verbal interpretation. This essay does not attempt to postulate an ultimate interpretation of Weidt's dances but tries to make a historically distant field of movement and meaning accessible to today's reader. As such, I would like to propose a dance history that studies its object within its specific historical-sociological context, but pays equal attention to the traces of movement that remain. This is the only way to thoroughly problematize the relationship between ideology and movement practice.

A life for dance and politics

Weidt's dancing practice and his political orientation and theoretical reflections exemplify the heterogeneous and complex relationship between political identity and cultural practices of the left in the Weimar Republic. While his membership in the Communist party provides a clear indication of his political outlook, his political orientation cannot be understood so easily and as totally coherent. Weidt was born into a working class family in Hamburg in 1904. From early on he had to help provide for his family, but he also belonged to the first generation of working class youth that could take part in youth activities. This included singing in a Christian choir and, later on, participating in body culture activities. After Weidt had finished his training to become a gardener at the age of 19, he joined a gymnastics club, where he met Sigurd Leeder (who would later become the partner of the well-known choreographer Kurt Jooss). Leeder invited him to join his dance classes. Later on, Weidt would speak somewhat skeptically of his dances and his mode of teaching. While he was extremely inspired by the physical experience, he believed that, for instance, dances based on improvisations to themes like "strong" or "weak" did not adequately use the potential of moving bodies. Yet, I would argue that several of Weidt's choreographic patterns can actually be traced back to this early training.

Weidt started working on his own dances at the age of 21. He rented a gym for rehearsals and the Komödienhaus, a theater in Hamburg to stage his solo works. The evening was announced on posters that stated simply: "Weidt is dancing." Only 100 visitors saw this performance in 1925. It was a financial fiasco but marked the first step for Weidt in being recognized as a new dance artist who combined abstract themes to the music of Frédéric Chopin in solos with titles such as *Dance with a red flag*.[7] In his dances, the worker conquered the stage as a person/individual and a topic. The worker was simultaneously subject and object of his choreographies. Presenting his work as a solo artist is clearly linked to the practice that had been initiated by other *Ausdruckstanz* dancers. He did not, however, see himself primarily as a solo-artist but sought to link art and life, and art and politics – yet another characteristic aspect of the avant-garde of this time. The same can be said about the importance which he gave to the idea of the community and which he sought to establish by dancing with people of the same political orientation. Prior dance experience was not paramount, and the group was made up mostly of lay dancers from the working class. Weidt perceived them as a free artistic collective in which art and political vision should be inseparable. He rented an old factory hall (the Zementklotz) and transformed it into a studio for dance and other artistic events. For instance, it also became a meeting-point for intellectuals and an exhibition space. Weidt not only danced and led political discussions, he also recited poems by Rainer Maria Rilke, following yet another trend of the time.[8]

> We managed to create something like an experimental stage/theater, even though we did not use this term. In our discussions about paintings and posters, about literature and dance, about natural lifestyle [. . .] we were not so concerned with Expressionism or other similar artistic programs but proposed a sort of agit-prop-art, so to speak, a political propaganda that nonetheless had to be artistically convincing. Our goal was to create a new and proper form for issues that had previously been ignored.[9]

Weidt wrote this in 1968, when the political climate in the German Democratic Republic had banned the experimental and expressionistic art of the Weimar Republic as profoundly bourgeois. It might explain why Weidt distanced himself in retrospect so clearly from artistic programs concerned with Expressionism in favor of political themes. Nonetheless, in the Weimar Republic Weidt shared many political and artistic beliefs that he later on marked as bourgeois. For instance, his aim of linking life and art was also common in much more moderate socialist or even bourgeois *Lebensreformer* circles. This affiliation to the life reform-movement can be ascertained not only from his comments on natural lifestyle and the influence of "humanistic ideals" but also by the fact that he took courses on painting and architecture.[10]

Weidt's visions of dance make it possible to draw further parallels to the thinking of the cultural socialists and to their ideas about art's purpose and form in the context of the worker's struggle. This group of socialists, which was associated primarily with the social democrats (Sozialdemokratischen Partei Deutschlands, SPD), understood socialism as a political, economic, and cultural movement.[11] Given the reality that Weimar had neither achieved the desired revolution nor created better living conditions for workers, the cultural socialists wanted to bring a better future into the present, at least in part, by "culturally uplifting" the working class.[12] Modern dance, which was part of a new and sought-after sensual culture, seemed to be an appropriate means for reaching that end, especially because it was seen as an alternative to what was perceived as an all too elitist book culture. Modern dance also seemed attractive in light of its exclusion and rejection of other dance forms. Ballet was rejected on grounds of its aristocratic origin, and contemporary social dances like the Charleston were seen as having too much the air of the hectic, technical rhythm and beat associated with industrial work. Modern dance fit both into an ideal of an art focused on physical sensation, and a practice that could activate and mobilize the body while simultaneously rejecting notions of sports records and capitalistic performance standards. This sort of socialist interpretation of modern dance was exemplified by Martin Gleisner's book *Tanz für Alle* (Dance for Everybody),[13] and Gleisner's thesis on the purpose and goals of dance share many similarities to Weidt's ideas about dance.

Weidt's relationship to the cultural socialists existed not only on the basis of similar convictions but also through his contacts with members of the SPD active in dance. The most prominent of them was the artistic director of the Hamburg Ballet, Olga Brandt-Knack. She fought vehemently for the creation of the *Kulturbund* (cultural union) and for better social standing and rights for dancers. She was also active outside the theater in teaching dance to working-class children and in creating performances for *Jugendweihen* (an alternative initiation practice to Christian Communion offered by the socialists). Weidt had both working and personal contacts with Brandt-Knack and was probably aware of her support for dance in the SPD cultural associations. In his biography *Der rote Tänzer* (The Red Dancer), Weidt acknowledged that he had learned choreographic practices from her while dancing in works such as the *Dämonen*. He was also introduced to the speaking and movement choirs that Brandt-Knack staged jointly with Alfred Johannesson for the socialist cultural programs. This may be where Weidt found his initial inspiration on how to combine moving and speaking, which he later integrated in some of his agit-prop style dances.

Weidt's political contacts and sources of inspiration became further diversified when he moved to Berlin in 1929. Originally, he came because he wanted to work with the director Erwin Piscator. While they only collaborated on one project, Weidt stayed in Berlin and founded a new group: the so-called Die roten Tänzer (Red Dancers), with which he continued to pursue his ideas of political dance. At the beginning Hertha Feist, head of the Laban School in Berlin and then a member of the SPD, offered him her studio for rehearsals, and Margarete Wallmann, a student of Mary Wigman, cast him in the role of the demon in her choreography *Orpheus*. He was integrated into a politicized dance scene both as a dancer and as a political activist. He met with Jo Mihaly, a woman who also staged political dances, and the famous Valeska Gert, who was known for her satirical dance collages. Weidt's rehearsal space in the Kurfürstenstraße was a meeting place for politically organized artists from the *Rote Gewerkschaftsopposition* (Red Opposition Union of the Theaters). His dances, such as *Klage des Soldaten* (Sorrow of the Soldier), *Tanz für Lenin* (Dance for Lenin) or *Gesicht eines jungen Arbeiters* (Face of a Young Worker), received positive notices by such dance critics as Fritz Böhme. If there was criticism it hardly ever concerned the mixture of arts and politics or his political orientation but was based on a belief in different artistic standards and physical virtuosity, which Weidt's work seemed to lack for some.[14] He and other dancers organized dance events in order to collect for the poor or for political parties. His ties to the Communist party became stronger and, after participating in their party events and agit-prop theater, he eventually became a member of the Communist party in 1931. As an active member of the party, he was imprisoned for six weeks shortly after the election in January 1933, and many of his materials, including the masks with which he worked extensively, were destroyed by the Gestapo.[15]

After the Nazis came to power, it was impossible for Weidt to continue his political dance style. Pretending to travel to Sweden, he and his group set out for the Worker's Olympic Games in Moscow in the summer of 1933. Disappointed by the feedback on their performance style and warned by friends against returning to Germany, he did not know where to go next. He sought exile in Paris but did not settle there permanently until after another difficult visit to the Soviet Union. In Paris he founded the Ballet 38, and, later on, fought for the British pioneer corps, dancing even while imprisoned in camps to entertain the soldiers. After the war, he resettled in Paris and achieved notable success with his newly founded Ballet des Arts and the piece *Die Zelle* (The Cell), winning the international choreographic competition in Copenhagen in 1947 (the same competition Jooss had won in 1932 with his famous anti-war piece *Der Grüne Tisch* (The Green Table)).[16] *Die Zelle* resembled the style of the pre-war era in many ways, though it was apparent that Weidt had taken some ballet classes during his exile in Paris. In 1949 he returned to East Germany. However, his hopes to find here the place for his political modern dance art were only supported at the beginning. Especially when after March 1953 a resolution on the future of dance explicitly rejected *Ausdruckstanz* as a degenerate bourgeois art form.[17] Though some of Weidt's writings took a critical stance toward *Ausdruckstanz*, his vision of dance could hardly be integrated into a system that privileged ballet as the proper Soviet dance form. Further investigation of Weidt's situation in the German Democratic Republic would provide an interesting analysis of politics and dance. The focus of this article, however, is limited to the Weimar Republic and, specifically, to how Weidt's activity in the body culture movement and his actual dance practice fit ideally into the aesthetics of *Ausdruckstanz* in the Weimar Republic.

The ambivalent image of the worker's body

Despite his focus on content and narration, the dancer's body for Weidt played a major part in the way dance signifies politically. He believed that his work was simultaneously a formation and presentation of the worker's living conditions, which were significantly shaped by physical labor. Weidt himself had a very striking physical appearance that served to provide an example for the dualistic image of the worker's body. Photos of Weidt portray him as very thin and worn out, evoking the impression of someone on the verge of starving. His facial features are hard and his hands are enormous from manual work. At the same time, however, the photos depict a man with clearly developed muscles, who controls his body in precise movements and energetic jumps. In these shots, he takes up a lot of space, generating an almost heroic image. Moreover, it did not exactly suit the notion of what was commonly considered a beautiful dancing body. The very act of presenting his body on stage was both an artistic and a political revolution: in comparison to other male and female dancers of *Ausdruckstanz*, his harshness was still a provocation if one expected to see a beautifully swinging body in the sense of the new body culture that fostered a movement free of force and inhibition. Yet, its presentation was made possible by avant-garde dance practices and performances in the Weimar Republic that tackled issues of tension and distortion. This political climate provided the space for such experiments. While Weidt exposed the worn out and wounded body on stage, made the movements of suffering part of the dance vocabulary and the research for choreography, he was even more interested in presenting the strong and confident worker's body, which he believed could be reached through the act of dancing. Physical education and the presentation of strength were interwoven with a symbolic and felt emancipation of the worker. The gradual development from an oppressed to a liberated worker was a general theme in the worker's movement that influenced Weidt's choreographic practice. For instance, he created twelve different versions of his dance *Der Arbeiter*

(The Worker) before reaching a form that suited him: "I worked at it, until I had reached the point where the worker is not to be presented with his head down and hanging, but full of pride and secure about his future."[18] The representational aspects of dance were thus linked to a physical practice that actually helped evoke this strength.

Therefore, Weidt's collaboration with his dancers needs to be understood as something more than rehearsing for performances. Most of the "Red Dancers" came from an organized worker's youth group called *Fichte-Arbeiterjugend* (Fichte's Workers' Youth). They were politically active young men and women who practiced sports but did not have any practical prior contact with dance. This group also never managed to become a professional, fulltime dance group, because rehearsals could only take place on Sundays or, sometimes, on week nights. Nonetheless, this rehearsal process was as important as the performances themselves, because Weidt wanted to transform the workers into dancers, into people with agency over their lives and bodies. He wanted to offer them an alternative to their daily work. Much like those who engaged in the bourgeois life reform movement, Weidt took his collaborators on walks and offered nude gymnastic classes, as part of the commonly active *Freie Körperkultur* (FKK, Free Body Culture Movement) in Germany.[19] His dancers never achieved a systematic technique in the classical sense (which, by the way, is not unlike many other modern dancers of the time), and they were often quite the opposite of virtuosic. But they did acquire and create a movement and dance vocabulary that could not be used or explained in labor terms and that challenged, even more than that of other modern dancers, the contemporary understanding of what bodies were allowed to do and to symbolize on stage. Their movement vocabulary, which was clearly recognizable as dance, could not be used outside the realm of dance, in the sense that, unlike gymnastics, it did not aim at regenerating or enhancing physical labor capacities. Personal gain was achieved by discovering new spaces of movement and by perceiving themselves as active agents in this process, as being – quite literally – on the move.

All of this suggests further similarities between the work of Weidt, his group and that of other socialists, especially the activities of the cultural socialists. They too saw the body as a central vantage point for the reform of the worker's life and liberation. Anna Siemsen, Max Adler, Valtin Hartig, and many others associated with the cultural socialists believed that the *Entfremdung* (detachment) of the worker's body, which reduced him/her to a pure work object, was far more critical an issue than that of low income. Fighting this physical abuse became a proclaimed goal.[20] Like Weidt, they oscillated between two images of the worker's body: the first, the strong, thin, a muscular body that did not have to concern itself with the bourgeois problem of "dieting"; the second, the worn out dirty worker who generally tended toward drinking. What they all shared was the common belief that increasing the worth of the body and understanding its importance for society and regarding human development in general would lead to a better position of the worker. "We do want the culture of the body. Taking care of the body and honoring it must evoke appreciation for physical work and also enhance the standing of the worker."[21]

The cultural socialists associated this body culture with dance and the nudist movement. Otto Zimmermann, the politically active leader of movement choirs and a passionate nude dancer, remarked:

> The new dance culture has a deep relationship to the future culture of the workers for the simple reason that it gives needed meaning and admiration back to the *Leib* (human body), which everyone shares – without class difference – without the capitalists having any extra rights. The beautiful naked human body will have the right to explore itself in the new world of dance.[22]

At this point it should be said that the socialists and the protagonists of the nude body culture who had a more conservative or nationalistic standpoint shared the same belief in the body as a source for respect and admiration. They adored the tanned, muscular male body. An example can be found in Adolf Koch, who was one of the leading protagonists of the nude body culture and an activist in the worker's movement. He had a school where young proletarian and life reformer youth exercised in the nude, and he too favored the presentation of the strong worker's body. The movement vocabulary that can be seen in photos and is described by the subtitles included pushing, pulling, bending with clenched fists and reaching out, all of which remind one of movements actually used in work. Fighting both a possible skeptical notion toward nudism and the image of the loose, uncontrollable worker, Koch sought to erase any doubts proclaiming: "Show them pictures of the active big city youth at work."[23] Thus body, culture, and physical strength were also closely intertwined in socialist circles, and they bought into the belief of the superiority of the beautiful body. They did so, however, not necessarily for nationalistic reasons but to fight the image of the weak and dirty worker. This might also be one of the reasons why modern dance culture, aspects of which proposed to show the possessed and not always beautiful body, had a more difficult time in the workers' milieu. It was too close to their own physical reality and did not provide the distraction they sought.

It is not surprising therefore that there are many strong and dynamic movements in the photos of Weidt's work, which present thin and muscular, almost naked bodies. Acquiring technical and physical ability, creating differentiated muscular schemes, and increasing energy made it possible to present a new ideal of the worker. While it is important to mention the disciplinary tendencies that life reformers, gymnasts, and dancers shared (even though they would probably have denied this and talked about natural training or regaining natural movements), it is also significant to note, however, that the productive energies of this training created a new and independent movement style. The term discipline should be freed from a solely negative connotation, because the dancers courageously crossed conventional boundaries as to how people should present their bodies and who has the right to dance.

This expansion in possibilities of movement was characterized by a freedom to choose and, for the first time, it became possible for a class of people that had never had any contact with the sphere of artistic dance or the modern arts in general. An extensive number of people could begin to experience their bodies in actions they had voluntarily chosen. Weidt belonged to a very heterogeneous Weimar body culture in which there was democratic and controversial discussion about what body types, what sort of training, and what goals should be reached by body culture and dance. Clearly there existed an idealized image of the body and the strong body was still preferred over the more grotesque or those less easily identified as beautiful. Yet, the possibility of the co-existence of these different bodily presentations in life and art, the heterogeneity in general mark a clear difference to body culture as it was fostered in the fascist era. Weidt's artistic work also mirrored that diversity and the contradicting images of the worker's fate. In what follows, I will demonstrate how the ideas of movement in *Ausdruckstanz* were ideally suited for embodying this dualistic reality and physicality of the worker.

Ausdruckstanz and the making of a body aesthetic of the worker

I will focus on just two aspects of Weidt's work to illustrate how he combined his political ambitions and topics with the modern dance form of *Ausdruckstanz*. First, I will discuss his mimetic dance style and his use of masks in order to show that he was clearly influenced by the emotionally charged, ecstatic, and sensual movements of *Ausdruckstanz*. Second, I will demonstrate that the influence of *Ausdruckstanz* can also be discovered in the rhythmic and spatial structuring of his dances, which show parallels to the theoretical discourses about movement and space of Rudolf von

Laban's choreutics and the contemporary discourse on rhythm. Even though most *Ausdruckstanz* dancers would have rigorously rejected any source of monotonous or technical rhythms, Weidt worked within the framework of *Ausdruckstanz* in the rhythmical structure of his dances. Both strategies corresponded mimetically to the worker's reality. The explicit use of mimetic movements and masks, however, was more ideally suited to portraying suffering, while the rhythmic structuring could demonstrate strength and force, especially in group formations.

Weidt's dances were inspired by the obvious and appalling physicality of poverty and age: the shivering of an old woman perhaps or the way a man, who lost a leg during the war, moved forward. Weidt took this physical quality as much as the stories as a vantage point for his choreographies. As such, his dances were not only little narrative pantomimes but worked explicitly with the performative aspects of the moving body, especially with the quality of physical tension.[24] In his piece *Eine Frau* (A Woman), for instance, which was one of his most successful dances in the Weimar Republic, he embodied the history and suffering of a woman who had lost her children in the war through movement that relied extensively on the use of weight and tension. Photos of the dance show Weidt performing with a bent upper body, his head tilted to the side, covered by a big mask (Figure 5). His arms are awkwardly twisted. Any sort of clear line and the vertical axis of classical dance are absent. Similar creatures with heavy and hanging heads are found in his group choreography *Tanz der alten Leute* (Dance of the Old People). This dance has been reconstructed twice, once by Weidt himself in 1984 with young dancers from Berlin's Komische Oper and more recently by Dominque and Françoise Dupuy. Both versions show simple movements, a back and forth swinging of the upper body, shivering, walking in circles. The people appeared truly old and the embodiment of suffering was convincing. As such, the quality of the movement was the most important part of the dance.[25] Though there were also clear spatial patterns such as the walking in circles and, at the end, a line of interwoven bodies, it was the mimetic form of presentation that struck the critics. "Weidt is never a dancer of absolute or 'abstract' form, he is always a dance pantomime."[26] This should not, however, lead one to think that his dancing style should be placed outside the realm of the modern dance of his time. His movements representing daily life were more than just mimetic copies of suffering. Böhme noted:

> In all these dances there are parts that truly grip the audience, in which an almost unbearable violence is aroused by madly and

Figure 5
Jean Weidt in *Eine Frau* (1928). Permission kindly granted by Tanzarchiv Köln.

> ecstatically dancing characters. An access to the understanding of these dances lies here: his creations are expressions of human sorrow in contemporary society, they are not simply mirrors of this reality, but endeavors and attempts to uplift everyday reality by way of movement creation into the realm of the symbolic.[27]

The ecstatic body was a *topos* that dominated early *Ausdruckstanz*. In this respect, Böhme establishes a link between the meaning of and physical quality in Weidt's dances. It is the dancing and moving body, even though reality is present through mimetic aspects, that plays a central role in giving meaning as much as it is the source and center of his artistic form.

The mimetic communication was based on the symbolically stylized and frozen facial expressions of the masks as well as the movement. Though the masks drew attention to themselves as art works and expression, Weidt insisted that the dances were never to be a simple play of masks. He searched for the same intimate relationship between dance and the mask that was characteristic in *Ausdruckstanz*. This also meant that one could not simply hide behind a mask. Movements needed to be formed in such a way as to animate the mask. This must have been quite successful in his dance *Eine Frau* because the audience articulated the illusion that there really was an old woman behind that big pale mask.[28] The fact that Weidt actually embodied a woman on stage without even marginally trying to conceal his male identity is yet another daring trait of this choreography.[29]

The masks ended up playing a significant role in communicating with the audience, probably even more than Weidt actually wished. A critic commenting on a performance of *Tanz der alten Leute* in France after Weidt had fled to Paris noted:

> In this piece there is so much suffering, a heap of sorrow, which leaves deep traces in our memory that can no longer be erased. The use of pale masks, the frozen faces, and the hardened expressions caused by the lack of hope provide this scene with an incredible sculptured motif.[30]

The masks function thematically. To the same extent that they form and interact with the bodies, they create characters and open fields of associations. Like paintings, they evoke something that remains, something the ephemeral quality of dance is generally considered as lacking. The artist drew on expressionist motifs in creating the masks, as suggested by the enlarged eyes and mouths. The aesthetic of the masks shows also a similarity to sketches and prints by Käthe Kollwitz. The masks helped create an atmosphere, in which movement could evoke emotional states and appear more legible than some of the more "abstract" movements that *Ausdruckstanz* normally showed on stage.

The masks also created a coherent aesthetic appearance for the group. Though Weidt sought to portray individuals and each mask was different, the masks assured that all the facial expressions and mimetic components were coherent within a group of people that came from very different artistic backgrounds and in which elements of mime could easily look far more amateurish than the movement performed by inexperienced dancers. While awkward movements of the body could be interpreted in the context of *Ausdruckstanz* and its new movement quality, facial expressions could be problematic. For this reason, most dancers of *Ausdruckstanz* froze their facial features or tried to keep it "neutral." Böhme refers implicitly to this advantage of the mask when, at a different point, he regrets they have been taken off: "When the facial sphere is uncovered, there is often a moment of individual reality in these dances that disturbs the impact and the coherence of the imagined world."[31] Despite their expressiveness, the masks evoked an artistic reduction and helped form an artistic group out of lay dancers. In the interplay of these masks, movement could remain quite simple. The dancers walked slowly in a circle with heavy bodies and hanging limbs; they turned to the front, bent their upper bodies forward, lifted their arms and let them fall together again. Once in a while someone knelt down and was then guided upward by someone else. Repeated movements, like turning one's hands outward or the final marching in a line, also revealed a reduced and stylized vocabulary of movement. It was never dynamic. The weighted movements, the masks, and spatial and kinetic awareness placed this dance within the context of *Ausdruckstanz* while making it possible to visualize the suffering of the elderly and to make an empathic claim on their behalf that might provoke change.

The *Rhythmisierung* (rhythmic structuring) of Weidt's pieces established another mimetic link in (re)presenting the worker's everyday life and a movement form that could be characterized as modern dance. Rhythmic patterns worked especially well in group works. In keeping with the trend of the times, Weidt's dances perceived rhythm, industrialization, and work as mutually dependent. While many modern dancers clearly opposed industrial rhythms and distinguished between a free flowing cadence and industrial metrics, Weidt did not share these doubts because rhythmic beats made up the daily life of the worker he wanted to visualize. This experience provided the basis for the rhythmic structure in his dances, such as *Akkord Akkord*, *Passion eines Menschen* (Passion of a Human), or *Morgens-Mittags-Abends* (In the Morning – At Noon – In the Evening). It is the rhythmic structuring that clearly connotes Weidt's work as dance, that highlights the qualities of movement, and that guides attention toward it. Repetition, accumulation, and the endless continuation of movement (as in the titles of the dances themselves) represent the repetitive structure of work, which the economist Karl Bücher had already qualified as the basis of any form of rhythm. Rhythm is based on movement, a concept that many dancers of the time would have shared. It does not come from outside, but is generated by the inner flow of movements. The repetitive structure of the movements makes one focus on the action of moving; these repetitive movements draw attention to the physicality of work and dancing, rather than a possible narrative structure that a dance with a similar political intention might want to convey. The rhythmical structure highlights the works' dance and movement qualities by taking everyday movement and making it appear more stylized and abstract.

It is impossible to extract the stylized "work" rhythms from either the photos or the critiques. But it is quite likely that the dances used stepping rhythms, performed with a great deal of tension, far more often than the free swinging cadences favored by many modern dancers. Böhme, who wrote about "a group of excellent jointly, rhythmically, and expressively dancing group of dancers" also mentioned the use of broken rhythms and movement flows: "There are always interrupted swings, gestures that are held, spilling impulses, movements of the whole body that are ripped apart, generated not only as pure form or out of an ornamental interest, but as an ultimate form of the expression of the experience of the soul."[32] This did especially apply to those movements that expressed rhythmical tension, that tore the movement awkwardly, that revealed the force they required. Weidt took the ideals of *Ausdruckstanz* that sought to explore and expose the suppressed states of being much more seriously than many of the fashionable dancers of the time. This was to have an effect on many people. A critique from Paris, where, in 1938, modern dance was not as yet well known, read as follows: "These dance reformers seek to stylize the rhythm of effort, the rhythm of work, the rhythm of pain."[33] Showing effort on stage and the "non-beautiful" body had a political dimension in addition to the theme. Thus, physical and narrative (re)presentation of politics were tightly interwoven. Weidt varied the potential of what *Ausdruckstanz* had to offer. He took the tension from a purely physical dimension and emotionally subjective space and bound it symbolically to the worker's fate.

Photos of Weidt's choreographies also reveal forceful movements, poses, and tensions. They show men moving their upper bodies upward and then downward. These may be the movements that one reviewer described as "movements of sense: hitting, mowing, and harvesting." Women reach their arms to the side and lift their solar plexus and, though they do not seem to be portraying a gesture that symbolizes work, one anticipates that they will also bend down, making an opposing spatial movement pattern. Hands are often clenched in fists, increasing the impression of tension and force, and simultaneously charging them symbolically. There is a general tendency to present the "work" movements non-realistically, to transform them along choreographic patterns. Photos in which hands reach far out or are in positions above the head indicating a shaking or holding that seems to threaten from above evoke associations to gestures of fighting rather than working. In the same way, the upper bodies of some of the men, which are bent to such extremes that just their knees can be seen, not only indicate working movements but are clearly shaped in the interest of a dancing form that is aware of the levels of up and down. These movements are always more than a mimetic copying of work movements.

The movements are stylized with a clear spatial intention that emphasizes lines which make the movements appear more abstract. These spatial structures show parallels to the use of space in Laban's dance analysis. In a photo of *Morgens-Mittags-Abends*, two men stand, tilting slightly backward from their pelvises up. Their left arms reach out in a long, upward diagonal line as if pointing or aiming at something up there. Their right arms are pulled backward from the elbow into the opposite diagonal. The tension between these two poles is increased by their clenched right fists. This cannot be identified as a work movement; at most it might suggest the pulling of a bow made all the more abstract by emphasizing the diagonal. The importance of spatial structures in Weidt's work becomes apparent when one sees how he contrasts this by placing four women in a line facing the audience. Their arms are lifted up in the same frontal body sphere, standing, in Laban's terminology, in the *Türebene* (doorway). How much attention was generally given to these lines and forms

Figure 6
Jean Weidt in *Arbeiter*, Kammerspiele Hamburg (1925), in J. Weidt, *Der Rote Tänzer. Ein Lebensbericht*, Berlin: Henschel, 1968.

of abstraction – at least in the process of making these photos – is exemplified in Weidt's *Der Arbeiter*. In a photo shot in 1932 he stands with his two arms reaching backward, absolutely parallel, tilting his upper body slightly forward in a diagonal prolonging of the right arm, which reaches backward and, with a fist, adds a gesture of combat (Figure 6). In dancing he realizes and evokes both an abstract spatial concept and the idea of an idealized and aesthetically normed/normative body of the worker. Masks, forming rhythms, and spatial structuring could all have a mimetic component. They could have an effect that make the movements look more abstract or could emphasize the dancers' corporeality and their states of tension. Weidt's dances were always more than just simple copies of everyday life or agit-prop art, even though he ventured into that field and never intended to stay outside the literal realm. The body was the sight for artistic and political action. Thus simply focusing on the political narrations of Weidt's work – as it has often been done before – fails to see the complexity both of his work and how the body can acquire political meaning. Adapting the strategies of *Ausdruckstanz* he maneuvered between the presentation of suffering and the image of the strong and fighting worker. And Weidt was just one example of how *Ausdruckstanz* provided the means to embody left wing politics.

Notes

1 After Weidt fled to Paris in 1933, he changed his name from Hans to Jean and kept this name from then on.

2 See S. Manning, *Ausdrucktanz across the Atlantic*, in this volume, pp. 46–60.

3 I. Baxmann, *Mythos: Gemeinschaft. Körper- und Tanzkulturen der Moderne*, Munich: Wilhelm Fink Verlag, 2000; L. Guilbert, *Danser avec le IIIe Reich. Les danseurs modernes sous le nazisme*, Brussels: Complexe, 2000; L. Karina, M. Kant, *Hitler's Dancers: German Modern Dance and the Third Reich*, trans. J. Steinberg, New York and Oxford: Berghahn Books, 2003 (orig. edn *Tanz unterm Hakenkreuz*, Berlin: Henschel, 1996). This is true, of course, only for those who consider the political dimension of this dance form at all.

4 For a more comprehensive study of these left-wing dancers, see Y. Hardt, *Politische Körper. Ausdruckstanz, Choreographien des Protests und die Arbeiterkulturbewegung*, Münster: LIT, 2004.

5 The term *Lebensreformer* refers to a heterogenous group who believed that life would be made better by cherishing nature and the body. It included those who sought to emancipate women from the corset, those who championed the naked culture, those who organized a new walking culture, etc.

6 N. Jockel, P. Stöckemann, *Flugkraft in goldene Ferne . . . Bühnentanz in Hamburg seit 1900*, Hamburg: Museum für Kunst und Gewerbe, 1989, pp. 52–5; H. Müller, Stöckemann, . . . *'Jeder Mensch ist ein Tänzer'. Ausdruckstanz in Deutschland zwischen 1900 und 1945*, Frankfurt a.M: Anabas, 1993, pp. 45–6. Weidt also helped generate this image in his biography *Der Rote Tänzer. Ein Lebensbericht*, Berlin:

Henschel, 1968, which must be interpreted as a product of the political influences of the German Democratic Republic and its visions of the proper political dance form.

7 Jockel, Stöckemann, *Flugkraft in goldene Ferne . . .*, pp. 52–4; J. Weidt, *Auf der großen Straße. Jean Weidts Erinnerungen. Nach Tonbandprotokollen*, edited by M. Reinisch, Berlin: Henschel, 1984, p. 13.

8 For the significance of Rilke in the context of the life reform movement see C. Hepp, *Avantgarde. Moderne Kunst, Kulturkritik und Reformbewegungen nach der Jahrhundertwende*, Munich: Deutscher Taschenbuch Verlag, 1987.

9 Weidt, *Auf der großen Straße*, pp. 16–21.

10 Weidt, *Der Rote Tänzer*, pp. 10–11.

11 Hartig, 'Über die Möglichkeit proletarischer Kunst', *Kulturwille*, 1924, no. 1, p. 1.

12 W. Guttsmann, *Worker's Culture in Weimar Germany. Between Tradition and Commitment*, New York: St Martin's Press, 1990.

13 M. Gleisner, *Tanz für Alle. Von der Gymnastik zum Gemeinschaftstanz*, Leipzig: Hesse und Becker Verlag, 1928.

14 F. Niessen, 'Podiumsdiskussion: Dossier Weidt', lecture at the conference Laokoon-Festival auf Kampnagel, Hamburg, August, 2005.

15 Weidt, *Auf der großen Straße*, pp. 37–8.

16 P. Veroli, 'Nach dem Krieg. Die choreographischen Wettbewerbe 1945 und 1947', *Tanzdrama*, 2002, no. 5, pp. 18–21.

17 'Der sozialistische Realismus in der Tanzkunst. Thesen der Tanzkonferenz vom 23./24. März 1953', in H. Müller, R. Stabel, P. Stöckemann, *Krokodil im Schwanensee. Tanz in Deutschland seit 1945*, Frankfurt a.M.: Anabas, 2003, p. 89.

18 Weidt, *Der Roter Tänzer*, p. 10.

19 Ibid., pp. 16–18.

20 For example, A. Siemsen, *Politische Kunst und Kunstpolitik*, Berlin: E. Laubsche, 1927; V. Engelhardt, *An der Wende der Zeitalters. Individualistische oder sozialistische Kultur?*, Berlin: Arbeiterjugend-Verlag, 1925; M. Adler, *Die Kulturbedeutung des Sozialismus*, Vienna: Wiener Volksbuchhandlung, 1924; V. Hartig, 'Über die Möglichkeit proletarischer Kunst', pp. 1–2.

21 'Arbeiterbewegung und Körperkultur', *Kulturwille*, 1926, no. 5, p. 81.

22 O. Zimmermann, 'Gymnastik und Tanz vom Standpunkt des Arbeiters', *Kulturwille*, 1928, no. 1, p. 5.

23 A. Koch, 'Arbeitergymnastik', ibid.

24 *Spannung* (tension) and *Entspannung* (release) were key movement principles in Rudolf von Laban's early writings. See, for instance, R. von Laban, *Die Welt des Tänzers. Fünf Gedankenreigen*, Stuttgart: Seifert, 1920.

25 It is interesting to note that in the reconstruction by the Dupuys, who had both danced in the version created in France shortly after the war, emphasis was placed on developing certain qualities when it was recreated with very young dancers, while the setting of movements only happened in the later part of the rehearsal process. From an Interview/Panel with Dominique and Françoise Dupuy on August 27, 2005, Hamburg, Kampnagel on the memory of Jean Weidt. The reconstruction was shown here as well.

26 F. Böhme, 'Tanzgruppe Hans Weidt', *Deutsche Allgemeine Zeitung*, April 13, 1931, n.p.

27 F. Böhme, 'Tanzgruppe Hans Weidt', *Deutsche Allgemeine Zeitung*, December 17, 1930, n.p.

28 Interview with Jean Weidt in the documentary *Jean Weidt. Tanzen für ein besseres Leben* (1988), directed by Klaus-Peter Schmitt, Jean-Louis Sonzogni, Petra Weisenburger, and produced by Lieurac, La Sept, Télé-Europe, SWF Baden-Baden.
29 This provides quite a contra-point to his more athletic body images. For a longer discussion on issues of gender in his dances see Hardt, *Politische Körper*.
30 É. Vuillermoz in *Excelsior*, 1939, March, cited in Weidt, *Auf der großen Straße*, p. 164.
31 Böhme, 'Tanzgruppe Hans Weidt', December 17, 1930, n.p.
32 Böhme, 'Tanzgruppe Hans Weidt', April 13, 1931, n.p.
33 Vuillermoz in *Excelsior*, 1939.

5 *Ausdruckstanz*

Traditions, translations, transmissions

Susanne Franco

Definitions between history and memory

The term *Ausdruckstanz* (dance of expression) defines a heterogeneous group of choreographic languages and teaching methods that became known in the German-speaking regions in the early twentieth century.[1] Though these languages and methods covered a broad range of theoretical, practical, and aesthetic approaches (whose definitions emphasized their "new," "modern," "artistic," "free," "rhythmic," "plastic," and "expressive" character) they still agreed on certain major principles: dance was aesthetically independent from the other arts; body movement was closely bound to emotional and mental processes and reflected the rhythm of the cosmos; the dancer's role was that of creator–interpreter; and improvisation was of major importance. During the first international tours *Ausdruckstanz* was defined as "German dance," so as to differentiate it, in particular, from American modern dance. With the rise of Nazism, this foreign definition was transformed into *Deutscher Tanz,* and used in a nationalist and racist key by the regime and by the artists, critics, and cultural managers who followed their directives. From the Second World War on, the term *Ausdruckstanz* took on an increasingly broad hold and ended up conveying a falsely monolithic image of this tradition. The picture was further muddled when the term was erroneously translated into the Italian, the English, and the French as "expressionist dance," making it the equivalent of the expressionist movement in literature, painting, film, and theater. *Ausdruckstanz* was implicitly attributed an ideological and aesthetic affinity with expressionism (which history – though not without debate – had deemed revolutionary and anti-bourgeois), and banned by Nazism as a consequence. Unlike expressionist art, however, which was labeled as degenerate and then silenced, *Ausdruckstanz* continued to flourish with the regime's support after 1933.

The shifting definitions are only the first layer of a belabored cultural, artistic, and political history, the full complexity and ambiguity of which has only recently come to the fore and has not yet been fully examined. They neither resolve the ideological issues *Ausdruckstanz* raises nor explain how the movement was, or still is, perceived.

Interest in the history of *Ausdruckstanz* was first aroused in coincidence with important celebrations of its two major exponents: two publications on Wigman – a book by Walter Sorell[2] in 1973, and a biography written thirteen years later, in occasion of her centennial, by Hedwig Müller[3] – and an exhibition on Laban at the Tanzarchiv of Leipzig[4] in 1979. This historical rediscovery led in 1986 to the birth of an association named after Wigman (Mary Wigman Gesellschaft) that organized the first international conference on *Ausdruckstanz*[5] and founded the magazine *Tanzdrama*, which in turn rekindled the debate on dance in Germany.[6] The fact that early attempts to narrate the history of *Ausdruckstanz* were entrusted mostly to episodic monographs, biographies, often with a hagiographic slant, and exhibition catalogues[7] has to be seen in relation with the state of dance studies, which was then a discipline in search of identity.

Early research on *Ausdruckstanz* was also prompted by *Tanztheater* (dance theater), a genre that made a name for itself in the early 1970s. This label took in the rather heterogeneous choreographic research of a young generation of artists (including Hans Kresnik, Gerhard Bohner, Pina Bausch, and, later, Susanne Linke and Reinhild Hoffmann), who considered themselves direct heirs to *Ausdruckstanz*, in as much as they had been trained by one or more masters of this tradition (mostly Wigman and Kurt Jooss). The innovation launched in the same period in East Germany by pupils of Gret Palucca and/or Jean Weidt, such as Tom Schilling, Harald Wandtke, Dietmar Seyffert and Arila Siegert, and others, was also presented as *Tanztheater*. If scholars have reached no consensus on what the two currents of the new *Tanztheater* share in their aesthetics, there is no doubt about their ideological differences: in the West it was a tradition that aimed at subverting the status quo, in the East it was a tradition that supported it.[8]

The term *Tanztheater* had first been introduced by Rudolf von Laban and Kurt Jooss in the 1920s. It defined the trend in German modern dance that sought to integrate dance into the major theatrical circuits and adhered to a model of training which taught various techniques side by side. This trend was opposed by Wigman's ideal of *absoluter Tanz* (absolute dance), which demanded that dance assert greater independence in its narrative apparatuses, in respect to institutions (the opera houses, essentially) and, last but not least, from ballet. But for the generation of the 1970s, *Ausdruckstanz* became *the* source for the new *Tanztheater* as a whole. From this perspective, it had successfully nurtured the new avant-garde movement because it had managed to keep its artistic lesson alive and its ideological charge intact during the 1930s and the early 1940s (despite Nazi exploitation of its most irrational component) and even during the 1950s and 1960s (despite weak institutional support and scarce receptivity by new generations of dancers and audiences, a situation that Dore Hoyer's suicide in 1968 made emblematic). The label *Tanztheater*, used by artists and critics, but not explored by historians, had re-evoked the flourishing and eclectic years of the 1920s without questioning the fate of this art or its ideology. This was symptomatic of the uneasiness artists and critics felt in placing dance in a trajectory of history (and of memory) that included both the Nazi period and the years immediately thereafter.[9] The need to root the new in the old, which was felt by Jooss (who returned in West Germany in 1949 after sixteen years of exile in Great Britain),[10] and by the younger generation of the choreographers of the 1970s, revealed on one hand the nostalgia for an old tradition, and on the other hand the desire to learn about one's own fascinating past, whose real historical dimension was not as yet fully known. It also grew out of the process of invention (and re-invention) of the tradition that had traversed the history of *Ausdruckstanz* ever since its major exponents of the 1910s and 1920s had molded it as the essence of "authentic Germanness" and as the most complete realization of the Nietzschian ideal of community, which was a starting point for German cultural rebirth. How then, if *Ausdruckstanz* was able to shape the desire to regenerate the national body as an original form of knowledge and archaic traditions,[11] could such great oblivion have followed? How much of this tradition was transmitted and how much of it was forgotten or betrayed in the attempts to recover it on an artistic and a historical level? Which aspects of this process were repressed and which were re-worked? Where (in the East? in the West? in the diasporical dimension?) and when (after the Second World War? after 1949 in the West? after 1953 in the East?) does it break continuity with the past? What is the relationship between ruptures and continuities in the historical and memorial narratives? Which is the road to take between truth in history, faithfulness of memory and right of forgetting?[12]

After 1945 generations of dancers in both Germanies inherited a single tradition that was expressed differently according to the cultural politics of their respective governments. *Ausdruckstanz* still influenced the way in which dancers were trained but was rarely staged in either the East or the West, albeit for different political reasons. In the Federal Republic, Adenauer's cultural politics, in the spirit of Restauration and in the frame of a diffused Americanization, granted classical dance (as the universal language) a more or less exclusive monopoly. In the Democratic Republic at least two phases ensued: at the beginning the modern dancers who had settled in the East (including Gret Palucca, Marianne Vogelsang, Dore Hoyer, and Wigman until 1949) started working freely once again, but, in 1953, national dance politics officially endorsed socialist realism and *Ausdruckstanz* – deemed excessively mystical, obscure, and inclined to formalism – was banned. This ideological readjustment led to the triumph of ballet (following the Russian model) and to enormous support for folkloric dance, exactly as it had been in the final phase of the Reich, when ballet was considered the most suitable form of entertainment, and deemed capable of expressing the "essence" of Germanness, while folkloric dance was promoted for its more or less authentic proximity to the people. This shows, among other things, the degree of uncertainty and the experimental limits with which totalitarian regimes approached dance. This also shows, at another level, that the memory (or illusion) of what contemporary dance has inherited from the past does not always correspond to historical reality. For instance, the institutional support to dance, that was so fundamental for the new *Tanztheater*, is a model derived more from the Nazi regime than from the Weimar Republic, when private management prevailed.[13]

In what manner, then, has the data provided by archives and processed by historians "dialogued" with the artists' memories? To what extent have archives participated in the process of memorialization and production of a "sense" of dance history.

It was memorial reconstruction that informed the first study,[14] which came out in 1972, entirely devoted to analyzing the circumstances of *Ausdruckstanz* between 1927 and 1936, the years of its greatest diffusion and of the rise of Nazism. The study was written by Horst Koegler, a post-war dance critic, and is based primarily on his reconstruction of the story told by his colleague Joseph Lewitan. The founder of one of the major dance magazines of the late-1920s, Lewitan was a close observer of *Ausdruckstanz* who was opposed to its nationalist and irrational surge and who had to leave Germany because he was Jewish. Koegler's study, which does not contextualize this anomaly in the core of the art and society of the time, was the first to focus on the continuity of the careers of many exponents of *Ausdruckstanz* after 1933. The historical narratives that followed developed a theory according to which *Ausdruckstanz*'s approach to the regime was the consequence of a cultural politics that had denied any sort of freedom and had been able to instrumentalize an art of considerable potential but weak identity. The dancers' allegiance to Nazi ideology was seen as the concomitant result of an idealistic attitude, a presumed political ingenuousness and an opportunism dictated by precarious working conditions during the Weimar Republic.[15]

Other studies, carried out by a generation of militant critics in the 1970s and 1980s, underlined the aesthetic affinities between *Ausdruckstanz* and *Tanztheater* based on their common "essence." Some argued that *Ausdruckstanz* had a hard time surviving after the war on predominantly or exclusively political grounds (given its involvement with the regime), others concentrated on aesthetic motives (such as the changes in taste and fashions).[16]

This chronological and ideological version of the facts was questioned in the late 1990s by studies that outline a more problematic history of *Ausdruckstanz*, its protagonists, the individual choreographic works, and the political dynamics underlying the public management of dance.[17] Susan Manning, Marion Kant, Lilian Karina, Inge Baxmann, and Laure Guilbert have brought to light the degree to which this modernity was not only synonymous with artistic and social progress but also embodied certain reactionary and anti-democratic aspects.[18] Re-reading the ambiguous shift from the experimental phase of the 1910s and 1920s to the rise of Nazism has shown how *Ausdruckstanz* was the result of a long process of cultural maturation and the forerunner of compelling modern utopias. It has also uncovered the roots embedded in the vast and multi-faceted movement that reacted to an industrial civilization in which social and moral values were summed up in the antitheses *Kultur/Zivilisation* (culture/civilization) and *Gemeinschaft/Gesellschaft* (community/society). These studies have disclosed the massive number of dancers that adhered to Nazi cultural politics and, in some cases, their active militancy in support of its ideology in choreographic and teaching practices and in theoretical formulations. The urgency of reckoning with the political and ideological dimension of *Ausdruckstanz* and, in particular, with its relationship with National Socialism, inevitably catalyzed the historical debate, leading both to its investigation and to restrictions in the directions of research. In some cases information-famished readers found themselves face-to-face with an image of this tradition that was so controversial it was difficult to accept.[19] A sign that the times are now ready to open to new prospects is found in the research that has begun to explore the convincing presence of *Ausdruckstanz* in left-wing contexts, such as that of Yvonne Hardt.[20] In this case too, the generational turnover is one of the decisive factors for the individuation of the object of study (that openly enters a dialogue with the results obtained in the past) and the selected methodology (that hinges on the theoretical maturation in dance studies of the last twenty years).

These new studies have had a fragmentary and erratic reception in many countries, and in very few cases have been registered in the general histories or dictionaries of dance. This is due primarily to the lack of, or delay in translations, which has generated a great deal of misunderstanding and many false starts.[21] Many new issues have been raised but often without awareness of the responses that have already been given.[22] Establishing the historical and political framework of *Ausdruckstanz* has been further encumbered by the difficulty in accessing sources, many of which are unpublished, and by the "truths" transmitted by its protagonists, who continued to teach with mixed results in the public and private schools in East and West Germany. The legendary aura surrounding these and other exponents of *Ausdruckstanz* is one of the components of the emotional relationship that has always bound teachers and students in the transmission of dance theory and practice. In many cases, however, their memories have been at variance with those of their colleagues who were forced into exile, and their recollections are quite often irreconcilable with the new histories, which have broken taboos, reopened old wounds, and inflamed polemics. History and memory have ended up telling different truths, each one standing firm on the principle of non-negotiability. While memory represented a factor of cohesion in the post-war construction of a new individual and collective identity, albeit in different ways at different times, history has often been seen as a conflicting factor. The research that attempted to free itself from memory by de-legitimizing it was justifiably received as a mortification of subjective involvement, whose unavoidable contribution to historical narration has by now been fully recognized. The politics of memory and oblivion have limited each other. And yet, it is actually in the dynamic between the right to forget and the necessity of knowing that history and memory can find grounds for exchange in reconstructing dance's past.[23] It is by recognizing the role that memory plays alongside history in shaping mentality and corporeality that *Ausdruckstanz* could take on new meaning and new importance for scholars.

In the footsteps of Mary Wigman. Comparing methodologies

Surveying the main stages of Wigman historiography can be helpful to focalize the different methodologies employed by scholars, in particular as far as the political and ideological import of her practice and theory of dance is concerned.

Müller was the first to openly address a political question, tracing the portrait of an art form plagued by the Reich and of an artist driven to support the regime by opportunism, patriotism, and a sentimental relationship with a Nazi party leader. Manning's monograph came out about ten years later. It took advantage of a great deal of information made available by Müller and of documents coming in large part from the Wigman archives at the Akademie der Künste in Berlin, which were re-read through the lens of critical theory, at "a convergence of feminism and nationalism."[24] Manning maintains that Wigman's choreographic work underwent a progressive aesthetic transformation from the 1920s to the rise of Nazism and traces the causes to an ideological shift prompted by political opportunism. From this point of view, Wigman had gone from the use of collective improvisation and the exploration of spatial and corporeal dynamics expressing the vast range of relations inspired by the social democratic ideals of the 1920s to a more marked *Führerprinzip* (leadership principle). The conformist turn in feminine iconography was also emphasized by the educational purposes assigned to choreographic practice. The height of this process is identified by Manning in the works presented at the dance festivals in 1934 and 1935 and at the 1936 Olympics. Manning reaches these conclusions first and foremost through a socio-political reading of photographs from a few performances that privilege the transitional period from one political structure to the other, and focus her analysis either on creation, production, or reception. Her research challenges the theory of a drastic break between Weimar and the Third Reich, and points out new avenues for the analysis and contextualization of dance in culture, which aimed at drawing the attention of other disciplines to the potential of this field of studies. Manning offers a reading of the interplay among the different forces and motives (personal, artistic, and institutional) that, as Mark Franko writes in his state-of-the-art (Chapter 1), constitute the political level of dance. She does this by choosing a circumstance that was "conjunctural," to use Franko's terminology; one that was particularly controversial but one in which cultural politics takes on marked visibility. Another conjunctural circumstance was the then all-female composition of Wigman's company, which was marked by a more or less total generation turnover that favored its director's leadership. Manning also brings out the discrepancies between oral and written history, as in the case of the training programs that were officially changed after 1933 as a result of greater forces but which, in daily practice, remained quite faithful to those of the 1920s. Her book raises certain fundamental methodological issues that have become key in the wider debate on dance historiography. To what point is it possible to take an approach that implies a constant, albeit ever different, interdependence between ideology and artistic practice? Or between political vision and danced utopia? Is it useful or reductive to delimit Fascist aesthetics chronologically? To what extent can a choreography be considered the result of its creator's intentions? Is it possible to speak only of dance discourses or also of counter-discourses?

What is the relationship between dance texts and body movement? How else could it be possible to effectively combine the choreographic and narrative reading of a work and how it is rendered in dance?

New studies were undertaken to answer these questions. Some sought to disclose unknown sources, others placed emphasis on aesthetic analysis. An example of the former is provided by a musicologist and historian, Marion Kant[25] who devoted to Wigman two articles and many passages of a book she wrote in collaboration with Lilian Karina, a dancer who took exile in Sweden after the rise of Nazism. Kant's articles came out of research begun in the mid-1980s. Relying primarily on Wigman's unpublished diaries, she traced the choreographer's thoughts and feelings, which Kant defines as more patriotic than nationalistic, and goes on to compare this material to the choreographer's artistic work. In the book she co-authors with Karina, the reflections are cross-referenced with a massive amount of information from the archives at the Propaganda Ministry and many other sources, which provide the administrative background on the Reich's cultural politics. The discovery of this substantial documentary corpus has had a strong impact on dance research, opening new horizons and inciting a great deal of tension among dance scholars. Kant and Karina's research was complementary to Manning's in privileging cultural politics over choreographic practices. Kant concluded that Wigman had approached Nazism first on a rhetorical (and theoretical) and later on an artistic level. Published initially in German and only recently in English, the book has had major repercussions in the world of dance in very different national contexts. Some have criticized the tone of the categorical position it takes in the face of those who put their art in the service of the Reich. Others have appreciated its clear and lucid reconstruction of the administrative politics of dance. Undeniably it has offered scholars a fundamental tool for broadening the scope of research on dance and politics. The book's first section puts the reader into the memory of Karina, who traces a profile of emigrated dancers and of the birth and development of *Ausdruckstanz* through the eyes of an artist. The second section provides Kant's historical framework and the appendices include a wide selection of documents. This tripartite structure allows the book to offer testimony of the exceptional "case" of dance's alignment with the Reich and to provide new insight that points toward greater methodological awareness. Does such a closely knit structure leave enough room to develop an argument that considers the various relationships between mechanisms of consensus and seduction? Or between the professional and cultural motivations of dancers' political and artistic actions? What other synergies might be hypothesized between oral testimonies and written sources?

The work undertaken in the 1990s by Isabelle Launay[26] comes from the perspective of aesthetic analysis. Launay openly questions the conclusions reached by historians who, in her opinion, have used artificial time periods that force the interpretation of facts. From her point of view, the idea that the evolution of art follows close on the heels of political events provides the basis for the causal interpretations of *Ausdruckstanz*'s ideological charge. It does not consider the degree to which dance is ontologically protected from social and political contamination and the extent to which the choreographic work goes beyond historical contingency, ideological implications, and power relationships. In virtue of that impermeability, the lesson of modern dance would have passed through the dark tunnel of Nazism to arrive at nurturing the contemporary trend. This research suggests considering the political dimension of a choreographic project beginning from the practices and theories inherent to the art, and not vice versa. Following closely the lessons of Michel Bernard,[27] it has re-focused attention (in dance studies in general, even before more specific work on *Ausdruckstanz*) on the questions of corporeality and of the creative process. To support her theory, Launay makes reference to the poetics of Wigman, heir to the romantic myth of creative and visionary genius, according to which an artist is abstract with respect to his or her socio-political context and thus relieved a priori of responsibility in the name of creative autonomy. A similar reading of modernism, not completely immune to the risk of complying with the critical-theoretical models of the same era, avails itself of a range of sources that privilege thematic over linguistic and chronological choices. Priority is given to autobiographical and theoretical texts, which, however, remain centered solely on the problem of dance's modernity. The author also avoids the bottleneck and easy reductions of an iconographic interpretation by rejecting visual sources.[28] These choices are motivated by the conviction that dance archives are not limited to written and iconographic sources but include, also and especially, dancers' physical experience. Gesture, understood in its broadest possible meaning, is to be investigated with the epistemological acquisitions of dance. For Launay, this is the only way to overcome the limits of a narrative reading of form and content and to focus on the dynamics of the forces that confer meaning to movement. From this point of view, the confluence of *Ausdruckstanz* and Nazism and, in particular, of Wigman's and Laban's collaboration with the regime, was originated from the weak status and social legitimacy of the art of dance, from the uncertain professional identity of its protagonists, and, last but not least, from the difficult balance between pure experimentation and the velleity of consolidating a tradition. In opposition to the theory of ideological consubstantiality between *Ausdruckstanz* and Nazism, Launay identifies gaps in the concepts of body, technique, mimesis, and *Erlebnis* (lived experience) that have not emerged in other analyses because too little attention has been given to the narrative component of dance. Among the fundamental methodological issues raised by this study, the most evident has also been posed in Ginot's essay in the third section of this book (Chapter 15). Can the identity of dance be distinct from that of the artist? Can aesthetic analysis find equally ample space *within* history? How can one avoid the contradiction between choosing to examine only the theoretical works of a dancer-choreographer and aiming to understand the process of choreographic creation and the level of symbolic signification of body movement? Is there really an original and authentic core of *Ausdruckstanz* or is it in its continuous, often contradictory transformations that *Ausdruckstanz* can be grasped? And then, echoing the issues raised by Franko, to what extent can politically sensitive methodologies reveal more about dance than dance itself is perhaps "willing" to?

Guilbert's book was the second volume on *Ausdruckstanz* to be published in French. It reconstructs the history of an entire generation of dancers between the two world wars, in which the figure of Wigman appears in the background and as the focus of a few passages, offering an interpretation of politics as both a structure and a network of relations. Guilbert follows Kant and Karina's example in examining the institutional, ideological, and aesthetic politics of German modern dance, placing emphasis on the relationships between dancers and administrators and unveiling their many paradoxes. The ideological consubtantiality takes on form by cross-referencing sources from dancers' personal archives, criticism of the times, documents from political institutions, and, to a lesser degree, iconographic materials. Toning down the conclusions of Manning and Launay, Guilbert opts for a problematic confluence of an ethical and aesthetic imaginary in Wigman's practice and suggests identifying its traces in the culture that nurtured this dance and in what it produced. This is proposed in virtue of the workings of *Ausdruckstanz* as Wigman herself described them: organic forces that take on form in a visible gestural *Gestalt*. According to Guilbert, the germination of the content from the form has a more explicit (and thus more legible) will to signify in the phase in which it approaches National Socialism: in this process the movement capable of transmitting the mystery of the sacred gives way to ideological dogma. A similar change in the creative modes is compared with the theoretical formulations of the choreographer, who, from the 1930s on, re-read absolute dance as a new category co-inhabited by modern and classical dance under the guise of abstraction. Alongside this, Guilbert observes thematic variations in the 1920s repertoire, in which existential experience and the search for the sacred prevail until the 1940s, when the reference to Nordic rituality and legends becomes more decided. She identifies in the principle of improvisation the element of continuity, and in the relationship between form and content the discontinuity. Here, too, numerous questions come to mind. Within what limits is dance capable of exercising an ideological power without becoming its emblem? What is the relationship between dance and choreography? What bodies are implicated? What does this type of research gain and/or lose from an iconographic and textual analysis that also considers the qualities of movement?

This brief and surely not exhaustive overview demonstrates how important it is for the Wigman case to remain open and how it actually constitutes grounds for further investigation precisely because so many scholars with such different backgrounds have already begun to address it. It also exemplifies how new methodologies emerge through the circulation of questions and answers, which identify and shape the subject of research. It further illustrates how dance studies develop from the convergence of disciplinary perspectives and from constantly transforming cultural contexts.

Suitcases, backpacks, and trunks. The histories of archives and the archives of history

The politics of interpretation are never free from those of preservation, and the historiography of *Ausdruckstanz* has been especially fraught by the destruction and dispersion of a great deal of its documentary heritage, both during the war and in its re-allotment after the division of Germany. The logic that has determined selection and conservation criteria, as well as the accessibility of archives and libraries, has varied from place to place. The histories of these "storehouses"[29] of collective knowledge have conditioned, if not hindered, the work of historians active in both Germanies and of foreigners as well. The collections preserving the documents related to the work of Laban, provide a glaring example of the intertwine between historical interpretations and politics of preservations. The fact that the "evidence" of what is and what is not collected in these archives hasn't become central in Laban studies invites reflection.

Laban was a nomad and a polyglot. He left traces of his thought, his varied endeavors, and his private life in documents that are not only difficult to access but are also written in several different languages. Laban historiography is consequently marked by the quantity and quality of sources referenced but also by the oral transmission of his thought and practice, in Germany, and, to a greater extent, in Great Britain and the US. In most cases, the texts disseminating Laban's thought are the result of studies by his former students and collaborators, only a few of whom have done archival research, especially on the German period. The fact that there is still not a complete collection of Laban's essays in German, let alone in translation, is as surprising as is the diffusion of his method of movement analysis and notation, thanks in part to the promotion of the Laban Centre in London, which is one of the best-known places in Europe for training dancers. Of the impressive bulk of Laban's writings from between 1920 and 1937, only his autobiography and his first essay on dance notation have been translated into English. There is no translation of his theoretical manifesto, *Die Welt des Tänzers* (The Dancer's World)[30] which was a fundamental point of reference for an entire generation of *Ausdruckstänzer*, or of any of the other theoretical essays, published and unpublished, scattered about in magazines and archives.[31]

The dispersion of the Laban archives reflects both German history and Laban's personal and professional vicissitudes. Laban left Germany in 1937, after what had originally been an intense and vital relationship with the Reich had deteriorated. The mode and timing of his departure made it impossible for him to take all his personal papers, which were then at the theater of the Berlin Opera (where he was the *maître de ballet*). This material ended up in the hands of his collaborator Marie-Luise Lieschke. Sometime later it was rediscovered by John Hodgson, a student of Laban, who "transported" it to Great Britain stowed away in three backpacks, extracting it at one and the same time from both German jurisdiction and from the research of Lisa Ullmann, Laban's last assistant and partner, she too on the tracks of this patrimony. Upon Hodgson's death, this archive was left to his family and, to date, is still not accessible for consultation. What remained in Germany was inherited by Lieschke's sister, who, in the late 1970s sold it to the Tanzarchiv in Leipzig. The documentation regarding Laban's collaboration with the Nazi regime is found in various federal archives, while other materials are scattered about in various places including the Kurt Jooss Collection, Dartington Hall Records, the Albrecht Knust Collection (recently acquired by the Centre national de la danse), and the national archives of all the cities in which Laban lived or worked. Among the most famous private collections are those legendarily known as Laban's "trunk" and "suitcase." The former belonged to his second wife Maja Lederer, the latter initially to his companion and assistant Suzanne Perrottet and then finally, after various intermediary steps, to the Kunsthaus in Zurich.[32] Upon Laban's death the documents in his possession were passed on to Ullmann, who donated them and his personal archives to the National Resource Centre for Dance at the University of Surrey, where the Laban Archive was opened in the mid-1980s. Marion North, who took over for Ullmann, tried to bring these archives to the Laban Centre, embarking on repeated legal battles in which she claimed that the Centre was the only legitimate heir. She was unsuccessful and the archival resources at the Laban Centre, the only institution that carries his name, remain scant.

If institutional politics are key in the conservation of a documentary patrimony, they are equally so in the transmission of dance practices and their history. The Laban Centre provides an example of the incongruity between a political institution that claims to be a guarantor for antonomasia in transmitting Laban's heritage and a real commitment to specific historic research. The Centre's informative materials and, more macroscopically, the biography written by Valerie Preston-Dunlop, who directed the Centre at length, presents the best-known yet least historically accurate image of Laban.[33] The decision to publish this study without referencing other sources that would allow it to be placed within the broader debate on *Ausdruckstanz* has ended up freezing Laban's image within stereotypes that are of little use to either the general public or specialists. More encouraging signs of growing interest in the lesser known aspects of Laban's theory and practice, in the case in point the years he spent in Germany, seem to be coming, albeit sporadically, from independent scholars and the academic context.[34]

The politics of dance. Considerations and overtures

The three case studies in this section represent some of the numerous directions that research on the relationships between *Ausdruckstanz* and politics might further investigate. Guilbert's autobiographical reflection manifests a two-fold disorientation. It is emotional, for the person who is unveiling, first and foremost to herself, "another" history, finding answers to many questions that are at times unexpected and at times painful. It is also professional, for the dance scholar aware of the instability of a discipline still in the making. Here, writing history (the history of dance) reveals the key importance of the subjective contribution and all the layers of which it is composed (intuitions, discoveries, regressions, hesitations, impulses, and solitude). This reflection brings out the necessity of fully integrating personal experience, which previously tended to be judged rather than analyzed, into the dynamics that converge to define a subject and its attendant methodology.[35]

The essay by Hardt attempts to go beyond these works, considering first of all the effects of a linear and causal interpretation. Critical repositioning implies the need for a definition of *Ausdruckstanz* that can embrace ideological polyvalence and artistic variety, a shifting viewpoint (the militant-left context), multiple sources (dancers' memories, criticism, photographs, reconstructions), and a refinement of research tools (in the direction of an analysis of physical dynamics). These moves converge toward shaping a new methodological proposal, whose fruitfulness relies on decoding certain mechanisms of signification that can restore depth to the initial reasons for the success of *Ausdruckstanz* or that can visually and physically translate the most rankling cultural issues of its time (the crisis in writing, the importance of body culture, the fear and fascination of technology, a yearning for an original state, and, last but not least, cultural alternatives to bourgeois education). Hardt's study bursts open the antithesis between a progressive aesthetic practice and a reactionary ideology, which reveals itself to be more constrictive than productive. It intertwines with Manning's case study by identifying conjunctural situations, in which the same teaching method or choreographic genre promoted different communitarian projects. Manning's essay traces the fate of *Ausdruckstanz* in exile. It follows a trail blazed a few years ago by a few pioneering studies that today, reinforced by postcolonial theories on the Diaspora, can bring new information to the study of the politics of the transmission of tradition. Once again, constructing the research subject involves its redefinition, understood in the broadest sense of transcultural tradition. Following the trail of the Holm's school in New York, which trained an entire generation of left-wing dancers, it is possible to investigate the evolution of someone like Gertrud Krauss, who became a key figure in Israel after she emigrated. Her contribution to the *ex nihilo* creation of folk tradition (in collaboration with the Kibbutzim Dance Company) and the development of concert dance (as a consultant to the Batsheva Company and the Israeli Ballet) made her a protagonist in the Israeli dance born in the footsteps of *Ausdruckstanz*.[36] New insights may also be gained into the dynamics between political mythologies and the artistic imaginary or between the construction of a national identity and a process of modernization by comparing similar choreographic models under various totalitarian regimes, such as, in particular, the movement choirs in Germany, Russia, and Italy.[37] Other dynamics between history and memory (visual and corporeal, individual and collective) are emerging on the horizon, in the case in point those of the memory and history broken up and dispersed with the rise of Nazism. Future studies on how *Ausdruckstanz* was transmitted in the Diaspora will have to productively articulate the politics of denial and of myth making, of isolation and of integration, of preservation and of innovation, of spatial dissemination and of temporal rooting, of communitarian and of individual identity. They might probe beneath the surface of a non-linear process encompassing the multiple ways in which dance is transmitted, from instances in which a strong intention to hand down a tradition is manifest but ineffective to situations where a vague project results in a fully accomplished transmission.[38] They might probe the solutions found by individual dancers who sought to obey both the logic of practical efficiency and the relationship with the cultural social order from which they came and the one into which they placed themselves. It might also be quite interesting to reinterpret the impact of those who returned from exile or from long sojourns abroad to find a welcome that did not always meet their expectations. This is the case of Hoyer, who after influencing an entire generation of artists in Argentina, had to face the harsh reality of being unsuccessful in Germany. Or what about the round trips of the same tradition, such as that of Renate Schottelius, who emigrated to Argentina in the 1930s, where she trained Daniel Goldin, a Ukranian Jew born in Buenos Aires, who in turn emigrated to Germany after the war to teach at the Folkwang Schule.[39] Or the career of the communist choreographer Patricio Bunster, which is an example of the migration of dance vocabulary and of the ideological diaspora[40] between Chile and East Germany.

A certain critical distance might make it possible to open a new chapter in the historiography of *Ausdruckstanz* based on the comparative analysis of the reconstructions–recreations done almost contemporaneously in East and West Germany in the 1980s, in works by Siegert and Linke, respectively.[41] Reinforced by the recent conceptualization in the area of reconstruction as a project of practical–theoretical analysis active in dance history, and by the perspective of the *Wende*, these studies could shed new light on the process of embodying the tradition of *Ausdruckstanz* in its post-war ramifications.

These and many others are the roads not yet taken, roads that would enrich and articulate the debate on dance and politics. These are roads along which the threads of history and memory intertwine to weave the fabric of the investigation and representation of the past.

Notes

I would like to thank Susan Foster and Inge Baxmann for the insights they have shared in discussing these issues, and Laure Guilbert and Patrizia Veroli for a continuous exchange of ideas and materials.

1 On this issue see G. Oberzaucher-Schüller (ed.), *Ausdruckstanz. Eine Mitteleuropäische Bewegung der ersten Hälfte des 20. Jahrhunderts*, Wilhelmshaven: Florian Noetzel Verlag, 1992 (2nd edn 2004), p. XIII (the conference that originated this volume was held at the University of Bayreuth in 1986 and the volume includes papers that had originally been excluded from the programme for political and bureaucratic reasons); the introduction of the same volume by K. Peters, pp. 4–5; M. Huxley, 'European Early Modern Dance', in J. Adshead-Lansdale, J. Layson (eds), *Dance History. An Introduction*, New York and London: Routledge,

1994, pp. 151–68; G. Brandstetter, *Tanz-Lektüren. Körperbilder und Raumfiguren der Avantgarde*, Frankfurt a.M.: Fischer Verlag, 1995, p. 33.

2 W. Sorell (ed.), *Mary Wigman ein Vermächtnis*, Wilhelmshaven: Florian Noetzel Verlag, 1973 (2nd edn 1986; Eng. trans. *The Mary Wigman Book. Her Writings*, Middletown, CT: Wesleyan University Press, 1986).

3 H. Müller, *Mary Wigman. Leben und Werk der grossen Tänzerin*, Berlin: Henschel, 1986. In addition to the books discussed here see also A. Rannow, R. Stabel (eds), *Mary Wigman in Leipzig. Eine Annäherung an ihr Wirken für den Tanz in Leipzig in den Jahren 1942 bis 1949*, Leipzig: Tanzwissenschaft, 1994, and the brief biography G. Fritsch-Vivié, *Mary Wigman*, Reinbek: Rowohlt, 1999.

4 See *Die Tanzarchivreihe*, 1979, nos. 19–20 (double monographic issue), and H. Koping-Renk (ed.), *Positionen zur Vergangenheit und Gegenwart des modernen Tanzes*, Berlin: Henschel, 1982, pp. 30–5.

5 *Ausdruckstanz. Eine Mitteleuropäische Bewegung.*

6 The magazine started in 1987 and closed in 2002; in 2003 it merged with *Ballett-Journal/Das Tanzarchiv* and is now called *Tanzjournal.*

7 See among others Müller, *Mary Wigman*; in addition to the exhibition *Ausdruckstanz* and the exhibition mounted on Laban, see A. and H. Markard, *Jooss. Documentation*, Folkwang Museum of Essen, Köln: Ballet-Bühnen-Verlag, 1985; *Künstler um Palucca*, Dresden: Staatliche Kunstsammlungen/Kupferstich-Kabinett, 1987; N. Jockel, P. Stöckemann, *Flugkraft in goldene Ferne . . . Bühnentanz in Hamburg seit 1900*, Hamburg: Museum für Kunst und Gewerbe, 1989.

8 For a preliminary overview, though more focused on news than on the history of dance in the two Germanies from 1945 on, see H. Müller, R. Stabel, P. Stöckemann, *Krokodil im Schwanensee. Tanz in Deutschland seit 1945*, Frankfurt a.M: Anabas, 2003; on *Ausdruckstanz* in East Germany see also E. Winckler, 'Ausdruckstanz in der DDR', *Tanzforschung Jahrbuch*, 1994, no. 5, pp. 53–8.

9 Other than the two volumes cited, see H. Müller, N. Servos, 'Von Isadora Duncan bis Leni Riefensthal', *Ballett International*, 1982, no. 4, pp. 15–23; see also the re-elaboration for the Italian and the English versions: 'Espressionismo? L'Ausdruckstanz e il nuovo Tanztheater in Germania', in L. Bentivoglio (ed.), *Tanztheater. Dalla danza espressionista a Pina Bausch*, Rome: Di Giacomo, 1982, pp. 57–80; 'Expressionism? *Ausdruckstanz* and The New Dance Theatre in Germany', *Dance Theatre Journal*, 1984, vol. 2, no. 1, pp. 10–15; N. Servos, '*Ausdruckstanz* und *Tanztheater*. Erbe "unter der Hand"', in *Ausdruckstanz. Eine Mitteleuropäische Bewegung*, pp. 486–92; S. Schlicher, *TanzTheater*, Reinbek: Rowohlt, 1987; S. Schlicher, 'The West German Dance Theatre: Paths from the Twenties to the Present', *Choreography and Dance*, 1993, vol. 3, pt. 2, pp. 25–43. The first critical reinterpretation of this historiography is: S. Manning, 'From *Ausdruckstanz* to *Tanztheater*', in S. Manning, *Ecstasy and the Demon: Feminism and Nationalism in the Dances of Mary Wigman*, Berkeley, CA: University of California Press, 1993, pp. 221–54 (2nd edn *Ecstasy and the Demon*: *The Dances of Mary Wigman*, Minneapolis, MN: University of Minnesota Press, 2006).

10 See the historical biography by P. Stöckemann, *Etwas ganz Neues muss nun entstehen: Kurt Jooss und das Tanztheater*, Köln: Klaus Kieser-Tanzarchiv Köln/Sk Stiftung Kultur, 2001.

11 I. Baxmann, *Mythos: Gemeinschaft. Körper- und Tanzkulturen der Moderne*, Munich: Wilhelm Fink Verlag, 2000.

12 For these topics see P. Ricoeur, *Memory, History, Forgetting*, trans. K. Blamey and D. Pellauer, Chicago, IL: University of Chicago Press, 2004 (orig. edn *La mémoire, l'histoire, l'oubli*, Paris: Éditions du Seuil, 2000).

13 On this particular point see the first critical remarque by Manning, *From* Ausdruckstanz *to* Tanztheater, and for the later historical inquiries see the volumes by L. Guilbert, *Danser avec le IIIème Reich. Les danseurs modernes sous le nazisme*, Brussels: Complexe, 2000, and L. Karina, M. Kant, *Hitler's Dancers: German Modern Dance and the Third Reich*, trans. J. Steinberg, New York and Oxford: Berghahn Books, 2003 (orig. edn *Tanz unterm Hakenkreuz*, Berlin: Henschel, 1996).

14 H. Koegler, 'Tanz in die Dreissiger Jahre', *Ballett 1972*, annual review, 1972, re-worked in English with the title: 'In the Shadow of the Swastika: Dance in Germany 1927–1936', *Dance Perspectives*, 1974, no. 57 (monographic issue).

15 *Ausdruckstanz. Eine Mitteleuropäische Bewegung*; H. Müller, Stöckemann, . . . *'Jeder Mensch ist ein Tänzer'. Ausdruckstanz in Deutschland zwischen 1900 und 1945*, Frankfurt a.M: Anabas, 1993 (catalogue of the exhibition *'Weltfriede – Jugendgluck'. Vom Ausdruckstanz zum Olympischen Festspiel)*; *Ausdruckstanz in Deutschland. Eine Inventur*, Wilhelmshaven: Florian Noetzel Verlag, 1994. Along these lines see: K. Toepfer, *Empire of Ecstasy. Nudity and Movement in German Body Culture 1910–1935*, Berkeley, CA: University of California Press, 1997, which still remains the most informative text in English, and also G. Vetterman, C. Jeschke, 'Germany', in A. Grau, S. Jordan (eds), *Europe Dancing. Perspectives on Theatre Dance and Cultural Identity*, New York and London: Routledge, 2000, pp. 55–78.

16 Among these critics the most relevant for this topic are Susanne Schlicher, Jochen Schmidt, and Norbert Servos. For this particular aspect of continuity-discontinuity in the tradition of Tanztheater see Manning, *From* Ausdruckstanz *to* Tanztheater. For a different approach to this topic see A. Sanchez-Colberg, *German Tanztheater. Traditions and Contradictions. A Choreological Documentation of Tanztheater from its Roots in Ausdruckstanz to the Present*, Ph.D. dissertation, University of London, Laban Centre, 1992, that offers a choreological documentation and a comparative analysis of choreographies by Laban, Jooss, and Pina Bausch.

17 Karina, Kant, *Hitler's Dancers*; Manning, *Ecstasy and the Demon*; Guilbert, *Danser avec le IIIème Reich*; Baxmann, *Mythos: Gemeinschaft.*

18 See in particular A. Hewitt, *Fascist Modernism*, Stanford, CA: Stanford University Press, 1996.

19 See Manning's preface to the second edition of *Ecstasy and the Demon*, pp. xiii–xxx.

20 Y. Hardt, *Politische Körper. Ausdruckstanz, Choreographien des Protests und die Arbeiterkulturbewegung*, Münster: LIT, 2004.

21 The conference *Tanz und Politik* held in Cologne in 2003, and organized by the Mary Wigman Gesellschaft and the Tanzarchiv Köln, was useful for this dialogue. The session on the relationship between dance and National Socialism also presented the first documentary on these issues. See *Tanz unterm Hakenkreuz*, written and directed by A. Wangenheim, Cologne, WDR Fernsehen (2003).

22 To the often incomplete bibliographies of many important studies, which reveal all the shortcomings of this indirect dialogue, one can add questionable projects such as the re-edition of *Ausdruckstanz. Eine Mitteleuropäische Bewegung*, which was published without a new introduction that would place its conclusions within an appropriate historical framework. Among the texts that have ignited these polemics among scholars see I. Launay, 'La danse moderne mise au pas?', in *Danse et utopie. Mobiles*, 1999, vol. 1, no. 1, pp. 73–106; F.M. Peter, 'War Kreutzberg ein "alter nazi"?', *Tanzwissenschaft 2*, 1996, no. 2, n.p.; 'Diskussion', *Tanzdrama*, 1994, no. 4, pp. 28–33, and 1995, no. 1, pp. 32–4.

23 A. Assman, *Erinnerungsräume. Formen und Wandlungen des kulturellen Gedächnisses*, Munich: C.H. Back'sche, 1999.
24 Manning, *Ecstasy and the Demon*, p. xv.
25 M. Kant, 'Mary Wigman. Die Suche nach der verlorenen Welt', *Tanzdrama*, part I, 1994, no. 25, 14–19; part II, 1994, no. 27, pp. 16–21.
26 I. Launay, *A la recherche d'une danse moderne. Rudolf Laban – Mary Wigman*, Paris: Librairie de la Danse, 1996; see also her 'La danse moderne mise au pas?'.
27 See M. Bernard, *De la création chorégraphique*, Pantin: Centre national de la danse, 2001, and in particular 'L'imaginaire germanique du mouvement ou les paradoxes du "language de la danse" de Mary Wigman' (1984), pp. 225–33.
28 For a list of films on *Ausdruckstanz* made between 1925 and 1942 see 'Filme', *Tanzdrama*, 1992, no. 2, pp. 16–19.
29 M. Hill, *Archival Strategies and Techniques*, London: Sage, 1993, p. 2.
30 R. von Laban, *Die Welt des Tänzers. Fünf Gedankenreigen*, Stuttgart: Seifert, 1920.
31 R. von Laban, *Ein Leben für den Tanz*, Dresden: Reissner, 1935 (anastatic reprints: Bern-Stuttgart: Paul Haup, 1989; Eng. trans. L. Ullmann (ed.), *A Life for Dance*, London: Macdonald & Evans, 1975); the anastatic reprints of the magazine *Schrifftanz* (founded by Laban in 1928), of which the English version proposes only a few essays in thematic order on the basis of the subject treated and not the original chronological sequence, is among the rare exceptions: see *Schrifttanz. Eine Vierteljahresschrift*, Hildesheim, Zürich and New York: Georg Olms Verlag, 1991; and V. Preston-Dunlop, S. Lahusen (eds), *Schrifttanz. A View of German Dance in the Weimar Republic*, London: Dance Books, 1990. For a more singular than rare example of the way in which oral tradition is intertwined with specific references to German texts, of which ample selections in translation are also given: V. Maletic, *Body-Space-Expression. The Development of Rudolf Laban's Movement and Dance Concepts*, New York, Berlin and Amsterdam: Mouton de Gruyter, 1987. The research initiatives brought together in *Espace dynamique. Textes inédits de Rudolf Laban*, Brussels: Contredanse, 2003, are praiseworthy.
32 V. Preston-Dunlop, J. Hodgson, *Rudolf Laban. An Introduction to his Work and Influence*, Plymouth: Northcote House, 1990, pp. 123–5; J. Metz, 'Rudolf von Laban. Autentische Quelle', *Tanzdrama*, 1991, no. 15, pp. 30–1; P. Bassett, 'The Library of the Laban Centre for Movement and Dance', *Dance Research*, 1994, no. 1, pp. 48–59. Some of the details surrounding these events were confirmed by Preston-Dunlop during an interview at the Laban Centre in June 2000.
33 V. Preston-Dunlop, *Rudolf Laban. An Extraordinary Life*, London: Dance Books, 1998. By the same author see also 'Laban and the Nazis. Towards an Understanding of Rudolf Laban and the Third Reich', *Dance Theatre Journal*, 1988, nos. 2–3, pp. 4–7 (German trans. 'Rudolf von Laban und das Dritte Reich. Ein Beitrag zum Verständins eine problematischen Verhältnisses', in *Tanzdrama*, 1992, no. 5, pp. 8–13). Among the major studies on Laban see also J. Hodgson, *Mastering Movement. The Life and Work of Rudolf Laban*, New York: Theater Arts Book, 2001.
34 See for example the research that is highly varied from a methodological point of view but based on important archival works: E. Dörr (ed.), *Rudolf Laban. Das Choreographische Theater*, Norderstedt b. Hamburg: Books on Demand, 2004; E. Dörr, *Rudolf Laban. Die Schfrift des Tänzers*, Norderstedt b. Hamburg: Books on Demand, 2005; M. Kant, 'Laban's Secret Religion', *Discourses in Dance*, 2004, no. 2, pp. 43–62. See also the already cited studies by Karina, Kant, and Guilbert.

35 See for example the polemics that followed the publication of the volume by Kant and Karina, which attributed the outcome of the research to the ideological bias of the former (in as much as she is a Jewish scholar who was trained in East Germany) and to the grudges of the latter (in as far as she is an artist who was forced into exile because of her marriage to a Jewish man). On the authors' considerations regarding their subjectivity see also M. Kant, 'German Dance and Modernity. Don't Mention the Nazis', in A. Carter (ed.), *Rethinking Dance History. A Reader*, New York and London: Routledge, 2004, pp. 107–18; S. Manning, 'Modern Dance in the Third Reich: Six Positions and a Coda', in S.L. Foster (ed.), *Choreographing History*, Bloomington, IN: Indiana University Press, 1995, pp. 165–76.

36 G. Manor, 'Der Weg zu den Wurzeln. Die Anfänge des *Ausdruckstanzes* in Eretz Israel', *Tanzdrama*, 1990, no. 13, pp. 7–11; G. Manor, 'Influenced and Influencing. Dancing in Foreign Lands. The Work of Choreographers/Dancers Persecuted by the Nazis in Emigration', in *Ausdruckstanz. Eine Mitteleuropäische Bewegung*, pp. 471–85.

37 E. Souritz, *Soviet Choreographers in the 1920s*, Durham, NC and London: Duke University Press/Dance Books, 1990; N. Chernova, J. Bowlt (eds), *Experiment*, Los Angeles: Institute of Modern Russian Culture, 1996; N. Misler (ed.), *In principio era il corpo. L'Arte del movimento a Mosca negli anni '20* (Rome: Acquario romano), Milan: Electa, 1999; P. Veroli, 'Docile Bodies and War Machines', in *The Annual of CESH. European Committee for Sport History*, 2004, pp. 28–46; and P. Veroli, 'Dancing Italian Fascism. Bodies, Practices, Representations', *Discourses in Dance*, 2006, vol. 3, no. 2, pp. 46–70.

38 C. Choron-Baix, 'Transmettre et perpétuer aujourd'hui', *Ethnologie française*, 2003, no. 3, pp. 357–60.

39 On these topics see among others V. Preston-Dunlop, 'Rudolf Laban and Kurt Jooss in Exile: Their Relationship and Diverse Influence on the Development of 20th Century Dance', in G. Berghaus (ed.), *Artists in Exile*, Bristol: Bristol University Press, 1990, pp. 167–78; C. Hoffmann, 'Deutsche und Österreichische Ausdruckstänzerinnen in der Emigration', in D. Hirschbach, S. Nowoselsk (eds), *Zwischen Aufbruch und Verfolgung. Künstlerinnen der Zwanziger und Dreissiger Jahren*, Bremen: Zeichen and Spuren, 1993, pp. 191–206; P. Stöckemann, 'Tanz in Exil', *Tanzdrama*, 1998, no. 42, p. 13; and the useful panorama in 'Emigranten und ihre Zufluchtsorte', ibid., pp. 19–21.

40 Patricio Bunster was a leading choreographer in Chile, trained by Jooss and Leeder. After the Pinochet putsch in 1973 he sought political asylum in East Germany where he taught at the Palucca School and introduced his own interpretation of *Audruckstanz* based on the Palucca system and the Jooss–Leeder tradition. In 1985 he went back to Chile where he became director of the Chilean National Ballet, combining *Audruckstanz* approaches with Chilean folk dance vocabularies. In 1968 he founded the first dance department in Chile. See J. Giersdorf 'From Utopia to Archive: A Dance Analysis', in *Proceedings of the Society of Dance History/Congress on Research in Dance Conference* (Centre national de la danse, June 2007), forthcoming.

41 H. Müller, 'Zwei rück, eins vor. Zur Frage der Rekonstruktion von Ausdruckstänzen', *Tanzdrama*, 1990, no. 11, pp. 4–6.

Part II

Keyword: **FEMININE/MASCULINE**

Topic: **THEATRICAL DANCE IN THE EIGHTEENTH CENTURY**

6 Feminine/Masculine

Linda J. Tomko

Féminin/Masculin. These words sat on my desk, tugged at my peripheral vision, and scrambled through my meditations from the first point in which I began to imagine this essay. For the standing equivalents of these words, at least in the scope of my academic "day to day," is gender. That is, their theoretical and methodological investments are typically or conventionally telegraphed by the term "gender," or just as often by the dyad "gender and sexuality." My academic "day to day" takes place in the United States, in a department at the University of California, Riverside, where conjoined pursuit of dance theory and dance history are framed in the title of the doctoral program we initiated there in 1993. I am aware, however, that the word "gender" can seem to invoke too limited a range of issues and contestations in cultural contexts different from mine, such as those of France and Italy. Thus I acknowledge the Anglo-American cast to the assessment I offer here of "the state of the field" with regard to *Féminin/Masculin* and also with regard to the structure of dance as a discipline in which notions of gender, feminine and masculine intervene.

I see gender as an interventionary stroke in the academic study not just of dance, but also of history – history history as I sometimes term it. For, like consideration of gender, historical analysis as a subject came later to the university study of dance. As scholars like Nancy Lee Ruyter and Janice Ross have demonstrated, the early additions of dance to university curricula in the 1910s and 1920s centered on emergent movement techniques and the study of composition.[1] Some thirty to forty years later, dance notation and dance history began to be added to dance curricula at the same time that study of dance started to move out of US Physical Education departments, sometimes to theater or music departments, sometimes to stand-alone dance departments. The modes for research and teaching dance history in the 1960s and 1970s in the US were substantially inflected by the person and approach of Selma Jeanne Cohen,[2] but other scholars need to be recognized. Certainly Christena L. Schlundt[3] (University of

California, Riverside), Angelika Gerbes[4] (Ohio State University), Shirley Wynne[5] (University of California, Santa Cruz), and Julia Sutton[6] (New England Conservatory of Music); influential independent scholars like Ingrid Brainard[7] and Wendy Hilton;[8] and highly visible journalists and researchers like Marcia B. Siegel[9] and Suzanne Shelton.[10] The approaches to history writing that they pursued issued in chronologies of performing careers, biographies, and choreographic analyses, the latter frequently favoring exploration of musicological issues. Largely absent here, or perhaps relegated to a distant background, was analysis and theorizations of change through time, a focus fundamental to "classical" academic history. When writers like Siegel investigated the "shapes of change" in a book by the same title,[11] she used a modified Laban Movement Analysis perspective as powerful aid to perception, but without recursion to models for theorizing causation that history writing offered.

University professors in US dance programs typically took their advanced degrees in fields like Literatures, Music, Anthropology, or English, in part because no Ph.D. degrees in Dance or Performance Studies existed. Christena L. Schlundt was one of the few in her cohort to pursue graduate work in history history. Her work in chronology was shaped in part by the impact of Curt Sachs's *World History of the Dance.*[12] "We wanted some *facts*," she once explained to me, indicating thereby a dissatisfaction with the lofty *Kulturkreis* model that Sachs floated in that book. Readers perusing Schlundt's chronologies of Ruth St Denis, Ted Shawn, and Helen Tamiris, for instance, should note the meaty analyses of phases and shifts in emphasis in the choreographers' careers. These are sandwiched among the rolling lists of dates, cities, venues, and performers that comprise the touring routes of itinerating performers. Buried deeply, perhaps, but not to be forgotten.

In the last two decades of the twentieth century, US academic study of dance has sustained the intervention of new writers trained up in the energizing enterprise of critical theory. As the new wave in the academy, they opposed previous models of "doing history," despite the only partial resemblance that then current dance history writing bore to other and longer standing models of writing history. Bringing critical theory to the table, their twenty-year engagement with the field has resulted in an intensification of theoretical scrutiny, a waning of recuperation and documentation efforts, and a re-nomination of the field as "Dance Studies." This shift was substantially assisted by a burgeoning interest in "the body" that animated a broad range of humanities disciplines. Dance Studies was, and is, at once reaching out toward and finding common concern with other fields in terms of critical theory while reciprocally receiving overtures from allied disciplines.[13]

I backtrack to the 1980s, when gender appeared on the radar screens of the established academic disciplines like history as well as the academic disciplines still in formation, like dance. In history departments, a new women's history emerged at the same time that the new social history and the new labor history were achieving wide recognition. All were concerned to read back into the historical record those people marginalized or silenced by master narratives of consensus history or intellectual history. All three were powered by new social critical movements – civil rights, feminist movements, labor movements.[14] Women's history writing rapidly moved from writing women back into the historical record to endeavoring to recast the frameworks through which the historical record was written. Here historians of women articulated gender as a category of historical analysis, and the conceptualization of gender grew to encompass the study of women *and* men in society.[15] Still today, in the first decade of the twenty-first century, it is not uncommon to read work that talks about "the subject" as "she," which may be recognized as a persisting political effort to place women in language in a way that was so long denied them.

The situation was quite different in dance, where women occupied the preponderance of faculty positions in dance departments in the US. As well, women had constituted much of the executant base in past nineteenth- and twentieth-century Western theater dance practice. Further, women had claimed creative power in the twentieth-century genre of modern dance and had rewritten the sexual division of labor therein.[16] Gender as a focus seemed ready-made for both the occupational profile and the research topoi of American dance academics. By 1994, for example, when the Congress on Research in Dance devoted a conference to the topic of dance and gender, floods of papers resulted.

Doing gender

What it means to "do gender" has been far from stable, in dance writing as in history writing, and I sketch here in large terms some of the conceptualizations and positionings that gender has received. I follow gratefully, and in part, on scrutinies fielded by David Glover and Cora Kaplan, Joseph Bristow, and Iris M. Young, and also by Susan Foster with regard to gender as choreography.[17]

Two early conceptualizations of gender pushed hard to discern the relation of gender to biological sex. A cognitive notion of gender was voiced by Robert Stoller in *Sex and Gender: On the Development of Masculinity and Femininity*.[18] Here gender is psychological, or cultural, rather than biological. Where sex is formulated as male or female, for Stoller gender was the amount of masculinity or femininity found in a person. Yes, persons could have quantums of both masculinity and femininity, but in this view usually one preponderated within a person. Gender identity constituted awareness that one belonged to one sex or the other, and gender role was the normative behaviors one displayed. Gender identity and gender role subscription could be at odds, could conflict with one another, and while they frequently were found to be mutually reinforcing, this was not always the case.[19]

Gayle Rubin's anthropological work on conceptualizing gender was extremely important to further separating gender from biological constructs and for forwarding the notion of gender as social, established in particular cultures. Rubin's "The Traffic in Women: Notes on the 'Political Economy' of Sex,"[20] helped posit the divide between sex and procreation as "nature," and rooted in the world of biology, on one hand, and gender as "culture," rooted in the makings by various societies, on the other. Gender as culture was rooted in the conventions those societies established for relations between men and women and it was rooted in the mutually exclusive categories that societies devised for men and women. Glover and Kaplan point to the important idea here that, "far from being an expression of natural differences, exclusive gender identity is the suppression of natural similarities."[21]

Rubin recognized not only that gender was constructed, but that sex was constructed too: that "what counts as sex is culturally determined and obtained."[22] Such determinations are made in areas of knowledge production like law, medicine, and science. They are also made in areas of self-fashioning that have grown increasingly visible and current in our time as the baby boom generation has aged: through surgeries; physical trainings, or disciplines; and drugs.[23] The "made-ness," the fabricated quality of gender, and the detachment of gender from any biological given, seem to me to have supplied the ground floor, the ground zero, if you will, for inquiries in Dance Studies that since the 1980s have taken notions of gender and run with them. Notions of gender identity and gender roles still persist and offer ways to think through the connection between gendered individuality and social agency. Resting on this foundational premise, at least two additional approaches seem to have won significant following.

Teresa de Lauretis's work in *Technologies of Gender*[24] is exemplary of theorizing that sees gender as representation and as a representation, one that circulates through technologies of media, advertising, schools, and the legal system, but also in the university system and experimental artistic work. Judith Butler's work is readily linked with notions of gender as performance or performativity. As performativity, gender in Butler's *Bodies that Matter*[25] depends on the subject's repeated citations and iterations of socially given codes, and the notion that gender is confirmed and construed *in* the repeating. Butler emphasizes the enunciation that is achieved by the iteration; here agency or the possibility for change is held in abeyance.[26]

The notions of gender as representation and gender as performativity or performance have been generative for dance scholars since the 1980s. Gender as representation, indeed gender as constituted *in* representation, comports with a sense and analysis of dance making wherein by making dances, we represent ourselves to ourselves, we comment upon our situatedness, our dilemmas, our ways of being in the world. Gender as representation further resonates with an approach to dance's past that Foster argued in *Reading Dancing*.[27] That is, dance, specifically choreography, can be read, but also created, through signs and codes whose salience derives from and possibly challenges issues and debates, ontologies and epistemologies, in particular historical moments. This she detailed in analysis of late Renaissance, eighteenth-century, and twentieth-century dance formations and epistemes of representation, linking theory with history in ways new for that period's dance history writing.

Foster's notion of codes, of when and how they are activated, also bears on Butler's notion of gender as performative. Foster's 1998 "Choreographies of Gender"[28] takes Butler as exemplary of scholars who too readily invoke the notion of performance in theorizing subjectivity, but fail to dip in any substantive way into the research findings and understandings that dance and theater disciplines can offer with respect to "performance" and "choreography." Butler in *Bodies that Matter* takes pains at one point to say she does not equate performativity with performance, cautioning that the reiteration of norms required by gender performativity precludes any fabrication by will or choice on the subject's part. The question of agency is precisely the question that Foster raises with regard to Butler's theorizing. She points out the panoply of decision-making that the activity of choreography requires. Foster's model of gender as choreography makes room for a querying stance within the production of representations. It positions subjects with elbow room to revise norms of behavior that Butler sees as given, constraining, and so controlling of sexual desire as well.[29]

The possibilities have been numerous, and they have been acted upon, for Dance Studies analyses to invoke and query gender as representation, performance, and choreography. This scholarly concern with gender is manifestly a twentieth-century phenomenon, and it has been deployed to substantial analytical gain with regard to twentieth-century topoi. I mention only two of many possible examples. Susan Manning unpacked feminism and nationalism in Mary Wigman's choreography in the book *Ecstasy and the Demon*.[30] She showed how the choreographic strategy of *Gestalt im Raum* upended gender norms and representations of gender as Germany engaged in World War I. And Manning addressed the different representations of femaleness that Wigman articulated with her group in the 1920s, also in her solo choreography in the 1930s, as these navigated and responded to changing political situations and, indeed, Wigman's changing personal situation in Nazi Germany.

Mark Franko's "Where He Danced" looked at the cross-dressing and what he terms through-dressing by, respectively, the female impersonator Barbette, on French stages in the 1920s, and butoh artist Kazuo Ohno in the late twentieth century. In this assessment, it is Kazuo Ohno in *Suiren* who is shown to hold polarities of sexual differentiation at bay and to create a third space, and a third kind of body, one which reconceptualizes the commonly available binaries of gender and sexual polarity. In this third space, Franko suggests, Ohno posited a way for sexual identities to interface, not blending, and not doubling two sexes in one body. Ohno performed a through-dressing that contributed to a depth model, one in which any and all gender attributes might be available for recombination at any kind of intervals, to any degree. I see Manning and Franko scrutinizing choreographic routes for creating spaces of social and sexual possibility through production of gender as representation and, effectively, through the choreographer's agency.[31]

To the eighteenth century

What of the state of the field in eighteenth-century dance research with regard to the key words *Féminin/Masculin*? I leave the twentieth century as a topos to look at twentieth-century studies regarding an eighteenth century in which neither gender nor the dyad *Féminin/Masculin* was designated or wielded as a principal category for scholarly analysis in dance. To be sure, eighteenth-century dance writers did promulgate analytical paradigms, and I can speak best to those of the first half of the century. These can be seen, for example, in the taxonomic energy that a Raoul Auger Feuillet expended on theorizing the ur-units of French noble style dancing, an energy that produced the ur-texts of *Chorégraphie*, a systems explanation for the style but also one that offered chart after graphic chart naming and registering steps and composite step-units for the style.[32] Some seventy-nine years later, Gennaro Magri's treatise on dancing *Trattato Teorico-Prattico di Ballo*[33] illuminated a continuing interest and drive toward taxonomy, although it produced textual registration of step variants more on the order of Pierre Rameau in *Le maître à danser*[34] in 1725. And, it was contredance choreographies that Magri's book captured for print circulation. Analysis of expression in dance received no less treatment by period dance writers. Treatment included not only the textual theorizing but also the material choreographic endeavors of John Weaver, in the 1710s and 20s, to formulate pantomimic expression, performed examples for which audiences largely failed to clamor at the time. Treatment of expression in dance included the greater success, achieved after the mid-century, by Jean Georges Noverre and peers Gasparo Angiolini and Franz Hilverding, in winning a place for pantomimic and narrative expression in the *ballet d'action*, in production and, subsequently, on the page.[35] Certainly the thematics of taxonomy and expression in dance outweighed other topics of print discussion or theorization by dance writers in the first half of the century. As new research advances into the latter part of the eighteenth century, we have the opportunity to check for such patterns in the revolutionary period. In *Choreography and Narrative*, Foster's scrutiny of French ballet and revolutionary festivals in the 1790s has shown the moment when danced characterization and political theory dallied, however briefly, with the concept of "la citoyenne."[36] Outright discussion of masculinity and femininity in dance writing occurred most consistently at micro levels, I think, wherein dancing masters turned scrupulous attention to say, the differences in height for rendering of a *demi-jeté* by man or woman, or the sequence and quality of the man's taking of the woman's hand. I want to emphasize that continued research that pursues questions of gender throughout the century, and the focusing of more research in the second half of the eighteenth century, stands likely to qualify this.

I will return to how twenty-first-century scholarship might choose to proceed in these circumstances. First I am obliged to limn some of the ways in which previous research in eighteenth-century dance has or has not invoked notions of gender or masculinity or femininity. I see Marian Hannah Winter and Lincoln Kirstein as two figures who contributed substantially to mid-century scholarship on the eighteenth century while pursuing quite different aims. In *A Short History of Classic Theatrical Dancing*, Kirstein's study of individual dancers was always subsumed in the perpetual quest to show how ballet emerged, waned, and renewed itself through phoenix fires, ever the premier form of classical theatrical dancing. Thus, even while he perceptively articulated a period production type – geographic ballets – to discuss a work like *Les Indes galantes*, and clearly though he saw the connection between shifting production types and mercantile colonization, questions of masculinity and femininity did not figure for him as part of the nation/race/capital equation.[37] Hannah Winter addressed an equally impressive number of dancers, breathing them to life as well. It seems to me that a unifying link in much of her work was to elaborate how spectacle figured in eighteenth-century dance. And, as the title of her book *The Pre-Romantic Ballet*[38] shows, she was equally convinced of the periods and practitioners who counted most in ballet's history. One of the least recognized benefits of her work was the clear picture she gave of the way that families constituted (institutional) structures for transmitting dance, for fomenting innovations, and for robing dance practices in the continuities of tradition as well. From whence did the female dancers come who ascended the stage of the Paris Opera – in the 1650s, per Régine Astier, or in the 1680s, per Susan Au's dance history text?[39] Hannah Winter's work gives us plausible cause to point to the dancing families of fairground performers. Neither Kirstein nor Hannah Winter plumbed the perspectives of gender/masculinity/femininity per se.

I can address only briefly the choreographic studies and the musicological studies that have constituted so much of the scholarship on eighteenth-century dance in the latter part of the twentieth century. My own mentor, Wendy Hilton, and scholars like Ingrid Brainard, Rebecca Harris-Warrick, Carol Marsh,[40] Meredith Little,[41] Anne Witherell,[42] and Richard Semmens pursued diligently the musico-dance matrix, the imperative for dance and music, each, to understand the temporal and spatial workings of the other's artistic forms. I see this bent, in large, as being conditioned by the emphasis on tough form promulgated via high modernist rankings of genres through the mid-twentieth century, and echoed in the conduct of academic musicology as well.[43]

Apprehension of the rise and fall of genres (be they *opéra-ballet* or *ballet d'action*), the social location of new dancers, the formal axes of musico-dance composition: these are the legacies of mid-century, modernist-infused investigations of eighteenth-century dance. Countering and complicating them have been work by Franko and Foster. Both have addressed specifically the identification of choreography *as* theory, and Foster has sounded the depths of certain choreographies of gender at moments of the eighteenth century. Franko is well known for his work on Renaissance and early Baroque bodies and choreographies, and also for analyses of modernist dance, including one referenced earlier in this essay. One of his most important theoretical insights has been the identification of choreography *as* theory, a point cogently argued in "Repeatability, Reconstruction and Beyond."[44] Not only can dances of the past yield up the premises on and through which they are composed, so do choreographies in whatever our present both index the suppositions about bodies and sociality and also comment upon them. Franko makes this case in assessing dance reconstruction projects he had witnessed through the time of the article's writings (I gauge this point to be about 1988), but also to argue for new choreography as a strategy for investigating the past. I see this initiative as an effort to retain the force of choreography for the shifting shaping of the new Dance Studies. I also witnessed one of Franko's choreographies in this vein, titled *Operratics*, in the Roman setting of the J. Paul Getty Museum in June 1995 before it became the new Getty building upon the hill in West Los Angeles, California. Particularly memorable for me was the section of the work which mobilized in several registers the oppositional use of arms that Pierre Rameau so achingly and painstakingly tried to set out in *Le maître à danser*. As it plays back in my mind, I see the opposition arms ascend and crest and stretch and skew the torso (that was the erratic dimension, I thought) and yield and sluice and pass from dancer to dancer, in a liquidity that differed not by sex or gender of dancer. This commented expressly on a different era and its different or non-polarized assignment of bodily attributes and energies to male and female dancers.[45]

Foster has argued with equal force and duration for choreography as theory. In *Reading Dancing*, for example, she pinpoints the shift from resemblance as mode of representation in allegorical dance of the late Renaissance to imitation as mode in neoclassical dancing, which she appraises with focus on Weaver and Noverre. In one dimension of her book *Choreography and Narrative*, she turned her eye on instances of the *Pygmalion* story in the eighteenth and nineteenth centuries, to illuminate constructions of femininity, crafted by woman in the case of choreographer Marie Sallé, or crafted for woman, in the case of Arthur St-Léon's 1847 *La fille de marbre*. The structure of the narratives, the contraventions of codes for who can initiate or give cause for social congress, and the compositional construction of a kind of female interiority, these are grounds for the choreography of gender that Foster unpacks en route to an ultimate focus on the Romantic ballet in Paris.[46]

For the concluding passages of this essay I want to return to some very recent re-formulations of gender for the catalyst they might offer to thinking about *Féminin/Masculin*. Here I turn to the dialogue between Iris Young and Toril Moi, and the insights of two young scholars, John Jordan and Derek Burrill. Iris Young views approaches to gender from the past decade or so to be closely focused on matters of subjectivity and identity. She takes Judith Butler's notion of gender as performative to be exemplary of this focus. Well enough, she says, except that the focus on subjectivity fails to consider the constitution of being achieved through people's interaction with structures of everyday life. Young elaborated this in a 1997 essay that talks about gender as serial.[47] The gist is this: that abstract yet practical structures generate a milieu of gendered existence that people traverse, the structures both "enable and constrain action but they do not determine it or define it."[48] Gender structures include heterosexuality, the sexual division of labor, and the power structures of a society. The individual experiential relations that people have to the gender structures are variable, she thinks; choice in response exists. As framed here, gender is comprised in serial interaction with structures of the social. Limitation of gender theory to formation of the subject is both too limiting and bound to fail in terms of conceptualizing agency. I take a moment to suggest that attention to gendered structures might enable scholars to revisit scenes of previous assessment. Consider the design by Jean Bérain (Figure 7), initially striking for the ambiguous gender assignment of its principal figure.[49] To what structures might those shadowy elements in the receding perspective of the image point us? Not the literal traces of symmetrical formal gardens and jetting fountains that one can just pick out. Rather, the interactions that such garden spaces enable, the calibration of experiences gained thereby for social identifications, even the ways they fashion desire. Further to this point are two images depicting public congress in Paris.[50] The contrast they offer should remind us to consider the differences that exist between spaces for social interaction and the connection with forms of masculinity and femininity that different spaces make possible.

Young maintains the need to attend to the social positioning of lived bodies, to the institutions and processes through which people find themselves gendered, in "Lived Body vs Gender,"[51] where she weighs Toril Moi's contention in the essay "What is a Woman?"[52] that the day for gender is over. Moi proposes instead the notion of the lived body as all that one needs to attend to questions of identity and subjectivity. Here the lived body is a physical body, located in and reacting to a specific historical and cultural moment. The lived body is actually a situation: it encounters material facts, has a relation to the environment, and has choice. "Situation, then, is the way that the facts of embodiment, social and physical environment appear in light of the projects a person has," Young writes. To nominate the body a "situation" as Moi does is to say that the "meaning of a woman's body is bound up with the way she uses her freedom."[53] The lived body, in large, allows description of habits and interactions "in ways that can attend to the plural possibilities of comportment, without necessary reduction to the normative heterosexual binary of masculine and feminine."[54] The lived body enables focus on the socio-historical differentiation of bodies. It relieves us of relying on the/or a distinction between biological sex and historically variable embodiment and gender. Young concurs that the notion of "the lived body" is useful for precisely the matters of identity and subjectivity Moi emphasizes. But Young maintains, as above, that gender remains a necessary conceptualization for thinking through such things as structural inequalities of opportunity, oppression of women and oppression of people who transgress heterosexual norms.[55]

Figure 7 *Habit des Nymphes de la suite d'Orithie du balet du Triomphe de l'amour*, staged by Jean Bérain, engraved by Jean Dolivar, Paris (1681), Bibliothèque Musée de l'Opéra. Permission kindly granted by Bibliothèque Nationale de France.

Figure 8
The first *Fête de la Liberté*, 15 April 1792 (Première fête de la liberté à l'occasion des Suisses de Château-Vieux; 15 avril 1792) by Jean-Louis Prieur (1759-95), Paris, Musée Carnavalet. © Photo Jean-Gilles Berizzi. Permission kindly granted by Réunion des Musées Nationaux.

These recent pulls and tugs at the utility of gender constructs, even to the utility of masculinity and femininity, bring me to the work on masculinities by John Jordan, for the eighteenth century, and Burrill, for digital interactive software in the twenty-first century. In his dissertation *Light in the Heels: the Emergence of the Effeminate Male Dancer in Eighteenth-Century English History*,[56] Jordan looked at the dancing Frenchman as constructed in English Restoration comedies, and at dancing as construed by period images and the publication *The Spectator*, the latter an early serial that offered more a sequenced essay than actual newspaper reportage. Jordan's analysis offers new purchase on what has long been understood as England's cultural anxiety about the French, the very people from whom English dancing masters borrowed and emulated the French noble style of dancing, and next to whom the English were the most avid choreographers of new work in that style. Reading beyond the receptivity to French models that the English prescriptive dance literature seems to offer, Jordan locates substantial ambivalence on the part of English people about the French, and about what constitutes proper masculinity. Jordan reads this ambivalence in connection with street thuggery by so-called "Mohawks," which *The Spectator* also reports, for example, and links this to period concerns about male sexuality and same sex relations. Jordan discerns a period concern with proper manhood not so much from dance writers of the day as from writings about dance in the day. It may be too early still to throw away the vectors of masculinity and femininity for a period such as the early eighteenth century.

In related vein, Burrill's recent work on interactive digital games impels me to consider a new way in which people might rehearse or try on identities and interaction in the social, albeit while sitting at the controls of digital games, making oneself one with the interface, the joystick, the medium of navigation and kinesthetic apprehension of a video game's ongoing-ness. As Burrill shows, video games provide different possible masculinities for the game player to inhabit, from the reversion to adolescence offered by James Bond films and video games to the repressed homoeroticism he sees on offer in action/adventure games such as *Metal Gear Solid* (Konami).[57] The very playing of the games requires a kind of iteration stipulated by Butler's notion of performativity. What's different, perhaps, in Burrill's *mise-en-scène* is both the range of enactments from which the game player might select, regardless of the player's gender, and the space (sometimes) afforded for choice. Burrill maintains that while the design and structure of the game deliver the options, more so than the at-one-ment with the avatar (the lead character, that other theorists have foregrounded), some games do exist that promote creation of new rules and structures *as part of play* (for example SONY's *Ultima Online*). However few these "open" games may be in comparison to the other, more numerous "closed" games, where choice is illusory, and "flat" games, where maintenance of a (in my word, dynamic) equilibrium is the goal, the possibility to play/create some choice is available.[58]

Jordan and Burrill together help us see at least two things. They offer salutary reminders that the rhetorical and historical female subject of so much feminist theory circulates in moments when, patriarchy notwithstanding, men too face the necessity to compose the self, in terms of its subjectivity and also its social interactivity. And, they remind us that at the very least pluralities of masculinities and femininities are needed, conceptually, for scrutinizing dancings in the eighteenth century, for assessing their cultural operation, and accounting for change through time. In this vein I point to ask which masculinity might have been invoked by the *Canaries* for two men, composed by the choreographer and virtuoso French dancer, Anthony L'Abbé. To twentieth-century eyes, it might signal a same-sex duet. We still need to be at work on what and how it signaled in 1725. And not just for this choreography.[59]

I do not think we have exhausted the gains to be had from investigating how actual choreographies might have choreographed gender. And this is especially important because of the period shift in theorizing the social that took place by the end of the eighteenth century. The new ideology of framing radical distinction between male and female took rhetorical and cultural form as the ideology of separate spheres, an ideology that deemed space either public or private, and that distributed men to the public sphere and women to the private. The force and sway of this ideological construction was not total, of course, and had different implications for different classes of people. But it is quite clear that this troping of social organization effectively spatialized gender, gave it a geography.

Shifts in theatrical dance practice at century's end confirm the salience of gender analysis. This shift is the well-documented revision of performers' functional duties such that men acquired responsibility for partnering, supporting and presenting women, and women gained added imperative to be the supported and presented. It is premature to relinquish gender, I think, for a period in which conceptualization and recalibration of dancers' duties foreground it. Further, by the end of the eighteenth century, shifting conceptions of race came to emphasize the role of biology in constituting identity. Historians of dance have been long accustomed to seeing and reading the visage and gestures assigned to "exotic" characters on the eighteenth-century dance/theater/opera stage. But previous scholarly cohorts have neglected to parse the constitution of racial ordination in dance on these stages. Whatever the intentions, the effects of this treatment have enacted a mid-twentieth-century approach to race

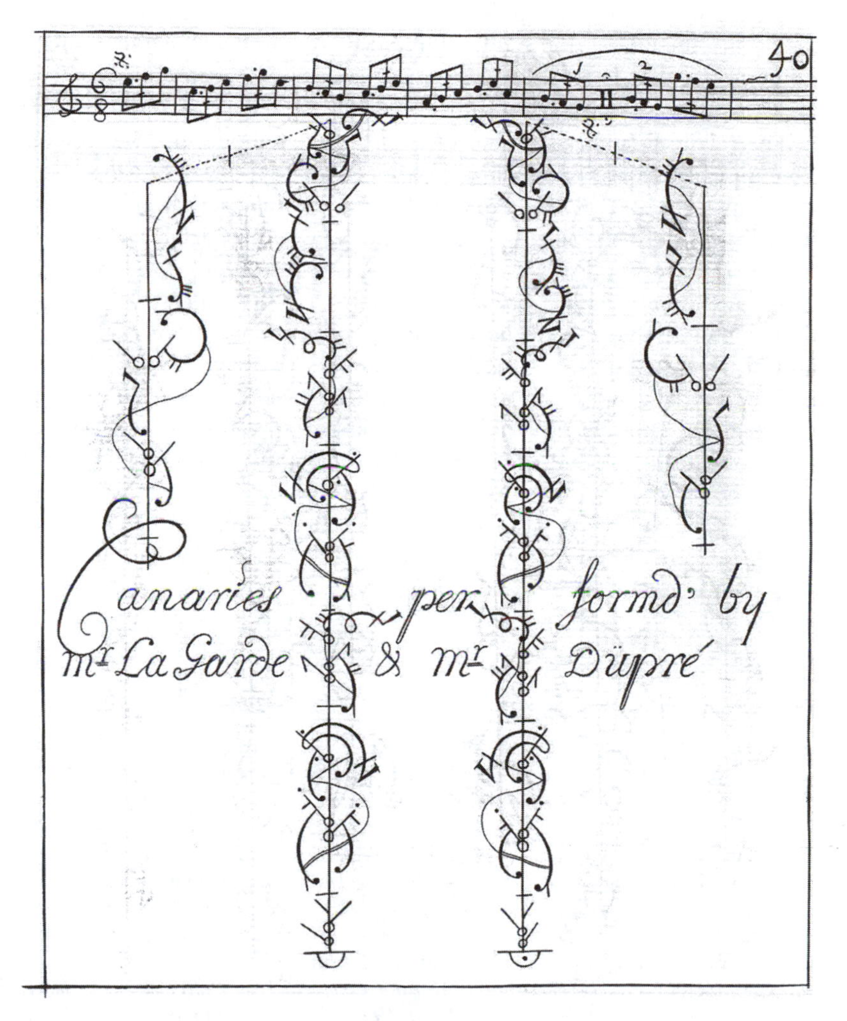

Figure 9 Canaries perform'd by Mr La Garde & Mr Dupré, in F. Le Rousseau, *A New Collection of Dances, containing a great Number of the best Ball and Stage Dances, composed by Monsieur L'Abbé*. Permission kindly granted by Derra de Moroda Dance Archives, University of Salzburg.

that Michael Omi and Howard Winant have called color-blindness. What is important for Dance Studies now is to retain the ability to suss out the choreography of gender while also scrutinizing the way in which gender formation or enactment may be coextensive with racial formation, enactment, and theorizing. Put a little differently, researchers have the opportunity to ask how gender and race may be coextensive for constructions of subjectivity and interaction in the social.[60]

There is a disconnect, then, between previous modernist assessments of eighteenth-century dance and the relatively few assessments of eighteenth-century dance that invoke critical theories of gender and sexuality. We are on the cusp of investigating whether, or how much, the nature/culture divide that, in Moi's view, so troubles contemporary theorizing about gender, characterized either eighteenth-century ways of thinking about dancing, or the findings of subsequent cohorts of theorists and historians. We do not know yet whether, following Young's lead, a notion of serial gender comprised in interaction with social structures best offers insight into social inequalities, this in an eighteenth century replete with colonial drives and shifts in models of political economy. In some ways, the disconnect leaves the eighteenth century – the long eighteenth century – a rich field for testing both the challenges mounted to previous models of gender and the binary (still) implicit even in the pluralizing of "masculini-ties and feminini-ties." That seems to me to be the opportunity before us.

Notes

1 N.L. Chalfa Ruyter, *Reformers and Visionaries: The Americanization of the Art of Dance*, New York: Dance Horizons, 1979; J. Ross, *Moving Lessons: Margaret H'Doubler and the Beginning of Dance in American Education*, Madison, WI: University of Wisconsin Press, 2000.

2 From 1960 to 1976, Selma Jeanne Cohen edited the *Dance Perspectives* monograph series, which provided a platform and helped emerging scholars circulate their research. Cohen's own *Next Week, Swan Lake: Reflections on Dance and Dancers*, Middletown, CT: Wesleyan University Press, 1982, modeled her parallel and continuing commitment to investigation of aesthetics.

3 C.L. Schlundt, *The Professional Appearances of Ruth St Denis and Ted Shawn: A Chronology and an Index of Dances 1906–1932*, New York: The New York Public Library, 1962; C.L. Schlundt, *The Professional Appearances of Ted Shawn and His Men Dancers: A Chronology and an Index of Dances, 1933–1940*, New York: The New York Public Library, 1967; C.L. Schlundt, *Tamiris: A Chronicle of her Dance Career 1927–1955*, New York: The New York Public Library, 1972.

4 A. Gerbes, *Gottfried Taubert on Social and Theatrical Dance of the Early Eighteenth Century*, Ph.D. dissertation, Ohio State University, 1972.

5 S. Wynne, 'Complaisance. An Eighteenth-century Cool', *Dance Scope*, 1970, vol. 5, no. 1, pp. 22–35; S. Wynne, 'The Minuet', in *Institute of Court Dances of*

the Renaissance and Baroque Periods, New York: Congress on Research in Dance, 1972, pp. 41–57; S. Wynne, D. Woodruff, 'Perspective Three: Part I, Reconstruction of a Dance from 1700', in *Dance History Research: Perspectives from Related Arts and Disciplines*, New York: Congress on Research in Dance, 1979.

6 Thoinot Arbeau, *Orchésographie*, Langres, 1588 (trans. and ed. by M.S. Evans, with new introduction and notes by J. Sutton, New York: Dover, 1967).

7 I. Brainard, *Three Court Dances of the Early Renaissance*, New York: Dance Notation Bureau Press, 1977. Leading historians of Renaissance dance, Sutton and Brainard also contributed significant articles on eighteenth-century topics. See J. Sutton, 'The Minuet, Elegant Phoenix', *Dance Chronicle*, 1985, vol. 8, nos. 3–4, pp. 119–52; I. Brainard, 'New Dances for the Ball: The Annual Collections of France and England in the 18th Century', *Early Music*, 1986, May, pp. 164–73.

8 W. Hilton, 'A Dance for Kings: the 17th-Century French Courante', *Early Music*, 1977, April, 161–72; W. Hilton, *Dance of Court and Theater: The French Noble Style 1690–1725*, Pennington, NJ: Princeton Books, 1981; W. Hilton, *Dance and Music of Court and Theater: Selected Writings of Wendy Hilton*, Stuyvesant, NY: Pendragon Press, 1997.

9 M.B. Siegel, *The Shapes of Change: Images of American Dance*, Boston, MA: Houghton Mifflin Co., 1979.

10 S. Shelton, *Divine Dancer: A Biography of Ruth St. Denis*, Garden City, NY: Doubleday, 1981.

11 Siegel, *The Shapes of Change.*

12 C. Sachs, *World History of the Dance*, trans. B. Schönberg, New York: W.W. Norton, 1937 (orig. edn *Eine Weltgeschichte des Tanzes*, Berlin: Dietrich Reimer/Emst Vohsen A.G., 1933). See also S. Youngerman, 'Curt Sachs and His Heritage: A Critical Review of *World History of the Dance* with a Survey of Recent Studies that Perpetuate his Ideas', *CORD News*, 1974, July, pp. 6–19.

13 The early publications of Susan Foster, Mark Franko, and Susan Manning in particular made this model visible. Thomas Laqueur's *Making Sex: Body and Gender from the Greeks to Freud*, Cambridge, MA: Harvard University Press, 1990, to take just one example, illuminates a mutual concern with "the body" that emerged in several disciplines at the time. See also S.L. Foster (ed.) *Choreographing History*, Bloomington, IN: Indiana University Press, 1995, which issued from a conference bearing the same title convened by Foster at the University of California, Riverside in 1992 to traverse and test some limits of just this common ground of "the body." The shift in nomenclature that the US experienced over twenty years was already in force at the Dance Studies Department of the University of Surrey in the early 1990s.

14 For an example of new social history see G.B. Nash, *The Urban Crucible: Social Change, Political Consciousness, and the Origins of the American Revolution*, Cambridge, MA: Harvard University Press, 1979; for new labor history see S. Wilentz, *Chants Democratic: New York City and the Rise of the American Working Class, 1788–1850*, New York: Oxford University Press, 1984. Studies of slave culture similarly upended ways in which histories of slavery as an institution operated and figured in US history. See for example J. Blassingame, *The Slave Community: Plantation Life in the Antebellum South*, New York: Oxford University Press, 1973; and E. Genovese, *Roll, Jordan, Roll: The World the Slaves Made*, New York: Pantheon Books, 1974.

15 J. Wallach Scott, *Gender and the Politics of History*, New York: Columbia University Press, 1988 and K.K. Sklar, *Catherine Beecher: A Study in American Domesticity*, New Haven, CT: Yale University Press, 1973 offer two vivid examples.

16 On executant base see Ruyter, *Reformers and Visionaries*; B. Barker, *Ballet or Ballyhoo: The American Careers of Maria Bonfanti, Rita Sangalli and Giuseppina Morlacchi*, New York: Dance Horizons, 1984. On women choreographers as self-authors, see S. Manning, *Ecstasy and the Demon: Feminism and Nationalism in the Dances of Mary Wigman*, Berkeley, CA: University of California Press, 1993 (2nd edn *Ecstasy and the Demon: The Dances of Mary Wigman*, Minneapolis, MN: University of Minnesota Press, 2006); A. Daly, *Done Into Dance: Isadora Duncan in America*, Bloomington, IN: Indiana University Press, 1995; and L.J. Tomko, *Dancing Class: Gender, Ethnicity, and Social Divides in American Dance, 1890–1920*, Bloomington, IN: Indiana University Press, 1999.
17 D. Glover, C. Kaplan, *Genders*, London: Routledge, 2000; J. Bristow, 'Whatever Happened to Gender? One Story of a Theory, 1964–1999', lecture given at Feminist Research Seminar, University of California, Los Angeles, March 14, 2000; I.M. Young, 'Lived Body vs Gender: Reflections on Social Structure and Subjectivity', *Ratio* (new series), 2002, vol. XV, no. 4, pp. 410–28; S.L. Foster, 'Choreographies of Gender', *Signs*, 1998, vol. 24, no. 1, pp. 1–34.
18 R.J. Stoller, *Sex and Gender: On the Development of Masculinity and Femininity*, New York: Science House, 1968.
19 Ibid.; Bristow, 'Whatever Happened to Gender?'; Glover, Kaplan, *Genders*, pp. xx–xxiii.
20 G. Rubin, 'The Traffic in Women', in R. Reiter (ed.), *Toward an Anthropology of Women*, New York: Monthly Review Press, 1975, pp. 157–210.
21 Glover, Kaplan, *Genders*, xxiii–xxv, quotation p. xxiv. Bristow, 'Whatever Happened to Gender?'.
22 Glover, Kaplan, *Genders*, pp. xxv–xxvi, quotation p. xxv; also Rubin, 'The Traffic in Women', p. 165.
23 See A. Jones, *Body Art/Performing the Subject*, Minneapolis, MN: University of Minnesota Press, 1998, especially Chapter 5.
24 T. de Lauretis, *Technologies of Gender: Essays on Theory, Film, and Fiction*, Bloomington, IN: Indiana University Press, 1987, see particularly Chapters 1 and 2, pp. 1–50; Bristow, 'Whatever Happened to Gender?'.
25 J. Butler, *Bodies That Matter. On the Discursive Limits of Sex*, New York: Routledge, 1993; see also J. Butler, 'Performative Acts and Gender Constitution: An Essay in Phenomenology and Feminist Theory', *Theatre Journal*, 1988, vol. 40, no. 4, pp. 519–31.
26 Bristow, 'Whatever Happened to Gender?'; Glover, Kaplan, *Genders*, pp. xxvi–xxviii.
27 S.L. Foster, *Reading Dancing: Bodies and Subjects in Contemporary American Dance*, Middletown, CT: Wesleyan University Press, 1986.
28 Foster, 'Choreographies of Gender'.
29 Butler, *Bodies that Matter*, p. 234.
30 Manning, *Ecstasy and the Demon*.
31 M. Franko, 'Where He Danced', in *Dancing Modernism/Performing Politics*, Bloomington, IN: Indiana University Press, 1995, pp. 93–107.
32 R.A. Feuillet, *Chorégraphie ou l'Art de décrire la dance par caractères, figures et signes démonstratifs*, Paris: chez l'auteur et chez Michel Brunet, 1700 (facsimile reprint New York: Broude Brothers, 1968. A second edition, published in 1701, includes supplementary charts).

33 G. Magri, *Trattato Teorico-Prattico di Ballo di Gennaro Magri*, Naples: V. Orsino, 1779 (I.E. Berry, A. Fox (eds), *Theoretical and Practical Treatise on Dancing*, trans. M. Skeaping, London: Dance Books, 1988).

34 P. Rameau, *Le maître à danser*, Paris: chez Jean Villette, 1725 (facsimile New York: Broude Bros., 1967; for an early Engl. transl. see J. Essex, *The Dancing-Master: or, The Art of Dancing Explained . . . Done From the French of Monsieur Rameau*, London, 1728).

35 For a close study of Weaver's professional and personal lives, and reproductions of his texts, see R. Ralph, *The Life and Works of John Weaver*, New York: Dance Horizons, 1985. Moira Goff's continuing research on Hester Santlow reappraises the sole credit typically given to Weaver for forwarding pantomimic dance via his early eighteenth-century stage productions. See for example, 'Coquetry and Neglect: Hester Santlow, John Weaver, and the Dramatic Entertainment of Dancing', in *Dancing in the Millennium: An International Conference*, Conference Proceedings, Madison, WI: The Print House, 2001, pp. 207–12. Among numerous treatments accorded to Noverre, see B.A. Brown, *Gluck and the French Theatre in Vienna*, Oxford: Clarendon Press, 1991; J. Chazin-Bennahum, *Dance in the Shadow of the Guillotine*, Carbondale, IL: Southern Illinois University Press, 1988; D. Lynham, *The Chevalier Noverre*, London: Dance Books, 1972; and S.L. Foster, *Choreography and Narrative: Ballet's Staging of Story and Desire*, Bloomington, IN: Indiana University Press, 1996. That credit endues to Noverre's peers Angiolini and Hilverding was argued by A. Michel in *Dance Index*, 1947, March, pp. 57–72.

36 Foster, *Choreography and Narrative*, p. 150.

37 L. Kirstein, *Dance: A Short History of Classic Theatrical Dancing*, 1935, p. 204 (reprint New York: Dance Horizons, 1977).

38 M. Hannah Winter, *The Pre-Romantic Ballet*, London: Pitman, 1974.

39 During the question and answer period for a panel devoted to Costume and Photography at the 1982 Society of Dance History Scholars conference at Harvard University, historian Régine Astier challenged the conventional recognition given the 1681 production *Triomphe de l'Amour* as the occasion on which women dancers first performed professionally at the Opéra. Susan Au continues use of this dating. See S. Au, *Ballet and Modern Dance*, New York: Thames & Hudson, 2002, p. 26.

40 Carol Marsh and Rebecca Harris-Warrick, two scholars who independently have published extensive article literature, collaborated on *Musical Theatre at the Court of Louis XIV: Le Mariage de la Grosse Cathos*, Cambridge: Cambridge University Press, 1994.

41 Marsh with Meredith Little published an indispensable *catalogue raisonné* of choreographies in the French noble style, *La Danse Noble*. A French approach to cataloguing these scores is F. Lancelot, *La Belle Dance*, Paris: Van Dieren, 1996. See also Little, N. Jenne, *Dance and the Music of J.S. Bach*, Bloomington, IN: Indiana University Press, 1991 (2nd edn 2001).

42 A. Witherell, *Louis Pécour's 1700, Recueil de Dances*, Ann Arbor, MI: UMI Research Press, 1983.

43 R. Semmens brings together musicological and choreographic considerations for querying the *bal publique*, a major form of public sociability, in *The Bals Publics at the Paris Opéra in the Eighteenth Century*, Hillsdale, NJ: Pendragon Press, 2004. Semmens, Moira Goff, Jennifer Thorp, Ken Pierce, and Linda Tomko are

contributing to an article literature that capitalizes on musicological questions and findings while articulating still other questions.

44 M. Franko, *The Dancing Body in Renaissance Choreography (c. 1416–1589)*, Birmingham: Summa Publications, 1986; M. Franko, 'Repeatability, Reconstruction and Beyond', *Theatre Journal*, 1989, vol. 41, no. 1, pp. 56–74, republished as 'Epilogue', in ibid., *Dance as Text; Ideologies of the Baroque Body*, Cambridge: Cambridge University Press, 1993, pp. 133–52.

45 Rameau speaks directly to the principle of opposition in Chapter 6 of *Le maître à danser*. He devotes part 2 of this treatise to a discourse on the use of the arms, set out in sixteen chapters via both textual description and line drawing.

46 For shifts in modes of representation, see Foster, *Reading Dancing*, pp. 100 and 121–45; for Sallé and St-Léon, see Foster, *Choreography and Narrative*, pp. 1–12.

47 I. M. Young, 'Gender and Seriality: Thinking About Women as a Social Collective', in *Intersecting Voices: Dilemmas of Gender, Political Philosophy, and Policy*, Princeton, NJ: Princeton University Press, 1997; Bristow, 'Whatever Happened to Gender?'.

48 Bristow, 'Whatever Happened to Gender?'.

49 *Habit des Nymphes de la suite d'Orithie du balet du Triomphe de l'amour*, staged by Jean Bérain, engraved by Jean Dolivar (Paris). Hilton's *Dance of Court and Theater* has used this image as text and cover illustration and called attention to the fluid embodiment and appropriate carriage of arms that it conveys.

50 The image "Dancing as the head of the Princesse de Lamballe is paraded through Paris" suggests close quarters of city streets and spontaneous eruption of dancing in response to execution (see Foster, *Choreography and Narrative*, p. 141, figure 46). The image "The first Fête de la Liberté, April 15, 1792" shows the city's revolutionary festival as designed and orderly, itself contained by an expansive but still clearly defined vista (Figure 8).

51 I.M. Young, 'Lived Body vs Gender: Reflections on Social Structure and Subjectivity', *Ratio* (new series), 2002, vol. 15, no. 4, pp. 410–28.

52 T. Moi, 'What is a Woman?', in T. Moi, *What is a Woman and Other Essays*, Oxford: Oxford University Press, 2001, pp. 3–120 (1st edn 1999).

53 Young quotes Moi, in 'Lived Body vs Gender', p. 415.

54 Ibid., p. 417.

55 Ibid., pp. 411, 420 and 427.

56 J.B. Jordan, *Light in the Heels: The Emergence of the Effeminate Male Dancer in Eighteenth-Century English History*, Ph.D. dissertation, University of California, Riverside, 2001.

57 D. Burrill, '"Oh, Grow Up 007": The Performance of Bond and Boyhood in Film and Videogames', in G. King, T. Krzywinska (eds), *Screenplay: Cinema/Videogames/Interfaces*, New York: Wallflower Press, 2002, pp. 181–93. On repressed homoeroticism see D. Burrill, 'Watch Your Ass: The Structure of Masculinity in Video Games', *Text Technology*, 2004, no. 1, pp. 89–112.

58 On the revisionist emphasis placed on design and structure of games, see Burrill 'Watch Your Ass'. For closed, open, and flat games see D. Burrill, 'Out of the Box: Performance, Drama and Interactive Software', *Modern Drama*, 2005, vol. 48, no. 3, pp. 492–512.

59 'Canaries performd' by Mr LaGarde & Mr Düpré', in Anthony L'Abbé, *A New Collection of Dances*, London: Stainer & Bell, 1991, p. 40 (orig. edn London, *c.*1725, n.p.).

60 M. Omi, H. Winant, *Racial Formation in the United States: From the 1960s to the 1980s*, New York: Routledge & Kegan Paul, 1986.

7 Dido's otherness

Choreographing race and gender in the *ballet d'action*

Susan Leigh Foster

There are fourteen scenes in Jean Georges Noverre's production of *Dido and Aeneas*, documented in his 1766 anthology of ballets *Théorie et Pratique*.[1]

Scene 1: As the ballet opens, Dido wrestles with her feelings of love for Aeneas. Even as she strives to release herself from this growing passion, Amour, appearing in disguised form, re-enflames her desire so that she can only think of "pleasing her conqueror."

STAGE DIRECTIONS: *Receive e-mail inviting me to participate in a conference with a contribution that brings feminist methodology to bear on an eighteenth-century case study.*

In *Choreography and Narrative*[2] I argued that the emergence of the *ballet d'action* was partnered by a radical re-definition of the division of labor between male and female roles. Where early in the eighteenth century, masculine and feminine were distinguishable based on the size and number of steps and the relative force with which they were executed, by the end of the century, male and female vocabularies began to diverge so that they shared fewer basic elements of vocabulary or style. As story ballets came to dominate dance offerings on the Opera stage, male and female roles transformed from a hierarchical relationship, in which male dancers exhibited strength and force while female dancers displayed delicacy and finesse, to an organic relationship in which male dancers supported but also controlled female dancers' charisma. These changes culminated in the genre of the Romantic ballet with its use of the female character as a dazzling yet insubstantial object of desire.

In *Choreography and Narrative* I also argued that the *ballet d'action*'s need to narrate using movement alone not only pressured gender roles to assume an organic configuration, but also disciplined the body to become the storyteller. Thus, not only did gender roles each assume a unique function, but the underlying aesthetic premises on which training and performance were based also radically altered. Rather than trace graceful lines in space through the arc of an arm or the circling of the foot, dancers began to internalize these geometric forms and to display them as a manifestation of their physicality. The arm no longer circled, but instead displayed a half-circle in the way that its musculature adhered to and promoted an imaginary line at the core of the limb. This change in the basic aesthetics of movement signaled a new role for the body as a danced character on which the story was mounted. Movement no longer carried along with it the affective state of the danced character but instead conveyed the inner feelings and motivations of that character. The dancing thus demonstrated rather than evoked the body's sentiments.

Not only did narrative re-define gender roles and the dancing body, but it also remapped the representation of cultural difference. The geometrization evident in the evolution of ballet technique effected criteria of technical competence and also ballet's treatment of world dance forms. Where eighteenth-century versions of Indian or Chinese dances incorporated signature gestures such as a particular use of the hands into the standard Baroque vocabulary, late-eighteenth- and early-nineteenth-century depictions of these dances borrowed foreign vocabularies but then subjected them to a geometrizing transformation. By counting out rhythmic phrases and spatially mapping gestural sequences from these other traditions, ballet dominated them and made them its own.

With this essay I want to supplement my argument about ballet's colonization of the Other by inquiring into the potential for narrative to accomplish this same subjugation. How did the Other figure within *ballet d'action* narratives? At the same time, I want to speculate about how the female character was drawn into complicity with this colonizing project. I will do so by focusing on a single ballet – Jean Georges Noverre's version of the story of Dido and Aeneas. Bringing together feminist and post-colonial perspectives on this ballet, I hope to demonstrate how the *ballet d'action* supported France's political and commercial agendas.

Scene 2: Aeneas, likewise enflamed by Amour, discovers Dido, and they dance out their growing love for one another.

STAGE DIRECTIONS: *Dust off cartons of notes from archival research conducted from 1988–94 in Paris librairies.*

In tracking the development of the *ballet d'action*, I find evidence to support the critique of narrative put forth by feminist scholars such as Teresa de Lauretis who deploys both Lacanian and semiotic analytic frameworks to illuminate the gendered relations embedded within narrative and the gendered logic that propels narrative along its trajectory and toward its inevitable conclusion.[3] In order to have a story, de Lauretis, Catherine Clément, and others argue, the woman must not only be fucked, but also fucked over.

Throughout Noverre's ballets there is much confirmation of de Lauretis's assertion that a masculine desire drives narrative. His heroines are either killed off or married off in conformance with the masculinist specifications for tragedy and comedy respectively. Of the eleven *ballet d'action* scenarios in Noverre's *Théorie et pratique*, four end in marriage celebrations; one leaves the heroine abandoned near death onstage; and six end with the female lead committing suicide. Remarkably, each of these heroines stabs herself to death.[4]

Scene 3: Moving from the sacred woods to the grand hall of the palace, Dido, now on her throne receives gifts from King Iarbas, a neighboring monarch. She declines his offer of marriage, and he endeavors to mask his resentment. Hoping to appease his apparent jealousy, Dido proposes a hunt.

STAGE DIRECTIONS: *Seize on the intersection of feminist and post-colonial theories as a way to deepen and enliven the project, and then remember theater historian Joseph Roach's interest in Dido as part of the circum-Atlantic aesthetic and political exchange.*[5]

Dido, who appears in several classical texts, most notably Virgil's *Aeneid*, was a widowed princess, who fled from her brother Pygmalion, King of Tyre, to current day Libya, where she founded and ruled the illustrious city of Carthage. In one prevalent version of her history, she throws herself on a funeral pyre in order to resist the repeated advances of Libyan King Iarbas. In Virgil's account, she has already rebuffed the offer of a second marriage from Iarbas when she meets Aeneas. In the midst of their romance, however, Aeneas is summoned by the gods back to Italy where he founds the city of Rome. Most accounts of Dido focus on her relationship either with Iarbas or with Aeneas. One of Noverre's striking innovations was to incorporate both male characters into a single plot.

Scene 4: In the forest where the hunt will take place, Juno, Venus, Amour, and Hymen plot Dido's defeat. During the hunt, Juno will create a storm; Venus will lead the couple into the cave; Amour will ensure Dido's happiness; while Hymen promises nothing.

STAGE DIRECTIONS: *Look for evidence of a ballet by Marie Sallé, because she is neglected as a historical force in the development of the* ballet d'action, *but find only notes for Noverre's version of Dido; in the process, become interested in Henry Purcell's opera.*

Renowned story ballet choreographers Noverre and Gasparo Angiolini both produced versions of Dido's story in 1766 and 1765 respectively. As a historian living in California, I was unable to obtain for this paper a copy of Angiolini's scenario, and this is a pity since I'm sure it would make for a fascinating comparison.

But it is also interesting to compare Noverre's version with that staged in the Purcell opera of 1689.[6] Purcell's *Dido and Aeneas* premiered at Josiah Priest's School of Young Ladies and was subsequently produced during the early years of the eighteenth century at Lincoln's Inn Fields, where John Rich first hired Marie Sallé to perform in 1725. Did Sallé ever hear about Purcell's opera? Might she have imagined choreographing a danced version of this story? Did Noverre, who took much inspiration from Sallé, hear about the opera through her or from his colleagues in London when he visited there in 1755?

A connection between Noverre's *ballet d'action* and Purcell's opera is unlikely since the opera fell out of production after 1706, and was not revived as a full production until the twentieth century. Although there is no record of the music Noverre used for his production, it was undoubtedly not Purcell's. Still, it is worthwhile to compare the two scenarios, since they bookend the transformation in gender roles that I outlined earlier.

Scene 5: Dido, in her chariot, with Aeneas and Iarbas on horseback, enter for the hunt accompanied by their entourages. They dance a pas de trois in which Dido's preference for Aeneas is obvious and Iarbas' frustration and resentment grows stronger. There follows a general divertissement performed by members of the courts. A storm erupts and Dido and Aeneas run into a cave.

STAGE DIRECTIONS: *E-mail eighteenth-century historian Lynn Hunt and ask her about Dido's status as Other. She responds that she doesn't know, but she recommends a few search engines.*

Did Dido read as Oriental or exotic in eighteenth-century France? Or did she affiliate as part of the civilized world? How did she figure in the French cultural imaginary? In *Poétique Francaise*, Jean François Marmontel couples Dido with Armide and Calypso, both exotic enchantresses who live on islands and waylay heroes who ultimately abandon them.[7] Voltaire, in contrast, imagines her as a real life personage by observing the differences between her Syrian origin and the local Muslim culture and religion with which she is confronted when she moves to Carthage.[8]

Whether as exotic temptress or as practitioner of a distinctive religious and cultural matrix, Dido signals a part of Africa whose influence and importance expanded dramatically over the course of the eighteenth century. Ruled by elected governors, but also heavily occupied by pirates who dominated a considerable trade with Europe, Carthage loomed as a powerful portal for European access to slaves and raw materials from Africa. Along with Egypt, which Napoleon invaded at the century's end, Carthage glowed with an ancient and contemporary foreigness to which Europeans were strongly attracted.

Scene 6: Juno, satisfied with his storm, dances with Venus, Hymen, and Amour in front of the cave, as if suggesting what is going on inside. Following Aeneas' "romantic" victory over Dido, they celebrate, all except Hymen who is in despair.

STAGE DIRECTIONS: *Read several books on post-colonial theory as it engages with feminism.*

Art historian Kay Dian Kriz argues that eighteenth-century Europe constructed Carthage as "a heterotopia [whose] elisions of past and present and of female bodies and geographical spaces are linked to this site in order to form a male colonizing consciousness based upon intellectual mastery, physical domination, and sexual pleasure."[9] According to Dian Kriz, depictions of Carthage in art and performance enhanced the Enlightenment project of rendering the Orient "ripe for penetration."[10]

Following this argument, Noverre's decision to depict Dido as the object of both Aeneas' and Iarbas' desires works to feminize Carthage in order to make it available for subsequent colonization. Both Dido and the city she stands for become something that must be conquered. The ballet's opulent *décor* and lavish dances undoubtedly invited and supported this conquest by sustaining the image of Carthage as given over to luxury. Such scenes of opulence, according to Dian Kriz, reinforced the impression that both Egypt and Carthage were in a state of decline and therefore in need of Western economic, military, and political intervention.[11]

Scene 7: Aeneas and Dido emerge from the cave happy and in love.

STAGE DIRECTIONS: *Do nothing on the project.*

Such a sexual objectification of both Dido and Carthage is not at work in Purcell's opera. In Purcell's version Dido is given more agency at several crucial points, most notably, when she chooses to enter the cave with Aeneas. The lovers are not driven into the cave by the storm, as in Noverre's ballet, but instead actively choose to enter it because of their love for one another. Purcell's storm erupts after Dido and Aeneas emerge from the cave, as the vehicle for separating them in their return to Carthage. It is at that point that the sorceress appears in disguise as Mercury to call Aeneas to Rome. In Noverre's version, Dido does not act, but instead reacts to the storm that, as the gods' pantomime suggests, allows Aeneas to conquer Dido emotionally and physically.

Scene 8: Iarbas discovers them and throws himself on Aeneas in a rage. All three enter into a fight with Dido helping Aeneas.

STAGE DIRECTIONS: *Get idea to coordinate critical analysis of ballet with specific scenes from the scenario.*

Purcell's opera also imbues Dido with a heroic stature by depicting her, from the beginning, as a strong political leader. Purcell's Act I begins with Dido's premonition that things will not go well in her romance with Aeneas, yet she is encouraged by ladies in waiting to pursue her desire for him. They argue that the union will make for a strong and hence fortuitous political alliance. Dido's decision to pursue Aeneas is thus based in part on her political sense of her country's future. Furthermore, Dido's strength as a leader is matched by that of the sorceress who engineers her downfall. Musicologists Wilfred Mellers and Joseph Kerman note that the sorceress, far from a grotesque figure, is accorded a grandeur in her arias that intimates her role as the dark side of Dido herself.[12] Never given a single solo, Aeneas, who Kerman describes as an "ineffectual booby," functions more as the prop or vehicle through which Dido meets her own inevitable tragic destiny.

Scene 9: Soldiers on both sides come to the rescue, and Aeneas' army, with Dido's assistance, soon triumphs over Iarbas and his troops. Rather than kill Iarbas, Aeneas breaks his own sword in two, releasing his rival. This only compounds Iarbas' rage and despair as he exits in defeat.

STAGE DIRECTIONS: *Realize that inter-referentiality between critical analysis and scenario will require a re-examination of the full text.*

In one sense the gods not only rob Noverre's Dido of her agency but also function as puppeteers who control the destinies of all the characters. Yet I would argue that the two male characters in Noverre's ballet attain agency and subjecthood by fighting over Dido. This rivalry, even as it fleshes out their characters, objectifies her as a potential prize, the bounty that will be rewarded to them for their efforts. Dido might appear intrepid, fighting alongside Aeneas, yet the fact of the two armies, thrown into conflict with one another because of her, renders her actions more charming than efficacious. As the object of two men's desire, she serves to fortify and enhance their masculinity, providing an opportunity for them to duel, and, importantly, for Aeneas to demonstrate magnanimity by releasing Iarbas.

Scene 10: Dido and Aeneas, happily reunited, relive the battle, celebrating their victory and their love.

STAGE DIRECTIONS: *Discover that a microfilm of the original scenario exists in California, at Berkeley. Coerce graduate student into xeroxing it and sending it to me. Fall in love, again, with archival manuscripts.*

Purcell's version, tragic, and spare, gives Dido majesty as a heroic figure, yet the sexism in that version, no less rampant, is only configured differently. The sorceress, as the dark side of the feminine, enables Aeneas to look good at everything he does. It is not his fault that he falls in love with Dido and it is simply his duty that he must leave for Rome. Thus in Purcell's version, Aeneas is ineffectual and Dido emerges as preeminent, yet her alter-ego, the sorceress, embodies all the destructive and malevolent impulses that have haunted the feminine for centuries.

Scene 11: Back in Dido's palace in Carthage, Aeneas dreams that he must abandon Dido in order to fulfill his destiny. He struggles in his sleep with the conflict between his desire and his duty.

STAGE DIRECTIONS: *Determine, with relief, that notes on the ballet from ten years earlier are accurate.*

In Purcell's opera, Aeneas is accosted by the sorceress disguised as Mercury, who commands him to abandon Dido and leave for Rome. Here, Aeneas' dream that he must leave redoubles the depth of his subjectivity by revealing the turmoil he feels. Whereas Purcell's Aeneas is duped by a female in disguise, Noverre's Aeneas, conflicted from within, attains a depth of character that also fortifies his masculinity. He must struggle heroically with the contradictions inherent in his fate, moving back and forth between his love for Dido, and his patriotic and statesmanly duties.

Scene 12: On the peristyle of the palace, overlooking the sea, Dido accosts Aeneas as he is leaving. Her tears and supplications initially draw him to her side, but remembering his mission, he continues toward the ship. She faints into the arms of her ladies in waiting, and he loses resolve, running toward her once again, but he soon returns toward his fellow soldiers. As the boat sets sail, Dido awakens and runs toward it, pointing her dagger toward her breast to show her suicidal intentions, but Aeneas is unmoved. As the ship sails out to sea, she curses Aeneas' infidelity.

STAGE DIRECTIONS: *Re-reading notes more carefully, discover that Angiolini also choreographed a version of Dido. Endeavor to obtain copy of his scenario.*

In scenes such as Aeneas' dream and this one, Noverre is able to build the inner life of the character, narrating through movement alone an entire sequence of feelings. The couple's struggle with their relationship enables their complex emotions to unfold in a long series of tableau-like images that reveals the autonomy of their subjectivity and its impact on the body. The bodies do not feel; the characters do. The pantomimic movement does not suggest feeling, but instead demonstrates it. Dido, abject and desolate, responds to Aeneas by threatening suicide, yet Aeneas remains resolved in his decision. Thus, even her life does not match his manly call to duty. In this way both Dido and the body are disciplined and subjugated by the narrative.

In Purcell's opera, both story and the heroine make a different move: once Aeneas announces his departure, Dido denounces him immediately. Calling him a "deceitful crocodile," a traitor who is merely using the gods as an excuse, she dismisses him and then sings the famous "remember me" aria to her faithful servant Belinda. Not the product of masculinist desire, her downfall is caused by her own tragic flaw.

Scene 13: Dido starts to kill herself when she sees a group of Moors set fire to her palace. Realizing that she has nothing left to govern, she helps fan the flames.

STAGE DIRECTIONS: *Failing in last minute efforts to procure Angiolini, proceed with idea to match analysis to scenario using Purcell for comparison.*

Returning now to the question of whether Dido figures as white or as Oriental, we can apprehend Noverre's "genius": if she reads as white, then she preserves French dignity by refusing the sexual advances of an African; if she reads as Oriental, then she is rightfully rejected by Aeneas who needs to go and found a nation. Either interpretation combines effectively with her status as objectified woman to "lower" the status of the Other and raise up the valor of the male character.

Although France did not actively colonize Algeria until the nineteenth century, Noverre's treatment of Dido prepares the way for that invasion by constructing Carthage as a kind of liminal space in between the Orient and the feminine. It rationalizes military incursions into the region designed to protect, maintain, and expand trade with the exotic Other. And it projects a happy outcome from such an invasion: Dido's Carthage can either be rescued or raped as "she" deserves.

Scene 14: Iarbas arrives, repentant for the destruction his men have caused, and offers protection and marriage. Dido refuses him once again, thrusts her dagger into her chest, and throws herself into the flames. Filled with remorse, Iarbas follows her.

STAGE DIRECTIONS: *Decide that it is important to stage the research for this essay as part of a feminist mandate to probe the political agenda underlying any historical investigation.*

Not unlike Dido, I refuse narrative's offer of marriage in this essay. I will not make a single-voiced argument that moves from dynamic tension to climactic resolution. Instead, these fourteen scenes of writing are choreographed to form a feminist analytical pastiche that partially unravels Dido's gruesome story so that another kind of narrative might be imagined. What if Dido shrugged her shoulders at Aeneas' departure and eloped to the Canary Islands with her faithful servant Belinda? What if she uttered a sigh of relief and continued to promote the artistic and intellectual achievements of her people so as to render Carthage the greatest civilization in the ancient world (far surpassing the Greeks and Romans, by the way)? What if she and Iarbas determined that through their union they might equalize trade relations with Europe and thereby foreclose the future traffic in human flesh?

These are resolutions to the story that Noverre, in his eagerness to usher in the *ballet d'action*, could not envision. Even as he "liberated" dance from sung or spoken lyrics in order that it might tell its own story, he constructed the docilized dancing body of the storyteller to convey the story's content. Feminist and post-colonial theories can show us how gendered and racialized identities depicted in the ballet overlap and reinforce one another. Dance Studies contributes to this analysis through its insistent interrogation of the corporeal and its role in constructing identity. With such choreographic tools as these, perhaps contemporary artists will be able to project a vision of the dancing body that defies current attempts at appropriation and conquest.

Notes

1 J.G. Noverre, *Théorie et pratique de la danse simple et composée; de l'art des ballets; de la musique; du costume et des décorations*, Louisbourg, 1766. According to Cyril Beaumont, Noverre's *Dido and Aeneas* was produced for the first time in Vienna in 1767. If this is the case, then Noverre had already devised the scenario but had not yet realized it when, thanks to the Duke of Wurtemberg, he published his anthology in 1766. See C.W. Beaumont, 'Introduction' in J.G. Noverre, *Letters on Dancing and Ballets*, trans. Beaumont, Brooklyn, NY: Dance Horizons, 1966, p. ix.
2 S.L. Foster, *Choreography and Narrative: Ballet's Staging of Story and Desire*, Bloomington, IN: Indiana University Press, 1996.
3 See T. de Lauretis, *Technologies of Gender: Essays on Theory, Film, and Fiction*, Bloomington, IN: Indiana University Press, 1987; T. de Lauretis, *Alice Doesn't: Feminism, Semiotics, Cinema*, Bloomington, IN: Indiana University Press, 1984.
4 There are four additional ballets described in *Théorie et pratique*, but these are divertissements with no clear leading characters.
5 See J. Roach, *Cities of the Dead: Circum Atlantic Performance*, New York: Columbia University Press, 1996, specifically pp. 42–8.
6 For a detailed discussion regarding uncertainties of the exact date of Purcell's opera, see E.T. Harris, *Henry Purcell's 'Dido and Aeneas'*, Oxford: Clarendon Press, 1987, pp. 4–10.
7 J.F. Marmontel, *Poétique Française*, Paris: Lesclapart, 1763, p. 298.
8 See Voltaire, *La Princesse de Babylone*, in P. Van Tiegham (ed.) *Contes et Romans*, tome 3, Paris: F. Roches, 1930, p. 185.
9 K. Dian Kriz, 'Dido versus the Pirates: Turner's Carthaginian Paintings and the Sublimation of Colonial Desire', *The Oxford Art Journal*, 1995, vol. 18, no. 1, p. 129.
10 Ibid., p. 117.
11 Ibid., p. 120.
12 Whereas Belinda predicts that Dido's fulfillment of private love will lead to public prosperity, the sorceress, as Wilfred Mellers observes, inverts this trajectory by announcing that she will destroy Dido and hence Carthage through an assertion of public duty. Thus, the sorceress evinces a grandeur that matches Dido's own. See 'The Tragic Heroine and the un-Hero', in C. Price (ed.), *Henry Purcell: 'Dido and Aeneas', an Opera*, New York: W.W. Norton and C., 1986, p. 209.

8 Danseuses and danseurs at the Opéra de Paris (1700–25) according to the cast lists in the libretto-programs

Nathalie Lecomte

This essay presents some of the preliminary results of an extensive study begun in 1996 under the auspices of the Théâtre Baroque de France[1] and continued in collaboration with the musicologist Jerôme de la Gorce until the Théâtre closed in 1998.[2] The study was devoted to the troupe of the Académie Royale de Musique, otherwise known as the Opéra, and aimed at producing an annotated catalogue of the casts from all the works staged by the Opéra between 1699 and 1733.[3] To accomplish this, we established the calendar of performances and then began collecting all the corresponding libretto-programs.[4]

Researchers had already been aware of these libretto-programs as source material, but the information they contain had rarely been exploited and then only partially so for specific purposes such as the biography of an important figure or to determine who had performed for the era's composers. We applied ourselves to a systematic and synthetic study of the cast lists with the goal of reaching a thorough understanding of the Opéra's troupe during this thirty-four year period.[5] This meant tracing the company's evolution over a period that scholars had previously overlooked primarily because of the limited number of extant archival sources.[6] The only way to compensate for the lack of necessary information and to learn about the composition of the troupe and gain insight into its organization during these years was through methodic scrutiny of the cast lists printed in the libretto-programs sold to the public at the theater entrance before performances. The majority of these libretto-programs were found in the collections of major libraries in Paris and the surrounding region.[7]

This essay is based on the documentation gathered in this research. It focuses on one issue in particular: the masculine/feminine relationship within the Opéra's dance troupe between 1700 and 1725. The dates that begin and end this period correspond, respectively, to the publication of Raoul Auger Feuillet's *Chorégraphie* and Pierre Rameau's *Le maître à danser*,[8] two of the essential sources for contemporary research on eighteenth-century dance in France. The analysis takes a historical approach and, from a methodological point of view, relies essentially on statistical tools. Wherever possible, I have tried to cross-reference the information in the libretto-programs with other available sources.

The corpus and problems of interpretation

My analysis is limited to performances staged in Paris. The corpus is made up of 148 libretto-programs;[9] the first was printed for the revival of *Ballet des Saisons* (31 July 1700) and the last was published for the revival of *Atys* (23 December 1725).

Whether printed for first productions or restagings, the libretto-programs were generally published for the first of a performance series and, as such, do not include possible alternations in the interpreter of a given role. Typeset and printed well in advance of the opening performance, they could not account for last minute changes. Sometimes, however, several editions were printed for the same performance series and included variations in the text and/or in the cast lists.[10] For some works, the libretto-program had to be reprinted several times to include new *entrées*[11] or changes made in response to a poorly received opening.[12] This requires the utmost vigilance in tracking the possible and sometimes even minute variations that exist between one edition and the other, variations that, as far the casts are concerned, occur first and foremost in the spelling of the artists' last names.[13]

All of the libretto-programs were published[14] on a standard 18 × 24.70 cm format following the same model. The following description of the exemplar printed for the 1705 restaging of Jean-Baptiste Lully's musical tragedy *Bellerophon* is typical.[15] The libretto-program has a total of 70 pages (from i to xvj and from 1 to 54). The date of the first production is followed, on the title-page (Figure 10), by the date of the first of a series of performances (in this case, 10 December 1705). The last names of the dancers are listed for the prologue, on page viij (Figure 11), and for each of the five acts of the tragedy, on pages xv and xvj.

The performers' first names are not given. This is a problem in those cases in which more than one member of the same family was cast in the same work or even in the same divertissement, or when some of the performers had the same last name even if they were not related. It was actually quite common to have more than one member of a family in the troupe. Brothers and sisters were traditionally distinguished by their last

BELLEROPHON,

TRAGEDIE,

REPRE'SENTE'E

PAR L'ACADEMIE ROYALE

DE MUSIQUE,

l'An 1679.

Remiſe au Théatre le Jeudy dixiéme Décembre 1705.

A PARIS,

Chez CHRISTOPHE BALLARD, ſeul Imprimeur du Roy pour la Muſique, ruë S. Jean de Beauvais, au Mont-Parnaſſe.

M. DCCV.

Avec Privilege de Sa Majeſté.

LE PRIX EST DE TRENTE SOLS.

Figure 10 Frontispiece of the libretto-program for *Bellerophon* (1705), Fonds Gilberte Cournand. © Mediathèque du Centre national de la danse, Pantin. Permission kindly granted by Centre national de la danse, Pantin.

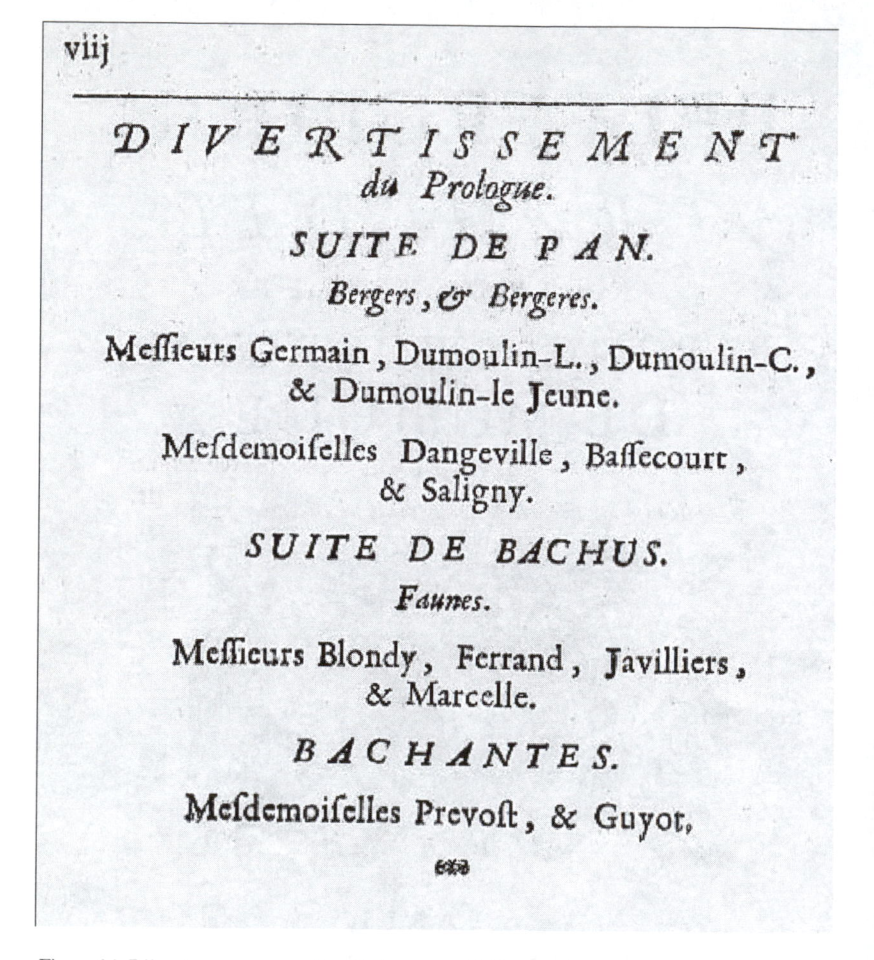
viij

DIVERTISSEMENT
du Prologue.

SUITE DE PAN.

Bergers, & Bergeres.

Messieurs Germain, Dumoulin-L., Dumoulin-C., & Dumoulin-le Jeune.

Mesdemoiselles Dangeville, Bassecourt, & Saligny.

SUITE DE BACHUS.

Faunes.

Messieurs Blondy, Ferrand, Javilliers, & Marcelle.

BACHANTES.

Mesdemoiselles Prevost, & Guyot,

Figure 11 Libretto-program for *Bellerophon* (1705): casting of the dancers for the *Prologue*, Fonds Gilberte Cournand. © Mediathèque du Centre national de la danse, Pantin. Permission kindly granted by Centre national de la danse, Pantin.

name followed by an initial, "L." for the elder ("l'aîné(e)") and "C." for the younger ("le/la cadet(te)").[16] Sometimes, but unfortunately not systematically, the initial of the first name was also mentioned and makes identification easier.[17] In other instances, however, the initial was left out or the name was misspelled and the same person was mentioned twice in the list of an *entrée*. This can make identification uncertain. The same problem arises for namesakes.[18]

The way in which the performers' names are placed on the page is important because it makes it possible to study how the roles in the divertissements were attributed. The soloists are highlighted and are most commonly distinguished from the corps de ballet by the fact that their names are placed on a separate line.[19] Sometimes, however, this distinction is also emphasized by the type itself, with the names of the soloists printed in capital letters.

The relationship between male and female troupe members

Danseuses appeared on the Opéra stage for the first time in May 1681, ten years after the troupe's first performance.[20] The occasion was a restaging of *Le Triomphe de l'Amour,* and that evening the evolutions of the danseuses, Mlles Caré, Pesant, Le Clerc, and La Fontaine, refreshed the performance set to music by Lully.[21] Until then, the corps de ballet had been exclusively male, but the danseuses quickly established the place to which they were due. Over the course of the year 1700, 14 women danced alongside 26 men.

In order to study the relationship between the casting of male and female troupe members and to be able to perceive the evolution of this relationship over a quarter of a century, I divided the corpus into synchronic subsections of four years each (Figure 12). In all of these years, there are always fewer danseuses than danseurs in the cast (broken lines on the graph). The most recurrent differences between the two groups are a deficit of three danseuses (in 20% of the cases), four danseuses (22%), and five danseuses (17%); the smallest deviation is one danseuse less (one instance) and the greatest is 14 danseuses (one instance). In the entire period, the total number of danseuses appearing in a performance is relatively constant and goes from a minimum of 7 to a maximum of 14. The group is most often composed of 11 women (in 24% of the cases). The total number of the troupe of danseurs varies a bit more but, when all is said and done, it too is relatively constant, going from a minimum of 12 to a maximum of 22. In most cases the male group is made up of 16 danseurs (in 26% of the cases). After 7 August 1717 (*Venus et Adonis*), the difference between the two groups leveled out and their relationship evolved in a parallel manner.

In further refining this analysis, I was interested in the number of roles played in a single performance, given that artists could actually appear in different roles in the same piece over the course of the various acts. Thus, to cite extreme examples, Mademoiselle Rose played as many as six characters in *Canente*, as did Henry Dumoulin in *Hesione* and

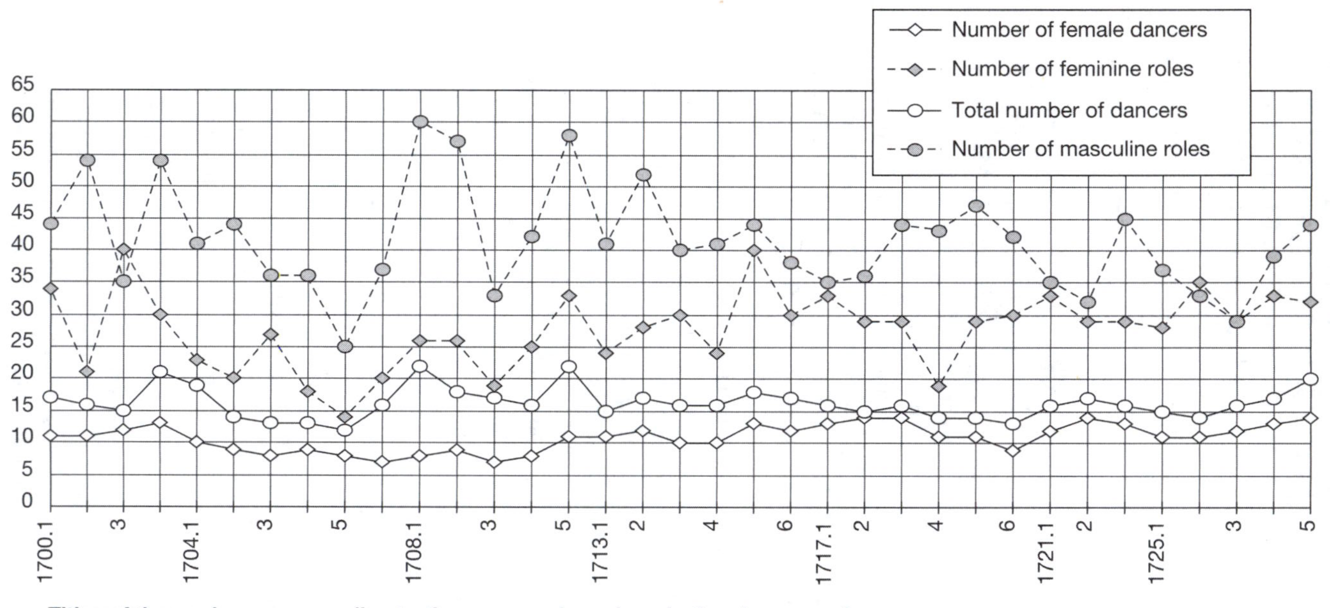

Titles of the works corresponding to the years and numbers in the above graph:
1700 : 1. Les Saisons ; 2. La Grotte de Versailles et le Carnaval Mascarade ; 3. Canente ; 4. Hesione.
1704 : 1. Le Carnaval et la Folie ; 2. Isis ; 3. Iphigénie en Tauride ; 4. Didon ; 5. Acis et Galathée ; 6. Telemaque.
1708 : 1. Hippodamie ; 2. Thétis et Pelée ; 3. Les Fragments de M. de Lully ; 4. Issé ; 5. Atys.
1713 : 1. Médée et Jason ; 2. Psyché ; 3. Les Amours déguisés ; 4. Médée et Jason ; 5. Telephe ; 6. Armide.
1717 : 1. Fragments ; 2. Ariane ; 3. Tancrède ; 4. Venus et Adonis ; 5. Isis ; 6. Camille reine des Volsques.
1721 : 1. Omphale ; 2. Les Fêtes vénitiennes ; 3. Phaëton.
1725 : 1. La Reine des Péris ; 2. Les Eléments ; 3. Les Fêtes de lété ; 4. Telegone ; 5. Aty s.

Figure 12 Evolution of female–male dancers' ratio. © Nathalie Lecomte.

Jean-Baptiste Guyot in *Isis* in 1717, which implies that they danced in all of the divertissements.[22] Here too the curve of the number of feminine roles comes out much lower than that of the masculine roles, with three exceptions: it is the same in *Les Fêtes de l'été* (29 roles for both men and women) and higher in two instances, in *Canente* (40 opposed to 35) and in *Les Éléments* (35 opposed to 33). A balance is almost struck twice, in *Omphale* and in *Les Fragments* (33 roles for women and 33 roles for men).

Examining the casting for the divertissements more closely, one notes that some of the roles were danced exclusively by one sex or the other. This was the case in the restaging of *Bellerophon* in 1705, in which acts II and V were danced by men and act III was danced by women. An analysis based on the same time frame as Figure 12 (Figure 13 and Table 1) shows that 21 (60%) out of the 35 works performed have at least one, two, or even four exclusively male divertissements. This phenomenon holds true for both revivals and first productions. Divertissements reserved for women only were less common, but 5 works in the same section include one. For 3 of these (*Iphigénie en Tauride*, *Didon*, and *Omphale*), an entirely female *entrée* follows an entirely male *entrée*, as though intended to reestablish a certain balance.

From whatever point of view one takes, therefore, it appears that the masculine/feminine relationship is always to the advantage of the men. But the difference in the number of the company's male and female dancers is not excessive and does tend to diminish.

The hierarchy: soloists and elective partners

We have already seen how the placement of names on the page makes it somewhat easier to understand the division of the troupe members within the performance. From this perspective, the troupe hierarchy is already quite clear. A certain number of dancers, both male and female, are clearly distinguished from the rest. Based on this, it was possible to draw up a chronological list of soloists, including:

> for the women, Catherine Du Fort, Mademoiselle Desplaces, Marie-Thérèse Perdou de Subligny, Michelle Dangeville, Marie-Catherine Guyot, Françoise Prevost, Mademoiselle Le Fevre, Mademoiselle Chaillou, Madeleine Menés, Mademoiselle La Ferriere, Mademoiselle Petit, Mademoiselle Corail, and Mademoiselle Delisle the elder;
>
> for the men, Louis Lestang, Guillaume-Louis Pécour, Romain Dumirail, Claude Balon, Michel Blondy, Henry Dumoulin, David Dumoulin, François Dumoulin, Pierre Dumoulin, Denis Dumoulin, Louis Dupré,

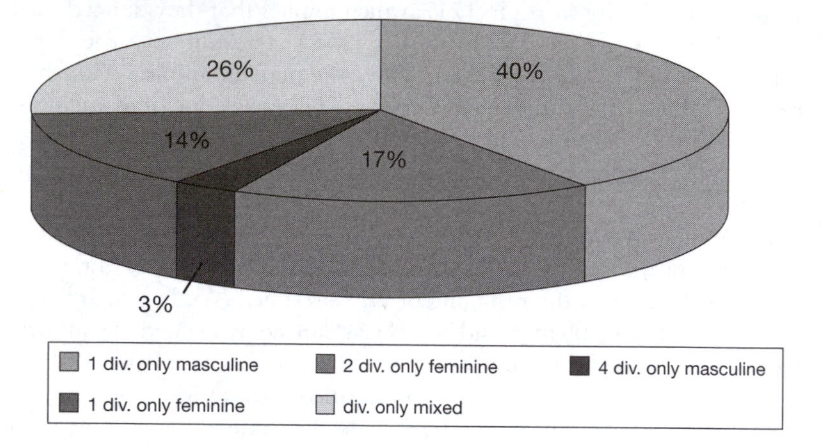

Figure 13 Percentage of *divertissements* according to sex division. © Nathalie Lecomte.

> Antoine Dangeville, François Robert Marcel, Malter the elder, Mion and Antoine Laval.[23]

These soloists appeared in three different formations: trio, duet, and solo. The first could be mixed, danced by two men and one woman (*Arethuse*, III, 1701) or by two women and one man (*Polyxène et Pyrrhus*, V, 1706). It could also be completely female (*Thetis et Pelée*, I, 1712), but this kind of trio was prompted especially by the introduction of the three Graces. The duets could be female, male, or mixed. The solos permitted the best artists of both sexes to demonstrate their talent and win the audience's favor.[24]

The layout of the cast lists also makes it possible to deduce the existence of elective partnerships (Table 2). Balon made a name for himself as the almost exclusive partner of Subligny. After she retired in 1705 and before he himself retired in 1710,[25] he danced with Prevost who, in turn, danced with both François and David Dumoulin. Guyot sometimes appeared with Blondy, whereas Mademoiselle Chaillou danced with Henry Dumoulin, as did Menés at the beginning of her career. From 1715 until 1724, however, Menés and Marcel were particularly in demand as a couple. This is further confirmed by Pierre Rameau: "Mademoiselle Menese who generally dances with Marcel in *pas de deux* of certain style, always adds to the attraction of a performance and excites the acclamations of the public."[26]

Male couples also emerge. Blondy's first accomplice was Marcel (between 1715 and 1717); later on, he danced with Dupré (between 1720

Table 1 List of *divertissements* interpreted exclusively by dancers of each sex. © Nathalie Lecomte

Title of the work (act)*	*Date of the* première	*Characters in the* divertissement
Exclusively masculine divertissements		
Le Carnaval mascarade, I	11 July 1700	Polichinelles
Le Carnaval mascarade, VII		Arlequin, Trivelins et Scaramouches
Le Carnaval mascarade, VIII		Matassins
Le Carnaval mascarade, IX		Dervis et Turcs
HESIONE, IV	21 December 1700	Vents souterrains et Vents de l'air
Isis, III	14 February 1704	Bergers et Faunes
Isis, IV		Hommes gelés et La Guerre
IPHIGÉNIE EN TAURIDE, I	6 May 1704	Scythes
Didon, III	18 July 1704	Furies
Didon, IV		Jeux et Plaisirs
Acis et Galatée, II	5 October 1704	Suivants de Polyphème
TELEMAQUE, III	11 November 1704	Démons
Thetis et Pelée, III	16 April 1708	Suivants du Destin
Thetis et Pelée, IV		Borée et Vents
Atys, V	29 November 1708	Dieux des bois
MÉDÉE ET JASON, II	24 April 1713	Magiciens et Démons
Psyché, II	22 June 1713	Forgerons
Psyché, IV		Démons
Armide, III	26 December 1713	Suivants de la Haine
ARIANE, IV	6 April 1717	Sacrificateurs
Tancrède, I	8 June 1717	Magiciens
Tancrède, IV		Démons
Venus et Adonis, II	7 August 1717	Suivants de la Jalousie
Venus et Adonis, V		Peuples d'Amathontes
Isis, IV	14 September 1717	Hommes gelés et La Guerre
CAMILLE REINE DES VOLSQUES, II	9 November 1717	Guerriers conjurés
Omphale, IV	21 April 1721	Magiciens
Phaëton, I	13 November 1721	Tritons
LA REINE DES PÉRIS, II	10 April 1725	Chasseurs indiens
TELEGONE, IV	6 November 1725	Démons et Furies
Exclusively feminine divertissements		
CANENTE, Pr.	4 November 1700	Diane, Flore et leurs Suivantes
IPHIGENIE EN TAURIDE, II	6 May 1704	Nymphes
Didon, V	18 July 1704	Nymphes
TELEPHE, II	28 November 1713	Prêtresses d'Apollon
Omphale, V	21 April 1721	Prêtresses de l'Amour

* First productions in capital letters, revivals in small letters.

Table 2 Privileged partners. © Nathalie Lecomte

Subligny	Balon	1700	*Le Carnaval mascarade*
Subligny	Balon	1702	*Tancrède*
Subligny	Balon	1703	*L'Europe galante*
Subligny	Balon	1703	*Armide*
Subligny	Balon	1704	*Le Carnaval et la Folie*
Subligny	Balon	1704	*Didon*
Subligny	Balon	1704	*Telemaque*
Subligny	Balon	1704	*Roland*
Subligny	Balon	1705	*Mort d'Hercule*
Subligny	Balon	1705	*Philomele*
Menés	H-Dumoulin	1712	*Médée et Jason*
Menés	H-Dumoulin	1713	*Psyché*
Menés	H-Dumoulin	1713	*Armide*
Menés	H-Dumoulin	1714	*Arion*
Menés	H-Dumoulin	1714	*Armide*
Menés	Marcel	1715	*L'Europe galante*
Menés	Marcel	1715	*Alceste*
Menés	Marcel	1716	*La Mort Alcide*
Menés	Marcel	1716	*Hypermnestre*
Menés	Marcel	1716	*Roland*
Menés	Marcel	1717	*Fragments*
Menés	Marcel	1717	*Ariane*
Menés	Marcel	1717	*Tancrede*
Menés	Marcel	1717	*Venus et Adonis*
Menés	Marcel	1717	*Isis*
Menés	Marcel	1718	*Amadis de Gaule*
Menés	Marcel	1718	*Le Jugement de Paris*
Menés	Marcel	1718	*Acis et Galatée*
Menés	Marcel	1719	*Iphigénie en Tauride*
Menés	Marcel	1719	*Le Carnaval et la folie*
Menés	Marcel	1719	*Issé*
Menés	Marcel	1720	*Polidore*
Menés	Marcel	1720	*Les Amours de Protée*
Menés	Marcel	1720	*Scylla*
Menés	Marcel	1721	*Omphale*
Menés	Marcel	1721	*Phaëton*
Menés	Marcel	1722	*Renaud*
Menés	Marcel	1723	*Pirithous*
Menés	Marcel	1723	*Philomele*
Menés	Marcel	1723	*Les Fêtes grecques et romaines*
Menés	Marcel	1724	*L'Europe galante*
Menés	Marcel	1724	*Armide*
La Ferriere	Pécour	1717	*Ariane*
La Ferriere	Pécour	1717	*Tancrede*
La Ferriere	Pécour	1718	*Le Jugement de Paris*
La Ferriere	F-Dumoulin	1720	*Thésée*
La Ferriere	F-Dumoulin	1722	*Les Saisons*
La Ferriere	F-Dumoulin	1722	*Les Fêtes deThalie*
Delisle	Mion	1724	*L'Europe galante*
Delisle	Mion	1724	*Les Ages*
Delisle	Mion	1725	*Les Fêtes de Thalie*
Chaillou	H-Dumoulin	1708	*Fragments de M. de Lully*
Chaillou	H-Dumoulin	1709	*Philomele*
Chaillou	H-Dumoulin	1710	*Phaëton*
Chaillou	H-Dumoulin	1711	*Iphigénie en Tauride*
Chaillou	H-Dumoulin	1711	*Nouveaux Fragments*
Chaillou	H-Dumoulin	1712	*Idomédée*
Chaillou	H-Dumoulin	1712	*Creuse*

Table 2 Privileged partners *(continued)*

Prevost	Balon	1705	*Bellerophon*
Prevost	Balon	1706	*L'Europe galante*
Prevost	Balon	1706	*Le Professeur de folie*
Prevost	F-Dumoulin	1706	*Polyxène et Pyrrhus*
Prevost	F-Dumoulin	1706	*Alceste*
Prevost	Balon	1707	*Amadis*
Prevost	F-Dumoulin	1707	*Bradamante*
Prevost	D-Dumoulin	1707	*Les Saisons*
Prevost	Balon	1707	*Thésée*
Prevost	Balon	1708	*Issé*
Prevost	Balon	1708	*Atys*
Prevost	Balon	1709	*Sémélé*
Prevost	Balon	1709	*Philomele*
Prevost	Balon	1709	*Roland*
Prevost	F-Dumoulin	1710	*Phaëton*
Prevost	Balon	1710	*Diomede*
Prevost	Balon	1710	*Les Fêtes vénitiennes*
Prevost	D-Dumoulin	1711	*La Grotte de Versailles*
Prevost	F-Dumoulin	1712	*Médée et Jason*
Prevost	F-Dumoulin	1713	*Les Amours déguisés*
Prevost	D-Dumoulin	1714	*Les Fêtes de Thalie*
Prevost	D-Dumoulin	1715	*Proserpine*
Prevost	D-Dumoulin	1716	*Ajax*
Prevost	D-Dumoulin	1716	*Roland*
Prevost	D-Dumoulin	1719	*Le Carnaval et la Folie*
Prevost	D-Dumoulin	1720	*Les Amours de Protée*
Prevost	D-Dumoulin	1720	*Thésée*
Prevost	D-Dumoulin	1722	*Les Saisons*
Prevost	D-Dumoulin	1722	*Renaud*
Prevost	F-Dumoulin	1722	*Les Fêtes de Thalie*
Prevost	D-Dumoulin	1723	*Pirithous*
Prevost	D-Dumoulin	1723	*Philomele*
Prevost	D-Dumoulin	1723	*Les Fêtes grecques et romaines*
Prevost	D-Dumoulin	1724	*Amadis de Gaule*
Prevost	D-Dumoulin	1725	*Les Fêtes de l'été*
Prevost	D-Dumoulin	1725	*Telegone*
Guyot	F-Dumoulin	1706	*L'Europe galante*
Guyot	F-Dumoulin	1706	*Le Professeur de Folie*
Guyot	F-Dumoulin	1707	*Les Saisons*
Guyot	Blondy	1708	*Fragments de M. de Lully*
Guyot	D-Dumoulin	1708	*Fragments de M. de Lully*
Guyot	D-Dumoulin	1708	*Issé*
Guyot	D-Dumoulin	1708	*Atys*
Guyot	D-Dumoulin	1709	*Hesione*
Guyot	D-Dumoulin	1709	*Philomele*
Guyot	D-Dumoulin	1710	*Phaëton*
Guyot	D-Dumoulin	1710	*Diomede*
Guyot	D-Dumoulin	1711	*Manto la fée*
Guyot	F-Dumoulin	1714	*Les Fêtes de Thalie*
Guyot	D-Dumoulin	1715	*L'Europe galante*
Guyot	D-Dumoulin	1717	*Fragments*
Guyot	D-Dumoulin	1717	*Camille reine de Volsques*
Guyot	D-Dumoulin	1719	*Le Carnaval et la Folie*
Guyot	D-Dumoulin	1721	*Les Fêtes vénitiennes*
Guyot	Blondy	1721	*Phaëton*
Corail	Laval	1723	*Pirithous*
Corail	Laval	1723	*Thetis et Pelée*

and 1722). When Dupré and Marcel were not dancing with Blondy, they danced together (between 1719 and 1722). François and Pierre Dumoulin were together several times (between 1708 and 1716). Finally, after 1724, the youngest of the Malters was systematically associated with Antoine Laval. The female duets of the period are less systematic, with the exception of the one formed many times between 1715 and 1718 by the soloists Guyot and Prevost.[27]

Invaluable accounts of these elective partnerships are found in the choreographies notated in the Feuillet system, composed for many of the Opéra's artists.[28] Several of these annotated choreographies confirm and conserve traces of these combinations.[29] Reading through the choreographies, it also becomes evident that both the men and women were often quite technically skilled.[30] Most of the male *entrées*, in particular, are full of ornamentations and difficult steps (battus, entrechats, *equilibres*, and so on).[31] Likewise, the numerous leaps and jumps, battus, turns, *pas soutenus* and *balancés* in the four solos Pécour choreographed for Marie-Catherine Guyot attest her talent, and allow one to assume she had the flexibility, agility, and precision they required.[32]

Choreological analysis has not as yet been done on the masculine/feminine relationship in the works performed by Opéra artists. It can be quickly pointed out, however, that in Pécour's choreographies for a man and a woman, such as *L'Entrée espagnole* in *L'Europe galante*,[33] both dancers perform the same steps and the same ornamentations, more often than not in mirror symmetry, crossing and alternating, coming together and coming apart, according to the volutes of the composition, all of which seem to indicate a real concern in maintaining a balance between the two dancers.[34]

Male and female salaries

Some of the information discerned from the libretto-program about the troupe's hierarchy can be further corroborated by comparing it with two archival sources regarding the months of October 1704 and January 1713 respectively.[35] These documents include a list of the artists employed on these dates and their annual salaries.[36] This has made it possible to compare the earnings of the men with those of the women (Table 3). In 1704 annual salaries reached 800 livres for four of the male soloists and 700 livres for the other two, with the exception of Balon who enjoyed a special status (he was paid 14 livres "each day of performance" and 7 livres "when he was ill") and Pécour who was both a dancer and the ballet master (for which he received 3,000 livres). Two of the four danseurs in the corps de ballet were paid 500 livres and the other two 300 livres.

Table 3 Comparison between masculine and feminine salaries. © Nathalie Lecomte

Masculine	*livres*	*livres*	*Feminine*
1704			
Claude BALON			
Guillaume Louis PECOUR	3000	1500	Marie-Thérèse de SUBLIGNY
Antoine GERMAIN	800	700	Michelle DANGEVILLE
Louis BOUTEVILLE	800	700	ROSE
Michel BLONDY	800	700	VICTOIRE
François DUMOULIN	800	500	LA FERIERE
Michel FERRAND	700	450	TISSARD
(Henry ?) DUMOULIN	700	400	Françoise PREVOST
Antoine DANGEVILLE	500	400	LE FEVRE
LEVESQUE	500	300	DU PLESSIS
Jean-Baptiste DANGEVILLE	300	300	NOISY
Claude JAVILLIERS	300		
1713			
Guillaume-Louis PECOUR	1500		
Michel BLONDY	1000	900	Françoise PREVOST
François DUMOULIN	1000	900	Marie-Catherine GUYOT
David DUMOULIN	800		
Antoine GERMAIN	800		
François-Robert MARCEL	800	500	Madeleine MENES
Pierre DUMOULIN	800	500	Anne LEMAIRE
Henry DUMOULIN	600	500	Marie-Louise ISECQ
Antoine DANGEVILLE	600	500	Anne-Julienne HARANG
Michel GAUDREAU	600	400	Renée-Julie FLEURY
Claude JAVILLIERS	600	400	Françoise MANGOT
Henry-François PIERRET	400	400	Anne LE ROY
Jean-Baptiste GUYOT	400	400	NADAL

As far as the women are concerned, the company's female soloist earned 1,500 livres, or almost the equivalent of what Pécour earned as a dancer, though she did not have the right to the same privileged salary as her colleague Balon. The other soloists were paid 700 livres each, or the equivalent of the salary earned by each of their two male counterparts. The women in the corps de ballet were paid either on equal terms as or slightly less than the men, with a right to 500 livres, 450 livres, 400 livres (including the well-known Prevost, who was just beginning her career), and finally 300 livres.

In 1713 the progress of the entire Opéra troupe is accompanied by a decrease in the highest salaries (especially for the singers) and by a more equitable division of these resources. Regarding dance, Pécour (who no longer danced but continued to work as the ballet master) still received 1,500 livres a year. The two best soloists were paid 1,000 livres, the other four earned 800. Four of the danseurs in the corps de ballet earned 600 livres, the other two 400. The scale of the women's salaries was the lowest: the two soloists – Prevost and Guyot – each received 900 livres, or slightly less than Blondy and François Dumoulin. Four of the young women in the corps de ballet, who sometimes danced lead roles, earned 500 livres, which was less than their male counterparts at the same level. Overall, therefore, the women were paid somewhat less than the men, but the differences between the salaries earned by the men and by the women are not excessive.

A typology of roles

Relying once again on the cast lists in the libretto-programs, I tried to determine which roles had been assigned to which dancers on the basis of their sex. There were three different possibilities: roles that could be assigned to both male and female dancers, roles that were reserved to women alone, and roles that were solely for men (Table 4).

In the mythological realm, many characters accompanied the gods. Venus, Diana, and Flora were three of the major goddesses whose praises were extolled by numerous attendants (men and women). Venus could be accompanied by a mixed suite, even though it was often made up exclusively of women, as was that of Diana, Astraea, and Minerva. On the contrary, the followers of Cupid,[37] Zephyr, Mars, and Medusa were made up entirely of men. The same was true for the Cyclops who trail Polyfemus. But there were also characters like the Vestals, the Hesperides, the Muses, and the Graces that did not have male equivalents.

Nymphs, bacchantes, dryads, nereids, sirens, priestesses, and huntresses completed this feminine mythological typology, which, in most cases, however, had a male *pendant* of fauns, satyrs, tritons, priests, and hunters. The same was true for the whole gamma (male and female) of the Greeks and other inhabitants of ancient cities or regions (Athenians, Cretans, Ionians, and so on). The *entrées* of male warriors, combatants, and heroes were far more numerous than those of the female warriors, amazons, and heroines, though they did exist.

Table 4 Typology of roles. © Nathalie Lecomte

Feminine roles	*Mixed roles*	*Masculine roles*
Suivantes de Diane	Suivant(e)s de Venus	Suivants de l'Amour
Suivantes d'Astrée		Suivants de Zephire
Les Grâces		Suivants de Mars
Vestales		Cyclopes
Nymphes		Faunes
Bacchantes		Satyres
Dryades		
Néréïdes		Tritons
Sirènes		
Prêtresses		Prêtres
Chasseresses		Chasseurs
	Grec(que)s	
	Athénien(ne)s	
	Crétois(es)	
	Ionnien(ne)s	
Amazones	Guerrier(re)s	
	Héro(ïne)s	
	Jeux et Plaisirs	
Suivantes de la Vertu	La Danse	Suivants de la Jalousie
	La Folie	Suivants de la Victoire
	Suivant(e)s de la Jeunesse	Suivants de la Gloire
	Suivant(e)s de la Paix	Suivants de la Haine
	Suivant(e)s de la Sagesse	Suivants de la Fureur
	Suivant(e)s des Quatre Continents	Suivants du Destin
Les Heures		Les Arts
Fontaines		Fleuves
		Vents
Fées		Enchanteurs
		Génies
		Lutins
		Démons
		Furies
		Sorcières
Ombres heureuses		
	Songes agréables	Songes funestes
	Berger(e)s	
	Pâtres/Pastourelles	
	Paysan(ne)s	
	Vendangeur(euse)s	
Sultanes		Icoglans
	Chinois(e)s	
	Maure(sse)s	
	Espagnol(ette)s	
	Bohémien(ne)s	
	Ethiopien(ne)s	
	Matelot(te)s	
	Gondolier(e)s	
	Masques	Matassins
	Arlequin(e)	Polichinelle
	Scaramouche(tte)	
	Pantalon(e)	

As far as allegorical characters are concerned, Dance was incarnated by both men and women, as was Folly. Though women were excluded from the suites of Jealousy, Victory, Glory, Hate, Fury, and Destiny, they alone comprised that of Virtue. They were included in the mixed corteges accompanying Youth, Peace, Wisdom, and the four continents. The Hours were their exclusive domain, but they were prohibited from the Arts, the Games, and the Pleasures, which, once cast exclusively to men, tended to become female from 1709 on. The "happy shadows" were female; pleasant dreams were mixed; nightmares were male.

In general, the figures associated with the underworld or the destructive powers of nature, such as the winds, were male specialties. Women could be called upon to interpret the fates (female equivalents of the enchanters in whose company they generally appear), but there were no female genies or elves. The gods of the underworld and demons were generally male, with the exception of those instances in which they were transformed – and thus in part softened – into nymphs[38] or into the Pleasures.[39] Sorcerers and the furies were always embodied by men.

The pastorale induced the presence of innumerable *entrées* of shepherds and shepherdesses, and sometimes farmers, always accompanied by their suitors, as they celebrated the sweetness of reciprocal love. Men and women grape-pickers and gardeners completed this typology tied to the rural world.

Exoticism brought on various men and women from far-away places, such as China and the Orient (sultans and their officials). On the whole, both women and men were cast in these picturesque roles, in particular those that enlivened the numerous sea-related feasts (men and women sailors as well as gondoliers). In the scenes of masked balls and carnivals, women had a chance to interpret the traditionally male characters of the Commedia dell'Arte, such as Arlecchina, Scaramouchette, and Pantalona, but not Punchinella. Likewise the *Matassins*[40] were always a male prerogative. Both men and women, therefore, had a chance to take on a wide range of characters.

Some of the evidence we possess leads one to believe that dancers of the era specialized in certain types of roles. Study of the cast lists confirms this. Among the men, Blondy systematically embodied the roles of the furies, demons, and other creatures of the underworld.[41] François and Pierre Dumoulin were generally cast as grotesque characters. And, after Balon and before Antoine Laval, David Dumoulin seems to be the ideal incarnation of the tender shepherd.

Fewer women seem to have specialized in a given role, perhaps because the female troupe was numerically smaller than that of the men. Nonetheless, Mademoiselle Du Fort seems to have been designated to interpret characterized roles, such as Arlecchina, who, according to the Parfaict brothers,[42] was the first to dance at the Opéra. The role of Arlecchina was later given to Mademoiselle La Ferriere. Guyot and Prevost interpreted a wide range of characters, but were distinguished above all as shepherdesses and nymphs. Unlike Blondy, Prevost owed a part of her success to her capacity to interpret various characters with equal brilliance.[43] As Pierre Rameau attests: "She is endowed with the same power as fabled Proteus. She assumes all manner of forms at will, with the difference that, while Proteus generally employed them to frighten curious mortals who came to consult him, she makes use of them to enchant the eager eyes that watch her and to conquer all hearts."[44]

It would be interesting to analyze this data in greater depth, especially from a sociological point of view. Unconsciously or not, the attribution of a certain type of character to one sex or other can actually refer to an ideal of different behavior, especially as far as allegorical roles are concerned. Thus women had to demonstrate qualities of reserve, modesty, and virtue, while the dancing of their male counterparts, relying on a muscular vigor held to be virile, was destined to evoke extreme characters or emotions, all the way to the malefic forces.

The role *en travesti*: a very targeted use

As clearly demonstrated by the typology of sex-based roles (Table 4), few feminine roles were interpreted by men *en travesti*. From 1671 until May 1681 cross-dressing was the rule on the Opéra stage given that the corps de ballet was then exclusively male. This convention was inherited from the tradition of the *ballet de cour* and was void of sexual ambiguity.[45] As women became part of the troupe, they quickly took on these roles.

This is what happened, for example, in the successive restagings of *Atys*. The first production in Saint-Germain-en-Laye in 1676 was performed exclusively by men, who played the nymphs *en travesti*.[46] When it was staged again on 7 January 1682 in Saint-Germain-en-Laye (by a mixed cast of professionals from the Opéra and noble amateurs), most of the female characters had been cast to women.[47] Roles *en travesti* were still danced in act II (the Phrygiennes) and in act IV (the nymphs of the ancient fountains)[48] but, by the time the production was performed in Paris in 1708, 1709, and 1725, even these had disappeared completely.

Over the course of the first quarter of the eighteenth century, cross-dressing at the Opéra always followed the same practice, persisting only in particular cases and solely in relation to evocations of the underworld. In the *entrées* of the furies and the sorcerers, the costumes actually made it possible for the audience to immediately and unequivocally identify the male interpreters. Cross-dressing was never used ambiguously for dramatic purposes as it might have been in certain comedies, with the intention of deceiving or of challenging one character regarding the sexual identity of another. The fact that cross-dressing ceased as soon as the company opened to female dancers, fully confirms the purely conventional aspect of the custom of an exclusively male corps de ballet. One notes, however, that not a single cast from this era bears witness to a male role interpreted by a woman.[49]

Conclusions

At the conclusion of this essay, it appears evident that the lists of the performers' names open numerous possibilities for investigation. For this study alone, the cast lists have been an invaluable source of information, given the rarity of extant sources on the dancers of the Opéra in the early eighteenth century.

Analysis of these lists further confirms the standing already given to danseurs, such as Pécour, Balon, and Blondy, and to danseuses Subligny and Prevost, who, even in posterity, are still represented in all the dance dictionaries. Yet this analysis also, and perhaps even more significantly, reveals the presence and absolutely determinant role that certain danseuses and danseurs who have long since been forgotten may have had in their time.

The data also shows that, at the turn of Grand Siècle, women dance professionals were quite capable of rivaling their male counterparts, which is to say, long before the arrival of Sallé and Camargo, two emblematic figures who reigned from the 1730s on. Though statistical tools demonstrate that there were clearly fewer female than male dancers, it is also evident that, once the transition period of the 1680s to 1690s was over, there was also a clear shift toward an equilibrium in both the first productions and revivals staged at the Opéra from 1700 on. The hierarchy within the troupe was the same for both male and female dancers and, even if male stardom remained strong, it did not inhibit certain danseuses from becoming quite well-known.[50] Through a systematic analysis of the cast lists it has been possible to trace, for the first time, a typology of roles attributed to dancers, demonstrating how some were exclusively reserved for one sex or the other, even if the majority of them could be played indifferently by both sexes or could find masculine–feminine equivalents. When all is said and done, the will to offer both groups equal opportunities seems to reign in the spirit of the librettists who invented the divertissements and the choreographers entrusted with composing them, from the ballet master Pécour on.

The scope defined by a historical approach does not include the possibility of exploring other approaches. But the information we have gathered urges investigation by researchers in other disciplines (sociology, dance movement analysis, musicology, aesthetics, and so on) in the hopes of bringing new light to the subject from various points of view.

Notes

1 The Théâtre Baroque de France in Rueil-Malmaison (Centre des Arts de la Scène des XVIIe et XVIIIe siècles) ran a research atelier with a twofold mission: on the one hand, applied research for the performances staged by its troupe of dancers, singers, and actors and, on the other, more fundamental research.

2 Research continued under the U.R.A. 1012 (Centre de Recherche sur l'Histoire de l'Art) of the CNRS, thanks to a research grant I received from the French Ministry of Culture in 2000–2.

3 The catalogue, which hopefully will be published soon, includes all the performances by the Opéra's artists on the Paris stage, as well as those held privately or at the Collège Louis-le-Grand.

4 These small objects served both as a libretto (including the whole text of the opera) and as a program (listing the names of the entire cast, role by role).

5 A work of this sort was recently completed on a mid-eighteenth-century composer. See S. Bouissou, D. Herlin, *Jean-Philippe Rameau. Catalogue thématique des œuvres musicales,* tome 2, Paris: CNRS-BNF, 2003.

6 This changes after 1753 when the veuve Duchesne began publishing the *Spectacles de Paris,* small almanacs that, each year, listed the names of all the artists employed at the Opéra. From here on, there is also an increasing number of documents in the archives regarding the theater's management and operation.

7 Several large collections are conserved at the Bibliothèque-Musée de l'Opéra, at the Bibliothèque Nationale (Imprimés, Réserve and Musique), at the Bibliothèque Municipale de Versailles (fonds ancien), and at the S.A.C.D. (the authors' and publishers' association). These are the most important collections, but there are also other more modest resources, such as those of the Bibliothèque Historique de la Ville de Paris, the Médiathèque du Centre national de la danse in Pantin (fonds Gilberte Cournand), or those of certain private collectors. Numerous libretto-programs are conserved in regional libraries or abroad, but the scope of our study was limited to materials in Paris and its surrounding region.

8 R.A. Feuillet, *Chorégraphie ou l'Art de décrire la dance par caractères, figures et signes démonstratifs,* Paris: chez l'auteur et chez Michel Brunet, 1700 (facsimile reprint New York: Broude Brothers, 1968. A second edition, published in 1701, includes supplementary charts); P. Rameau, *Le maître à danser,* Paris: chez Jean Villette, 1725 (facsimile New York: Broude Bros., 1967; for an early Engl. trans. see J. Essex, *The Dancing-Master: or, The Art of Dancing Explained . . . Done From the French of Monsieur Rameau,* London, 1728).

9 There were 63 first productions and 85 revivals.

10 There are two for *Manto la fée,* for example. The second was printed because the first production of the work was postponed from 29 January to 5 February 1711. It registers the omission or the addition of a duet by David Dumoulin and Marie-Catherine Guyot in the second act and corrects Françoise Prevost's

role to that of a dryad instead of a faun. See *Manto la fée*, Paris: Christophe Ballard, 1701, FPo. Liv. 18 [R 14 (4).

11 This is particularly true for *Les Fêtes vénitiennes*. The first production of this opéra–ballet on 17 June 1710 included a prologue and three *entrées*. The addition of a new *entrée* on 8 July, 8 August, 5 September, and 14 October made it necessary to publish supplements that were printed separately or inserted as best as possible in the first publication.

12 This was the case for *Les Muses*, which was not received well when it premiered on 28 October 1703. The new version, presented at the beginning of November, required reprinting the libretto-program to reflect the changes that had been made.

13 In the eighteenth century the spelling of proper names was not fixed, and the name of the same artist can vary from one edition to another and even from one act to another within the same edition.

14 Between 1700 and 1725, three successive Parisian publishers had the privilege of printing the Opéra's libretto-programs: Christophe Ballard (through June 1713), Pierre Ribou (through May 1716), and the latter's widow (through November 1727).

15 Based on a libretto by Thomas Corneille and Fontenelle, it was first produced at the Paris Opéra on 31 January 1679 and revived in July 1680. See *Bellerophon*, Paris: Christophe Ballard, 1705, FPo. Liv. 18 [R 21 (8).

16 We know from other sources that the two Dangeville brothers in *Bellerophon* are Antoine François (the elder brother) and Jean-Baptiste (the younger brother); Mademoiselle Dangeville, who was their sister, is called Michelle. The Dumoulin case is very difficult to resolve: at that time four brothers performed at the Opéra, designated in *Bellerophon* by the initials "L." [which we identify as Henry] and "C." [François] or by a descriptive adjective (Dumoulin the younger) [Pierre] or by a number (Dumoulin the fourth) [David].

17 In 1713–14 there was a fifth Dumoulin (whose relation to the other four is not clear) and who was explicitly called Denis.

18 This is the case, for example, for the Duprés: there are at least two, perhaps three. The cast lists can be interpreted by attributing the role of soloists to Louis (the famous God of dance), nicknamed "the Great Dupré" – but unfortunately not in the librettos – to distinguish him from Jean Denis, who seems to have been relegated to the *corps de ballet*. This interpretation is plausible but has not as yet been cross-referenced. The same problem exists for the Pécours. Which one appears only in the prologue alongside Mlle Delisle between 1715 and 1718? Is it the illustrious Guillaume-Louis, the ballet master whose choreographies Feuillet published and who would have been making a comeback to the stage given he had retired in 1702? Or is it the humble Georges, then in the *corps de ballet*, who, on these occasions alone, may have accompanied the soloist? The question is not easy to resolve.

19 In *Bellerophon*, this is the case for Françoise Prevost and Marie-Catherine Guyot (in the prologue) – see Figure 11 – Dangeville the elder (act I), Michel Blondy (act II), Claude Balon and Françoise Prevost, as well as Dumoulin the younger (act IV) and once again Claude Balon (act V).

20 The first production of *Pomone* on 3 March 1671.

21 See C. and F. Parfaict, *Histoire de l'Académie Royale de Musique depuis son établissement jusqu'à présent*, manuscript (FPn, Ms. Fr. nouv. Acq. 6532), tome 1, fol. 48.

22 A small number of dancers often played an entire host of characters. As far as the women are concerned, there were 12 danseuses for 40 roles in *Canente*, 13 for 40 roles in *Telephe*, and 11 for 35 roles in *Les Eléments*. The phenomenon is even more frequent for the men: the most evident cases are *Hippodamie,* where 22 male dancers interpreted 60 roles, *Thétis et Pelée*, with 18 dancers for 57 roles, and *Atys* in 1708, a production in which 22 men danced 58 roles.

23 For the majority of these dancers see the corresponding entries in M. Benoît (ed.), *Dictionnaire de la musique en France aux XVIIe et XVIIIe siècles*, Paris: Fayard, 1992 and Ph. Le Moal (ed.), *Dictionnaire de la danse*, Paris: Larousse, 1999.

24 This is clearly the case for Antoine Dangeville (act I) and Blondy (act II) in the 1705 restaging of *Bellerophon.*

25 As in act IV of the restaging of *Bellerophon*.

26 Rameau, *The Dancing Master*, p. xv.

27 This is the case for *Bellerophon* from 1705 on.

28 Found easily thanks to appendix 6 of the catalogue by F. Lancelot, *La Belle Dance*, Paris: Van Dieren, 1996, pp. xxxviii–xci.

29 There are eleven for de Subligny and Balon; five for Guyot and David Dumoulin, and two for the former with François Dumoulin; three that associate Chaillou to Henry Dumoulin; one for Menés and Marcel; and finally five that bring together Guyot and Prevost.

30 See for example the analyses of the passacaglia in *Scylla* danced by Mademoiselle de Subligny in 1701: C. Bayle, 'The Meanderings of Interpretation', *Dance Research*, 1997, vol. 15, no. 2, pp. 170–99.

31 See C.G. Marsh, M.E. Lutz, 'Gender Differences in Baroque Dance', *Ballet International/Tanz Aktuell*, 1998, August–September, pp. 44–5. On a group of only eight choreographies analyzed, of which only one is dedicated to a danseuse of the Opéra (Subligny) (numbered FL/1704. 1/05 in Lancelot, *La Belle Dance*, p. 2), the authors note a difference in the compositions and establish that those for men are technically more difficult than those for women.

32 On this subject see P. Whitley-Bauguess, 'The Search for Mlle Guyot', *Proceedings of the Eleventh Annual Conference, Society of Dance History Scholars,* Riverside, 1988, pp. 32–67; M. Goff, 'Surprising Monsters: The First Female Professional Dancers', in B. Ravelhofer (ed.), *Terpsichore 1450–1900, International Dance Conference Ghent*, Ghent: The Institute for Historical Dance Practice, 2000, pp. 179–87.

33 Choreography published in 1704 by Feuillet, classified FL/1704. 1/2 in Lancelot, *La Belle Dance*, p. 59.

34 See the analyses in *L'Entrée espagnole . . . dansée par M. Balon et Mlle de Subligny au Ballet de l'Europe galante* in C. Bayle, 'Les ornements de la danse baroque', *Les Goûts-réünis: la danse baroque,* conference proceedings, Besançon: IMDA, 1982, pp. 79–89.

35 The first (FPan, minutier central XXVI-219, 18 March 1705) is found in a series of accounts (from October 1704) put together to evaluate what the director, Francine, owed the Opéra personnel; the second (FPan, AJ13 1) is one of the handwritten documents attached to the new theater regulations promulgated by Louis XIV on 11 January 1713. On these two documents, see J. de La Gorce, *L'Opéra à Paris au temps de Louis XIV*, Paris: Desjonquères, 1992, pp. 127 and 159. A page of the record of 1713 is reproduced in M. Hannah Winter, *The Pre-Romantic Ballet*, London: Pitman Publishing, 1974, p. 69.

36 It should be noted that, in these two documents, the number of artists reviewed is less than the number listed in the casts for the same dates. This leads one to

believe that the theater also employed extra dancers that these two archival documents do not take into consideration.

37 With one sole exception in *La Mort d'Alcide* in 1716.

38 In the second act of Quinault-Lully's *Armide* for the replicas in 1713, 1714, and 1724.

39 In the second act of Duché de Vancy-Gatti's *Scylla* in 1701. On this, see the analysis of the passacaglia danced by Mademoiselle de Subligny in Bayle, *The Meanderings of Interpretation.*

40 Grotesque characters, armed with a sword, often associated to those of the Commedia dell'Arte, that one can suppose did a *bouffonne* dance. In his *Dictionnaire* Antoine Furetière defines the term *Matassins* as: "A sort of frolicsome dance. These Masks dance the *Matassins*. Also used for those who dance it." A. Furetière, *Dictionnaire universel*, La Haye and Rotterdam: chez Arnout & Reinier Leers, 3 vol., 1690.

41 To the extent that he was, according to Bonin, incomparable in the *entrée* of the furies, his reputation in this sort of role goes beyond limits. See L. Bonin, *Die Neueste Art zur Galaten und Theatralischen Tantz-Kunst,* Frankfurt-Leipzig: Johann Lochner, 1712, p. 165.

42 C. and F. Parfaict, *Dictionnaire des théâtres de Paris,* Paris, 1767, tome 2, p. 344.

43 She herself showed off this talent by creating *Les Caractères de la danse,* the choreographic divertissement set to music by Jean-Féry Rebel in 1715.

44 Rameau, *The Dancing Master*, p. xv.

45 All the more considering that the costumes of the men *en travesti* (short skirts, necklines) were clearly distinguishable from those worn by the women.

46 *Atys,* Paris: Christophe Ballard, 1676, FPo. Liv. 17 [R 1 (9).

47 The dancers included eight ladies in waiting (among which there were two illegitimate daughters of Louis XIV, Mademoiselle de Nantes, and Princesse de Conti) and two professionals (Le Peintre and Le Clerc).

48 *Atys,* Paris: Christophe Ballard, 1682, FPo. Liv. 17 [R 2 (10).

49 This aside, it should be noted that there is a print, published in Paris by Mariette between the late seventeenth and early eighteenth century, that portrays Mademoiselle Desmâtins in a very curious way, dancing dressed as a man: see F. Lesure, *L'Opéra classique français,* Genève: Minkoff, 1972, p. 79. To date, it has not been possible to identify the work in which she appeared dressed as a man, though we do know she danced at the Opéra until 1701.

50 On this see N. Lecomte, *The Female Ballet Troupe of the Paris Opéra from 1700 to 1725*, in *Women Making Dance in Early Modern Europe* (monographic issue of Studies in Dance History, ed. L. Brooks), Madison, WI: University of Wisconsin Press, forthcoming.

9 A balance lost

Staging the body and controlling social mobility during the French Revolution

Inge Baxmann

A cultural break and a new aesthetics of movement

Over the course of the French Revolution there was a profound change in the way in which communication and social interaction were represented. Inventing a new sociability meant creating national habits that would replace all prior categories: from the attire of the members of social hierarchies (the Estates) to the republican *tu*[1] between citizens, from a haircut or a name taken from ancient Rome to new rituals of fraternizing (such as the frugal outdoor feasts), from the revolutionary catechisms that propagated maxims and models of virtues (they too often taken from Roman antiquity) to the start of a new era based on the republican calendar. These changes marked a cultural break with the Ancien Régime and with the entire course of prior history. This is why abolishing the many signs of social distinction that had determined the society of the Ancien Régime was so much easier than responding to the question of how to replace them.

The new norms of social communication and behavior established by republican civility (*civilité républicaine*) were claimed to rest on moral maxims that conformed to human nature and universal values. These "natural" codes – derived, in part, from the theater, painting, and literature of the Enlightenment – were only intelligible against the background of what they moved away from or rejected (implicitly or explicitly). In this way, they provided the basis for the political imaginary of a new "art of being together," with its own forms of theatrical production and representation. The revolutionary mentality was fraught by a profound contradiction. On the one hand, it was marked by an ideal of communication and interaction tied to the free flow of information and the free circulation of citizens; on the other, it was anguished by the idea of liberating mobile social forces and the fear of chaos and collective violence. The relationship between mobility and order became a fundamental issue of revolutionary politics.[2] The Revolution defined itself as a "regeneration," a return to a state of society close to nature. The goal was not permanent revolution but a stable political order that could defend the utopian project of a social order based on nature against the contingencies of history. To the dread of the revolutionary politicians, however, society was to reveal itself as "eminently mobile."

The ballet master Pierre Gardel directed the Opéra from 1787 to 1829. During the Revolution, he and the painter Jacques-Louis David took a leading role in organizing the numerous mass productions for public *fêtes* and commemorations. Their task was to put the "eminently mobile nation" into organized forms or, rather, to model a collective body that was mobile but well structured (and thus inoffensive). The mission of the "choreographer of the masses" was to plan parades and processions and to orchestrate the movement and ritualized gestures of the crowd.

Gardel's mass choreographies for revolutionary *fêtes* and opera always repeated the same scenarios. The Revolution strove to fuse the *fête* and everyday life and to give the stage an educational role in the revolutionary reorganization of collective life. Gardel's mission was to forge citizens. Revolutionary *fêtes* were rehearsed on stage, and republican hymns were sung at the theater by actors and spectators alike. The *Fête de la Fédération* held on 14 July 1790 at Notre Dame began by re-staging the taking of the Bastille, re-enacted by actors, musicians, singers, and dancers from various theaters in Paris and the Opéra. The following day a procession crossed Paris and, in the evening, people danced in front of the Bastille transforming the square into an immense ballroom. On 30 September 1792 the Opéra presented *L'Offrande à la Liberté*, an operatic divertissement that re-staged the Revolution with enormous success.[3] *La Marseillaise* was sung on stage, and groups of women, children, and soldiers flocked to the temple of *Liberté*, dancing in homage to freedom and, later, raising arms in its defense.[4]

The revolutionary politicians' ambition of organizing *fêtes* that projected a "dynamic image of gathering" was expressed in processions, in the way in which space and dance were staged, and in the ritual actions and gestures composed by famous choreographers, some of whom, such as Gardel or his assistant Sébastien Gallet, were from the Opéra. The era's culture of movement established a counter-model to Louis XIV's *ballet de cour* and a vehicle for the republican culture of sentiment that provided the basis for the new social order.

Gardel's choreography for *La réunion du 10 août* (5 April 1794) included dance scenes that projected a positive new image of market vendors or villagers.[5] The choreographer employed everyday movements, danced in everyday clothes. He incorporated dances like the *Carmagnole*, in which performers formed a large circle, sang, made slow rotations, moved in place, and accelerated their movement on the refrain, evoking the ecstatic energy of the masses.

The provocation expressed by these dances can only be understood as a counter-model to the ideal of the geometrically-stylized movement and corresponding spatial conceptions of the culture of the Ancien Régime. Commentators of the era saw these popular dances as a threat: they were ecstatically disordered and chaotic, and went against the dominant movement culture of the Ancien Régime, which is to say, the disciplined body and the aristocratic style that was paradigmatically achieved in Louis XIV's *ballet de cour* (and would remain the model under successive French kings until the late eighteenth century).[6]

The new aesthetics of the Enlightenment and the French Revolution could only be understood in comparison to its opposite figure (which was often implicit). If the nation of the Ancien Régime was symbolized by the "artful body" endorsed by the king and his courtiers (the ruling classes), the counter-model of the Enlightenment was the "natural body," a direct expression of universal human feelings and free of "affectations" and "masquerades." "Nature" and "artifice" had been a founding opposition of Enlightenment thought, and the Revolution strove to create a social order that proclaimed what was true to human nature and stood against the arbitrariness of all the schemes that had been handed down by tradition and were based on social hierarchy.

The revolutionary *fêtes* were an attempt to apply the ideal of the Enlightenment to the political reality: the invention of the "natural body" and its movement as an expression of a natural way of life was part of this attempt. The codes of natural simplicity were part of a reconstruction of civility, seen as a "republican civility," that was reorganized on the basis of a set of norms intended for the aristocracy so as to promote interaction among the various social groups through the internalization of these norms. In lieu of being bound to a network of social obligations and prohibitions, civility was to be anchored to the immutable and universal truth of natural human feeling alone. The change in the structure of the culture of movement was, therefore, part of the fundamental shift in the structure of the culture of sentiment. Bringing the daily life of the French Revolution into the realm of theater and aesthetics was part of an attempt to instill these new, still inconceivable, forms of life and values into reality. The theater and the revolutionary *fêtes* were to provide republican education and to mold republican sensibility. The era's aesthetic debates, in painting and theater in particular, offered cultural codes that were to become guidelines for the organizers of the revolutionary *fêtes*.

These historical processes had been announced prior to the Revolution, especially in the arts of the Enlightement. They had paved the way for the change in structure of social codes, especially in the domain of the culture of sentiment, and for the historical transition from fundamentally constrained social interaction to broader communication throughout the varied layers of society. For theater, this occurred in bourgeois drama and melodrama; for the figurative arts, through the re-evocation of ancient values seen in David's neo-classical works or Jean-Baptiste Greuze's genre painting;[7] and for dance, in the *ballet d'action* as conceived by Jean Georges Noverre in the second half of the eighteenth century. All of these experiences were part of the search for new models of social interaction and communication. From Noverre on, the *ballet d'action* bet on dance's capacity to express and evoke natural feelings and to stir the soul through movement. The *ballet de cour*, with its elegant way of moving through space around an invisible central axis, was replaced by danced drama that exposed natural passions and human conflicts. In their staging of the Revolutionary *fêtes* and Opéra performances Maximilien and Pierre Gardel followed Noverre's example, developing an aesthetics of movement and a choreographic concept that ceased to rely on already elaborated techniques. They conceived movement as the expression of "natural" human sentiments and of the *ballet d'action* as the staging of dramatic conflicts based on human passions, all of which conformed to the ideas developed during the Enlightenment and elaborated most thoroughly in Diderot's theories on drama. Technique was subordinated to dramatic action, and a gestural expressiveness and style of movement similar to pantomime prevailed. Costumes were modified such that the corsets, heavy wigs, and thick brocade fabrics characteristic of the *ballet de cour* were replaced by less inhibiting attire styled after antiquity (tunics made of light fabrics, worn with sandals or tight jackets) and by "everyday clothes" similar to those worn by the Sansculottes. This, in turn, liberated movement technique, permitting higher jumps, the development of the *demi-pointe*, and new possibilities for dramatic expression on stage.

Fraternal space or the difficult relationship between nature and history

The French Revolution attributed an educational function to public space. Models derived from antiquity, such as the amphitheater and the circus, made it possible for masses of citizens to congregate together outdoors and created a non-hierarchical order among whoever participated in the *fête*. The conception of space also reflected the era's debates on natural order and its models. The most common topographic forms were circles, globes, and spheres. Taken as a spatial model, the circle strove to inscribe the Revolution in the "order of nature" (conceived as cosmic order), as a way of coping with anarchy and violence. In Gilbert Romme's *Rapport sur l'ère de la République: histoire des hommes et histoires des astres*, one reads: "Natural regularity bound to the return of the solar phases is the model."[8] Beauty, perfection, simplicity, wholeness, order, equality in relations, precision, regularity, and, finally, infiniteness in the dimension and the multiplicity of forms (as the surface was conceived as a polyhedron) were all reflected. Through the primary symbol of the sphere, astronomy, geometry, physics, biology, natural law, social policy, the building of the State, and the structure of society all put themselves in service of the same scientific knowledge. In "fraternal space," citizens had to immediately recognize the unity of society and the principles on which it was founded. They had to know how to relate to other individual members of the "great human family." By making an analogy with the harmonious order of the universe, the representation of social order drew society outside of history, suggesting the immutability of nature's laws and the a-temporal validity of the principles of social order.[9]

The model of a harmonious order of society required a rigorous spatial division between individuals based on their "nature" and, in particular, between masculine and feminine spaces. At the *Fête de l'Être Suprême* organized by David and Gardel in June 1794 at the Champ de la Réunion in Paris, the procession of men and the elderly was placed at the right of the mountain and that of the women and young girls at the left. The "troops of adolescents" encircled the mountain, while the "national delegation" rose toward the top. The groups were arranged according to a principle that sought to suitably picture the harmony of the new community through the use of contrasts. The participants were separated either by banderoles, banners reflecting the respective ideas of the individual groups, or by the way in which the different groups were spaced in the order of the march. Any mixing of groups or any unchecked suppression of differences in the midst of "confusion" was seen as a danger, and a commissioner had to watch over the maintenance of order so that "bad citizens" and dishonest people would not have a chance to disrupt social order[10] (Figure 14).

The revolutionary *fêtes* staged the body in such a way as to control the mobile imagination by means of new collective symbols. At the same time, they deferred social mobility through the culture of movement. Reconciling the need for equality among citizens with the need for a stable social order, the *fêtes* exemplified the major issue at stake in society's own conception of itself.

Figure 14 Pierre-Antoine Demachy, *Fête de l'être Suprême* au Champ-de-Mars, 20 prairial – 8 juin 1794, oil on canvas (*c.* 1794). © Gérard Blot/Christian Jean. Permission kindly granted by Réunion des Musées Nationaux.

A quick look at the era's iconography is enough to see how the historical censorship that operated within the Revolution – the ambition of beginning the history of humanity over from scratch – was correlated with the fear of an "open future," of anarchy and violence. "Égalité" as a dangerous source of chaos and violence was the leitmotif put forth in preference to the paradigm of "femininity." An etching named *The Contrast* depicts the British Liberty as a woman, seated, dressed in red bonnet and an antique frock. She holds Magna Charta in her left hand and the scales in her right. A lion rests at her feet and a ship (a symbol of commerce) can be glimpsed in the background. Facing her, the French Liberty steps over a decapitated body, with a threatening gesture, her face distorted with aggression. In her left hand, she holds a pike, dripping in blood; in her right, she grasps a sword poised for combat. Her features and her arms are masculine. Snakes grow in the place of the hair on her head and on the belt of her tattered dress, while clouds of smoke rise in the background where a man, clothed like an aristocrat, has been hung from a lamp post. The caption "*Which is the Best?*" invites the viewer to choose between the two versions of liberty: on the one hand, the British Liberty, subtitled with the predicates "Religion, Morality, Obedience to the Law, Independence, Personal Security, Justice, Inheritance, Protection, Property, Industry, National Prosperity," summed up by the word "Happiness," or, on the other, the French Liberty, defined by "Atheism, Perjury, Rebellion, Treason, Anarchy, Murder, Equality, Madness, Injustice, Famine, National and Private Ruin," summarized by "Misery."

The masculine figuration and the aggressive pose of the woman representing French Liberty can be related to the assimilation of equality to anarchy and to the rebellion suggested by the caption. The concept of equality is symbolized by an inversion of natural order due to the suppression of sexual difference. "Natural" femininity is no longer identifiable; the figure is a newborn monster, half-man, half-woman, stylized like Medusa. The social bearers of this notion of freedom present the new French Liberty as disorder because, unlike its English counterpart, it is not legitimized by tradition ("inheritance").

The history of the Revolution was further recounted by the counter-revolution and by foreigners as a parricide that set off an irreversible succession of trespasses against traditions and values, and of violence against the members of society. In English commentaries, the king's beheading was associated with the loss of tradition and paternal authority, which was the only thing that could assure social order. This criticism made reference to a tradition that presented the State and relations between state and society through the metaphor of the family.

Society in a "tableau"[11] or the lessons of nature

The aesthetics of the Enlightenment had conceptualized both presentation and reception as part of a science of sensory perception. Subsequent research brought about a change in the aesthetic codes of various genres such that theater and painting became the major references for festive representation. Despite the multiple aspects of the concept of nature in Enlightenment philosophy, there was a common presumption that the core of human nature could be represented and that this representation with its many differences aimed at standardizing nature with the goal of knowing it in its entirety. As a result, humanity divided into various ideal types, whose diversity and contrasts nonetheless implied the possibility of apprehending their differences (historical, national, cultural, and other), while confirming the existence of a nature common to all men. The scale that classified human nature and behavior according to the way the passions were expressed in various situations is one example.[12] The task of aesthetic representation was not, therefore, that of describing men that pre-existed empirically, but of picturing them in the idealized form of the *belle nature* and its variants. Even the domain of reception could be explained scientifically, through the classification of emotional reactions.

The aesthetics that society employed in staging itself through the *fêtes* corresponded to the contemporary understanding of human perception. Based on the idea that the spectator's soul could be penetrated through vision, Jean-Baptiste Gence conceived the festive parade as a "moving picture":

> [. . .] the ideal would be not to mix the subjects nor to scatter them about, not to isolate the perception and the idea of the different groups nor to let them overlap [. . .]. Finally, it would be good if the movement of the procession [was] uniform, better slow than hurried, so that the eye has time to understand the stories and, in consequence, to comprehend and store their underlying lessons in memory.[13]

In painting as well, the attempts to construct a typology of human sensations and feelings was codified on the basis of the Cartesian hypothesis of a correspondence between moods and body movements.[14] Alongside modes of behavior and movements that corresponded, respectively, to every variable of human nature, there were also different kinds of meditation known through painting and theater. These were codified in specific signs such as the expression of a certain emotion in front of the represented subject, which could be attributed to different groups participating in the *fête*, allowing gestural and mimic expressions to be differentiated by age and sex. Tears, "cries of exhilaration" or "pain," and "joyous steps" visibly externalized emotions appropriate to the represented subject while, at the same time, documenting the coherence of the meaning that was sought. *Fête* costumes and accessories also provided symbols that referred to the social role attributed to every "variant" of human nature. The women, for example, wore white dresses styled after the ancients and braided their hair (a reference to the ancient Republic and symbol of chastity), while the men and boys carried sabers (a symbol of their disposition toward combat). By stylizing individuals on the basis of "natural" difference, everyone's social role and their implicit relationships to others were simultaneously established.

At the *Fête de l'Être Suprême* in Nancy, the wagon of a "good family" paraded amidst the others: the mother leaned over a cradle, while the father taught a small child sitting on his knee how to read; a third child hugged the first two and a fourth crowned the scene. This "living picture of morality and patriotism" described the way in which the society of the Revolution chose to depict itself. It was inspired by Greuze's "moral painting" and by literary theory of the Enlightenment. It pointed to the unity of the pathetic summit of a scene in which the action was in some way immobilized. In a single concentrated instant, it placed the order of human nature before the eyes of the spectator, characterizing beings generically, independent of any individual difference.

By establishing a typology, the unifying principle of the painting made it possible to express the basic anthropological constants that were inherent in human nature (drawn somehow from history), and the morality that corresponded to this nature could be deduced and recognized at a glance. The undisputed presupposition of this kind of conception is that the perspective from which the order is established as a figure of human nature does not become an issue in any way, because the subject described is considered to have an a-temporal value. In commentaries on the *fêtes*, one often finds a successful festive representation compared to a painting, as, for instance, in the comparison between the *Fête de la Fédération* in 1790 and a "painting of Roman order." The picture of the new society stylized *fête* participants according to the criteria of a biology perceived as nature (sex and age), completed by a repertoire of figures that imitated the ancient republics (like those figures devoted, for example, to the representation of State as "magistrate"). The simplification obtained by stylizing social relationships had to simultaneously reveal the direct and transparent aspect of social interaction that was the new principle of "political sociability."

The theory of the social contract established, first and foremost, new models of national and political bodies. The Ancien Régime had already developed new interpretations and new practices in the culture of movement, which had risen up against the "artful body." In the aristocratic culture of movement typical of the *fêtes* at the courts of Louis XIV and his successors, the boundaries between masculinity and femininity disappeared in this ideal of the "artful body." The court *fêtes* had developed a culture of masquerade and, from the seventeenth century on, theatrical cross-dressing with masks rendering individuals unrecognizable became a fashionable phenomenon at court and in the upper echelons of the Parisian bourgeoisie. Guests would change parts of their attire several times over the course of an evening, so as to remain incognito. With the exoticism then in vogue, these disguises ranged from Chinese despots, to Turks or "Negros," all the way to idyllic shepherds and villagers, passing through mythological figures like amazons and witches, to arrive at the characters of the Commedia dell'Arte. The dissolution of identity made it possible to break through the barriers between the sexes, and cross-dressing became common practice at court *fêtes*. In her memoirs from the mid-eighteenth century, the king's cousin, Anne-Marie Montpensier, writes of having appeared in a costume identical to that of Philippe D'Anjou, the king's brother, who was disguised as a woman, a masquerade he was fond of throughout his life.

In contrast to this, the Revolution gave utmost weight to the masculine/feminine difference as a crucial model of order. Against the "crisis of difference" that, along with the invalidation of the conventional hierarchy, brought the fear of the dissolution of order, and of chaos and anarchy, the staging of difference between the sexes was carried to the extreme in the Revolution's culture of movement.

Ritual oaths: a barrier against social mobility

In the Enlightenment antiquity was the "utopian past" from which the model for new values and new forms of life could be drawn. Social upheaval was understood in terms of "regeneration," as a return to a former state of social equality and freedom, which was projected onto Greek and Roman antiquity. Gardel's ballets (*Le jugement de Paris*, *Psyché*, *Télémaque*) staged ancient myths and stories quite similar to the *ballet de cour* of the Ancien Régime, while his productions for the *fêtes* relayed political content in a neo-classical style (*L'Offrande à la Liberté*). What was actually new in Gardel's ballets, such as *Psyché,* must be sought on another plane. The *ballets d'action* were focused on representing the feelings of humans (as well as those of the gods), such as anger, love, and so forth, and they played a role in the re-structuring of the culture of sentiment that was taking place in the transition from the Ancien Régime to bourgeois society.

Antiquity – as a cultural model that tended toward unity, symbolized in the neo-classical style – offered itself as an effective symbology for the Revolution's political culture. Perceived as it was in the Enlightenment (which contemplated architecture, art, and, in a broader sense, the "sentiments of life" alongside history), antiquity became the realization of a unity of human nature and society. The heroes of the Roman republic became the embodiment of the republican virtue of the bourgeois state. The revolutionaries did not use antiquity as a cultural legitimization of the will for domination (as in the cultural politics of Louis XVI), but as a model for an egalitarian society. This implied a fundamental shift in how antiquity was perceived, allowing it to serve as an efficient model for interpreting contemporary political experiences, on the one hand, and, on the other, to provide an idealized vision of the future.

David's painting *Le Serment des Horaces* (1785) was a model of republican adhesion to the virtue of the Republic. It prefigured the place of the State as sacred, a transcendental idea typical of the Revolution, and the corresponding spirit of unconditional sacrifice. Its influence on the way in which the French revolutionaries represented themselves was far greater than that of any other work of art, and, later on, David went on to create a new interpretation of antiquity based on the concepts of the Enlightenment. *Le Serment des Horaces* was actually staged in the form of a *tableau vivant* by those present at a *fête* organized by David and Robespierre. The painting functioned emblematically to evoke unshakeable loyalty toward the new State, which evidently could not be understood without the knowledge of the era's complex historical stakes. The theme that emerges is the emotional breakdown of the family unit, and its staging of the duality of the sexes dramatically emphasized the moral requisites of the republicans. The scene is taken from Roman history and describes the disputes between Rome and Albe. It depicts the Horaces' pledge to fight against the Curiaces, despite the family ties binding the adversaries, which represent the opinions of the different States. Camille, sister of the Horaces, is in love with a member of the Curiace family. The men's moral strength (the father holds the swords while the three sons take oath) is expressed in their posture and their gestures. The fixed gaze and energetic carriage of the head, the arm energetically outstretched in taking oath, and the taut leg muscles serve to accentuate the contrast between the group of men standing at the painting's center and the group of women and children seated on the right. The impotent and resigned desolation of the Horaces' mother and her daughters, Sabine and Camille, is imprinted in their half-closed exhausted eyes and in their drained posture. Staging republican values and ideals in a model that reduced femininity to an object and a mirror of the virtue and strength of masculine will is a

Figure 15 Jacques-Louis David, *Le Serment des Horaces*, oil on canvas (1784), Paris, Musée du Louvre. © Gérard Blot/Christian Jean. Permission kindly granted by Réunion des Musées Nationaux.

predominant theme in the revolutionary society's representation of itself (Figure 15).

Given the danger to which the maintenance of new social order was tendentiously exposed by the uncertainty of history, the rituals of the revolutionary *fêtes* can be seen as an attempt to assure, through a sort of "controlled movement," the laboriously established balance between the forces making up the new society and the leveling of social relationships. The rituals expressed society's relationship to history by attempting to "stop" time and to definitively establish recognized values as a reaction to the rapid changes in orientation caused by a sense of the acceleration of time.

Article 2 of the Constitution of 1791 obliged every "active citizen" to take a "civic oath." Everyone had to pledge their belonging to a new community (the new political institution) with the Constitution and the Declaration of the Rights of Man at its core. The enthusiasm for these bonding rituals with the fatherland translated into spontaneous oaths of loyalty to the nation, the law, and other republican values. Staging a contractual model of society through this oath was founded on the fear of social movement. Asking an eminently mobile nation to respect, by oath, the social roles already determined by nature became a promise for the future. How could the operation of the egalitarian power model not gain in verisimilitude?

Reuniting the masses in immediately visible blocks was the task of familialism, the principle of the allegedly natural order that determined the way in which the new society represented itself. In the philosophy and in the theory of public law inspired by the Enlightenment, the family was constantly proposed as a sort of primary community at the heart of collective life, and the metaphor of the family as a model of social relationships was to have many variants over the course of the Revolution. In its early phases, the aristocrats and the wealthy remained part of the family, as their awareness could be broadened through republican education. In staging the family of the new society, however, the representation of social contradictions eventually became taboo. From the moment in which every citizen conducted him or herself according to the laws of nature and exerted mutual control over one another, the paradox of the modern theory of state and the models of egalitarian power, which attributed citizens the double role of subject and sovereign, was assumed to have been resolved. This paradox was eased in the familialism derived from Jean-Jacques Rousseau: "I made the fathers of families kings. With this completely natural rule, I established a salutary harmony among men and I spared them the shame of having to obey their fellow creatures."[15]

The familiarist staging of bodies in the *fêtes* had to form "within" that which was simultaneously represented on the exterior. Bodies served as living allegories, as bearers of an idea that took on specific meaning through a global production in which the participants perceived themselves not as individuals but as representatives of a group. At the core of this model of society, femininity had a dual role. On the one hand, it had to further the conception of the new society as a natural harmonious order by representing a natural difference and the consequent civic designs (which were also true to nature). On the other, it had to establish a sort of natural control at the center of a power model based on a network of connections. Above all, however, feminine nature, which had been the object of completely contradictory definitions in the philosophical discourse of the Enlightenment, had to be defined without ambiguity. The excesses of egalitarianism offered by its integration in the familiarist domain had to be eliminated, after which feminine nature had to be de-sexualized or its sexuality oriented along the tracks of familiarism.

Channeled into forms determined by rituals, social movement (the ritualized aspect of which always leads back to the starting point or original state) had to impede real movement from breaking the fragile balance between nature and history. The rituals of the revolutionary *fêtes* had a broadly symbolic character and corroborated the existence of the values they represented to the extent in which they staged social utopia (or the behavior required to bring it about). "Equilibrium" in the place of "Mobility" was the ideal of this social model and the true goal of the rituals. A hymn from the *Recueil des chants philosophiques, civiques et moraux* was worded as follows: "A free people can be born from your ranks. Love it, love each other, that this be the happy support for your balance."[16] The forms of movement at the core of this new public space, the festive parade, and the succession of rituals obeyed a model of "natural order" based on "natural differences" and on clearly delimited spaces and orders of movement. This, too, was a stage for the conflict between the ecstatic and "chaotic" movement of the general fraternizing (something no *fête* fully achieved) and the need to present the Revolution as an order. The rituals of assembly had the right to follow only those rituals that underlined the difference.

The celebration of the Revolution as a return to nature became a constant demarcation, a univocal simplification, and an elimination of ambivalence, precisely in that, according to the era's understanding, it functioned as a clear sign of the order of nature. Femininity, in consequence, in its role as a representation of nature, became more and more artificial. The anxiety of the historical rupture was transmuted in a fury of order. Nature became an all-defining social code that excluded the heterogeneous and claimed to immobilize it in the familiarist model of nature liberated by the Revolution. This construct of a normative nature provided a glimpse of an ideology of order bound to a new power model: at the same time, power became omnipresent, invisible, and, as nature, unquestionable.

Notes

1 To be on first-name terms with someone [eds].

2 This insuppressible ambivalence was expressed in the formula of J. Grenier, a Revolutionary politician in his *Opinion sur la question de savoir si l'on doit supprimer de la formule du serment civique les mots de haine à l'anarchie*, Paris, year VII: "We had to be revolutionaries in order to found the revolution, but, in order to preserve it, we must cease to be." See M. Ozouf, *Festivals and the French Revolution*, trans. A. Sheridan, Cambridge, MA: Harvard University Press, 1988, p. 281 (orig. edn *La fête révolutionnaire*, Paris: Gallimard, 1978).

3 With music by François-Joseph Gossec and sets by Pierre Gardel. "The dance technique in this work is negligible, but the choreographed parades, processions, and huge crowds that mill around and make gestures or uniform movements have importance. Previously, the emphasis in dance was on the small, elegant,

attitudinizing; now the accent is on mass movement. Thus the Opéra became a serious organ of propaganda for the government; and even if one did believe in revolutionary principles, it must have been obvious that fine talents were being wasted on such repetitious and empty exercises." See J. Chazin-Bennahum, *Dance in the Shadow of the Guillotine*, Carbondale and Edwardsville, IL: Southern Illinois University Press, 1988, p. 104.

4 Gardel produced numerous danced choral plays, most of which interpreted episodes of the Revolution patriotically. For example, *La Réunion du 10 août*, the work that adapted the *Fête de la régération* of 10 August 1793 into a dramatic action, staged the various stations of this *fête* and narrated the Revolution as the freeing of the poor and the innocent from slavery. One of the last *fêtes* was the *Fête de la raison*, on 10 November 1793, and included the (not always voluntary) participation of the singers and dancers from the Paris Opéra. See I. Guest, *Ballet under Napoleon*, Alton: Dance Books, 2002, pp. 17–18.

5 Ibid., p. 20.

6 "Aristocratic appropriation of the court ballet" sensuous techniques likely reinforced the overall image of royal authority, but it also established a fascination with bodily display and attraction that would catalyze the art forms associated with "aristocracy" in the following decades. See S. Cohen, *Art, Dance and the Body in French Culture of the Ancien Régime*, Cambridge, Cambridge University Press, 2000, p. 122.

7 See I. Baxmann, *Die Feste der Französischen Revolution. Inszenierung von Gesellschaft als Natur*, Weinheim and Basel: Beltz, 1989.

8 G. Romme, 'Rapport sur l'ère de la république: histoire des hommes et histoires des astres, imprimé par ordre de la Convention nationale', Séance du 20 septembre 1793, Paris: Imprimerie Nationale, n.d.

9 In *What Is the Third Estate?*, a text that articulates the pretence of the third state of the exercise of political power, Seyès develops the following image: "I represent the law as the center of vast sphere: all of the citizens without exception are found, on its surface, at an equal distance from the center and occupy equal places. Everyone depends on the law in equal measure and puts under its protection their liberty and their property. It is what I define the rights common to all citizens, rights thanks to which they are all equal." See E. J. Seyès, *What Is the Third Estate?*, New York: Praeger, 1964 (orig. edn *Qu'est-ce que le Tiers-État?*, s.l. 1789), p. 162.

10 "Everyone in their place. Everyone holds a large branch, an ear of corn or a flower in hand. To put every group in order there are as many commissioners as groups. The bad citizens and the dishonest people can be recognized by the fact that they want to create confusion and disorder in this parade of a respectable *fête*." See *Plan de Fête à l'Etre Suprême, qui sera célébré à Tours, le 20 Prairial en exécution du Décret du 18 Floréal, l'an second de la République, une et indivisible*, Paris: Bibliothèque Nationale, p. 6; see also 'Anarchie', in H.F. Gravelot, C.-N. Cochin, *Iconologie ou Traité de la science des allégories à l'usage des artistes*, tome 1, Paris, 1791, plate 4.

11 In Diderot's *On Dramatic Poetry* (1758) the notion of "tableau" refers to the unity of the action expressed in a meaningful immediateness. See D. Diderot, *On Dramatic Poetry*, in D. Diderot, *Selected Writings*, ed. by Lester G. Crocker, New York: Macmillan, 1966 (French edn *Discours sur la poésie dramatique*, in Diderot., *Oeuvres esthétiques*, ed. by P. Vernière, Paris: Garnier, 1988, pp. 179–290), pp. 287–93.

12 C. Le Brun, *A Method to Learn to Design the Passions*, William Andrews Clark Memorial Library, Los Angeles, CA: University of California, 1980 (1st Engl. trans. London: J. Huggonson, 1734; orig. edn *Méthode pour apprendre à dessiner les passions*, Amsterdam, 1702).

13 J. B. Gence, *Vues sur les fêtes publiques et application de ces vues à la fête de Marat*, Paris: Imprimerie de Renaudière, 1793.

14 See Cohen, *Art, Dance and the Body*.

15 *Dame Nature à la barre de l'Assemblée Nationale*, Paris: Chez les marchands de nouveautés, 1791; *Jean-Jacques Rousseau dans la Révolution Française*, Paris: Éditions d'Histoire Sociale, 1977.

16 *Chants Révolutionnaires et patriotiques à l'usage des fêtes nationales et décadaires*, Paris, 1790, p. 23.

10 Gender underway

Notes for histories yet to be written

Marina Nordera

A double paradox

The keyword and the topic of this section reveal a double paradox, which has an impact on methodological issues valid for dance studies in general. The first regards the topic: eighteenth-century dance. How are we to write the history of dancing bodies that have long since passed away and belong to a time so distant from the researcher's own body? Posing this question helps one to think that studying dance always means making history out of bodies that are phenomenologically lost, even if technology captures the movement, written and oral sources capture the testimonies, photography captures the forms and volumes, and so on. The presence of the living source is nothing more than an epistemological illusion or a methodological shortcut that is sometimes able to bridge the gap that separates it from the scholar. How can we compensate for this void: through the retrieval and rigorous analyses of new sources, through sensibility, imagination, and the invention of narrative strategies? Far from minimizing the pre-eminence of archival research and fieldwork, the scholar's subjectivity and the way in which he or she is intellectually and politically implicated in constructing a discourse or fascinated by the research topic are constitutive aspects of the dance historian's work. The process of reconstructing a work from documents presupposes the researcher's sensitive and political involvement as the choreographer of the historical text.[1] This holds true regardless of the chronological gap that separates the researcher from the object of investigation.

The second paradox regards the keyword Feminine/Masculine. One of the most common objections one faces in applying a recently elaborated methodological approach to a subject from the past is that of putting into practice illegitimate anachronisms.[2] Why rely on feminist or even post-feminist theories in analyzing a phenomenon or an event from a time when feminism did not exist? Why apply the category of gender, which has only been in use for about thirty years, to the eighteenth century? Why impose the social and political issues with which we labor today onto men and women who had concerns of their own?

In light of recent studies, the application of new critical theories appears to have brought about a general methodological renewal in dance research by exploring previously overlooked documentary archives and by formulating other interpretative schemes. The introduction of the category of gender, in particular, has brought to the fore a wide range of masculine and feminine lives and experiences, revealing some of the forms their relationships have taken on in the social and theatrical practice of dance, as well as the discourses they have produced or been produced within. This has made it possible to further question and to historicize the implication of gender subjectivity in a researcher's work.

The essays in this section, including this one, which is simultaneously a summary, an assessment, and an outline for the future development of the issues at stake, propose to study how masculinity and femininity are inscribed in eighteenth-century dance through the category of gender. The eighteenth century is not conceived here as a static and homogeneous entity but rather as a chronological frame of reference within which to focus the persistence, fragmentation, and at times substantial incoherence of certain phenomena. The century's manifest instability and its major historical upheavals provide a wealth of insight for a thorough reflection on the theory and methodology of dance research.

Gender's genres

In the dense and articulated essay that opens this section, Linda Tomko outlines the state-of-the-art in gender studies, placing particular emphasis on those studies addressing dance in the Anglophone and, in particular, the American context. Europe, though it has never ceased gazing across the Atlantic, has a different history and a different set of circumstances. The gender studies that reach us from the United States take root in ground that has been fertilized by the theoretical and historiographical experiences specific to each country.[3]

In England the studies on social and economic history that followed the Second World War and were guided by an impulse of Marxist origin relied primarily on demographic tools to make the active presence of women in the daily life of past centuries known. They took an interest in factors that the mainstream political history had not fully grasped, such as the history and economy of the family, the division of feminine and masculine roles, birth and death rates, and so on. In France the development of historical anthropology, the rise of the school of the *Annales* and, later on, Michel Foucault's writings disclosed the niches of public space in which aspects of feminine existence could no longer be ignored, placing particular attention on the social dynamics of sex and affectivity. In Italy gender studies took hold in the feminist movement that, from the 1970s on, sought to create a space for itself within an academic male-dominated context. Early studies focused on bringing to light the feminine life which had been overlooked in social, cultural and artistic milieus, and it was not until the late 1970s that the category of gender (*genere*) was introduced and granted an epistemological and exegetic status equivalent to that of race and class.[4]

The category of gender was not readily accepted in Europe. In the first place, European feminism feared that adopting the category would conceal the issue of masculine domination and thereby jeopardize the political grounds on which it had been founded. In the second, the Romance languages, such as French or Italian, give rise to a terminological problem that has yet to be resolved, as our choice of Feminine/Masculine as the keyword of this section instead of "gender" demonstrates. In the most frequently used Italian dictionary, the first meaning of *genere* (gender) is a "comprehensive notion of various species" and a "group of essential distinctive characteristics of a category." The second meaning refers to "each one of the various forms of artistic expression according to the canons of tradition" and, finally, the third defines a "grammatical category that, depending on the language, opposes an animate to an inanimate *genere*, or a masculine, a feminine, and a neuter (as in the German), or just a masculine and feminine (as in the Italian)."[5]

In Italy, the English "gender" has been traditionally translated as "sexual difference." This choice is debatable in that it essentializes a binary dichotomy that is rooted in the biological sphere and that recent studies have articulated both as dynamic (bringing to light the variety of options existing between the two opposite poles) and as the fruit of a discursive process.[6] In France, in the 1990s, the definition that prevailed was the "social and cultural construction of the masculinity and the femininity." In the abstract dyad that comprises the keyword of this section, "feminine" and "masculine" are not essentialized but compounded by the slash in an articulated and dynamic relation that takes their structural instability into consideration. Giving precedence to the feminine is a precise choice, keeping well in mind that much of woman's history still remains to be written or re-written.

Using this conception of gender makes it possible to distinguish between sex – in most cases considered biologically determined and invariable – and the set of elements that concur to build an individual identity according to parameters that are both historically determined and individually elaborated. The interest in reading subjective experiences and phenomena in light of the dynamic category of gender lies in the relational value it presumes: femininity and masculinity are not built independently but by a reciprocal relationship through progressive adjustments that depend on culture, on social conditioning, and on the imaginary of a given time, as well as on the way in which individual desires and impulses take form. In an attempt to de-essentialize both the biological and cultural constructs, Judith Butler has proposed "in place of these conceptions of construction [. . .] a return to the notion of matter, not as a site or surface, but as a *process of materialization that stabilizes over time to produce the effect of boundary, fixity, and surface we call matter*."[7] Not even sex, therefore, is considered to be biologically determined and invariable, just as gender is not given once and for all, but is the outcome of a continuous process of acquisition by an individual over the course of a lifetime.

Feminist historiography of dance has taken several approaches: the decodification of images of women, the celebration of single individualities, the construction of sexuality in discourses on dance, and, from a post-structuralist perspective, the analysis of fragmentary and contradictory identities and subjectivities.[8] Scholars have brought to light previously unknown or forgotten women, they have studied the contribution of the pioneers of modern dance and have denounced the victimization or objectification in the staging of the female body, to the point of stigmatizing romantic ballet as the "worst enemy of womankin."[9] Most of the studies published in this field have focused on Western concert dance, of the twentieth century in particular, while next to nothing has been done on the social practice of dance and the period between the fifteenth and the eighteenth century. The overwhelming majority of sources from this period was produced by men and, quite often, for men, and those sources by or for women are not immune to the discursive construct that is produced by a dominant male culture. In the eighteenth century, cultural promoters, teachers, theoreticians, and choreographers were men. Women were the performers, who more often than not went down in history for their beauty or sensuality rather than for their technical or artistic talent. The current feminine connotation of the art of dance and the idea that it is unseemly for a man to dance are the heritage of this model.

Men in tights

A few years ago my son, who was 5 at that time, paused in front of the TV screen at home to watch the images of the first act of *Giselle* on which I was working and, after a few seconds of silent reflection, asked me, laughing, why a man would wear "woman's tights." Of all the images streaming before his eyes that seemed to be the only thing he was curious about and that made him laugh. He grew even more surprised and hilarious when he learned that the man in "women's" underclothes was none other than a prince dressed up as an ordinary farmer. My son had often drawn ballerinas in tutus, and I myself (who, in his early childhood, had been obstinately studying the relationship between dance and gender) never suggested he draw a male dancer. While the image of the ballerina in tutu and toe shoes has lived on in children's imagination since the dawn of language and picture making, the man in tights is a recent discovery. The predominance of females in dance schools is a given fact in contemporary Western culture, which raises prejudices against a male's choice of the art of Terpsichore as a profession or as a leisure activity. This phenomenon has grown out of the stereotypes that were formed regarding the dancer's body, attitudes, and sexual orientation, and had gone as far as to assert an analogy between dance and homosexuality and the relative homophobic reactions. The episode of the "man in woman's tights" further demonstrates how, from early childhood on, knowledge and the images tied to it are structured around stereotypes that pass over the biological differences between men and women to become fixed in the category of gender.

The first wave of gender studies in dance research was closely tied to women's or feminist studies. It was limited to examining the image and role of women, and it is only recently that the field has expanded to include masculinity. According to Ramsay Burt this depends in part on the fact that the traditions and conventions of the most important trends of concert theater have been built upon the reinforcement of heterosexual and masculine norms, and marginalize alternative forms of sexuality to the point of repression.[10] In certain moments of history, social restrictions on sexuality have shaped the ways in which dance is staged, demonstrating and reinforcing the power of homophobia. Thus, in dance as well, the introduction of gender studies marked a considerable departure from the feminist studies in which they had largely developed, by considering the masculine element not only as an agent of domination and as responsible for female oppression (of which there is undeniable historical evidence) but also as a relational term and a subject/object of alternative forms of sexuality.

Between biology and ideology

Throughout the history of Western culture, where do the categorizations of femininity and masculinity originate and how do they change in dance? If the biological difference between the male and female body is taken as an observable given, this difference has been explained and theorized over the centuries by the natural sciences, by medicine, and by common knowledge based on data that is drawn from the observation of nature but largely conditioned by ideology. It is embodied in social and theatrical practice and staged after having undergone a process of public semiotization.

The Aristotelian tradition relies on the theory of humors to explain woman's diversity – more often indicated as inferiority – by a lack of complete intrauterine development. As a result of this congenital weakness, the female body is unable to produce sperm and is only the passive receptacle of the act of generation. In this way the difference justifies the polarity required for procreation: a masculine active ingredient – the sperm, paradoxically immaterial – and a female passive ingredient – menstrual blood. In the Galenic tradition that follows, the male and female body are similar, except for the fact that the genital organs, which are external in the former, have remained internal in the latter due to a lack of warmth at the moment of embryonic development. A woman, therefore, is nothing more than an incomplete man. According to the Galenic theory of the plethora, the human body produces an excess of blood that has a negative influence on health and must be eliminated. Man does this by the sweat produced through physical exercise, woman through menstruation. For women, therefore, physical activity is not only useless, it is discouraged as well. In the relationship between gender identity and physical exercise, the feminine and movement are further bound in an association of symbolic order that has a negative connotation. The normative treatises demand gravity, composure, and control from women who dance; excessive, disordered and quick movement is symptom of a dangerous natural propensity toward instability, madness, and hysteria. Finally, whereas femininity is expressed by round forms, curved and limited space, flexibility, and softness, masculinity is characterized by angular forms, broad space, muscle tone, strength, power, and stability.

This explains in part how, from the fifteenth to the late eighteenth century, dance as a formative discipline, social practice, and theatrical art was predominantly a male domain. Men danced female roles; men developed and transmitted technique; men invented a system of dance notation; men created and produced ballets. What was it, then, that changed so drastically to prompt Théophile Gautier to write in the 1830s about the male dancer: "Nothing is more distasteful than a man who shows his red neck, his big muscular arms, his legs with the calves of a parish beadle, and all his strong massive frame shaken by leaps and pirouettes."[11] Gautier was disgusted by the feminization of technique and of the style that attempted – in vain – to negate the masculine features of the male body.

The profound political and social upheavals that had marked the transition from court to bourgeois society through the process of rationalization launched by the Enlightenment and characterized by a supposed natural order is the background for this transformation in mentality. A subterranean homophobic attitude thus crept into the history of dance, one that, as we have seen, has only recently been staged or studied. On the other hand, the figure of the Romantic ballerina and its myth indirectly reaffirm the masculine domination in the gaze and in desire.[12]

Choosing a death for Dido

The three case studies presented in this section demonstrate the significance of the relationship between the choice of sources and the methodological approach. Nathalie Lecomte comes out of a French tradition of rigorous historical and archival studies done in close relationship to musicological studies. Susan Foster draws on Anglo-American critical theory, on feminist theory in particular, and on her own personal experience in the practice of dance. Inge Baxmann's background brings cultural history and the history of mentality of German formulation, better defined by the term *Kulturwissenschaft*, together with critical theory. Each essay is based primarily on only one type of source: libretto-programs, ballet scripts or subjects, and *fête* descriptions, respectively. Other kinds of primary and secondary sources are evoked in a transitory or functional way as the argument unfolds. The analytical methods chosen are, respectively, statistical treatment of data, theory of narrativity associated with feminist and post-colonial criticism, and, lastly, cultural history and the history of mentality.

Foster's motivation for studying the launching of France's eighteenth-century colonial project grew out of her subjective political implication in the current redefinition of the concept of Empire, in the United States in particular. Her essay makes this implication explicit through the use of "stage directions," in which, though speaking of herself, she never uses the first person but relies instead on the infinitive of the verb, a strategy that shows how social forces oblige the author to resort to words and demonstrates how a subjective intuition becomes public writing. The "stage directions" also unveil the various aspects of the historian's craft: the unexpected surprises, the way in which a network of intellectual and personal connections works, the reading and re-reading of sources, the stalemates, and the makeshift solutions. The latter might actually explain renouncing a comparison to Gasparo Angiolini's libretto for *La partenza di Enea o La Didone abbandonata*.[13] What would the narrative analysis of the Italian libretto have revealed? Angiolini drew his subject from the first four books of Virgil's *Aeneid* and from Metastasio's *Didone abbandonata*, the era's best-known version of the story of the Carthaginian queen on the European stage.[14] Angiolini's Dido doesn't kill herself; she dies in the burning of Carthage provoked by Iarbas' jealousy. Aeneas is a weak character, split between his heroic duties and the queen's charms. The elements of Jean-Georges Noverre's libretto that lend themselves to becoming a show for the masses and to the intervention of the supernatural and wondrous – the hunt, the storm, the gods – are absent. Angiolini imagines a sentimental and human affair, driven by Iarbas' jealousy. Yet, however active Italian merchants may have been in Mediterranean trade, the colonization of North Africa would not take shape until the following century. Italy was not as yet a nation state endowed with a central power capable of throwing itself into a colonial project. From a methodological point of view, in the French as well as the Italian example, one might ask to what extent it is legitimate to base an interpretation on one source alone, the libretto, which is produced under particular conditions that are often subject to censure and which does not necessarily reflect dance. What distance should be assumed between the stage and the writing? Between literary work and scenic embodiment? And what impact did the writing and staging of a work have on the culture, the society, and the public opinion of the time? How many and what discourses does this impact produce?

From data to discourse and back

If subjective intuition and implication become method for Foster, Lecomte's subjectivity remains discreet and her interpretation appears in the form of circumspect hypotheses in strict relation to the time period and to the subject she has studied. Her work reveals extreme care in researching, elaborating, organizing, and presenting archival data that opens a wide gamut of interpretative viewpoints and a vast range of prospects for further research. Does, for example, the casting of certain mythological and allegorical roles to danseurs or danseuses respond to the dynamics of the technique itself or to other more symbolic motives? Are the furies, the natural forces, and the witches cast to men because they require high jumps, athletic figures, and bursting energy, or are there other image constructs between masculinity and these figures? Throughout the seventeenth century, at least, witches were the incarnation of uncontrollable feminine irrationality as opposed to masculine rationality. Is this a clue to the eighteenth-century turning point Foucault identified as an epistemological revolution?

Bringing Lecomte's data together with a sociological approach would make it possible to formulate hypotheses about the daily lives of the danseurs and danseuses (material conditions inside and outside the theater, places of residence, the existence of single or collective dressing rooms, relocations, relationships). It would allow us to gain insight into the family networks within which this art was handed down and the way in which this type of transmission was articulated in training at the Opéra (different programs for men and women, age groups, marriages and alliances).

If all of the directions of research we have indicated thus far use data to construct discourse, might it not also be worthwhile to question how discourses construct data? This could help us realize that Lecomte's quantitative data is in turn the fruit of the production of discourses and the diffusion of ideas on femininity and masculinity of that era. How, therefore, are we to situate within these discourses the identities of the danseurs and danseuses of the Paris Opéra between 1700 and 1725?

The crisis of difference

Baxmann's study examines the manifestation of the Republican *fêtes* and the public celebration of new political and social culture aimed at replacing the symbolic role of the monarchy deconsecrated during the French Revolution. The author uses the Feminine/Masculine dyad to study a crucial problem in the history of mentality: the crisis of difference revealed by the development of an egalitarian society. She does not look at dance specifically, but at the strategies through which the citizen body is staged and, especially, at the episodes in which the stage and the public square become confused, from the masses represented on stage to the choreographer's direction of the crowds for the public *fêtes*. This vision leaves open questions to which the analysis of more narrowly choreologic sources might respond. One such track, the *Volkskunde* (ethnography) briefly pointed out by Baxmann by the example of *Carmagnole*, is that of comparing staged dance expressions with more common social practices.

Baxmann embarked upon her study with the hypothesis that the Enlightenment and the French Revolution had constructed a form of feminine emancipation. The sources analyzed, however, did not support this intuition. The need to legitimize the egalitarian order had actually prompted revolutionary society to assign fixed roles to the masculinity and femininity, even while basing them on renewed values such as that of the family. The analytical model Baxmann applied to the representations supplied by the chosen sources relies on the theory of separate spheres, put forth by radical feminism on the basis of anthropological and ethnological data. Taking a different perspective, one might ask how the egalitarian utopia and the crisis of difference are articulated in embodied dance: do these separate spheres affect the way in which theatrical roles are divided? If "difference" is what moulds the bodies, what does its crisis produce in terms of technique and expression? Besides the *maîtres de ballet* who put themselves in the service of the new regime, what is the political implication of female and male dancers in the pre- and post-revolutionary movements? Before losing her fortune because of the Revolution, Marie Madeleine Guimard became a leader of and spokeswoman for her colleagues. She also demanded that the Opéra pay her the same salary as Vestris, allow her the privilege of deciding if and when she was to dance, and grant her an exclusive on certain roles. When she retired from the stage in 1789, she lived in precarious conditions due to the irregularity of the pensions under the new regime and she died in anonymity in 1816. What effects did the political upheavals and the changes imposed by the new regime have on the experience and the status of female and male dancers?

Reconstruction and embodiment

We have already seen how the gender studies that developed in the Anglo-American context of the 1980s were progressively affirmed in Europe. It was not until the end of the decade, however, that it became evident that the category of gender could have different meanings for different eras. In consequence, studies on dance and gender in modern times are still scarce, fragmentary, and generally not systematic.[15]

From the 1970s on, in the wake of the interest in the folk art and tradition popular at that time, amateur or semi-professional companies supported and accompanied by musicians and musicologists re-discovered or brushed up on the normative treatises and notation systems that had been worked out between the fifteenth and the eighteenth century, reconstructing and staging the dances they described or notated. Whereas the aim of this first generation was to stage these works, for today's scholars, who combine reconstruction with critical theory, it represents an obligatory passage in the attempt to flesh out documentary materials that take a critical position in the present.[16] Reconstruction makes it possible to test the way in which different dances are embodied according to their character (vocabulary, spatial schemes, dynamic qualities, the prevalent use of a certain part of the body, rhythm, accents, and so forth), their context, and the dancer's stylistic and interpretive choices. Carol Marsh, Meredith Little, and Francine Lancelot have provided essential tools for retrieving and classifying the scores in Beauchamp-Feuillet notation.[17] A systematic and comparative analysis of these documents, which passes through reconstruction and contextualization and comparison to other sources, remains an exciting field that has yet to be explored and one in which new research methodologies might be experimented. Detailed studies have been published on some choreographic scores in Beauchamp-Feuillet notation, which provide refined analyses of the recurrences, variations, and transformation of steps, and of the rhythmic and musical structures, and which sometimes, in a marginal way, take into consideration the similarities or differences between masculine and feminine roles.[18] Lecomte observes how, in the Opéra troupe between 1700 and 1725, specializing in a role is more evident for men than for women, hypothesizing that the latter might have been obliged to be more versatile because they were fewer in number. The scores in Feuillet notation intended for danseuses show how the vocabulary used was actually not very different from that of the danseurs. A few scores in Beauchamp-Feuillet transcribe the dances performed at the Opéra by Marie Thérèse Subligny and Marie Catherine Guyot. Choreological analysis of these scores shows the high technical level of these soloists: the compositions are rich in battus, leaps, turns, *pas soutenus* and *balancés*. In Feuillet's treatise, however, there is no hint of distinction between masculine and feminine execution of the steps. Pierre Rameau and, later, Gennaro Magri pause briefly on the behavior that, according to the rules of etiquette, women were to observe in society dances and their judgment of this type of feminine performance is anything but flattering!

What Tomko defines as Feuillet's and Rameau's taxonomic potential has often distorted the readings of scholars and reconstructors, who have taken their notation to the letter, often forgetting how attempting to reduce the dancing body to a written code implies losing the living and gendered body. It is on the basis of this that the conviction of the dominance of the formal in the eighteenth-century dance that preceded the *ballet d'action* (which was also transmitted negatively by Angiolini's and Noverre's reformist impetus) has taken hold in current historiography. The Feuillet system only makes it possible to codify (and de-codify) certain aspects of dance movement. How can we fill a void that lets very little surface regarding the differences of interpretation? How can we find our way out of the bottlenecks imposed by the code and penetrate the tried materiality of the dancing bodies in which gender is revealed? What can the body of a female dancer, today, performing a piece choreographed for Subligny tell us about the eighteenth century?

If the work of reconstruction were conducted alongside a thorough study of the process of embodiment[19] that took critical advantage of non-normative sources, it would contribute to filling the void left by taxonomic sources. It might bring us closer to that which regards the performance of individual female and male dancers and perhaps even break down the stereotypes on the formalism of what we call baroque dance.

The lives of female dancers

Professional female dancers emerged from anonymity in the eighteenth century, after a few decades of official presence on the stage. For a long time, all that had been known of them was, hardly, their name, last name, and the family relationships that identified them within a patriarchal society in which a woman's position was defined in relationship to a man – father, brother, husband, lover, patron. Though their contemporaries took an interest in how these women danced and in the innovations they introduced in technique and performance, a great deal more, morbid, attention was given to observing and elaborating stories about their private lives: encounters, love and power relationships, scandals, suppositions, dissimulation. Though from the mid century on new scientific knowledge about the female body and the movement of the *Précieuses* had put forth a new form of equality (albeit in a narrow social circle), eighteenth-century mentality still had a hard time accepting the embryonic attempts of feminine emancipation and looked for motivations and justifications in moral categories that carried the misogynist stereotypes which had persisted for centuries. An example of this can be seen in the article from an Italian journal that, in the second half of the eighteenth century, commented on Teresa Campioni, one of the most famous danseuses of the century, as follows: "She possesses the four qualities required of a great ballerina that is to say youth, beauty, stature and disposition."[20] There is no mention of intelligence, sensitivity, culture or even agility, technique, and expressive quality. . . For Italy's theater system, which was then managed prevalently by private producers, the fact that well-to-do men maintained danseuses was considered an indirect form of patronage, based on mechanisms of objectification of the female body through appearance, which also defined the realm of fashion.[21] Some recent studies have updated the biographical profiles of famous danseuses, but the portraits that emerge are profoundly conditioned by the masculine gaze that configured the coeval discourses.[22] An exemplary, though contradictory, figure that in itself sums up the effects of the ballerina's negative representation and the evidence of the will for ethical and social emancipation in the late eighteenth century, is that of Guimard: on one hand, her various well-to-do lovers, risqué parties in her elegant home, her exceptional seductive talents; on the other, her humble origins, misery at the beginning and the end of her existence, charitable acts, and corporative claims.[23]

Over the period taken into consideration in Lecomte's study, dancers' salaries rose progressively but still remained lower than those of the musicians and the singers in the comprehensive budget for an opera production. Dancers remained at the fringe of civic and theater society for a long time, and it would take the entire century for them to obtain dressing rooms of their own: progressing from the initial collective facilities, to separate rooms for women and men, and, finally, to private rooms for soloists. For the historian, one of the consequences of this marginalization is the scarcity of testimony on dancers' professional and private lives, with the exception of rare administrative documents (registers, wills, contracts) or summaries of events worthy of a police report, a public demonstration, an exchange of letters, or a line in a newspaper or journal. The sources for famous soloists and major theaters are more numerous and more readily accessible, and it is not mere chance that studies to date have focused here. The effort is more arduous and has yet to be made for the dozens of public and private provincial theaters in Europe, which flourished in the second half of the eighteenth century. Their archives are often dislocated, dismembered, inaccessible, or not catalogued and have discouraged more than one well-intentioned scholar.

Gender confusion

Throughout the eighteenth century up to the French Revolution *fêtes* and performances continued to be organized on the model established during the reign of Louis XIV, in which the use of masks and cross-dressing in the *ballet de cour* and in the *masquerade* added to destabilizing social categories and confusing gender identities. Being admired was considered a woman's prerogative and, to share in this pleasure, aristocrats appeared at their balls dressed in women's clothes and accessories.[24] Within this context, danseuses arrived late on the scene not only because of the prohibitions of social norms,[25] but also because danseurs performed female roles without reserve and without sexual ambiguity. The art of dance was a masculine prerogative and the process of feminization was not to be achieved until the end of the eighteenth century. As a consequence, feminine cross-dressing, which rarely occurred in *masquerade*, was completely absent from the *ballet de cour*. On the same stage where masculine cross-dressing made it possible to project actual or symbolic alternative and non-normative sexuality in representing the body,[26] femininity and its representation were fixed in a univocal vision. In other words, the male body could incarnate masculinity, femininity, androgynous, and neuter roles, while the female body was only assigned feminine roles.

In the period Lecomte's essay considers, not a single Opéra cast lists a masculine role performed by a woman, while masks and male cross-dressing were still used to play gender roles. They gradually disappear from the stage in the eighteenth century to make it possible for performers to embody characters through emotional experience and through the expression of passions perceptible by facial features. In theorizing this process, however, Noverre does not seem to question the stereotypes passed on through the Ancien Régime's convictions about gender relationships, masquerade, and cross-dressing. In the only passage devoted to female dancers in his long letter on facial expression and the drawbacks of masks, he maintains that it is easier for women to forsake masks because they are more skillful at concealing effort and at modulating expressions, being "naturally" gifted with the ability of pleasing and making themselves attractive.[27] Whereas masculine dissimulation passes through the mask, that of femininity is given by nature itself. Beyond the performance, the characteristics of the dancing body, and the role impersonated, identity, sexuality, and gender are imposed on the danseuse by the very nature of her being a woman. This is evidenced in the contemporary newspaper account of the episode that prompted Marie Sallé to return to Paris after a successful season in London. While impersonating the role of Cupid in her ballet production for Georg Friedrich Händel's *Alcina*, she had antagonized the audience by wearing a male costume that did not suit her[28] and was considered beneath her primary duty as a female dancer and as a woman, which was to please. Afterwards, in her private life as well, Sallé distanced herself from the stereotype ballerina, disappointing the public's curiosity and providing reporters with little to go on: no protector, no lover – a form of chastity that led her biographers to imagine Sapphic loves and female cohabitation.[29]

How are norm and transgression inscribed in the practice of cross-dressing that crystallizes the performative aspects of gender? How to bring to light the aspects that the normativeness inherent to eighteenth-century discourses has concealed? How to free oneself from the stereotypes that, constructed then, still hamper the way we look at things? A study that traverses the eighteenth century asking these questions would contribute to releasing the categories of gender from the fixity with which they have been used. It would help reveal alternative forms of sexuality and of gender performativity as well as different relational dynamics between femininity and masculinity, both on the plane of embodiment and on that which is identitarian, symbolic, social, and political.

Betting on a two-fold paradox has opened a wide range of research prospects that should not remain unexplored, but serve instead to stimulate studies, to enrich knowledge on theatrical dance and gender in the eighteenth century, to re-launch debate, and to pose ever new questions that can unsettle and invalidate those which today seem to be impregnable certainties. In other words, it is not enough to study dance history by limiting oneself to the lessons handed down by our predecessors; research must be fostered and challenged by inquiries and doubts that can re-open it and turn it into a self-conscious and active practice.

Notes

I would like to thank Patrizia Veroli and Ramsay Burt, whose pertinent and stimulating discussion of the essays in this section nourished some of my considerations.

1 See S.L. Foster, *Choreographing History*, in S.L. Foster (ed.), *Choreographing History*, Bloomington, IN: Indiana University Press, 1995, pp. 3–21.
2 Richard Ralph denounces the superficiality with which certain "new scholars" rehash already published materials according to the academic fashion of the moment. He urges the publication of sources and a sort of methodological neo-positivism, which reduces the dance historian's task to "the research and publication of information and data." See R. Ralph, 'On the Light Fantastic Toe. Dance Scholarship and Academic Fashion', *Dance Chronicle*, 1995, vol. 18, no. 2, 249–59. On this debate see also B. Sparti, J. Adshead-Lansdale, 'Dance History – Current Methodologies', *Dance Research Journal*, 1996, vol. 28, no. 1, pp. 3–6; and J. Adshead-Lansdale, 'The "Congealed Residues" of Dance History. A Response to Richard Ralph's "Dance Scholarship and Academic Fashion." One Path to a Pre-determined Enlightenment?', *Dance Chronicle*, 1997, vol. 20, no. 1, pp. 63–80.
3 For initial exposure to these issues in the Italian context see P. Di Cori, 'Dalla storia delle donne alla storia di genere', *Rivista di storia contemporanea*, 1987, no. 4, pp. 548–59 and more in general J. Wallach Scott, 'Gender: A Useful Category of Historical Analysis', *The American Historical Review*, 1986, vol. 91, no. 5, pp. 1053–75.
4 Thanks also to the publication in Italian in 1977 of the essay: N. Zemon Davis, 'Women's History in Transition: The European Case', *Feminist Studies*, 1976, nos. 3–4, pp. 82–102.
5 G. Devoto, G.C. Oli (eds), *Dizionario della lingua italiana*, Florence: Le Monnier, 1990, *ad vocem*.
6 Foucault introduces the element of desire and therefore of a relational dynamic that emphasizes the projection or the movement toward one or the other sex rather than essentializing them in the biological "trademarks." The dynamic of desire renders social conditioning productive and not only repressive: see M. Foucault, *The History of Sexuality*, vol. 1: *An Introduction*, trans. R. Hurley, New York: Pantheon, 1978 (orig. edn *Histoire de la sexualité*, vol. I: *La volonté de savoir*, Paris: Gallimard, 1976). On the developments in the notion of desire in relation to queer theory and to dance, see J.C. Desmond (ed.) *Dancing Desires. Choreographing Sexualities on and off the Stage*, Madison, WI: University of Wisconsin Press, 2001.
7 J. Butler, *Bodies that Matter. On the Discursive Limits of 'Sex'*, New York and London: Routledge, 1993, p. 9.
8 C. Brown, *Re-tracing Our Steps. The Possibilities for Feminist Dance Histories*, in J. Adshead-Lansdale, J. Layson (eds), *Dance History. An Introduction*, New York and London: Routledge, 1994, pp. 198–216.
9 See A. Daly, 'The Balanchine Woman: Of Hummingbirds and Channel Swimmers', *Drama Review*, 1987, vol. 31, no. 1, pp. 8–21. This article is an

example of feminist analysis that was later reformulated by the author herself (see A. Daly, 'Trends in Dance Scholarship. Feminist Theory across the Millenial Divide', *Dance Research Journal*, 2000, vol. 32, no. 1, pp. 39–41) and that has had the merit of pointing out a new direction in studies.

10 R. Burt, *The Male Dancer. Bodies, Spectacle, Sexualities*, New York and London: Routledge, 1995.

11 See T. Gautier, *The Romantic Ballet as Seen by Théophile Gautier*, trans. C.W. Beaumont, London: C.W. Beaumont, 1947, p. 24.

12 See S.L. Foster, *The Ballerina's Phallic Pointe*, in S.L. Foster (ed.), *Corporealities. Dancing Knowledge, Culture and Power*, New York and London: Routledge, 1996, pp. 1–24.

13 G. Angiolini, *La partenza d'Enea, o sia Didone abbandonata*, in *Merope. Dramma per musica da rappresentarsi nel nobilissimo Teatro San Benedetto il Carnevale dell'anno 1778*, Venice: Modesto Fenzo, 1778.

14 Metastasio's source is also book V of Virgil's *Aeneid*, hybridized with book III of Ovid's *Fasti* and insertions of parallel love affairs that thicken the plot. Metastasio's libretto was written in 1723 and printed the following year in Naples, where the opera was staged with enormous success. It was set to music by around seventy Italian and foreign composers, and performed regularly throughout Europe at least until 1760. See P. Metastasio, *Didone abbandonata*, in P. Metastasio, *Melodrammi e canzonette*, ed. by G. Lavezzi, Milan: Rizzoli, 2005, pp. 113–230.

15 Among the studies on dance and gender in the seventeenth and eighteenth century, in chronological order see: *L'homme et la femme dans la danse*, conference proceedings, Leuven: Association Européenne des Historiens de la Danse, 1990; M. Perreault, *Les changements dans les rôles des danseurs masculins depuis le XVIIIème siècle: un premier regard sociologique*, in C. Brack, I. Wuyts (eds), *Dance and Research. An Interdisciplinary Approach*, Leuven: Peeters Press, 1991; N. Lecomte, 'Maîtres à danser et baladins au XVII*ème* et XVIII*ème* siècles en France. Quand la danse était l'affaire des hommes', in *Histoires de corps. A propos de la formation du danseur*, Paris: Cité de la Musique, 1998, pp. 153–72; M. Goff, 'Surprising Monsters. The First Female Professional Dancers', in *Terpsichore 1450–1900*, Gent: The Institute for Historical Dance Practice, 2000, pp. 179–88; A.I. Tardif, 'Eighteenth-century Origins of the Social Debut in England and its Relation to Dancing', in *Terpsichore 1450–1900*, pp. 151–60; L.J. Tomko, 'Magri's Grotteschi', in R. Harris-Warrick and B.A. Brown (eds), *The Grotesque Dancer on the Eighteenth-century Stage. Gennaro Magri and his World*, Madison, WI: University of Wisconsin Press, 2005, pp. 151–72; and the *Women Making Dance in Early Modern Europe* (monographic issue of *Studies in Dance History*, ed. L. Brooks), Madison, WI: University of Wisconsin Press, forthcoming, which contains N. Lecomte, 'The Female Ballet Troupe of the Paris Opéra from 1700 to 1725'.

16 See M. Franko, 'Repeatability, Reconstruction and Beyond', *Theatre Journal*, 1989, vol. 41, no. 1, 56–74, republished as 'Epilogue', in M. Franko, *Dance as Text; Ideologies of the Baroque Body*, Cambridge: Cambridge University Press, 1993, pp. 133–52.

17 M. Little, C.G. Marsh, *The Danse Noble: An Inventory of Dances and Sources*, Williamstown, MA: Broude Brothers, 1992; F. Lancelot, *La Belle Dance*, Paris: Van Dieren, 1996.

18 See J. Thorp, K. Pierce, 'Taste and Ingenuity. Three English Chaconnes of the Early Eighteenth Century', *Historical dance*, 1994, vol. 3, no. 3, pp. 3–16; C. Bayle, 'The Meanderings of Interpretation', *Dance Research*, 1997, vol. 15, no. 2,

pp. 170–99; D.C. Colonna, 'Comparative Study of the Different Versions of the Passacaille of Armide', in *Proceedings of the Society of Dance History Conference*, 1997, pp. 93–101; D.C. Colonna, 'Le Chaconnes d'Arlequin', in F. Mòllica (ed.), *Aspetti della cultura di danza nell'Europa del Settecento*, Bologna: I libri della società di danza, 2001, pp. 41–56; D.C. Colonna, 'Variation and Persistence in the Notation of the Loure "Aimable vainqueur"', in *Proceedings of the Society of Dance History Conference*, 1998, pp. 285–93; M. Lutz and Marsh, 'Gender Differences in Baroque Dance', *Ballett International/Tanz Aktuell*, 1998, August, pp. 44–5; M. Goff, 'Imitating the Passions Reconstructing the Meaning within the Passagalia of Venüs and Adonis', in S. Jordan (ed.), *Preservation Politics. Dance Revived, Reconstructed, Remade*, London: Dance Books, 2000, pp. 154–65.

19 On these aspects of the process of embodiment see S.L. Foster, 'Dancing Bodies', in J.C. Desmond (ed.), *Meaning in Motion: New Cultural Studies in Dance*, Durham, NC: Duke University Press, 1997, pp. 235–58. Desmond speaks of "kinesthetics of sexuality" to indicate the new area of study the book she edited opens and shows how it is necessary "to analyze movement with precision. This level of kinesthetic detail is absolutely crucial. It allows us to take bodily motion as specific evidence, not as general referent. These theoretical and historical investigations must analyze dancing as an embodied social practice." See *Dancing Desires*, pp. 7 and 13.

20 *Notizie dal Mondo*, February 19, 1776, no. 15, p. 119.

21 See P. Perrot, *Le travail des apparences ou les transformations du corps féminin, XVIIIème-XIXème siècles*, Paris: Seuil, 1984.

22 See Goff, 'Coquetry and Neglect. Hester Santlow, John Weaver, and the Dramatic Entertainment of Dancing', in *Dancing in the Millennium*, CORD and SDHS, Washington, 2000, pp. 207–12; I. Alm, 'Profits and Perils: Professional Dancing in Early Eighteenth-century Venice', in *Aspetti della cultura di danza nell'Europa del Settecento*, pp. 78–83; M. Nordera, 'Au fil de l'exposition', in *La construction de la féminité dans la danse (XV-XVIIIème siècle)*, exhibition catalogue, Pantin: Centre national de la danse, 2004, p. 32.

23 Nordera, 'Au fil de l'exposition', pp. 35–7.

24 S. Cohen, *Art, Dance, and the Body in French Culture of the Ancien Régime*, Cambridge: Cambridge University Press, 2000, p. 156.

25 Prohibiting danseuses to tread heavily on the scene is a French and court phenomenon. Sources coming from public and private theaters testify to their appearance before the famous date of 1681 reiterated by books on dance history as the moment in which women began to be considered professional dancers. The importance of this date requires reexamining and verifying the presupposition that postulates the Parisian centrality – at court and at the Opéra – of an evolutionist and Francocentric vision of dance history. European and American publishers have recently produced more than one dance history book that is limited to recapitulating, re-working or re-writing the volumes published thirty or forty years ago, without integrating the results of recent research and obliging us to explain to our incredulous students that the manual we ask them to adopt recounts falsehoods.

26 Franko hypothesizes that the androgynous figure staged by the young Louis XIV unites the two bodies of the king: the masculine is meant to evoke the abstract and immortal body that is identified with the idea of state, while the feminine embodies the strength, the sexual and uncontrollable of the king's mortal body power. See M. Franko, 'Double Bodies, Androgyny and Power in

the Performances of Louis XIV', *The Drama Review*, 1994, vol. 38, no. 4, pp. 71–2. For Cohen instead the king does not have two bodies, but "two dresses – or, rather, many dresses, and a panoply of other costumes – male, female ungendered allegory [. . .] the monarchical body" is "inseparable from his artifice of display." See Cohen, *Art, Dance, and the Body*, p. 51.

27 J.G. Noverre, *Lettres sur la danse*, Paris: Librairie Théâtrale, 1952, p. 150.

28 *Le pour et le Contre*, t.VI, p. 287, cited in É. Dacier, *M.lle Sallé. Une danseuse de l'Opéra sous Louis XV*, Paris: Plon, 1909, pp. 168–70.

29 See Dacier, *M.lle Sallé*, p. 192.

Part III

Keyword: **IDENTITIES**

Topic: **CONTEMPORARY DANCE**

11 Dance, identity, and identification processes in the postcolonial world

Andrée Grau

In what way can identity be seen as one of the key ideas underpinning the study of dance? It is undoubtedly a central concept in western thought: from the aphorism *gnothi seauton* (know thyself) inscribed on the pediment of the temple of Apollo in Delphi and adopted as a motto by Socrates, to Amin Maalouf's late twentieth-century idea of *identités meurtrières* (deadly/ murderous identities)[1] many authors have chosen to engage with the issue. The notion has been debated in the fields of philosophy and psychology. It is found in psychoanalysis, anthropology, and sociology. Yet what can it bring to dance studies? Looking at dance and its many practices through the lens of identity may be helpful in our search for a better understanding of the phenomenon and of those engaged in it, as the concept brings together aesthetic and socio-cultural realms. This is especially pertinent in the postcolonial world we live in, when those involved in dance have to deal with issues of greater complexities than in any other historical period. An essay such as this, however, can certainly not be exhaustive. I will investigate only some of the key issues that are worth considering. Hopefully they will bring up useful ideas, which may help our analysis of dance works and dance practitioners as well as of their place within a web of power relationships in a globalized world.

Identity as a concept

In popular thought identity is first and foremost a set of information that allows us to recognize someone as an individual (surname, first name, filiations, date and place of birth, specific details of our physiognomy and so on). Bank clerks, police officers, and custom personnel check it on a regular basis, whilst the media warn us about identity theft and identity fraud. Identity is what makes one the being one is. It is made of those attributes that make one person unique as an individual and different from all others, indeed unlike anyone but her/himself. In respect, the popular usage of the term is close to its etymology, identity deriving from the Latin *idem* (the same).

Who, however, is this "same" one is identical to? Who is this "same," when one speaks of the identity of a group or of an object? Through what processes are the identities of dancers, choreographers, their works, and their techniques established? When and how are they formed? How do they mesh with the socio-cultural and historical spheres of dance practices? These are some of the questions this essay wants to raise.

Each human being is unique but never, it seems, in isolation. Individuality is often invoked in relation with other terms, such as *idiosyncrasy*, composed from the Greek *idios* (peculiar) and *sunkrasis* (mixture). Here again, the distinct is tied to the general; the *I* is bound to the *we*. One cannot be unique alone. The self can only be achieved through others, or to put it another way one can understand the self only through a process of alienation. As the poet Arthur Rimbaud once wrote:

> [. . .] I is an other. If brass wakes as a bugle, it is not its fault at all. That is quite clear to me: I am a spectator at the flowering of my thought: I watch it, I listen to it: I draw a bow across a string: a symphony stirs in the depth, or surges onto the stage.[2]

The sociologist and philosopher Alfred Schutz similarly insisted that one can only understand the self in terms of the other:

> In the we-relation our experiences are not only coordinated with one another, but are also reciprocally determined and related to one another. I experience myself through my consociate, and he [*sic*] experiences himself through me.[3]

Indeed he talked about "reciprocal mirroring." Similarly some anthropologists argue that, given that the self can only be achieved through others, anthropology is not the study of human beings but, rather, the investigation of the dyad "human beings/fellow human beings."[4]

The philosopher Michel Foucault explained it in this way:

> [. . .] the subject constitutes himself [*sic*] in an active fashion, by the practices of the self, these practices are nevertheless not something that the individual invents by himself. They are patterns that he finds in his culture and which are proposed, suggested and imposed on him by his culture, his society and his social group.[5]

If the recognition of similitude is brought about through the experience of the other, one can argue that identity is structured by otherness and vice versa. It is therefore *others* that render us *epistemologically* self-conscious. Similarly one could argue that the identity of a dance work exists always in relation to other dance works and each performance of a work in relation to all other performances of that work. Following this line of reasoning, identity is first and foremost dialogic, given that it is constructed through dialogue with the other, and it is constantly in construction, given that it is bound to the dynamics of interactions.

Identity and the everyday life

Individuals can belong to a virtually unlimited number of categories, which will contribute to the make up of their identities. They are born in a social group; they belong to linguistic, ethnic and gender groups. Stateless persons aside, they all have a nationality and, in some cases, more than one. They adhere to a profession. They belong to a union, a sports club, a group of friends, a religious group, or a political party. They feel close to a community of other individuals that share their passions, their sexual orientations, or their physical challenges. With this multiplicity, one might think of individuals having as many identities as affiliations, were it not for the fact that these affiliations are rarely autonomous, that they generally overlap, and that they are, above all, dynamic and ever changing.

Every social experience solicits principles of affiliation and differentiation. An affiliation can take on more or less importance depending on context. It can be rendered prominent or invisible. For one reason or another (such as a change in the political climate or a transformation in one's personal life), an affiliation can expand and even come to the point of hiding all others, creating, in some cases, a kind of fanaticism. It can also disappear forever, or only briefly to perhaps take hold again later on in life.

Maalouf describes the case of an imaginary inhabitant of Sarajevo.[6] In 1980 he would probably have proclaimed, "I'm Yugoslavian," adding maybe "I come from Bosnia-Herzegovina," and possibly, incidentally, "I was born in a Muslim family." At the heights of the war in the 1990s, in all likelihood, he would have answered first "I'm Muslim," adding immediately "Bosnian," whereas today he would probably say first "Bosnian" and then "Muslim," wanting to see his country enter the European Union. What will he say first in twenty years time? European? Muslim? Bosnian? Something else? Balkanic maybe? Over the course of his lifetime, our protagonist will have been told that he was a Slav from the south and, above all a proletarian; a Yugoslavian and nothing more; a Muslim and nothing more. At a certain point, he might even have been told that he had more in common with the inhabitants of Kabul than with those of Trieste. Over the years, social class, religion, ethnicity, language group and so on have been put forward and withdrawn to represent him. This fictitious example shows how the hierarchy established among the many elements making up an individual's identity varies according to the social-historical context and a person's individual circumstances.

The performing arts and the construction of identities

Although the discussion so far has been primarily about the identity of people rather than that of performance works, similar issues can be raised when discussing music and dance. The ethnomusicologist Ankica Petrovic[7] provides an example based on the same region as the one discussed by Maalouf. She shows how, in the 1970s, *ganga* music symbolized a rural and mountain identity that, shared by Croatians, Serbs, Muslims, Catholics, and Greek Orthodox, was capable of transcending religion and ethnicity. Before the Second World War, however, it had been tied to the ultra-nationalist Croatian movement of western Herzegovina, a role it took on again in the conflict of the late 1980s to early 1990s in response to Serbian nationalist music. *Ganga* remained recognizable throughout the entire twentieth century; its form did not change but its meaning did. Is it possible, therefore, to say that the cultural artefact, *ganga,* remained the *same* in its different historical embodiments? What, then, happened to its identity?

The waltz too is a case in point. When it was introduced to British high society at a ball at the English court, it created such a scandal that the *Times* wrote about it on 16 July 1816 arguing that "the voluptuous intertwining of the limbs and close compressure of the bodies" threatened the morality of English youth! For the journalist:

> So long as this obscene display was confined to prostitutes and adulteresses we did not think it deserved a notice, but now that it is attempted to be forced on the respectable classes of society by the evil example of their superiors we feel it is a duty to warn every parent against exposing his daughter [*sic*] to so fatal a contagion.[8]

Almost two centuries later this "immoral" dance is for many an example of decorum and elegance. Once again, the cultural object has maintained its form, while its meaning has been transformed to the point that, for some, the dance now represents the exact opposite of what it did, for some, when it first appeared in England.

What would be necessary to bring the existence of a cultural artifact to an end? What is necessary for it to persist? These issues will not be discussed in detail here as this debate belongs to the realm of philosophy,[9] suffice it to say that these three examples, fictitious and real, show to what extent affiliations and representations are rarely anodyne. In all their various manifestations, they are bearers of meaning and cannot be limited to their external manifestations. Made up of such multitudes of threads, identities are therefore extremely complex phenomena, difficult to apprehend because of their ever-changing nature, bounded as they are to individuals' histories and "stories."

The performing arts in general, and dance in particular, can be particularly useful as an entry into the realm of identities. Just as histories, they are always in the making. Similarly the anthropological approach with its emphasis on the dynamic nature of cultures as ways-of-being-in-the-world will be pertinent as an intellectual tool to help in the journey. Cultures and histories are embodied in all of our activities, in the sense that they are constructed through human beings' involvement in society and through their engagement in systems of beliefs that operate through and beyond discursive principles. As the philosopher Paul Ricoeur argued, "understanding" is not just a "mode of knowing" it is also "a way of being."[10] These in-corporations of world-views are often incarnated in a more "distilled" way in the extra-ordinary activities of dancers and other movement specialists. Whilst it might be useful occasionally to speak of multiple intelligences as Howard Gardner does, one must always keep in mind that these forms of intelligence are interwoven and that the verbal and corporal are not distinct from each other.[11]

Anthropologist Drid Williams has argued for many years that "dances are socio linguistic phenomena"[12] associated to physical actions. Similarly anthropologist Sylvia Faure has demonstrated that learning to dance – as well as other physical disciplines like sports and martial arts – is both linguistic and physical.[13] Dance training requires the acquisition of a technical vocabulary as well as physical practice, the latter often punctuated by the teacher's corrections, comments, and other verbal suggestions that provoke physical reactions in students, perhaps even without their direct awareness. Choreography is transmitted partly verbally and choreographers' comments inform the way dancers will interpret their choreographies.

Though often forgotten, this interpenetration of body and language has a long history in anthropology. As early as 1925 the linguist/anthropologist Edward Sapir argued that:

> The relational gaps between the sounds of a language are just as necessary to the psychological definitions of these sounds as the

> articulations and acoustic images which are customarily used to define them. A sound that is not unconsciously felt as "placed" with references to other sounds is no more a true element of speech than a lifting of the foot is a dance steps unless it can be "placed" with reference to other movements that help to define the dance.

In 1927 Sapir also wrote:

> [. . .] Our breathing habits are largely conditioned by factors conventionally classified as social. [. . .] The subdued breathing of those who are in the presence of a recently deceased companion laid away in a coffin [. . .], the style of breathing which one learns from an operatic singer [. . .] are [. . .] socialized modes of conduct that have a definite place in the history of human culture [. . .]. There is no hard and fast line of division as to class of behavior between a given style of breathing, *provided that it be socially interpreted*, and a religious doctrine or a form of political administration.[14]

Anthropology in its attempt to think about the relationship between "unity and diversity"[15] and to consider the modernity derived from the "dialectic it puts forth between differences and similarities, between continuity (tradition) and discontinuity (change, modernity)"[16] gives us analytical tools to examine identities. Its sub-discipline, the anthropology of dance generates a pertinent theoretical framework that gives us a better understanding of dance and dance practices in general and, more specifically, of their identities, with their different "narratives." The approach could also enter into a more sustained dialogue with and possibly enrich the philosophical discussions surrounding the notion of dance works.

Dance and the anthropological approach

It is worthwhile pausing here to speak briefly about the anthropological approach, of which many people still have a rather old-fashioned vision. Some still think that cultures exist outside of history and of the social and political contradictions that make them possible. They believe that anthropology is a discipline that only addresses so-called traditional and generally distant societies; that its focus is limited to reconstructing past societies and that this reconstruction is made without any consideration of their present and their insertion in the wider whole in which they exist. The discipline's ties to colonial empires also make it suspect.

This vision is not completely wrong from a historical point of view. Anthropology has clearly been engaged in the study of "exotic" societies but, as early as 1943, William Foot Whyte published *Street Corner Society: the Social Structure of an Italian Slum*,[17] a field study on an Italian-American neighborhood in Boston and by the 1970s Urban Anthropology was well established as a subfield of Anthropology. Today anthropologists are working on subjects as varied as the French National Assembly[18] or soccer.[19] If it is true that anthropology did pass through an evolutionist period and regarded contemporary societies characterized by simple technologies as relics of the past representing different stages of human development, it is also true that this way of thinking disappeared from the anthropological discourse in the second quarter of the twentieth century, whilst it still persists in popular thought, among many dance practitioners, as well as among some dance scholars.

Newspapers and their readers seem to relish discoveries of so-called primitive societies that somehow are seen to exist in the "Stone Age," having survived without contact with the west and therefore remaining "pure" and uncontaminated by "civilisation." Indeed an article in the *New York Times* on 11 May 2006 started:

> Since time immemorial the Nukak-Makú have lived a Stone-Age life, roaming across hundreds of miles in isolated and pristine Amazon jungle, killing monkeys with blowguns and scouring the forest floor for berries. But recently, and rather mysteriously, a group wandered out of the wilderness, half-naked [. . .][20]

Jean-Jacques Rousseau's "noble savage" is still quite present! Many artists and intellectuals still evoke a so-called "primitive" thought that westerners are supposed to have lost in the evolutionist progress toward scientific thought[21] and I would argue that the approach underpinning much of modern dance can be understood in part as a romantic search for a "natural" and "primitive" body as a counter-part of the "intextuation" – to use De Certeau's expression[22] – of the disciplined body of academic dance, where, as in competitive sport, "the ideal body, [. . .] exalted in its sculptural beauty [. . .], passes for the mortification of the real body."[23]

In an otherwise pertinent scholarly text on character dance, published in 2004, one can read, for example, without any evidence given to support the argument, that:

> The three stages of evolution in dance [. . .] reflect the functions and forms peculiar to the art: imitative in primitive dance, expressive for

> folk or popular dance, and finally, abstract, i.e. "scholarly" or *danse savante*. In primitive dance, there is no awareness of "steps." What counts is the overall picture, in its magical-religious aspect. Primitive dance played an incantatory role. Jointly repeating and speeding up the pulsation, brought the group to a trance-like state, a sacred phenomenon. Through the sacred, unity is achieved, the group becomes one, in a magical union with the object of the ritual – on which it confers a god-like quality, or even deifies. In popular dance, lines and steps appear. Each dancer declares his belonging to the group. Dance may reflect the image of social rank. As the dance is broken down into steps, virtuosity, and a sense of aesthetics emerge. Folk dance is created by the people for the people. Performance, as we know it today, does not yet have a place. No clear distinction is drawn between dancers and spectators. Whoever does not dance, takes part in the social event by his encouraging presence, by shouting or clapping his hands. [24]

An example, from a practitioner's perspective, could be that of Dominique Boivin's work of 1994 *La danse, une histoire à ma façon . . .*, which traces the history of dance "from its origin in prehistoric time to today."[25] As critic Patricia Boccadoro wrote: "With virtually nothing, Boivin retraces the story of dance via Isadora Duncan, Vaslav Nijinsky, Martha Graham to Merce Cunningham with humour and imagination."[26] The piece is extremely witty and clearly Boivin knows his dance history. It is a shame, however, that he starts with the usual clichés, which the audience does not question. If he had begun with Jean Georges Noverre, he would have eluded evolutionism and his performance would have had greater historical and artistic pertinence. Instead he fell into the trap of a vision of human evolution as a single linear process proposing that cultures evolve successively from a "primitive" to a more "evolved" state of development sometimes stopping along the way.

In this vision, the so-called primitive contemporary societies are presented as stages through which western civilization is supposed to have passed in its ascension toward the apogee of human intellectual development. This perspective is found in many books on dance history, which include a chapter on the "savages," another on social and folkloric dances, and perhaps another on classical Asian dances, concluding with western concert dance, the height of which is often seen as classical ballet. The length of each section is commensurate with the importance attributed to it and three-quarters or more of the book is devoted to the West. Captions of illustrations usually name performers of "art dances" whilst those who perform "non-art dances" generally remain anonymous.

Dance in a global perspective: a question of status

Like many others before him, the British choreographer and dancer Kwesi Johnson laments the fact that dances defined as "indigenous" or "traditional" are usually considered inferior to those falling under the label of western concert dance, such as contemporary dance or ballet. He argues that "vernacular and traditional dance forms are still classed as lesser than, for example, classical or contemporary dance forms – even though African dance [traditions] and b-boying have as much of a defined vocabulary as Cunningham or Graham technique."[27] As all dances they are choreographed around a technical vocabulary and an aesthetic of body, time, and space. They do not, however, comply with western canons and, because of this, are systematically marginalised. Academic dances from other parts of the world are also perceived differently.

Classical ballet born in the royal and imperial courts of Italy, France, and Russia has gone beyond its original boundaries to the point where it is danced and appreciated by an international community of dancers and dance lovers. This is why it is accepted as a transnational with a somewhat neutral ethnicity, even if it has undeniable European origins. In contrast bharatanatyam, a high-art genre from southern India, which has followed a comparable path, is perceived as inseparable from its socio-cultural origins.[28] Only the West has the right to the universal, as, in this world vision, it sets forth the norms of civilisation.

In order to elucidate a better understanding of the contemporary situation, it may be helpful here to compare two historical conceptions of race, published in the late ninteenth century and deriving respectively from the social sciences and from dance. The first comes from the sociologist/anthropologist Émile Durkheim and dates back to 1897:

> [. . .] the sociologist must be very careful in searching for the influence of races on any social phenomenon. For to solve such problems the different races and their distinctions from each other must be known. This caution is the more essential because this anthropological uncertainty might well be due to the fact that the word race no longer corresponds to anything definite.[29]

Let's compare Durkheim's cautious position to that of his contemporary, Lilly Grove.[30] In her treatise on dance, *Dancing*, published in 1895, the third chapter entitled "The Dances of Savages" begins as follows:

> The dancing among savages may be considered a just indication of their character; it plays a very important part in their daily life – so important that there are races who have special dances for every day in the year and for every occasion in the day. There are people – some African tribes might be instanced – who could not live a single week without their dances. Nations which are in their infancy dance with the greatest ease and pleasure; the Negro, for example, begins to skip at the mere sound of the most rudimentary music, even under a broiling sun.[31]

This sort of attitude is still echoed in comments that describe African dance as singular, treating Africa as a country rather than as a continent with over fifty countries with hundreds of dance traditions and techniques with very different ways of understanding the physical dancing body; African dancers as having dance or rhythm "in their blood"; or in the monolithic presentation of certain populations that "can't live without their dance." It fails to acknowledge that individuals outside of the western world can be dissidents or that the notion of a life in dance as if entering dance was like entering religion whilst being part of the worldview held by many western theater dancers is not necessarily a universal position.[32]

The anthropology of dance as an analytical framework for dance

Let's come back to contemporary anthropology and its pertinence to dance studies and to issues of identity. One could say that the first aim of the discipline is to question the contents of the modern imagination; that it is a discipline that re-examines everyday words and demonstrates, as the anthropologist Mondher Kilani asserts, how our categories "have nothing to do with the *nature* or the *essence* of things, but are *artefacts*, social constructs, historical products and, as such, arbitrary, conventional, and variable."[33]

As understanding the other also means attempting to understand oneself, anthropology offers a framework within which the debates between otherness and identity may be conducted. Anthropology puts different interpretations of the world face-to-face and, as Kilani demonstrates, proposes an "anthropology of possibility"[34] similar to what the philosopher Ludwig Wittgenstein outlined in *Philosophical Investigations*.[35] In the words of Silvana Borutti, a commentator of Wittgenstein, this anthropology does not say that "the other is just like me," but rather that "I am not the other," and that "I understand myself in relationship to the other as my possible other, by comparison and by difference [. . .] through the invention of the other, *precisely*, and according to the contrasting, non symmetrical, conception of identity."[36]

Through fieldwork the anthropologist puts his or her own identity into play. Doing field research means dialoguing with one's "real" self with one's "virtual" selves.[37] This is what differentiates anthropological fieldwork from that of other disciplines such as Cultural Studies, for example. Through the methodologies of participant observation and reflexive ethnography, anthropologists not only embody cultural knowledge but share different ways of apprehending the world. In the process they attempt to "dismantle Western-centrism, and open possibilities for a new reflexivity towards Western academic intellectual givens."[38] This is why anthropology, through its experiential dimension, can provide tools that are useful in studying dance generally, and identity in dance specifically. Furthermore one could argue that anthropologists translating field experience and sharing it with the public are similar to dancers translating a choreographer's vision with an audience.[39]

Identity and post-identitarian discourses

Some researchers influenced by post-modern and post-structuralist discourses maintain that we live in a post-humanist period. This implies that we live in a space "freed from humanism, where gender and essence are things of the past."[40] Ours is a time of "post-identity" and researchers engaged with identity are, in some circles, rather *passé*. In an article in 2000 on the state-of-the-art in the theory, sociology, and aesthetics of dance, dance scholar Ramsay Burt argued that examining choreographers and their works according to parameters of identity is reductive and negates their complexity. According to him, only a post-identitarian position allows us to take distance from the separatism tied to issues of identity and to move on toward new forms that permit a general consensus that works against the hegemony of the "normal."[41]

If identity is defined solely as "ethnic" or "sexual" or any other single identity, I would have to agree with Burt. But the term is not so reductive. As Maalouf writes:

> Identity can't be compartmentalized. You can't divide it up into halves or thirds or any other separate segments. I have not got several identities: I have got just one, made up of many components combined together in a mixture that is unique to every individual.[42]

Each one of us carries different, often contradictory, predispositions that form what is held to be our basic character. The elements that make up identity, ours or that of others, are drawn from a polysemic and ambivalent imaginary. The British choreographer Shobana Jeyasingh comments how her cosmopolitan life makes it possible for her to be described as "A Christian in India, a Tamil in Sri Lanka, an Indian in East Malaysia, an Indian in Britain."[43] In a similar way Kaijo Saariaho states:

> First, I was the woman composer in Finland, then I was a computer music composer, then I became the Finnish composer in Paris. But I really don't care about these categories. Because I'm partly all of those things – but I'm also left handed. There are so many things that make up one's personality: it's ridiculous to take just one to categorise a person, or their music.[44]

This irritation about being branded as a certain kind of artist is also expressed by the novelist Alex Wheatle who in an interview argued "I get annoyed when people call me a ghetto writer or a black urban writer. Why can't they call me a writer full stop? That's what I am reaching for."[45]

A study I conducted on the world of intercultural theater in the 1980s showed how artists manipulated their identity according to circumstances, generally presenting themselves as *actors*, but in some cases as *black dancers* or in others as *contemporary dancers*. In like manner, audiences often perceived their performances as *African* and as stylistically *homogeneous* when they were performed solely by black artists, even if the dancers were of different origins (United States, Jamaica, Brazil, or Nigeria). The same held true if the dance techniques were derived from traditional *Tiv*, *Hausa*, *Igbo*, and *Yoruba* dance cultures from contemporary Nigeria. If, on the contrary, the artists' skin colour varied, the works were perceived as the expression of an *intercultural* art and *heterogeneous* style.[46]

What is important is that every individual has the right to claim multiple origins in accordance with his or her individual path, often shaped in part by socio-historical events, without being forced in any sort of ghetto. Jeyasingh claims the legacy of Purcell, Shelley, and David Bowie,[47] just as the director and actor Djamel B. claims that of Anton Chekhov, Molière, and Jacques Prévert.[48]

Speaking of a post-identitarian period is similar to considering our times to be "post-race" or "post-gender" because the concepts of race and gender are social constructs like any other and these concepts are ideologically connoted, charged with historical significance, and should no longer exist. The problem is that people continue to use them and that racism and sexism are still highly prevalent in contemporary societies. As Annamaria Rivera provocatively states:

> Racism is not a marginal, pathological or conjunctural phenomenon. On the contrary, it is, as are universalism and egalitarianism, one of the constituent elements of European culture, destined to reappear periodically, and especially in moments of transition or crisis [. . .].[49]

Similarly Laura Lee Downs's discussion of the so-called postmodern vacuity of the concept of "woman" is highly pertinent here when she entitles an article "If 'Woman' Is Just an Empty Category, then Why Am I Afraid to Walk Alone at Night?: Identity Politics Meets the Postmodern Subject."[50]

Identity has to be seen as fluid and in the making. It cannot be reduced to fixed essences that confine individuals, and its edges must be considered part of the whole. An open history in which the intercultural and *métissage* are the norm might be seductive – as it would make a tolerant future radiate before our eyes – but one must not forget the conflicting relations that still exist between individuals, between groups, and between societies. These conflicts to me are significant not so much at an ideational level, but for the pragmatic responses that ensue, giving different access to resources to different artists not because of the quality (or not) of their work but because of the way they are perceived by those granting the resources.

Identity, power and access to resources

Identitarian positions open and close doors, and identitarian issues can rarely be separated from those of power or economics. In our hyper capitalist world, it can be said that we are that for which others are willing to pay, and that the way in which artists present themselves and their work has repercussions on the funding they can obtain and on the places in which they are welcome to perform. The questions we have to answer are: who creates the boundaries of identity, and how are these boundaries established both from within and without?

While studying at the University of Roehampton in London, Francesca Flamminger conducted a study among the teachers and students of a number of conservatories and universities teaching ballet.[51] She purposefully selected institutions whose focus was primarily on contemporary dance techniques and sought to explore the teachers' and students' perception of the artistic and technical contribution of ballet. Some of her results are pertinent to our current discussion. She demonstrated, for example, the extent to which contemporary Britain-based dancers find it difficult to accept that classical companies such as the Royal Ballet, the Scottish Ballet, or others establish contemporary repertoires that include works by Merce Cunningham, Twyla Tharp, or other contemporary choreographers. They feel as though their territory has been invaded, and they complain that classical ballet dancers already have access to the largest part of government funding for dance. In their eyes the ballet companies should not encroach on a choreographic territory that is not historically theirs. For their part, the directors and dancers of the classical companies express a desire to broaden their vision and to further develop their artistic potential. Both groups generally agree that they are *the only ones* capable of dancing *their own* repertoire and, as such, the only ones with the authority to validate it. This example demonstrates the extent to which the attribution of identity and its boundaries are often bound to a struggle for control over a territory against every form of usurpation.[52]

Who says I can't be a bharatanatyam dancer because I'm white? The dancer Bithika Chatterjee recounts how, once, at an Indian dance performance in which the dancers were not all from South Asia, she heard the person next to her whisper to her friend that "white women shouldn't dance; they look like *hijras*."[53] Artists like the Italian-born Odissi dancer, Ileana Citaristi, who has lived in India since 1978, also note that "it is not only the government but the Indian mentality, in general, which is not yet ready to accept the idea that a non-Indian may become the leading dancer of Indian dance in India."[54] In India the whiteness of one's skin is not necessarily the criteria for exclusion in dance, though it is undoubtedly of great significance in everyday life. The bharatanatyam dancer Navtej Johar, who graduated from the prestigious Kalakshetra school, in the state of Tamil Nadu in southern India where bharatanatyam originated, has also found it difficult to be accepted just because he is Sikh and originally from the Punjab, a region in the north of India.[55] Recently he commented, "at times, I have been made to feel small by the musicians who think that an 'outsider' like me does not know much about the dance or the music."[56] Why such reluctance? Is it because Johar is a northerner or because he is not Hindu yet wants to engage in an artistic practice with close links to Hinduism?

Who says I can't join the British Royal Ballet because I'm dark-skinned? In 1965 a Chinese student at the Royal Ballet School in London was told: "We don't employ coloured dancers in the company."[57] Perhaps this has changed now that the Royal Ballet exalts its star dancer, Cuban-born Carlos Acostas. But one could argue that he is the exception that confirms the rule, that whilst dancers of Asian descent have now become part of the company, it is exceptional in the UK to see ballet dancers of African ancestry in a subsidized ballet company and many such dancers have felt and still feel marginalized. Many comment, for example, that as dance students they were encouraged and directed towards jazz and musical theater rather than ballet.

Identity, politics, and ethics

Identity is not an obsolete concept. As Anthony Cohen argues "it is clear that identity (however inexplicit), boundary (however elusive and nebulous) and authenticity (however contested and contestable) are matters in which people invest huge value."[58] How can one make sense of the different genres and techniques of dance, if not in terms of the dancers that characterize them? And how can they be differentiated from each other if not by gestural movement, the use of energy and space or, in a word, by their movement identity? How can we analyze Kwesi Johnson's recommendation to dancers to "expand [their] horizons," but to "stay connected to [their] essence"[59] if not in terms of identity? As scholars of dance, how can we explain our implications in different countries, in different languages, in different cultural, intellectual and disciplinary traditions if not in terms of identity?

By wanting to be intellectually post-modern, negating the compartmentalization of everyday life, and for ever "deconstructing" the world of dance, "Dance Studies" end up creating another sort of intellectual imperialism, divorced from dancers' lives and their daily experiences. Rather than rejecting concepts of gender, race, or identity, and repudiating all notion of empiricism because it is linked to positivism and all its problems, I would argue that it is crucial to carry out more empirical research and listen to what dancers have to say about their experiences so as to better understand, through rigorous documentation and analysis, how they find their place in the world and how their experiences of gender, race, identity, or other, are, or are not, invoked in their artistic practices.

It is by listening to the other that we understand ourselves. As an anthropologist I want to reclaim identity and alterity as pertinent concepts to understand the world we live in as well as imagine other worlds. Similarly, because I have not yet found a better way of dealing with the moral aspects of human life I want to reclaim the concept of humanism. Repossessing these notions and researching the identities, values, and ideologies of those engaged in dance, dance scholars will find a rich territory, which will help us understand the postcolonial world dancers inhabit today.

Notes

1 A. Maalouf, *On identity*, trans. B. Bray, London: The Harvill Press, 2000 (2nd edn *In the Name of Identity: Violence and the Need to Belong*, London: Penguin, 2003; orig. edn *Les identités meurtrières*, Paris: Grasset, 1998).

2 A. Rimbaud, 'Letter to Paul Demeny, 15 mai 1871', in A. Rimbaud, *Complete Works*, trans. P. Schmidt, London: Harper Colophon Book, 1975, p. 102 (orig. edn A. Rimbaud, 'Lettre à Paul Demeny', in A. Rimbaud, *Œuvres complètes*,

Maastricht, Paris and Brussel: Stols éditeurs, 1931, p. 43). This theme has inspired numerous artists including choreographer-dancers Annabelle Bonnéry and François Deneulin in the company *Âne à belle*, which used it as the title of one of their productions.

3 A. Schutz, *The Structures of the Life-World*, trans. R. Zaner and T. Engelehardt Jr., London: Heinemann, 1974, p. 67 (1st edn Evanston, IL: Northwestern University Press, 1973).

4 See J. Blacking, 'Man and Fellowman' (Inaugural Lecture at The Queen's University, Belfast on 9 February 1972), *Queen University Belfast New Lectures series*, 1972, no. 71.

5 M. Foucault, 'The Ethics of Care for the Self as a Practice of Freedom', trans. J.D. Gauthier, in J. Bernauer, D. Rasmussen (eds), *The Final Foucault*, Cambridge, MA: The MIT Press, p. 11 (orig. edn in *Philosophy & Social Criticism*, 1987, vol. 12, nos. 2–3, pp. 319–88).

6 Maalouf, *On identity*, pp. 11–12.

7 A. Petrovic, 'Perceptions of ganga', in J. Baily (ed.), *Working with Blacking: the Belfast Years*, special issue of *The World of Music. Journal of the International Institute for Traditional Music*, 1995, vol. 37, no. 2, pp. 60–71.

8 See *Times*, 16 July 1816, p. 1.

9 The ontology/metaphysics of art has an established history within philosophy. See for example the comprehensive essay 'Ontology of Art', in M. Kelly (ed.), *Encyclopedia of Aesthetics*, vol. 3, New York: Oxford University Press, 1998, pp. 389–402, which includes a section (pp. 399–402) by J. Van Camp on the ontology of dance; as well as A. Thomasson, 'The Ontology of Art', in P. Kivy, *The Blackwell Guide to Aesthetics*, Oxford: Blackwell, 2004, pp. 78–92. From a dance perspective the most comprehensive and most recent discussion of dance ontology is undoubtedly: G. McFee, *Understanding Dance*, London: Routledge, 1992. On a more focused level, questions about the creatability of musical works too have been part of lively debates in the philosophy of music and much of the discussion applies to dance too; see for example J. Levinson, 'What a musical work is', in P. Lamarque, S.H. Olsen (eds), *Aesthetics and the Philosophy of Art: The Analytic Tradition*, Oxford: Blackwell, 1990, pp. 78–91 (orig. edn in *Journal of Philosophy*, 1980, vol. 77, no. 1, pp. 5–28) and J. Levinson, *Music, Art and Metaphysics*, Ithaca, NY: Cornell University Press, 1990; P. Kivy, *The Fine Art of Repetition: Essays in the Philosophy of Music*, Cambridge: Cambridge University Press, 1993; J. Dodd, 'Musical works as eternal types', *British Journal of Aesthetics*, 2000, vol. 40, no. 4, pp. 424–40. From a dance perspective it would also be worth mentioning the following texts: A. Armelagos, M. Sirridge, 'The identity crisis in dance', *Journal of Aesthetics and Art Criticism*, 1978, vol. 37, no. 2, pp. 129–40; McFee, 'Was that Swan Lake I saw you at last night?: Dance-Identity and Understanding', *Dance Research*, 1994, vol. 12, no. 1, pp. 21–40. It is worth noting however that when looking at art, analytic philosophers have tended to focus on questions of numerical identity, i.e. the somewhat narrow issue of what makes one performance count (or not) as a performance of a work. There are a few aestheticians, however, who have suggested that philosophy of art should really be interested in a more substantive conception of identity (and not confine themselves to questions of strict numerical identity). See B. Edlund, 'On Scores and Works of Music: Interpretation and Identity', *British Journal of Aesthetics*, 1995, vol. 36, no. 4, pp. 367–80. I thank my colleague Anna Pakes for sharing her knowledge on the subject and for directing my attention to these resources.

10 P. Ricoeur, 'The Task of Hermeneutics', in P. Ricoeur, *Hermeneutics and the Human Sciences*, trans. J.B. Thompson, Cambridge: Cambridge University Press, 1981, p. 44.
11 See for example H. Gardner, *Multiple Intelligences: The Theory in Practice*, London: Basic Books, 1993.
12 See for example D. Williams, *Anthropology and the Dance: Ten Lectures*, Chicago, IL: University of Illinois Press, 2004, pp. 174–5 (1st edn *Ten Lectures on Theories of the Dance*, Metuchen, NJ: Scarecrow Press, 1991).
13 S. Faure, *Apprendre par corps: socio-anthropologie des techniques de danse*, Paris: La Dispute, 2000, pp. 142–62.
14 E. Sapir, 'The Unconscious Patterning of Behavior in Society' (1949), in D.G. Mandelbaum (ed.), *Selected Writings of Edward Sapir*, Berkeley, CA: University of California Press, pp. 544–59 (orig. edn in E.S. Dummer (ed.), *The Unconscious: A Symposium*, New York: Knopf, 1927, pp. 114–42). Emphasis in original.
15 M. Kilani, *Introduction à l'anthropologie*, trans. A. Grau, Lausanne: Payot, 1989, p. 21.
16 Ibid., p. 45.
17 W. Foot Whyte, *Street Corner Society: The Social Structure of an Italian Slum*, Chicago, IL: The University of Chicago Press, 1943. Strictly speaking Whyte belongs to the Chicago School of *Sociology* rather than *Anthropology*, but one could argue that the way he approached his research, using the canonical anthropological method of participant observation, renting a room with an Italian family and participating in their social life for several years makes the work anthropological in its conception.
18 M. Abélès, *Un ethnologue à l'Assemblée*, Paris: Odile Jacob, 2000.
19 C. Bromberger, *Le match de football: ethnologie d'une passion partisane à Marseille*, Naples, Turin and Paris: Éditions des Sciences de l'homme, 1995; C. Bromberger, *Football, la bagatelle la plus sérieuse du monde*, Paris: Bayard, 1998.
20 J. Forero, 'Leaving the Wild and Rather Liking the Change', *The New York Times*, 11 May 2006, late edition, accessed online. I thank my colleague Stacey Prickett for pointing me towards this article.
21 This popular way of seeing symbolic thought as an early and incomplete form of rational modern thought echoes the convictions that the roots of theater are found in rites, that the history of dance follows a continuum from the primitive to the folkloric, to the theatrical, or that art has its roots in religion and is often part of the unquestioned belief system of many western (and non western) dance practitioners and researchers.
22 M. De Certeau, L. Giard, P. Mayol (eds), *The Practice of Everyday Life*, Berkeley, CA: University of California Press, 2002 (orig. edn *L'invention du quotidien*, vol. I, *Art de faire*, Paris: UGE, collection 10/18, 1980).
23 C. Detrez, *La construction sociale du corps*, Paris: Seuil, 2002, p. 90.
24 N. Loujine, 'Character Dance in our Own Time', *In the Name of Auguste Vestris*, virtual publication, 2004, auguste.vestris.free.fr/Essays/Character.html accessed 8 April 2006.
25 Listing in Culturagenda for the company's season at Centre national de la danse, Pantin, in February 2005, www.evene.fr/culture/agenda/la-danse-une-histoire-a-ma-facon-3778.php accessed online 13 April 2006.
26 'CultureKiosque Dance: Reviews', online publication accessed 13 April 2006, available at www.culturekiosque.com/dance/reviews.
27 K. Johnson, 'Rise of the independent dancer', *Dance UK News*, 2003, Winter, p. 15.

28 A. Grau, 'Bharata Natyam, communauté et héritage culturel', in C. Rousier (ed.), *Être ensemble: Figures de la communauté en danse depuis le XXème siècle*, Pantin: Centre national de la danse, 2003, pp. 285–96.
29 É. Durkheim, *Suicide: A Study in Sociology*, trans. J.A. Spaulding and G. Simpson, London: Routledge & Kegan Paul Ltd, 1968, p. 85 (1st Engl. trans. 1952; orig. edn *Le suicide: étude de sociologie*, Paris: Alcan, 1897).
30 Lily Grove was the wife of James Frazer, author of *The Golden Bough*, the monumental study in comparative folklore, magic and religion. This key text on evolutionism came out in twelve volumes between 1906 and 1915, and in abridged version (Frazer and Grove) in 1922. The latter edition was republished regularly throughout the entire twentieth century. The reference to her husband is not meant to negate Grove's worth as a scholar in her own right, but to show how her social environment gave her further access to the British intellectual world of her times.
31 L. Grove, 'The Dances of Savages', in L. Grove, *Dancing*, London: Longmans, Green and Co., 1895, pp. 65–92.
32 See for example R. Garaudy, *Danser sa vie*, Paris: Seuil, 1973 or J.P. Pastori, *La danse des vifs*, Lausanne: L'Age d'Homme, 1977.
33 R. Gallissot, M. Kilani, A. Rivera (eds), *L'imbroglio ethnique: en quatorze mots clés*, Lausanne: Payot, 2000, p. 5 (orig. edn *L'imbroglio etnico: in dieci parole-chiave*, Bari: Dedalo, 1997).
34 Kilani, *L'invention de l'autre: Essais sur le discours anthropologique*, Lausanne: Payot, 1994.
35 L. Wittgenstein, *Philosophical Investigations*, Oxford: Blackwell, 1974.
36 S. Borutti, 'La rappresentazione tra logica ed esperienza: le ragioni filosofiche dell'antropologia di Wittgenstein', in U. Fabietti (ed.), *Il sapere dell'antropologia*, Milano: Mursia, 1993, p. 258.
37 A. Grau, 'Fieldwork, Politics and Power', in T. Buckland (ed.), *Dance in the Field: Theory, Methods and Issues in Dance Ethnography*, London: Macmillan Press, 1999, pp. 163–74.
38 S. Howell, 'Cultural Studies and Social-Anthropology: Contesting or Complementing Discourses?', in S. Nugent, C. Shore (eds), *Anthropology and Cultural Studies*, London: Pluto Press, 1997.
39 See A. Peterson Royce, 'The anthropology of performance and the performance of anthropology', in E. Schultz, R. Lavenda, *Cultural Anthropology: A Perspective on the Human Condition*, New York: West Publishing Company, 1990 (2nd edn), pp. 184–5.
40 N. Badmington (ed.), *Posthumanism*, Hampshire: Palgrave, 2000, p. 149.
41 R. Burt, 'Dance Theory, Sociology, and Aesthetics', *Dance Research Journal*, 2000, vol. 32, no. 1, pp. 125–30.
42 Maalouf, *On identity*, p. 3.
43 S. Jeyasingh, cited in Grau, S. Prickett, 'South Asian Aesthetic Unwrapped: Symposium Report', 2002, online publication available at www.akademi.co.uk/productions.htm.
44 T. Service, 'All for Love', *The Guardian*, 21 November 2002, G2, p. 12.
45 'Sons of SW9: Novelist Alex Wheatle talks to Pendle Harte about music, books and Brixton', *Living South*, 2002, May, pp. 24–5.
46 See A. Grau, *Interculturalisme dans les arts du spectacle*, in J.-Y. Pidoux (ed.), *La danse art du XXème siècle?*, Lausanne: Payot, 1990, pp. 343–55 and 'Intercultural Research in the Performing Arts', *Dance Research Journal*, 1992, vol. 10, no. 2, pp. 3–29.

47 S. Jeyasingh, 'Imaginary Homelands: Creating a New Dance Language', in J. Adshead, C. Jones (eds), *Border Tension: Dance and Discourse. Proceedings of the Fifth Study of Dance Conference*, Guildford: National Resource Centre for Dance, University of Surrey, 1995, p. 193.
48 B. Djamel, 'Moi Djamel B., metteur en scène et acteur d'une nouvelle ethnicité', in A. Boubeker (ed.), *Les mondes de l'ethnicité: la communauté d'expérience des héritiers de l'immigration maghrébine*, Paris: Balland, 2003, p. 289.
49 A. Rivera, *Néoracisme*, in Gallissot, Kilani, Rivera, *L'imbroglio etnique*, p. 209.
50 L.L. Downs, 'If "Woman" Is Just an Empty Category, then Why Am I Afraid to Walk Alone at Night?: Identity Politics Meets the Postmodern Subject', *Comparative Studies in Society and History*, 1993, vol. 35, no. 2, pp. 414–37.
51 F. Flammiger, *Perceptions of Ballet: A Research Study to Investigate Ballet's Identity, its Status as a Creative Genre and its Role and Value as a Technical Training*, M.A. Thesis in Ballet Studies, Roehampton University, 2004.
52 A. Cohen, 'Discriminating Relations: Identity, Boundary and Authenticity', in A. Cohen, *Signifying Identities: Anthropological Perspectives on Boundaries and Contested Values*, London: Routledge, 2000, p. 1.
53 B. Chatterjee, 'Dancing the Colours of White', *Pulse*, 2003, no. 6, p. 8. *Hijras* are transvestites who live as women and who are marginalized in Indian society.
54 L.G. Singh, 'Desperately Seeking Shakuntala . . . er, Sharon?', *Pulse*, 2003, no. 6, p. 20.
55 Grau, 'Bharata natyam, communauté et héritage culturel'.
56 Singh, 'Desperately Seeking Shakuntala . . . er, Sharon?', p. 19.
57 F. Yeoh, personal comment shared during a course at Roehampton University, 2003.
58 Cohen, 'Discriminating Relations', p. 5.
59 Johnson, 'Rise of the independent dancer', p. 14.

12 Resistant identities

Anderson and Ruckert

Ramsay Burt

This essay investigates the relationship between innovative dance performance and some of the problematics of the corporeal nature of identity and identification. It does so through an examination of the Berlin-based choreographer Felix Ruckert's deconstruction of the performer–audience relationship, and Lea Anderson's uncanny uses of ironic citations that disrupt the normal and familiar. Focusing on Ruckert's *Hautnah* and Anderson's two pieces based on the drawings of Egon Schiele, it argues that dance performances which re-stage scenes of spatial projection and identification can sometimes discover inconsistencies and contradictions within the processes of identity formation. By doing so it thus draws attention to those aspects of experience and possibilities for identification that elude the compulsion to conform with the visible, the normative, and the same. It argues that these dance works have adopted strategies which deliberately draw attention to these aspects of experience in order to trouble and disturb normalizing discourses and processes and thus create new spaces for resistant or alternative identities.

While Anderson and Ruckert would have been aware of issues concerning identity and identification when they made these works, this was not their primary concern. To appreciate this, it is useful to position these pieces in the context of the changing relationship between cultural production and the politics of identity. Initiated in the aftermath of 1968 by the Black, women's and gay liberation movements, identity politics had become, by the 1980s, a motivating factor for many artists who used the privileged spaces of cultural production to give visibility to identities that were marginal to mainstream norms: hence the paintings of Judy Chicago, the photographs of Robert Mapplethorpe, the films of Yvonne Rainer and Isaac Julien, and, in dance, works by Emilyn Claid, Michael Clark, Bill T. Jones, and Lloyd Newson. Accompanying these developments were essays and reviews by writers who used varying combinations of feminist, Black, queer, and lesbian politics to generate the intellectual climate for the reception of these kinds of works. In doing so, they proposed identitarian readings of works by other artists who did not themselves directly associate their work with these particular social and political movements. Anderson's Schiele pieces and Ruckert's *Hautnah*, however, belong to a moment when this identity politics was already in decline.

To speak of this decline of the identity politics of the 1970s and 1980s is not to say that identity itself ceased to be an issue. The fact that identities are always fluid and continually in process of changing is an inevitable limitation on a politics that claims allegiance from individuals on the basis of a relatively fixed notion of identity. Furthermore, radical challenges to the status quo are always relatively transient and unstable. As Simon Critchley has pointed out: "What is so troubling about contemporary capitalism to many on the Left is its extraordinary hybridizing energy, its ability to assume new forms, to hegemonize itself, to recuperate what was originally intended as opposition and to sell it as a commodity, to renew and propagate itself not out of any reactive gestures but rather out of a cheerfully superficial affirmativeness."[1] As capitalism in its current globalized form has shifted from a Fordist economy of production into a post-Fordist economy of consumption, it has increasingly adopted approaches that recuperate the strategies from post-1968 liberation movements. Using focus groups and sophisticated marketing techniques, products have been promoted by exploiting an appeal to the kinds of individual aspirations and desires that were developed within these liberation movements. Although globalized culture seems to offer endless freedoms for creative self-invention, not everyone has equal access to these, and increasingly standardized and normalized modes of thinking and perception render possibilities for conceiving alternatives largely invisible and imperceptible. Individual agency is further circumscribed by the way that one is always already trapped within these power relations so that opposition or resistance can only come from inside them.

Edward Said has suggested that globalizing processes have had largely conservative effects on individuals' sense of their identities: "one way to defend yourself against the sense of an all-encompassing global atmosphere – represented by American to most people – is to return to comfortable symbols of the past."[2] "There is more of a concentration today on the affirmation of identity, on the need for roots, on the values of one's culture, and one's sense of belonging."[3] I shall argue that these pieces by Anderson and Ruckert do precisely the opposite. Whereas Said has suggested that many people have felt a need to reaffirm a sense of identity – a sameness that they share with others through shared cultural values – these dance pieces have problematized notions of identity. They have questioned the normativity of some cultural values and made the comfortable symbols of the past seem uncanny and disturbing. Rather than reacting against globalization in the way that Said describes through trying to get back to how things used to be (or to how people imagine they used to be), avant-garde dance works keep open possibilities for new and unpredictable experiences. Furthermore they suggest that instead of only identifying with sameness, there is a need not only to accept differences that may be visible but also to acknowledge the possibility of differences that for whatever reason are currently invisible but may not always be imperceptible.

A 1910 pencil drawing, *Schiele, Drawing a Nude Model in Front of a Mirror* exemplifies what is at stake within these identificatory processes. In this the artist, clothed, sits on a chair with a sketch pad across his knees while a nude, boyish, female model stands boldly in front of him, both of them facing the mirror. Reading the drawing from left to right, one sees first the comparatively small, reflected figure of the artist, frowning as he looks at his subject. In front and to the right of the artist's reflection, slightly obscuring it, the reflected model stands at a slight angle to the mirror, her fingers resting provocatively on her pelvis as she stares disturbingly out of the mirror at herself as if unaware of the figure close behind her. All the left side of the drawing is filled by the much larger back of the model, across which the viewer's eye is led to the reflections. The formal relationship between the model and her reflection prompts the viewer to place her or himself within the scene depicted, completing its conceptual symmetry by recognizing their position in front of the drawing as that which Schiele initially occupied. To do so is to put one's own awareness of one's bodily presence into a relationship with the bodies that are evoked by Schiele's taut pencil lines. But to do so is to enter an intimate, yet uncannily absent scene marked by a lack of any emotional current between the man and woman in it, despite their physical proximity. The drawing thus enacts a dialectic through attracting but at the same time disturbing the viewer, inviting identification but at the same time inhibiting it. It is not therefore just an examination of the relationship between artist and model but also of that between artist, model, and viewer in a manner that involves, in a complicated way, the viewer's own sense of their embodied presence as they look. The relationship between dancer and spectator within the moment of performance also enacts this dialectic, and it is this which is the subject of this essay. On a theoretical level, it chiefly investigates this through the phenomenological account of experience that Maurice Merleau-Ponty developed in his later writings. Although Merleau-Ponty was almost entirely concerned with the nature of individual experience, I shall reappraise some of his proposals in the light of recent philosophical discussions of the ethics of interpersonal relationships especially those implicit within the relationship between dancer and spectator.

Hautnah

I go upstairs to a waiting room where I meet the dancer, Catherine Jodoin, and agree a fee with her. On payment, she takes me up another floor and leads me through a labyrinth of screens behind which other dancers are performing their solos. Her small cubicle has a carpet that continues up the wall on one side. There are two lights at floor level, a red velvet chair, and on the carpet a pair of heavy, stack heeled boots and a thick, baggy cardigan. Jodoin has long, reddish hair and wears velvet trousers and a long-sleeved red and purple T-shirt. Her solo starts with sharp, precise gestures as she crouches on the carpet stretching her hands out toward a screen and staring at them. Then she gets up and comes to me. I am sitting on the chair with legs crossed and hands folded in my lap. Moving my leg and putting my hands by my side, she hugs my leg and places my arm round her shoulder. Then she gets me to my feet and we dance together for a while (though I respond rather woodenly, unsure exactly what I am supposed to do). At one point she places my hands on either side of her head and makes me press it hard. At another she parts my legs and crawls through them from behind me, squatting in front of me on all fours. Our "duet" ends when she does some movements that are much faster and more precise – a standing version of the opening sequence crouching on the floor. She dances on her own, ending with a more gestural, mimetic sequence, covering her eye then her mouth, then one hand closing over the fingers of her other hand. She puts on her boots and cardigan, hiding her face inside its high, zipped collar, and lays down very still. I speculate whether she is acting dead. Then she sits up, looks expectantly at me, says "Adieu" and smiles. This is my memory of a performance of Ruckert's *Hautnah.*

Having started with the invisible mirror in Schiele's drawing, I want to introduce two more mirrors, one psychoanalytic, the other phenomenological. These suggest what is problematic about the kinds of corporeal identifications that conventional dance performance invites and works like *Hautnah* disrupt. Jacques Lacan's mirror stage[4] describes a moment in an infant's development. Dependent on a primary care-giver because inadequately able to control what seems to be a fragmented bodily self, the infant, catching sight of itself in a mirror, imagines their image to be more complete and powerful than itself. Lacan describes a process that involves a spatial projection from inside one's subjective awareness of one's own body out onto another who is situated within mirrored and hence virtual space. The infant thus becomes aware of space outside itself and makes what Lacan calls an inverted projection from its sense of its own turbulent and uncontrollable movements onto a desire to become like and mimic the disturbingly powerful double in the mirror. The infant misrecognizes their own image, imagining an ideal with which reality can never compete. Events in later life that recall the resulting disappointment have the potential to bring back repressed memories of a sense of turbulence and fragmentation. There is a growing body of Lacanian criticism by Elizabeth Bronfen, Parveen Adams, Slavoj Žižek, and others that has identified images or themes in films, visual art, and literary texts which have the power to recall otherwise repressed, unconscious memories of such developmental traumas. Few dance scholars have so far explored these kinds of approaches. One could argue that some experimental dance performances have the power to bring back disturbing developmental memories that more conventional dance works do not evoke. Thus sitting in a theater watching highly trained and uniquely expressive dancers through the mirror of the proscenium arch can sometimes reassure one that wholeness and completeness are attainable. It is not, however, my intention to pursue this direction here. What interests me in this account of the mirror stage is the cognitive processes and the kind of mimicry that Lacan has described.

Hautnah systematically robbed one of the safe distance between auditorium and stage. By making one negotiate a price for the performance with the dancer and then hand over the money, the piece made one uncomfortably aware of how one's desire as a consumer had become implicated in a libidinal economy. On one level this aspect of the piece provocatively alluded to a transaction between a prostitute and client, one that is not normally associated with contemporary dance performance. The box office is generally the first port of call in a theater, has a fixed tariff, and seems entirely separate from the dancer. In *Hautnah* one usually had to wait one's turn downstairs for the dancer of one's choice – each one performed a different solo. Going upstairs was already going inside, and going up a second floor was going in even deeper. Then, in the cubicle itself, while the chair might have promised a clear distinction between dancer and watcher, this was almost immediately disrupted as Jodoin embraced and then drew one into the dance. I could detect garlic and nicotine on her breath and worried about how I myself might smell to her. It would be a mistake, however, to interpret this intimacy literally as a re-enactment of the prostitute–client relationship. First, to do so would be to ignore other aspects of the piece that clearly had nothing to do with the sex industries. Second, I suggest that any sexual aspects of the piece were used strategically to unsettle the spectator–participant, stop her or him viewing the piece in the kind of habitual manner usually adopted in dance performance, and to create a heightened physical sensitivity toward the movement material performed.

If for Lacan identification is a process of projection into a rarefied, virtual space the other side of the mirror, then *Hautnah* took away the mirror. Merleau-Ponty has proposed that one understands another's body in relation to one's own bodily schema. This suggests that the schemas that we use to make sense of a dancer's movements are the basis for a kind of corporeal identification between audience and performer. In Lacan's account, it seems to be through looking that the infant discovers their ideal other. Although vision is generally privileged over other modes of perception – saying "I see" is synonymous with saying "I know" – visual perception alone cannot account for what we think we know about another's movements. Vision is a distant sense in comparison with touch and smell, which operate closer to oneself. It is this feeling of being distant that *Hautnah* disrupted, but even in a conventional dance performance vision alone cannot be used to comprehend dance movement. In his account of the phenomenology of perception, Merleau-Ponty proposed that individual senses do not work in isolation from one another but that our perception is formed through their interdependence and chiasmic intertwining. Referring to this idea of the chiasm, Michel Bernard has suggested that as audience members we experience dance with a listening eye, in that we see dance in depth and watch it unfold in time just as the ear distinguishes sounds from one another by placing them in space and noting their temporal sequence. Bernard writes: "When one says 'the eye listens,' there is an investment of this temporality of the ear through my way of seeing. My glance finds itself crossed by a mode that transforms the space I have in front of me, into a temporalized space in the manner of sound. My glance produces a simulacrum, a fiction constituted by the play of the specificity of sound material."[5] Here Bernard, like Merleau-Ponty, finds himself chiasmically involved with space so that his glance is changed by the way the dance moves around it through time.

Within the perceptual continuum of flesh that Merleau-Ponty so intensely and beautifully described in his last essays, the body is a thing among things. If the body touches these things and sees them, Merleau-Ponty wrote, "this is because being of their family, itself visible and tangible, it uses its own being as a means to participate in theirs."[6] It is surely this sense of immersion within an experiential continuum that pieces like *Hautnah* sought to create. Within them one experiences what Merleau-Ponty called the reversibility of experience: "Not to see in the outside as the others see it, the contours of a body one inhabits, but especially to be seen by the outside, to exist within it, to emigrate into it, to be seduced, captivated, alienated by the phantom, so that the seer and the visible reciprocate one another and we no longer know which sees and which is seen."[7] Throughout my brief time with Jodoin during *Hautnah* I felt she was observing and evaluating me as much as I was doing the same for her. Indeed Ruckert later confirmed that the dancer uses their observations and responses to the participant to make each performance uniquely personalized. In order to determine the limits of this reversibility I turn to Merleau-Ponty and thus to my second mirror. Merleau-Ponty pointed out that whereas one can see an object or another person and locate them in relation to oneself, one cannot see oneself in the same way. "I am always," he wrote, "on the same side of my body; it presents itself to me in one invariable perspective."[8]

Feminists and others have criticized Merleau-Ponty's phenomenology for the way it universalizes experience[9]: his theory claims to speak for all bodies, irrespective of differences of culture, race, gender, and other components of identity. He provided tools with which to articulate the modes of embodying an existential relation to the world through sameness and differences that are both visible and invisible, but not for understanding how notions of universality can lead to a fear of visible differences that can in turn be used as a basis for discrimination. Merleau-Ponty analyzed the body as a thing among a family of things rather than investigating how embodied beings participate within society. Yet the mirror he described could become a way of investigating how dance stages the individual's relation to others. Looking at oneself in the mirror one is aware not only of the visible but also of what remains invisible to oneself about oneself. Perceiving the dancing body of another through the mirror of the proscenium arch, one understands the other's physical experience by identifying what one knows from one's own real and imagined experience. But one also recognizes the other as a person like and unlike oneself. One sees someone who, when they look in the mirror, knows there are certain things about themselves they cannot see. The experiential continuum is made up of both the visible and the invisible. Through its deconstruction of the performer–audience relationship, *Hautnah* made one aware of the affective power of some of these invisible differences.

Confronting the infinite difference that the other represents, as Emmanuel Lévinas pointed out, is always a question of ethics, a matter of respecting and bearing witness to the rights and obligations one owes to others and on which human sociality depends. Zygmunt Bauman has proposed a telling and useful analysis of the ways in which increasing globalization creates a disturbingly liquid economy within which the circulation of goods, services, and identities leads to the weakening of this sociality. For an individual to survive in the globalized job market, he argues, one needs to avoid being unduly conservative: one should refrain "from habitualizing to any particular bed, be mobile and perpetually at hand. To prove that one is the genuine article, one needs to be flexible, always at a beck and call, ready to start anew rather than conform and stick to the form once it has been taken."[10] We live in a mobile culture with our mobile telephones so that, as Bauman points out, "You stay connected even though you are constantly on the move, and though the invisible senders and recipients of messages move as well, all following their own trajectories." "Nowhere," he suggests is "the space without a mobile, with a mobile out of range, or a mobile with a flat battery."[11] The resulting new mobile relationships, he argues, mimic the consumer choices we make: "There is always," he points out, "the possibility of blaming choice, rather than an inability to live up to the opportunities it offered, for the failure of the anticipated bliss to materialize. There is always a chance to abandon the road along which fulfillment was sought and to start again – even, if the prospectus looks attractive, from scratch."[12] What Bauman calls liquid modern times seem therefore to loosen the responsibilities and obligations that underlie ethical commitments. Contemporary dance performance is in an ambivalent position, implicated within this economy but taking a critical stance toward it. In *Hautnah*, for example, the ease with which one entered an intimate relationship with a dancer uncannily mimicked the liquid sociality that Bauman describes. This might seem to come at a high ethical cost. However, its very uncanniness, its emphasis on the invisible, and its deconstruction of normative conventions gave it an alternative status, the position which experimental work claims as a site from which to reflect critically on its social context.

The Featherstonehaughs Draw on the Sketchbooks of Egon Schiele and *The Lost Dances of Egon Schiele*

Two recent works by Anderson similarly repeated the forms of our liquid modern times in ways that trouble the seeming normality of the kinds of identifications circulating within them. In 1998, she made a 60-minute live performance with her all-male dance company The Featherstonehaughs, called *The Featherstonehaughs Draw on the Sketchbooks of Egon Schiele*. In 2000, Anderson and the six Featherstonehaughs worked with director Kevin McKiernan to make a ten-minute dance film for BBC television called *The Lost Dances of Egon Schiele*. This was not a filmed record of the stage work but a reinterpretation of some of its themes through rearranged and newly choreographed movement material that took advantage of aesthetic possibilities offered by film. Both works referred to Schiele's drawings and paintings. The Featherstonehaughs wore costumes and heavy makeup which created the illusion that they were animated versions

Figure 16 The Featherstonehaughs Draw on the Sketchbooks of Egon Schiele, by Lea Anderson (1998). © Photo by Lea Anderson. Permission kindly granted by Lea Anderson.

of works by Schiele. Their faces, the suits that they wore at the beginning and end of the pieces, and the tight, all-in-one body suits that they wore during the central sections were hand painted with short, acid-colored marks that resembled Schiele's harsh, dry brush strokes in oil paint or gouache (Figure 16).

There is a highly idiosyncratic and recognizable way in which people seem to move within Schiele's self portraits, double portraits, and drawings of female nudes and couples. The recognizable patterns within the kinds of gestures and postures that Schiele and his models take up in these works provided Anderson and the dancers with a source of material which they closely worked on and interpreted as they created their choreography. The resulting movement style animated the distinctive distortions in Schiele's work which themselves arise from the way his drawings and paintings compress bodily posture within a narrow, frieze-like, pictorial space. Bodies in Schiele's work are often foreshortened through close observation, or looked down upon so that the picture plane is severely flattened. In putting this space on stage, the choreography was full of hunched shoulders, craned necks, awkwardly twisted arms, and hands displaying curiously separated fingers. Hampered by the need to maintain these awkward details, the dancers seemed precariously unstable as they picked their way along their carefully defined pathways. Anderson's two works drew attention to the artificiality of the scenes Schiele depicted. As spectators, it was through our own knowledge and experience of embodiment that we appreciated the difficulties that the performance of such movements must entail, but in doing so we recognized their dissimilarity from our ordinary, everyday experience. These difficulties were central to the way in which the film and live performance distanced the viewer. Furthermore, the strangeness of the personas performed by the dancers and the impersonality of their encounters with one another deterred the spectator from making any empathetic identification with them, and this distancing strategy troubled normative processes of identification.

Internationally, Schiele is probably the best-known Austrian painter, and his images circulate widely in books, postcards, posters, and reproductions. Anderson's Schiele pieces depend upon the familiarity that the market has produced and on which their own marketability in part depends. Nevertheless, because Anderson specifically chose key works by Schiele that themselves staged processes of identification, the resulting dance pieces exploited inconsistencies and contradictions within these processes and were thus able to suggest possibilities for resistant identities. Initially Anderson wanted to call the dance film *Mirrorman* because of a 1914 photograph of Schiele taking up a characteristic pose in front of a mirror. Mirrors were of course a recurring subject in Schiele's works, particularly where he depicted himself with others as he did, for example, in the pencil drawing discussed at the beginning of this paper. Anderson involved spectators of her dance in complicated ways that directly cited these pictures. At one moment in both the dance film and live performance, the Featherstonehaughs posed as life models in positions that resembled Schiele's drawings of his own nude male body. Drosten Madden's musical score at this point included the scratchy sound of a stick of charcoal drawing on a large sheet of drawing paper. During this section, two men in suits walked on at the back to sit down and gaze at these models, reflecting back to the audience their own gazes in a way that replicated the complex chains of gazes and identifications brought into play in Schiele's 1910 pencil drawing. In both the film and the live performance there are moments when two dancers move together in a physically intimate yet emotionally absent way, drawing on imagery from Schiele's double portraits. Through the use of close-up shots in the film, this sequence makes the viewer aware that while they look at the screen, the dancers are looking intently back at them as if they are looking at their own mirror images reflected in the camera's lens. But they seem unable to recognize themselves beneath their grotesque masks of heavy makeup. Identification with the dancers through spatial projection is thus both invited and repelled in a dialectic of sameness and difference.

The dance film starts and finishes with sequences based not on Schiele's drawings but on the 1914 photograph of him before a mirror. First two parallel hands, their backs facing each other, their fingers tautly extended, enter the frame on the left, as if the farther hand is a reflection of the nearer one. The arms and then heads and upper bodies follow these onto the screen, and it is as if one were looking over the shoulder of the nearer dancer at his reflection in a mirror. Both dancers raise their arms in unison to join above the head. Then both turn their heads as if looking toward one another in the mirror, but break the illusion by both turning to stare, somewhat complicitously at the camera and viewer. From being mirror reflections they become doppelgangers or clones. At the end of the film the same sequence takes place in reverse. The uncanny clones turn back into their slightly less disturbing mirror images and retreat out of the frame leaving their hands till last. Throughout both the film and live performance, each of the six Featherstonehaughs took the same role, "were" Schiele. Rather than reassuring spectators that wholeness and completeness are attainable, these Schieles recall the traumatic realization that reality always fails to live up to a fantasmatic ideal. For the Featherstonehaughs, the process of performing, of becoming Schiele, was one of becoming less like themselves, thus in effect becoming invisible. One understands the Featherstonehaughs's mirrored bodies through mapping the body of the nearer dancer onto the farther one, noting their reflected symmetry in a way that repeats the process through which one uses a schema derived from one's own embodied experience to understand that of another. Or one tries to understand it, because the more the two dancers try to become like each other being Schiele, the more one becomes aware of elements and qualities, both visible and invisible, that aren't quite right but remain irreducibly different. As I pointed out when discussing *Hautnah*, invisible differences can exert an affective power. When another and yet another Featherstonehaugh is introduced, each performing the same role, their individual differences become increasingly disturbing and uncanny. Anderson's two Schiele pieces engaged one in what seemed to be a straightforward, familiar succession of images from a popular, recognizable source, only to make one aware that it was not quite so simple. In doing so they made one aware of the necessity of recognizing the possibility that others may not be quite the same as oneself. Underlying this, I suggest, the pieces used a failure to become the same to investigate the right to be different and in doing so reminded one of one's ethical obligation to respect that right.

Conclusion

I began this paper with an account of the complicated interweavings of gazes and spatial relationships in Schiele's 1910 drawing of himself with a nude model in front of a mirror. The voyeurism in this drawing is troubled by the physical intimacy of the spatial relationship between the artist and the object of his gaze; it is further troubled by the fact that both are also looking at their own mirror images and thus involved in the kinds of psychological and phenomenological processes of projection and identification that Lacan and Merleau-Ponty described. I have demonstrated that Anderson's Schiele pieces performatively re-staged the complicated and troubling relationships mapped out in this drawing. These were also re-staged in a different way in *Hautnah* where the spectator–participant found themselves sitting on a chair in a relationship with a dancer that was both disturbingly intimate and yet demonstrably inhibited. Like the drawing, both *Hautnah* and Anderson's Schiele pieces involved the spectator's sense of their embodied presence as they looked. If identity is grounded in a dialectic of sameness and difference, both pieces uncannily defamiliarized normative assumptions about sameness. The kind of spatial identification that Lacan discussed involved mimicry. In this paper I have interpreted this in a socio-political way. *Hautnah* and Anderson's Schiele pieces, I have argued, mimicked the liquid sociality of our globalized times in ironic or uncanny ways in order to remind us of things we are in danger of forgetting. Their value lies in the way they evoke the affective power of what is otherwise invisible in order to remind us of ethical responsibilities and obligations that we cannot afford not to respect.

Notes

1 S. Critchley, *Ethics-Politics-Subjectivity*, London: Verso, 1999, p. 172.
2 D. Barenboim, E. Said, *Parallels and Paradoxes: Explorations in Music and Society*, London: Bloomsbury, 2004, p. 12.
3 Ibid., p. 11.
4 See J. Lacan, 'Le stade du miroir comme formateur de la fonction du Je', *Revue française de psychanalyse*, 1949, vol. 13, no. 4, pp. 449–55.
5 M. Bernard, 'Sens et fiction, ou les effets étranges de trois chiasmes sensoriels', *Nouvelles de danse*, 1993, no. 17, pp. 62–3.
6 M. Merleau-Ponty, *The Visible and the Invisible*, Evanston, IL: Northwestern University Press, 1968 (orig. edn *Le visible et l'invisible*, Paris: Gallimard, 1964), p. 137.
7 Ibid., p. 139.

8 Ibid., p. 148.
9 See for example E. Grosz, *Volatile Bodies: Towards a Corporeal Feminism*, Bloomington, IN: Indiana University Press, 1994, pp. 103–11.
10 Z. Bauman, K. Tester, *Conversations with Zygmunt Bauman*, Cambridge: Polity Press, 2001, p. 90.
11 Z. Baumann, *Liquid Love*, Cambridge: Polity Press, 2003, p. 59.
12 Ibid., p. 55.

13 Donald Byrd

Re/making "beauty"

Thomas F. DeFrantz

What are the terms of "beauty" as an action that may be achieved in dance? How do African-American artists approach the performance of "beauty?" In a preliminary consideration of these questions, this paper offers a case-study analysis of two works by choreographer Donald Byrd: *The Harlem Nutcracker* (1996), a revision of the Petipa–Ivanov ballet set to Duke Ellington's swing adaptation of Tchaikovsky's score, and *Life Situations: Daydreams on Giselle* (1995), a postmodern version of the quintessential Romantic ballet. Working through prisms of feminist and Africanist aesthetic theory, I suggest strategies to critique identity formation within dance performance as a function of aggressive irony, inversion, and the triumph of technical precision. Byrd's choreography constructs "beauty" as a function of black Atlantic[1] performance practice, as an act that may be socially progressive in its intentions, and an action that may hold material consequences for its performers and audiences.

Certainly "beauty" may be considered a constituent element of ethnic identity for all populations. In addition, "beauty" attracts ideological qualities that may be of exceptional value to minoritarian artists who work to construct social solidarity around issues of ethnic identity. Through particular choreographies, African-American dancers confirm markers of identity consistent with approaches to social formations that include the production of "beauty."

In order to construct an argument about African-American identity as it may be enabled through choreography, we must first review the history of African-American dance, and the emergence of black Atlantic theory. As Africans arrived in the United States via the Atlantic slave trade, music and dance remained foundational practices within emergent African-American cultures. An expansive range of performance practices connected African people in the new world, who found themselves living in diaspora, as they responded to the harshness of slavery and the potential of modern, hybridized life. For example, dances that echoed various spiritual practices became ring shouts[2] as well as cakewalks and aspects of Congo Square celebrations in New Orleans. Eventually, a wide array of dance emerged with a distinctly African-American ethos; dances tied by aspects of performance as well as social and situational contexts for dance.

African-Americans entered the concert dance arena in the United States in the 1930s. Recent scholarship indicates that while in the minority, African-American artists studied and performed concert dance alongside European Americans in the early part of the twentieth century.[3] Rampant racism limited the involvement of black Americans in artistic performance. By the 1940s, social tides turned, and African-American innovation in music and social dance appreciably influenced emergent modernist traditions, especially in the work of modern choreographers Katherine Dunham, Helen Tamiris, and ballet master George Balanchine.[4] Even as choreographers referred to these African-American dance practices as well as physical aspects of African-American corporeal identity in their creations, racist configurations regularly referred to black Americans as "unattractive" and "ugly" in everyday discourses.

Social upheavals in the 1960s allowed a reclamation of Africanist aesthetic practices in the United States, especially in the rise of neo-African dance forms studied on college campuses and in community centers nationwide. As civil rights legislation took effect, "Black is Beautiful" became a slogan of empowerment and ethnic destiny for millions of African-Americans who had been long stigmatized by race. Enlivened by the loosening of colonialist binds that placed ballet and classical arts above other performance traditions, African-Americans began to explore various Africanist popular music and dance traditions as worthwhile documents of American corporeal history. Black social dances and Africanist approaches to American concert performance began to take their place in the concert dance arena, most notably in works by choreographers including Alvin Ailey, Talley Beatty, Eleo Pomare, and Dianne McIntyre.

By the 1980s, cultural historians began to connect African diasporic performance traditions in academic work known as black Atlantic theory. This theory presumes an ontology of performance that reflects Africanist aesthetic and social concerns.[5] Although the majority of scholars creating this theory were British, their work inspired vigorous conversation in the American academy that has continued in the twenty-first century. Concerned largely with the articulation of modernity that precluded an African ontology of any import, these scholars exposed an epistemological fault line wherein "it is unproblematically assumed that the modernist consciousness which really matters belonged to Europe rather than to its formerly imperial and colonial subjects."[6] The "problem" with modernism as it had been conceived had to do with the place of black consciousness within it. According to leading British cultural theorist Paul Gilroy, modernism, as it had been largely understood in the realm of cultural studies, offered a stark binary in which Africans figured either peripherally, along the margins, or "as the repressed, primitive counterpart to an undifferentiated modernist consciousness."[7]

Black Atlantic theory sought to connect markers of cultural formation across various African diasporas, to suggest commonalities of corporeal practices that could accommodate shifts in idiom, geography, historical moment, and political sensibility. In terms of performance, black Atlantic theory offers a way to consider aesthetic commonalities in relationship to political circumstances surrounding black life and black identities in diaspora. This formulation of black corporeality holds an implicit concern with the material circumstances of black identity and its key features, which include the construction of "beauty."

Where is "beauty" in African-American identity?

Surely identity, like performance, may be engaged by individuals as a moving target: contingent, porous, at times transparent or inconsequential. But all identities are not equivalent, and racial identities, in particular, support political narratives that hold material consequences for their inhabitants. Racial identities foreground historic convergences of power dynamics between groups of people. For example, for many North Americans a "black American" racial identity might suggest corporeal affiliation with the slave trade as well as various historical narratives of ancestral trauma, material lack, and political disenfranchisement. In a North American context, these assumptions correspond to visible black identity. As with gender, the visibility of race adds an overlay of presumptions and expectations that charge relationships, and accord special significance to whose identity is in question when, where, and by whom.

Because we bother to learn to see "black," we learn to see it first as a racial identity, and only thereafter as a social or political condition. As art historian Richard Powell notes, blackness is less a porous and changeable identity marker of skin tone than "a metaphor for struggles against economic exploitation and cultural domination."[8] For most black people, "black" is a visible racialized identity, seldom unmoored from social and political stigmas of, at least, minority status and historically contingent material lack. It may be argued that race no longer constructs an essentialized, totalizing or singular identity, but its contingencies emerge at particular moments with particular consequences for many, including the many African-Americans involved in concert dance.

But black identity is by no means solely a catch-all metaphor for the miseries of exploitation and social oppression. In his 1993 study of black Atlantic cultural formations, Gilroy proposed that black identity is "lived as a coherent (if not always stable) experiential sense of self. Though it is often felt to be natural and spontaneous, it remains the outcome of practical activity: language, gesture, bodily significations, desires."[9] Gilroy's work from this era details a global circulation of black diasporan identities rooted simultaneously in social forces exerted on black people, as well as, significantly, generative actions performed by black people. Ten years later, his articulation of a black Atlantic tradition as "an irreducibly modern, ex-centric, unstable, and asymmetrical cultural ensemble" resounds for dance theorists working on Africanist performance practice.[10]

Gilroy suggests contingencies of black identity that are ambivalent: simultaneously reductive and productive in terms of performance. As a reductive marker, this seemingly-coherent black identity leads quickly to stereotype. The recognition of blackness by audiences sets in motion a reductive chain of significations that overwhelms performance, and can only be overcome by the dancer's force of will and technical elan. In its pro-ductive force, visible black identity can predict heightened mastery in "recognizably black" dance formats: jazz dance, hip hop, African dance, tap dance, and the like. Visible blackness may also predict "recognizably black" socio-political narratives of racial and gender oppression or economic and cultural domination. Ultimately, this productive black identity becomes similar to the stereotype as it cannibalistically reproduces itself as a signifier of an impossible fetish. To paraphrase Homi Bhabha, black identity becomes recognized by its eternal ambivalence as an object of colonial discourse.[11]

A discussion of how black identity might become manifest in dance performance will benefit from a consideration of how identity is perceived. The key concept here is not a flexible but recognizable "black identity" present in dance produced by black people in performance, but rather the act of recognition that allows blackness to become visible. This act of recognition coheres black identity to dancers in a flash of the visible for some and a flash of the spirit for others. Black identity here is born of action on the part of both the dancer and the audience member; for some its currency is visual recognition, while for others its presence arrives in something of Gilroy's "practical activities" of gesture, bodily significations, and desires. I want to focus now on this latter action of recognition, as a currency passed between productive gestural efforts by the dancer that are received as spiritually effective by its audience.

By invoking the spirit here, I do not make reference to the religious or the sentimental, even if we may all have witnessed performances by black

Americans that refer to either or both of these categories. We may think of Ailey's *Revelations* as a quintessential example of this mode of work, as Ailey's dance coheres visible blackness to both North American slavery and social disenfranchisement as well as a non-confrontational, fundamentalist portrayal of historical black American religious practice. Rather, I make reference to the contingent presences of immaterial, animating, vital forces that allow human beings to recognize incorporeal actions. The spirit "flashes" in Africanist performance to momentarily confirm incorporeal action enabled by the performance, and not bounded by the performer's body. In the flash of the spirit we find what African art historian Robert Farris Thompson has described the motivating feature of successful Africanist performance.[12]

"Successful" performance here emerges in the communal recognition of excellence in action that culminates, at times, in a flash of the spirit. Performance "succeeds" as it is recognized to be Africanist through the enlivening flash of the spirit; this flash marks the performance in terms of its efficacy and its durability. Effectiveness of performance may be monitored by gathered audiences and performers through the recognized engagement with Africanist aesthetics and the flash of the spirit; performance that does not arrive at both aesthetic excellence and the intermittent or singular flash of the spirit will not likely be considered either successful or Africanist. The flash of the spirit constitutes a component aspect of performance engaged by African diaspora artists trained to engage its particular "improvisatory drive and brilliance."[13]

I intend to expand Thompson's paradigm of successful performance to encompass the revelation of "beauty." "Beauty" here is an action achieved through a parity of honesty of intention and accuracy of gesture. In this flash of the spirit, we may experience the contingent creation of "beauty," recognized as an animated black identity, revealed through dance performance.

Beauty through Africanist aesthetics

To be clear, I intend to arrive at an articulation of "beauty" as an action recognized in dance by audiences through an engagement with Africanist aesthetics. I am inspired by Gilroy's argument that the "intensity of the slave experience" marked out blacks as the first truly modern people, "handling in the nineteenth-century dilemmas and difficulties which would only become the substance of everyday life [in Europe] – for others – a century later."[14] One of those dilemmas involves the enunciation of "beauty" and its nature as a necessary aspect of everyday life in late-capitalist societies. From at least the nineteenth century forward,

African-Americans engaged hybrid constructions of group and individual identity that allowed "beauty" to flourish in everyday traditions of song, dance, language, gesture, bodily signification, and desires. These traditions involved the effective transmission of information through action performed accurately, purposefully, and in the service of communication. As stated above, an ability to act "in the spirit" provided the overarching mark of achievement of Africanist aesthetic balance. This action became manifest as an ability to temporarily blur the boundaries of everyday communication, and incarnate the liminal space at the edge of consciousness; to release the flash of immaterial spirit into the space of performance. African-Americans engaged this action with great regularity in performances of religion, social ritual, and artistic expression.

"Beauty," a necessary component of any ethnic group's self-awareness, surely became manifest in various guises for African-Americans, including within the contexts of dance performance. But "beauty," as a productive aspect of African-American performance practice, seldom arrived in any discourses of the West. Surely "beauty" exists as a contingent possibility for African-Americans that may be accessed through dance performance. I propose to discuss beauty in this paradigm as an action that may be released by way of successful Africanist performance, with that "success" tied to Africanist aesthetics and the "flash of the spirit." To reiterate my main points, black identity is contingent, and its recognition cannot be based solely on the visual appearance of blackness. For audiences who appreciate Africanist artistry, "beauty" is produced in the sensorial recognition of dance gesture that enables a flash of the spirit.

"Beauty" as sensation, not visible identity

To characterize beauty as an action recognized in dance performance, we must move beyond the realm of the visual as the dominant signifier of aesthetic meaning. An Africanist aesthetic achievement of "beauty," as I explore it here, refers to the visual as only an aspect of the sensorial. To recognize "black beauty" in motion, we engage intuition born of an awareness of social and political circumstance as well as the perception of fullness of gestural execution and the manifestation of spirit.

Here, "beauty" is not manifest through stillness or the visual consumption of the dancer as an object in repose, or even within the codified postures of classical dance themselves. "Beauty" is an action that may be recognized through its performance. This proposition contradicts the most prevalent assumptions of "beauty" and dance, which converge around balletic lightness and verticality: concepts rooted in ideologies that are obviously racialized and gendered. In 2000, dance writer Sally Banes offered a discussion of Aristotle's attempts to equate slavery with an immorality embodied by certain physical postures as evidence that "ballet's verticality has an ethical dimension whose origins are sociopolitical."[15] In the same essay, she set out André Levinson's articulation of "beauty" in classical dance, which prized verticality, the proportion of the five classical positions, and the turnout of the body, especially the legs, as the bases for motion. Together, these restrictions and possibilities enable qualities of "equilibrium, symmetry, harmony, and unity of line." Banes notes how these possibilities are contingent, "because in ballet, [. . .] they are achieved, distributed, and found again in the flow of motion."[16] Banes continues to recount postmodern ballet choreographer Karole Armitage's concept of "A new kind of beauty for our time," one that, according to the choreographer, "demanded a kind of passion, because it had a troubled spot at the center." This "troubled spot" that Armitage and Banes refer to might be a place where Africanist and feminist aesthetics collude, a place to resist a politic of "beauty" as a commodity that may be consumed by a stationary beholder.

Differences in Africanist and feminist paradigms

Africanist and feminist aesthetics must diverge at several crucial points. First, feminist aesthetics resist the totalizing paradigms that characterize analytic aesthetics, while Africanist aesthetics struggle to make sense of the egregiously under-theorized origins of black Atlantic hybridity. Feminist aesthetics are necessarily encountered within the social context that feminism struggles to overcome. In this paradox, its approaches may seem anti-theoretical and polemical. But feminist aesthetics seek to dismantle master narratives of universalism, to seek contingent theory that is, to quote Hilde Hein, "saturated with experience."[17] Africanist aesthetics seek to align aspects of divergent practices according to performance commonalities that are dispersed across genres, geographies, social locations, and configurations of participants and audiences. Africanist aesthetics attempt to suture palpable approaches to art-making to disparate forms; to tie complex rhythm, apart-playing,[18] percussive attack, ubiquitous flow, and an essential category of derisive performance to the analysis of performance including church orature, breakdancing, gospel singing, ragtime piano syncopations, carnival adornments, beatboxing, cakewalking, and strains of postmodern concert dancing. To construct a binary tension, feminist aesthetics dismantle, while Africanist aesthetics assemble.

More importantly, feminist aesthetics refer to an eternal past of masculine domination that is inseparable from experience in any historical era, while Africanist aesthetics arise from a totalizing historical moment that is the rupture of the middle passage – the forced enslavement of Africans brought to the "New World." A prolonged but identifiable historical action produced Africanist aesthetic practices within the crucible of the slave trade; there is a real and fetishized pre-Africanist historical moment that of necessity gives way to contemporary black Atlantic cultural formations and black identities. Given the historical possibility to explore both pre- and post-Africanist aesthetics, it would seem probable that these paradigms would be fully enunciated by now. Ironically, I think it is fair to assess that feminist aesthetics have exposed the contingencies of gender identity in performance more fully than Africanist aesthetics have been able to account for the broad diversity of performance modalities recognized as "black." Still, Africanists and feminists have many reasons to collaborate. As cultural theorists including Gilroy, Stuart Hall, and bell hooks have pointed out, gender is a modality through which race is lived, and by extension, Africanist aesthetic theory must be in unavoidable collaboration with feminist aesthetics.

Donald Byrd

To offer a case study of feminist and Africanist aesthetic theory in action, I want to turn now to the work of Byrd. Born securely in the visibly black middle class of the 1950s, Byrd has participated in a concert dance tradition framed by the proscenium stage.[19] In all, Byrd's choreographic project explores the expressive limits of classical ballet technique sutured to the weightiness of modern dance. His work tends to be highly kinetic – almost excessively so – in an effort to align compositional rigor with a patently discursive physicality. Highly literate in terms of dance compositions, his works always reference other dances, and he enjoys a choreographic game in which he challenges his audiences to recognize trace elements of other choreographies as they are played out in his own constructions, including his versions of *Giselle* from 1995 and *The Nutcracker* from 1996.

Byrd's choreography consistently engages a recognizably black identity in its fierce deployment of Africanist aesthetic principles throughout, including: the percussive attack of the dancers as they repeatedly pierce the space above their heads with pointed feet; an antiphonal phrasing that constructs gestural responses to various movement calls; and the complex rhythm and apart-playing of dancers whose asymmetrical spatial alignments repeatedly challenge their audiences to choose a focal point. More important than these obvious compositional strategies, though, is the intense finish that Byrd encourages from the dancers. As if to coax all possible tension from the dancers' taut performances, his movements are phrased to emphasize an unimpeachable mastery of physical technique in terms of, at least, flow, depth of spatial field, and rhythmic intensity. This performed "finish" contributes to the engagement of "beauty" as it might be aligned to an aesthetic of the cool.

Giselle

Byrd's fascinating three-act work *Life Situations: Daydreams on Giselle* offered a patently feminist re-articulation of the Romantic ballet, simultaneously concerned with an essentialized black identity in concert dance. In Byrd's version Giselle is danced by a ferociously accomplished African-American woman, the lone black woman in the company of twelve dancers. As danced by Leonora Stapleton, Giselle finds herself constrained by her ties to the local multi-ethnic community, which included her black male partner (her Hilarion). Adventurous in spirit, she enters a relationship with a traveling white male "outsider" figure, against the admonitions of her friends. Giselle falls in love with her Albrecht, but he simply abandons her after their tryst, and she goes mad – for a time. In Byrd's version, Giselle's friends accost Albrecht, physically attack him, and beat him into submission. The first act ends with Giselle restored to her community, all the wiser for her poor choice of a lover, grouped defiantly with the others as they wave Albrecht along his way.

For Byrd, "beauty" often comes to be tied to the triumph of physical technique, or excellence in form. Form is tied to finish, with most jagged edges of movement smoothed into a seamless performance persona. The ruptures of Byrd's rhythmic phrasing makes clear principles of percussive attack or complex meter, but without breaking an overall flow of movements performed to their physical ends. In pushing his dancers to work at the ends of physical possibilities, he forces them to respond in the physical crucible of the spirit. He extracts a "beauty" of dancing in the spirit by overloading physical challenges posed to his dancers. The dance proceeds as rife with Africanist aesthetic assemblage to arrive with an unavoidable honesty of intention and precise execution. Here, "beauty" is evoked in the spirit, born of the tension between the execution of balletic movements with a low-to-the-ground weighted stance.

The second act of Byrd's Giselle features only four Wilis – Myrtha, Giselle, and two other women – and a hapless man who is the object of their evening's fury. The man who dances in the second act is neither the Albrecht nor the Hilarion of the first act, suggesting that Byrd imagines some alternate reality for Giselle. The act is enveloped by ruthless, drag-show humor, as the Wilis are depicted as four automatons with black wigs, red turtlenecks, and filmy white Romantic-length tutus, who vogue-dance, then sputter and dissemble through mechanical shoulder and neck isolations, then freeze as Myrtha repeatedly struts around the perimeter of stage in a quintessential diva promenade. The other Wilis answer with a volley of furious full-bodied gesticulations. The effect is hysterical, like classical ballet on speed. Again, Byrd flips the narrative script in this act, as he has Giselle plead passionately for the man's life, but when outranked by Myrtha and her minions, she ultimately joins into the rapacious plunder. As in the first act, the community proves to be more powerful than the individual's desire. The man dies, and the Wilis leave the stage together, triumphant in their completed task.

The third act of Byrd's work may be the "Daydream" of the entire evening's title. Four additional guest artist ballet dancers appear in this act, two men and two women who dance *en pointe.* They perform Byrd's postmodernist extensions of movement phrases derived from the original nineteenth-century choreography for Giselle. The opening gesture of Byrd's revision featured a solo man, clad simply in black, who paraphrases Giselle's introductory solo variation – augmented by Byrd's distinctive rhythmic and percussive emphases. As the guest artists work through extensions of balletic vocabulary, the modern-dance cast of the previous acts witnesses from the corners of the stage space, on rare occasion jumping into weighted unison passages with each other and the other dancers. Throughout this section, the ballet dancers suggest Balanchine's suture of classical technique and Africanist aesthetic devices of downward-directed weight, percussive attack, and flexible, rolling articulations of torso, necks, and hips uncommon in ballet.[20] The work ends as the ballet artists dance offstage, again shadowed by the modern dancers, leaving Stapleton – the sole black woman, who had danced the first two revised acts of the work as Giselle – standing center stage, trapped in a pool of light, somehow unable to dance, seeming to ruminate on her palpable absence from the classicism of the third act's abstraction.

This final image resounded with a poignancy born of asymmetrical race relations in American dance, which have never produced an African-American prima ballerina in a majority-white company. For many audience members, Stapleton seemed to be barred, by virtue of her visible racial identity, from participating in the third act's choreographic innovations. As a black woman with obvious facility in ballet, she would seem to be an inevitable presence in the "jazzy" pointe-shoe variations. But, as though dancing Giselle at all had depleted her usefulness to the evening as a whole, Stapleton was forced to the sidelines, a hungry witness to her own displacement in a post-colonial ballet built, ironically, around her presence on stage. As the final curtain falls on Byrd's Giselle, "beauty" cannot be accessed by its principal dancer because she is not allowed to dance (Figure 17).

Figure 17 *Life Situations: Daydreams on Giselle* by Donald Byrd (1995), dancers: Elizabeth Parkinson and Fabrice Lemire. © Photo by Julie Lemberger. Permission kindly granted by Julie Lemberger.

Harlem Nutcracker

Byrd's revisioning of *The Nutcracker* begins from a startling narrative inversion: on Christmas Eve in a mythic Harlem brownstone, Clara, a recently widowed grandmother, waits alone for her family and friends to arrive. She remembers her husband, who appears as a ghost, and the large nutcracker that he had given her before he died. As in the many earlier versions of the story, Clara's family arrives for a long sequence of pantomime and social dancing. In a second scene, as everyone else sleeps, Clara has a mild stroke, and faces Death, who appears with his army of rat minions. The Nutcracker comes to life to defend her. But when he begins to lose the battle with death, Clara rallies herself and beats death away. She uncovers the Nutcracker, who is, of course, the ghost of her husband, and together they are transported to a magical Nightclub for Act II (Figure 18). After enjoying a long series of divertissements, Death reappears to show Clara vignettes from her life. She weakens, and the scene returns to her home on Christmas morning. Clara's daughter finds her lying on the living room floor, and family members rush to help make her comfortable. As the children begin opening Christmas presents, Death returns, unnoticed by all but Clara. This time he reveals himself to be Clara's husband, and she takes his arm to leave with him. As the curtain falls, Clara and her husband are joined together in death, seemingly happy among the unaware Christmas celebrants.

Here, Byrd's feminist project enlivens Clara's centrality, allowing her a physical resilience, in her fight with death, as well as an age-based authority in the scenario, as the family matriarch. Byrd's generational adjustment re/makes Clara from an ostensible subject of the ballet as a dreamy-eyed young girl, to an undisguised initiator of the work's actions. Byrd reconciles Clara's seemingly divergent desires suggested by her roles as mother and woman, allowing her to both celebrate with her family as its matriarch, and then party with her husband in a nightclub. In all, Clara's journey is configured as personal and cultural, as well as allegorical.

Choreographically, Byrd employs his signature kinetic attack and slyly ironic movement juxtapositions to engage the story. The second act divertissements feature humorous African-American versions of various "national" dances set to the Duke Ellington–Billy Strayhorn arrangement of the Tchaikovsky score. For example, Byrd recasts the "Dance of the Sugar Plum Fairy" as an Orientalist dragon-lady attended by two cavorting, minstrel-era clowns in a scene of patently stereotyped gendered stage identities. In this acidly humorous section we notice both a capitulation to gendered and raced identities on the theatrical stage, as well as a teasing

Figure 18 *The Harlem Nutcracker* by Donald Byrd (1996), dancers: Eleanor McCoy and Gus Solomon jr. © Photo by Susan Kuklin. Permission kindly granted by Susan Kuklin.

of the divertissement format, the whole framed by an undercurrent of kinetic danger. The fairy's brash ferocity pushes against the sinuous undulations of the musical score, even as her precision is at odds with the slap-happy trembling of her two male attendants. The overall effect is both provocative and derisive, engaged with Africanist and feminist aesthetics on the levels of choreography and narrative impact.

Socially progressive possibilities of "black beauty" in concert dance

Byrd's project to re/make classical ballets proposes an obviously politicized gesture to align Euro-Western dance classicism, and its unavoidable connotations of proportion, formalism, and "beauty," with Africanist aesthetics. Among other works, he created versions of Balanchine's *Prodigal Son* and *La Valse*; before he disbanded his company due to economic crises in 2002, he had begun work on an Africanist *Sleeping Beauty*. His project to rethink these classical works troubled longstanding assumptions separating dance traditions, with a hybridity that marked his work as Africanist, and within that paradigm, often "beautiful." These works present vistas of movement that enable a-temporal flashes of the spirit in their very structure. In this, I find Byrd's vision of "beauty" to be unique and engaged in a progressive aesthetic politics, one that retrieves "black beauty" from the realm of racial dispossession. I can say this only because I believe in the possibility of an aesthetic politics that might construct "black beauty" as a process to be fulfilled by dance performance on the concert stage. Here, "beauty" is not an idea contained by the metaphor of classical allusion, rather it is an action, addressed in concert with others, capable of charging the air with spirit in the moment of its emergence.

Notes

1 P. Gilroy, *Black Atlantic: Modernity and Double Consciousness*, Cambridge, MA: Harvard University Press, 1993.
2 See S. Stuckey, 'Christian Conversion and the Challenge of Dance', in T.F. DeFrantz (ed.), *Dancing Many Drums: Excavations in African American Dance*, Madison, WI: Wisconsin University Press, 2004.
3 See S. Manning, *Modern Dance, Negro Dance: Race in Motion*, Minneapolis, MN: University of Minnesota Press, 2004 and J. Perpener, *African-American Concert Dance: The Harlem Renaissance and Beyond*, Springfield, IL: University of Illinois Press, 2001.
4 Ibid. See also B. Dixon Gottschild, *Digging the Africanist Presence in American Performance: Dance and Other Contexts*, Westport, CT: Greenwood Press, 1996 and *Waltzing in the Dark: African American Vaudeville and Race Politics in the Swing Era*, New York: Macmillan, 2000.
5 Prominent among these cultural theorists are Paul Gilroy, Stuart Hall, and Kobena Mercer. See P. Gilroy, *Small Acts: Thoughts on the Politics of Black Cultures*, London: Serpent's Tail, 1993; Gilroy, *Black Atlantic*; S. Hall, 'New Ethnicities', in K.H. Chen, D. Morley (eds), *Stuart Hall: Critical Dialogues in Cultural Studies*, London: Routledge, 1996, pp. 441–9; and K. Mercer, *Welcome to the Jungle: New Positions in Black Cultural Studies*, New York and London: Routledge, 1994.
6 Gilroy, *Small Acts*, p. 155.
7 Ibid., p. 157.
8 R. Powell, *Black Art and Culture in the Twentieth Century*, London: Thames and Hudson Ltd., 1997, p. 10.
9 Gilroy, *Black Atlantic*, p. 102.
10 Ibid., p. 198.
11 H. Bhabha, 'The Other Question', in P. Mongia (ed.), *Contemporary Postcolonial Theory*, London: Arnold, 1997, p. 38.
12 R.F. Thompson, *Flash of the Spirit: African and Afro-American Art and Philosophy*, New York: First Vintage Book, 1983. Thompson's inventory of "guiding principles" of Africanist performance have been frequently recounted, but bear repeating here. They include dominance of a percussive performance style; multiple and

complex rhythmic meter; overlapping call and response in singing; an inner pulse control that retains a rhythmic common denominator; suspended accentuation patterning that allows for cross-rhythms; and the performance of songs and dances of social allusion.

13 Ibid., p. xiii.

14 Gilroy, *Black Atlantic*, p. 221.

15 S. Banes, '"A New Kind of Beauty": From Classicism to Karole Armitage's Early Ballets', in P. Zeglin Brand (ed.), *Beauty Matters*, Bloomington, IN: Indiana University Press, 2000, p. 267.

16 Ibid., p. 268.

17 H. Hein, 'The Role of Feminist Aesthetics in Feminist Theory', in C. Korsmeyer, P. Zeglin Brand (eds), *Feminism and Tradition in Aesthetics*, University Park, PA: The Pennsylvania State University Press, 1995, p. 450.

18 The concept of apart-playing and dancing refers to the tendency in African forms to allow each artist a unique contribution to the whole. Strict unison is seldom desired; rather, dancers and musicians "unite music and dance, but play apart." See R.F. Thompson, 'An Aesthetic of the Cool: West African Dance', *African Forum*, 1966, vol. 2, no. 2, p. 93.

19 The "official" biography Byrd circulates stresses his studies at Tufts and Yale Universities, the Cambridge School of Ballet, the London School of Contemporary Dance, the Alvin Ailey American Dance Center, and with Mia Slavinska. He danced, briefly, with Twyla Tharp, Karole Armitage, and Gus Solomons Jr. before he founded his company Donald Byrd/The Group in 1978 with a commitment to the idea that "dance can change and enrich the lives of many people." Prolific, he has created over eighty works for his own company and others including a 1998 production of *Carmina Burana* for the New York City Opera. In 2002 Byrd dissolved his own company and assumed artistic directorship of the Spectrum Dance Theater of Seattle, Washington.

20 Brenda Dixon Gottschild has argued that Balanchine works such as *Agon* (1957) and *The Four Temperaments* (1946) employ Africanist principles in their choreographic structure. See B. Dixon Gottschild, 'Stripping the Emperor', in *Digging the Africanist Presence*, pp. 59–79.

14 *Dispositif* trouble

When what is said is not what is shown

Hélène Marquié

In contemporary dance in France today one notes a sharp increase in the number of performances and discourses on gender identity and sexuality. Stereotypes of masculinity and femininity, in particular, are being claimed as subversive forms. In the absence of a real reflection on the social relationships between sexes and in the frequent confusion between biological sex, gender, and sexuality, this evolution appears quite ambiguous.

This case-study[1] focuses on *Dispositif 3.1*,[2] a work choreographed by Alain Buffard in 2001, which is particularly representative of a trend led by male choreographers who affirm both an identitarian research on gender and sexuality and a subversive will or "militant dimension."[3] This trend constitutes a sort of intellectual elite in contemporary dance, the productions of which are aimed at a target audience, pre-selected by the places in which they are performed, such as Centre Pompidou in Paris (which co-produced this work). *Dispositif 3.1* is an apparatus (*dispostif* in French)[4] that includes a choreographic work and all the discourses that accompany it and are intended to guide its reception. In this respect, it is exemplary of the workings of a current fringe of choreographic production.

The para-choreographic apparatus (introductory texts, reviews, interviews . . .) is essential for a work that sometimes appears to be a pretext. Reference is made to postmodernism, to the visual arts of the 1970s and 1980s in the United States,[5] and to new technologies; Michel Foucault, Gilles Deleuze, Jean Baudrillard, Judith Butler, or Jacques Derrida are cited, even if often allusively. The works of this trend are amply commented on and have been the object of frequent articles in magazines such as *Art Press* or *Mouvement*. As such, it has become difficult to ignore *Dispositif 3.1* within the sphere of contemporary dance and in certain intellectual milieus. Reviews, interviews with the choreographer, articles . . . the copious comments by the psychoanalyst Sabine Prokhoris (who devotes several passages in her book *Le sexe prescrit* to Buffard and is, herself, cited in the program),[6] the participation of the dance scholar Laurence Louppe, and so on. Even before seeing the work, much of the audience knew what it was about, what references it drew upon, its structure, and, especially, its intent.

The purpose of this book is to question dance discourses and to propose new research tools. I will focus in particular on the discourses created around *Dispositif 3.1* (those of Buffard, Louppe, and Prokhoris) and, especially, on the discrepancy – and quite often the contradiction – between what could be seen and the discursive apparatus that surrounded it. This discrepancy reveals the ideologies that are troubling the world of dance and makes it possible to put the subversive import of these works into perspective. The references and the quotations help us decipher the performance and, even before this, to place it within a register. The discourse produces the signs of an elitist culture but, above all, the signs of distinction itself.[7] As such, the quotations and allusions in the program of *Dispositif 3.1* are taken for granted, at times not even referenced, and are clearly intended for the initiated.[8] The highly ambitious style of the comments envelops the work in a postmodern aura but does nothing to render it accessible to the audience at large, nor to make it any easier to approach the work. Moreover, this process actually contradicts a part of the discourse itself, which expresses interest in making the audience active, in modifying its habitual vision. (This is why the audience of *Dispositif 3.1* is seated in two blocks on separate sides of the stage space facing each other.) What we shall see, however, is that, rather than rendering the audience autonomous, the discursive apparatus tends to dictate its own perception and interpretation.

In the impressive program of *Dispositif 3.1* distributed at Centre Pompidou (five 8½ by 11 pages), Buffard presents his work as follows: "Learning presupposes a model or at least a referent. This condition necessitates a framework of control, conformity and effectiveness. The subject must find his/her own points of reference, sometimes keeping to the sidelines, sometimes playing out his/her own bewilderment with respect to conditioning. These are the frameworks *Dispositif 3.1* tries to trouble, or to make them troublesome."[9] Said in another way, the performance tries to cloud the normative framework that conditions the subject. The subversive intention has been announced, making subtle reference to the language of Foucault (*dispositif*) and of Butler (the repetition of the concept of "trouble" recalls *Gender Trouble*.)[10] We are in a postmodernist perspective; everything happens and will happen, on stage, in signs and signifiers, leaving the meaning unchanged, especially where the relationship between sexes is concerned. Buffard provides a brief index of themes in the piece's program.[11] The only reference that appears in the "Difference between the sexes" is from Prokhoris's *Le sexe prescrit*. In relation to feminist production, listing this one reference alone on the issue of the difference between sexes suggests an ideological choice.[12] The performance illustrates the confusion that reigns in this artistic trend between biological sex, gender, sexual identity, and sexuality, as well as that between a claim to identity and a gay "culture" and political homosexual vindication. If post-modern or queer theories are widely evoked/invoked, those of materialist feminism are never brought to the fore. Generally speaking, the issue of the social relationships between the sexes is never broached. This in itself would not be reproachable, if the discourses did not lead one to believe that it has not only been addressed in the piece but actually surpassed in a "beyond genders." Thus Buffard's statement: "The fact that I'm a fag[13] determines quite a few things. What has been put into play in *Dispositif 3.1* regarding the role of women in our society, for example."[14] Let's see exactly what has been put into play.

"Things are not necessarily what they would like us to believe"[15]

The audience is seated in two blocks on separate sides of the stage space, which forms a relatively wide corridor between them. The four performers are dressed identically. They wear blond wigs, the hair of which falls down in front of their faces, and are bare-chested under long white aprons with low necklines in the back and on the sides. They have on black bikini underwear, black knee pads, and black ankle and elbow guards. Everyone – male and female dancers – plays the same role designated under the generic term of *Little Girl*. For the first twenty minutes or so, the hair from the blond wigs conceals their faces. In the first sequence (15 minutes), three of the *Little Girl*(s) traverse the space in numerous parallel comings and goings amidst the two groups of spectators. They walk, crawl, or squirm along the floor at different speeds, following the instructions of the fourth *Little Girl*, who, standing at a distance, calls out orders, encouragement, or reprimands in English.

Prokhoris presents the roles as follows: "Three generations of women and one man are brought together in the figure of the *Little Girl*, in an allegory of training and its risks."[16] Prokhoris sees this performance as a "summary history of embodiment. This history, following the convention of the piece, which is (and not without reason) in some ways a feminine plural version of Buffard's 1998 solo *Good Boy*, passes through the far from straightforward path of trying to attain the docile (?) state of "becoming-a-girl."[17] Perhaps it has something to do with the psychoanalyst's slightly complicated style, but the project seems unclear. If the "docile (?) state of becoming-a-girl" leaves one perplexed, one could maintain that the choreographer wants to move on from the investigation of male identity begun in *Good Boy* and further developed in 2001 for the quartet in *Good for* – which oscillated between the exhibition of a certain virility and the reappropriation of camp (see below) – to a female identity that he would embody through three women. "*Dispositif 3.1*, *Good Boy* and *Good for* take a militant stance in relation to institutionalized dogmas and normative power by the way they present the biological sex and certain aesthetic forms," says Buffard.[18] Here, the subversive aesthetic claimed is camp.[19] Susan Sontag defined camp as a sensibility and an aesthetic that was particularly widespread within gay communities in the US and UK during the 1960s and 1970s.[20] Camp is characterized by a parody of the signs of femininity, by artifice, and by exaggeration. It connotes effeminacy. As an individualist and apolitical stance, camp was nonetheless credited as subversive in gay circles. Andrew Britton,[21] however, has challenged this vision of camp as a subversive and avant-garde attitude, demonstrating that it was never anything more than a play on normative signs, that it never proposed a radical critique of that norm, without which it would not exist because it would have no definition.

"Laurence [Louppe] doesn't have to do anything, she's already 'camp.' I had a vague idea of doing something on femininity."[22] Femininity . . . or effeminacy? If we follow the logic of this reasoning, then for Buffard femininity is part of camp. What femininity? From this perspective, it would be a cultural construct for men who can appropriate it, but its essentialist character for women remains implicit.

"Sharing or erasing borders, especially between masculinity and femininity, is a recurring aspect of my work,"[23] says Buffard, who, in speaking of *Dispositif 3.1*, refers to the "masculine-feminine comings and goings."[24] In what is shown to us, however, the problem is not that of sharing or erasing borders. We are deliberately far from any sort of limit and placed at the core of a male fantasy of femininity, the effeminate. "One no longer knows who is who, perhaps there is a third gender. Things are not necessarily what they would like us to believe."[25] Is this third gender camp? Does it abolish the boundary between the other two? On the contrary, it emphasizes it, because its very definition is based upon it. It represents the quintessence of the iconic and abstract femininity with which men play at representing themselves, without ever locking themselves into the apparatus. No to-and-fro, the only gender treated in *Dispositif 3.1* is the "feminine camp," over-invested and embodied by three women and one man. But, you might say, this is the subversion. The choreographer himself plays one of the *Little Girl*(s) and, if one believes Louppe, "everything [is done] to free oneself from identitarian dictates, to find in 'carnivalesque' zones a certain undifferentiated state of the subject: an abandonment of the identity of the biological sexes, a momentary abolition of the dualism that rules, institutes and instrumentalizes bodies, desires."[26]

But what does one actually see? In the first place, in *Dispositif 3.1,* only the male sex has any freedom from prescribed gender identities, while the female sex remains assigned. In the second place gendered identities are not abandoned but, on the contrary, gender (and only one gender) is actually staged. Third, the dualism isn't abolished and, what is more, attention is focused on one of the two terms, and the excess exacerbates the dualism.

Finally, if we set to one side for the moment what the cross-dressing signifies, what we are confronted with is neither an undifferentiated state of subjectivity nor an abandonment of fixed sexual identities in the motilities. The three performers moving about at length before us offer us raw material, "natural" and "everyday" variations within their corporeal experience, and thus within the markers of gendered identities. Far from leading us back to "a certain undifferentiated state," the way the dancing bodies move through space and the movement qualities they produce, especially in the transitions between scenes, are especially revealing of the performers' identitarian constructs – according to his or her biological sex.[27] Thus, and this is the key point, despite what the para-choreographic apparatus strongly asserts, sexual identity is not abandoned. The choreographer says: "You no longer know who's who."[28] But yes you do, from what he shows us. Not even for a single second does his theatrical apparatus leave the slightest ambiguity about the performers' biological sex, even when the performers' faces are concealed by the hair falling over them from their wigs. From the very start of the performance, in the numerous displacements on the floor and on their knees, presenting themselves in profile between the two blocks of the audience, the apron neckline does nothing to conceal the women's breasts: it's impossible not to see them. Moreover, despite his cross-dressing, Buffard's body is never confused with the female bodies of the other three *Little Girl*(s): he is distinguished by his stature, which amply exceeds that of his partners, and by a muscular build marked by a male structure (Figure 19). As the performance continues, only the women speak, in a texture that "conforms" with what is traditionally expected of their biological sex. Nothing surprises us or troubles conventions. Nor does anything in the discursive apparatus allow for ambiguity; neither the program we are supposed to have read, nor the choreographer's remarks, nor the review lets us forget that the choreographic work calls for three women and one man, who is identified as the "author of the concept." Everything is designed to stop us from forgetting who's who. Even the title itself is *Dispositif 3.1,* not *Dispositif 4.* A critic,

Figure 19 Dispositif 3.1 by Alain Buffard (2001), dancers: Alain Buffard, Laurence Louppe, Claudia Triozzi and Anne Laurent. © Photo by Marc Domage. Permission kindly granted by Alain Buffard.

Anne van Hove, described it as "a game between 4 players one of whom is a pitcher."[29] The masculine role is, in fact, the pillar of the apparatus.

Prokhoris writes: "And each of these bodies that are so visibly modeled on 'little girl,' but all the same led back, through the interwoven bonds that have produced the 'little girl,' toward the flesh common to all, because it is exposed equally, is intensely moving and alive."[30] Exposed equally? No, because we know who is a woman and who is a man. A man cross-dressed as a woman always attracts more attention than three women masquerading . . . as women. It is a classical scheme of disguise. To over-determine the stereotype of femininity and masculine "transgression," it is important to know who's who in order to adopt a strategy for ignoring this. We know in advance that the performance is based on the 3 + 1 apparatus. On the one hand, three representatives of the group "woman" that inflect "feminine camp" at three different ages and, on the other, one man, a single individual, who plays this role. One can't say that a cross-dressed man in an avant-garde performance, at the beginning of the twenty-first century, subverts any norm at all, particularly when he maintains a singular and dominant position. The women form a group[31] of individuals who are ultimately interchangeable[32] and, above all, implacably fixed in that feminine from which they cannot escape. Their function is to draw attention to the transgressive man who, like them, can embody this masculine fantasy of camp femininity. He interprets it even better, because camp only takes on meaning in the male-centered circles originating in gay culture, which define it as transgression. Transgression remains a male privilege and is not even a possibility (how could it be?) for the women who seem to accept this state of affairs. This is revealed in a scene with the three women performers. Louppe plays a little girl, a docile doll, whose eyes are blindfolded. She is seated at a table between the legs of another *Little Girl,* who manipulates her hands from behind, forcing her to grab and squash and throw tomatoes, making a mess of herself. At the same time, the third *Little Girl,* seated in front of her, makes her obediently repeat fragments of a German text referring to *Heidi*: "Heidi is young, Heidi is healthy, Heidi is innocent, Heidi is obliging, she refuses nothing, nothing to anyone . . . ."[33] This segment could have constituted an "allegory of training and its risks," a critical primer for the construction of the feminine, or, as Prokhoris has put it, a "prescription of identity," but it doesn't go beyond the game, as if the limit of what women can achieve rests solely in showing off, with the intention of provoking laughter from the audience. When the scene ends, the three *Little Girl*(s) are still *Little Girl*(s); nothing has evolved and they rejoin the masculine figure. The latter remains outside of this entire scene, to which he actually turns his back, while the "training" is done by the women. It is a woman who manipulates Heidi, and another who makes her repeat the "prescription of identity." All of this takes place as if the social conditioning transmitted by the women operated *ex nihilo*, independent of masculine presence and the relationship between sexes. Moreover, the scene is not conceived directly as a critique or as a simple reference to the novel *Heidi* (whose author, Johanna Spyri, is not acknowledged in the program). According to the index, this is a homage to Paul McCarthy who, in 1992, made a video with Mike Kelley on this theme in which the two men played the roles of Heidi, Peter, and the grandfather. Buffard picks up on certain aspects of this. In McCarthy's work, however, it is a man, the grandfather, who educates Heidi by making her repeat the same phrases. In the trends of current discourses on gender, one notes the disappearance of bodies, whose materiality and experience are turned into discursive notions (while, paradoxically, one often nevertheless sees that the genders are implicitly essentialized). Too many discourses on corporeality have ended up replacing their objects. This exclusion of the body is not, however, independent from the extent to which the questioning of the actual social relationships between sexes has been excluded to the advantage of gender discourses. On stage, the bodies become projections of signs, behind which the flesh disappears. In this, one observes still another dissonance between what is said and what is shown. Prokhoris has spoken of an "allegory of training and its risks: subversive experience of a non-disciplinary eroticism."[34] I personally did not sense any experience of eroticism in this work. On the contrary, I saw signs of a "disciplinary eroticism," or rather the non-critical staging of the representation of eroticism within a male-dominated social order. For it to have been eroticism, work would have had to be done on bodies, feelings, relationships with others and with oneself. Instead, the bodies disappear simultaneously behind the discourses and the image. Buffard asserts that he wanted this beginning "to render more sensitive the singular spaces of the bodies [. . .] to reveal the multiple inventions that our singularity forces us to find"[35] by standardizing costumes and wigs, by making the bodies walk, crawl, and slither on the floor. What is produced is the exact opposite. The bodies are not revealed under the costume, despite their nudity. Only the disguise makes sense. Nudity would have made it possible to "render more sensitive the singular spaces of the bodies." Here all one sees is the space limited by the masquerade of gender, which screens the individuality of the bodies, except for what they pretend to hide – their biological sex. The apparatus does not work as it was meant to and delivers quite another message. A stereotypical image replaces the bodies. And this image evokes an eroticism . . . a disciplinary eroticism. The apron emphasizes more than it conceals, and the breast is a voyeuristic apparatus, void of any implicit or explicit critical perspective. With a blond wig and a white apron, the *Little Girl* is a girl–woman; the Lolita, the obedient and blinded housewife, who creeps and crawls on all fours, in the classic postures of pornographic fantasy. White aprons, but black bikinis, black knee pads, and black ankle and elbow guards evoke images of a sadomasochistic universe and its leather accessories. If the intention was to experiment with movement, from the perspective of purely kinetic analysis, the context and the staging denote quite different meanings. Connotations cannot just be swept aside by statements of intent. To neutralize them at least, it would have been necessary to grasp and to work with them, otherwise we are left with what is implicit.

Privileging a game of signs over real experimentation with bodies and identities in movement participates in the lack of any real transgression. What Gilles Deleuze has called a "Becoming woman," remains in the form of caricature. There is no experimentation with "being woman," nor any transgression of gender that might pass as an even temporary experience of living, as, for example, in the work of Michel Journiac.[36] The body produced is a body for masquerade.[37] One might join Nicole-Claude Mathieu in asking "if the monopolizing of femininity by men at the level of symbolic game is not more possible than the impossibility of their lowering themselves to the feminine in reality at the level of a symbolic game is more feasible precisely because they would never consider debasing themselves to the lowly status women occupy in real life."[38]

Like other choreographers who are part of this trend, Buffard affirms his own homosexuality. "The fact that I'm a fag determines quite a few things. What has been put into play in *Dispositif 3.1* regarding the role of the woman in our society, for example. Working together with Anne [Laurent], Laurence [Louppe] and Claudia [Triozzi], we often agreed about this. We belong in the same way to a minority."[39] In the same way? Put in relation to the history of the gay and feminist movements, the last statement seems rather naive.[40] Yet this claim poses another problem. Here, as in many current French productions, gender and sexuality are confused, while homosexuality and cross-dressing become interchangeable terms. The framework of the homosexual milieu is extremely limited; homosexuality seems to have only one biological sex, male, and one gender, effeminate. Does this subvert any moral order at all? Can we, today, still think that the claim of a male homosexuality which passes for effeminacy and/or that of cross-dressing necessarily carries with it a radical change in the heterosexual order, in the representation and in the situation of women, to say nothing of those of lesbians who are especially invisible in contemporary dance? The subversive character of a practice can only be evaluated within its context. If, more than thirty years ago, camp was able to constitute a form of communitarian resistance and a way for gay men to re-appropriate discriminatory discourse (and it is in this context that its significance must be assessed), its meaning becomes completely different today, in a much more complicated context. Cross-dressing is very much in vogue on the French scene; it is almost exclusively related to effeminacy and predominantly addresses masculine concerns. Over this asymmetry of fact can be superimposed a symbolic asymmetry that Mathieu has identified in modern and traditional societies and that rests on the hierarchy between the two genders and on the power relationships between the two sexes.[41] In momentarily assuming the position and the gender that they themselves attributed to the dominated, in becoming "difference," and "other," the dominators have always had the pretext of subverting the norms of their class. They have not done anything but confirm the "other" in its difference, even if the "other" also comes to play with its own caricature. They have never, on the other hand, subverted the relationships of domination. And today, when gay visibility in mass media passes almost exclusively through the caricature of the effeminate man, these images end up reinforcing the norms they claim to fight.

If the remarks surrounding these productions sometimes demonstrate a will toward subversion that one can suppose is sincere, the performances themselves attest to a lack of fundamental discussion of the dominant masculine order. Thus any real discussion of the norms of sexuality becomes equally impossible. "These are the social structures that *Dispositif 3.1* seeks to trouble, or to make them troublesome," asserted Buffard. The masculine gender is not at all troubled, and the framework of the dominant order that forms the basis for the binary, hierarchical structure of gender and produces homophobia remains intact.[42]

Dispositif 3.1 has interesting aspects from yet another perspective of analysis (I am thinking in particular about the *mise en abîme* of the empty postmodern discourse on contemporary art.) But the apparatus constructed by its conceivers imposes this framework of interpretation, and it is actually the dual language, the contradiction between what is said and is shown that makes trouble. Here as elsewhere, far from presenting itself as a reflection that encourages one to experiment with alternative approaches to gender, bodies, and social relations of sex that lead toward original creation, everything takes place as if the discourse was trying to justify individualist identitarian expressions *a posteriori* by applying them to an ambitious – and fashionable – project of politics. The result might be interesting and innovative from a choreographic perspective, which is something I don't intend to discuss here, but far from shaking up the values of a hierarchical order of domination, it comforts them, doing nothing more than modifying the appearances it claims to subvert. In today's dance performances and discourses, it seems that the question of gender and of sexuality actually renews and often accentuates "restrictive forms of gender categorisation."

Masculinity at breaking point[43]

Though *Dispositif 3.1* does not trouble any normative framework, it should be recognized that it does at least reveal the existence of such a framework and the necessity for its subversion. This is far from the case of many productions that currently question issues of gender and sexuality.

Gender is in vogue, but the concept is still vague. Essentialist ways of thinking remains preponderant, even if it is often accompanied by references to postmodern discourses. If genders are considered constructs, they are assumed to be equivalent, and as such may be freely modified, simulated, exchanged, and played upon. Femininity and masculinity become interchangeable. The issue of explicit and implicit hierarchies, of the system of domination that underlies the very qualifications of femininity and masculinity is not approached. Would femininity and masculinity become interchangeable? Certainly not, because only men are involved in this circulation.

"The boundaries of gender have the tendency, where men are concerned, to fall apart, to explode and for masculinity to reveal itself at breaking point," states Daniel Welzer-Lang.[44] Contemporary dance in France illustrates this evolution. "Men in their skin – Choreographers and dancers in search of male identity,"[45] "Immersed in eternal masculinity"[46] are revealing titles from articles written for the press at large. In the past few years, one notes an explosion of choreographic works focusing on masculinity.[47] The existence of genders themselves is not contested, but reaffirmed in the extreme. Men claim the right to choose their gender from the range of what is made available by a system they do not question. It seems, however, that only the male sex has this choice.

In conclusion, I would say that representations of the masculinity can be placed on an axis between virility[48] and femininity or camp. They are always played by individuals of the male sex. The feminine gender can be interpreted by the two sexes, as the accent is placed on (and even further enhanced by) transgression – which, for a man, consists in exposing "his femininity." Studies by Mathieu have amply demonstrated how the hetero-social system of male domination can be reinforced by diverse forms of gender transgression.[49] This is particularly clear, given that only men exercise this transgression. It is obvious that the gender – here feminine – can be represented by the opposite biological sex – men – and very effectively so, so as to perpetuate its existence. This means of representation legitimizes the dualism and the hierarchy of the genders and, by implication, the socio-cultural construct they reflect and maintain. Women, in any event, are excluded from this right to transgress gender norms just as they are from challenging heterosexual ones. Masculine identities are often affirmed within homo-social contexts, such as performances with all male casts. When women are present, they are in the service of a search for, or demonstration of, masculinity; that is to say, they participate in the constitution of masculine self-sufficiency. There has not been any circulation of questions, and the point of view is constantly male-centered. The current dominant production in France is always found within the order it intends to fight. It remains, therefore, ineffectual and, above all, provides an alibi for the lack of re-opening (or opening) of any real discussion. A comparative study still needs to be made between these French productions and those of artists such as the English choreographer Lloyd Newson, whose intellectual, artistic, and political process is completely different.

A new identitarian, social, and cultural phenomenon is emerging. In male circles, the masculinity has obtained the right to be expressed "dans tous ses états." Though the stereotypes of classical virility and its countertypes (the effeminate, the homosexual, and the foreigner as well) may not be new, what has changed is their alliance, which unfortunately ends up reinforcing the order of masculine power. Visible in both high and mass culture, from contemporary dance to television programing, and passing through literature, film, and advertising, this evolution translates into a more general phenomenon. Making reciprocal use of the contrast, the two versions of masculinity transmit the same ideology, inflecting[50] it and addressing it to different audiences.

"Will contemporary dance soon give birth to a new man?" asks Rosita Boisseau.[51] If we consider the new alliances of masculinity, this may be the case. But this new man does not "trouble" the framework that normalizes the relations between sexes and genders. Analyzing the forms of masculinity proposed, one actually notes – behind a discourse that claims to be politically or aesthetically subversive – the development of novel forms that actually perpetuate existing imbalances in the relations between men and women.

Notes

1 This article is part of the work presented at the seminar "Culture et rapports sociaux de sexe" held at the Université de Saint-Quentin-en-Yvelines in 2002–3.

2 Presented as follows: Conception: Alain Buffard. Production and interpretation: Alain Buffard, Anne Laurent, Laurence Louppe, and Claudia Triozzi. Co-production: Espace Pier Paolo Pasolini, Valenciennes; Centre Pompidou, Paris; Le Quartz, Brest; Centre national de la danse, Pantin; Association pi:es. The work was realized in collaboration with the following national choreographic centers: Ballet Preljocaj, Aix-en-Provence; Ballet Atlantique, Régine Chopinot, La Rochelle; Centre chorégraphique de Rennes et de Bretagne, Catherine Diverrès. The project received the assistance of DRAC Nord-Pas-de-Calais during its residence at the Espace Pier Paolo Pasolini, Valenciennes.

3 'Ils s'exposent. Entretien avec Jennifer Lacey, Nadia Lauro et Alain Buffard', *Art Press*, 2001, no. 270, p. 36.

4 Throughout this essay, the French term *dispositif* introduced by Foucault has been translated by the English term "apparatus": as Paul Rabinow and Nikolas Rose point out, "the apparatus embodied a kind of strategic *bricolage* articulated by an identifiable social collectivity. It functioned to define and to regulate targets constituted through a mixed economy of power and knowledge." See P. Rabinow, N. Rose (eds), *The Essential Foucault: Selections from the Essential Works of Foucault, 1954–1984*, New York: New Press, 2003, p. 11. For a definition of "dispositif" by Foucault see ibid., pp. 10–11 (orig. edn M. Foucault, 'Le Jeu de Michel Foucault', in *Dits et écrits,* Vol III, Paris: Gallimard, 1994, p. 298): "a resolutely heterogeneous grouping composing discourses, institutions, architectural arrangements, policy decisions, laws, administrative measures, scientific statements, philosophic, moral and philanthropic propositions; in sum, the said and the not-said, these are the elements of the apparatus. The apparatus itself is the network that can be established between these elements." [eds/trans].

5 In particular to gay artists. It should be noted that the artists invoked are often illustrated through rather sexist representations (Bruce Nauman, Vito Acconci, Dan Graham, Jeff Koons, etc.) and that, in equal measure, there is no reference to women artists from the same period whose works, on the contrary, are characterized by feminist considerations.
6 S. Prokhoris, *Le sexe prescrit. La différence sexuelle en question*, Paris: Aubier, 2000.
7 P. Bourdieu, *Distinction: A Social Critique of the Judgement of Taste*, trans. R. Nice, Cambridge, MA: Harvard University Press, 1984 (orig. edn *La distinction*, Paris: Éditions de Minuit, 1979).
8 Take, for example, the "Index" at the end of the program of *Dispositif 3.1*, where one reads: "Gilda: see text by Alain Ménil" without further comment. See *Programme*, Paris: Centre Pompidou, 20–4 February 2002, n.p.
9 See *Programme*, n.p.
10 See J. Butler, *Gender Trouble: Feminism and the Subversion of Identity*, London and New York: Routledge, 1990.
11 They appear in the following order: Camp, Différence des sexes (the difference between the sexes), Gilda (with a reference to the text by Alain Ménil), Heidi, Phylogenèse (Philogenesis), Smith [Jack], Smith [Patti], White Cube, Gilda (for the second time, now with a reference to the movie).
12 The work addresses an original critique of certain postulates of psychoanalysis and raises the issue of the legitimacy of interfering in social debates and in political decisions, and of aspiring to uphold a new morality and establish our laws in the name of a truth it sustains. The author criticizes the essentialist vision of the difference between sexes, but does not question the making of this difference, or how it works in social or cultural terms.
13 Buffard uses the French term *pédé* (short for pédérast) in this and in the quotes that follow [eds/trans.].
14 'Ils s'exposent', p. 36.
15 Ibid., p. 35.
16 Prokhoris, 'Le chant des gestes indomptés', *Mouvement*, 2001, no. 12, p. 54.
17 Ibid., p. 57.
18 'Ils s'exposent', p. 36.
19 Buffard gives the following definition of camp, avoiding the essential dimension of the gay environment: "Camp: notion or characteristic consecrated by Susan Sontag, which can be applied to every manifestation or personality that mixes Hollywood glamour, the transgression of social and artistic codes, and a propensity for excess and aberration. 'Camp' was particularly fashionable in the 1960s in New York in those artistic circles close to the underground and to alternative trends related to minimalist aesthetics." See *Programme*, n.p.
20 S. Sontag, *Against Interpretation and Other Essays*, New York: Farrar, Strauss and Giroux, 1966.
21 A. Britton, 'For interpretation – Notes Against Camp', *Gay Left*, 1978–9, no. 7, pp. 11–14.
22 'Ils s'exposent', p. 35.
23 Ibid.
24 Ibid., p. 36.
25 Ibid., p. 35.
26 Louppe, in *Programme*, n.p.

27 Even the final curtain call brings to light a clear difference between the male "conceiver" and the other three female performers, both in posture and in the projection of their gaze.
28 'Ils s'exposent', p. 35.
29 A. van Hove, 'Singulier', *Les Saisons de la Danse*, 2001, no. 341, p. 12.
30 Prokhoris, 'Le chant des gestes indomptés', p. 56.
31 On the representation and the perception of the identity of men as single individuals and of the women as the representation of their sexual category, see F. Lorenzi-Cioldi, *Individus dominants et groupes dominés. Images masculines et féminines*, Grenoble: Presses Universitaires de Grenoble, 1988.
32 Thanks to her brilliant performance, Louppe nonetheless makes the group of women lose their homogeneity and take on weight with respect to the masculine role. It should be noted that Buffard and Louppe's intentions are fairly well-known but we know little about what the other two performers felt.
33 The programme translates these phrases and explains that the text was written by the four performers.
34 Prokhoris, 'Le chant des gestes indomptés', p. 54.
35 See *Programme*, n.p.
36 In particular the performance *24 heures de la vie ordinaire d'une femme* (1974).
37 In *INtime/EXtime* (1999) Buffard had already donned a stocking filled with Styrofoam balls, which produced a fluid form, a "pregnant" body that, according to Claudine Colozzi, went "to the point of the ultimate temptation of man experiencing the body of pregnant woman." See C. Colozzi, 'Mon corps cet inconnu', *Les saisons de la danse*, 1999, no. 319, 27. This is not an 'Intime' experience, which would be a work of feeling and flesh, but an 'Extime' experience of the projection of an image, of a masquerade of pregnancy.
38 N.-C. Mathieu, 'Dérive du genre, stabilité des sexes', in M. Dion (ed.), *Madonna, érotisme et pouvoir*, Paris: Editions Kimé, 1994, p. 64.
39 'Ils s'exposent', p. 36.
40 On this, see, among others, M.-J. Bonnet, 'Gay Mimesis and Misogyny: Two Aspects of the Same Refusal of the Other?', *Journal of Homosexuality*, 2001, vol. 41, nos. 3–4, 265–80; J.-Y. le Talec, *L'éveil d'une nouvelle 'conscience gaie' – Liens entre la problématique proféministe et la question gaie*, in D. Welzer-Lang (ed.), *Nouvelles approches des hommes et du masculin*, Toulouse: Presses Universitaires du Mirail, 2000, pp. 141–61.
41 Mathieu, 'Dérive du genre, stabilité des sexes', pp. 44–70.
42 On the common ground between sexism and homophobia, see M. Dorais, P. Dutey, D. Welzer-Lang (eds), *La peur de l'autre en soi. Du sexisme à l'homophobie*, Montréal: VLB éditeur, 1994.
43 In French the author used the expression "dans tous ses etats" that has the idiomatic meaning of being all worked up or in a terrible state about something [trans.].
44 D. Welzer-Lang, 'Les transgressions sociales des définitions de la masculinité', in *La place des femmes. Les enjeux de l'identité et de l'égalité au regard des sciences sociales*, Paris: La Découverte, 1995, p. 450.
45 See R. Boisseau, 'Mâles dans leur peau – Chorégraphes et danseurs à la recherche de l'identité masculine', *Télérama*, 2002, no. 2736, pp. 74–5.
46 See R. Boisseau, 'Plongée dans l'éternel masculin', *Télérama*, 2002, no. 2722, p. 81.

47 The study of these masculine identitarian productions of contemporary dance was presented at the seminar "Culture et rapports sociaux de sexe."
48 The most convincing example is clearly that of Angelin Preljocaj with, among others, the performance *MC 14/22, ceci est mon corps* (2001).
49 N.-C. Mathieu, 'Identité sexuelle/sexuée/de sexe? Trois modes de conceptualisation du rapport entre sexe et genre', in N.-C. Mathieu, *L'anatomie politique (Catégorisations et idéologies du sexe)*, Paris: Côté-femmes, 1991, pp. 227–66.
50 The author uses this term in its grammatical meaning [trans.].
51 See Boisseau, 'Mâles dans leur peau', p. 75.

15 Identity, the contemporary, and the dancers

Isabelle Ginot

Identity and dance studies. State-of-the-art, history, effects . . .

The singular composition of this section clearly reflects the singularities of its subject and its field of study. The keyword "identities" crystallizes the theoretical efforts of the several decades of research in the human sciences, outlined by Andrée Grau in her introduction. From work in anthropology to the various aspects of cultural studies approach, the last few decades of social science research have given the field of dance new insights into the customary boundaries between high-brow and low-brow dance, between concert and social dance, and between western and non-western dances. It is no longer possible to think of dance as anything but a human and social practice, to ignore the bonds between dance's staged forms and its everyday practices or, even more, to ignore the fact that dance, like any other human practice, is subject to the pressure of political relationships and is in itself a place in which power is exercised.

This aside, numerous theoretical boundaries continue to operate in both choreographic practices and theoretical research, as attested in the introduction to this section regarding the anthropological perspective and in the three case-studies focused on contemporary "avant-garde" dance works. Take, for example, the analyses of "identitarian" issues in contemporary dance orienting the three studies devoted to performances and representations of identity in selected works (masculinity/femininity, Black Atlantic/European American, and so forth). But what about contemporary dance as a social environment and a place where identity is formed, beginning, for example, from a dancer's education and training? This issue has been explored by Hubert Godard and Isabelle Launay, who, investigating contemporary dancers' memories, have shown that one of the key guiding factors of their training is identity. The question is whether to succeed or not in "becoming a dancer," in conforming to real or fictional images of this "being a dancer" and its identity, perceived as both repressive and desirable. And, starting from these very same stratagems, how to come to terms with these norms to preserve or to invent one's own identity as a dancer? These are the issues that come out of this study,[1] which, paradoxically, owes nothing to research on the concept of identity, but rather to an ethnological process that uses French contemporary dancers as a field of inquiry.

What I would like to consider in the following pages is how the dyad identity/contemporary dance condenses a certain number of theoretical issues that are part of dance research in general and go beyond, or actually traverse, methodological variations and the choice of subjects. I will begin this discussion with the problem of analyzing contemporary choreographic works and hope to show how this is tied to the issue of identity.

The field of the contemporary dance seems to pose different issues than those of more or less distant historical periods. In historical dance research the question of sources is always a problem, whereas contemporary choreographic works are clearly better and ever more documented. Yet the question regarding the relationship between the "analogous" document (film or video) and the work itself is rarely raised. And theorization is rendered more difficult (perhaps?) by the necessarily live relationship between the scholar and the subject in its context. It seems harder to isolate and compartmentalize, for example, the frameworks of reference, to separate the cultural, political, and theoretical context, the spectator's experience, and so on. Nonetheless, the questions raised about contemporary dance and the relationships between theory and experience seem to be the same regardless of the period in question. What changes is the way in which the relationship between the researcher and the subject is organized.

Three case-studies

The history of theories of identity is a succession of analyses of relationships between the ruler and the ruled, be it through feminism, post-colonial, gender, or cultural studies. In France, and through the work of the research team of which I am a part,[2] other relationships may also be included, such as the relationship between dancers and the individuals producing discourses on dance or the disciplinary relationships between practitioners of gesture and masters of discourse, the latter of which was first analyzed by feminists based on the norms assigning women to the sphere of body and feeling and men to the mastery of discourse. All of these relationships are successive variations of the same model derived from feminism and, as such, I will allow myself to group them under the generic term of "culturalism." Though the subject varies, the major characteristic of these theories is the consideration of identity as a cultural as opposed to natural construct, the fruit of power relationships that have to be analyzed and deconstructed. Obviously, the common scope of these many theoretical currents is political and ideological. And it should also be remembered that this theoretical body is not at all limited to contemporary dance and that many studies have investigated dance history from the perspective of feminism, gender,[3] ethnic identity, and so on.

The three case-studies presented in this section take into consideration culturalist practice as applied to contemporary dance. They approach identity from a theoretical point of view and attempt to see how this operates in dance. Starting from a given point of reference, which varies for each study, they attempt to observe how dance reproduces, re-invents, reflects, or contradicts the identitarian productions and the inter-identitarian relationships that have been described by others. In their analyses Ramsay Burt, Thomas F. DeFrantz, and Hélène Marquié each rely on a specific theoretical corpus (Burt on Jaques Lacan/Maurice Merleau-Ponty, DeFrantz on Paul Gilroy, and Marquié on materialist feminism). In addition to their choice of subjects, there is an essential difference between what I would call their posture. The first two use the choreographic work to demonstrate or illustrate the pre-selected body of theory; the third does the opposite, using her own theoretical framework to criticize the work and to demonstrate its contradictions.

Whatever the motive of same and other in identitarian analysis may be (man/woman, white/black, homo/hetero, western/non-western, dancer/spectator), these three analyses reunite the two major poles of the definition of identity that organize the entire theoretical field and that Grau addresses in her introduction. I would define the first as geographic. This notion of identity organizes territories, establishes a sense of belonging (to a community), and signals through recognizable signs of a certain "sameness." It is identity in terms of cultural, national, ethnic belonging. On a theoretical plane it is constructed primarily from semiotic models and is focused on signs. It confers primacy to predominantly visible and discursive signs of identity. It defines a community on the basis of a set of common signs (skin color, physical features, territory, religious belonging) and considers individual variations secondary in relationship to primary belonging. DeFrantz, for example, introduces David Byrd's *Giselle* by immediately opposing the interpreter of Giselle, "a ferociously accomplished African woman, the lone black woman," to the rest of the company. For her part, Marquié is interested in a work situated explicitly in the territorial issue of its choreographer Alain Buffard: "Sharing or erasing borders, especially between masculinity and femininity, is a recurring aspect of my work."[4]

Marquié's analysis, in turn, seeks to show how the gender frontiers held to be erased have actually been consolidated in the work:

> But what does one actually see? In the first place, in *Dispositif 3.1*, only the male sex has any freedom from prescribed gender identities, while the female sex remains assigned. In the second place gendered identities are not abandoned but, on the contrary, gender (and only one gender) is actually staged. [. . .] [T]he dualism isn't abolished and, what is more, attention is focused on one of the two terms [. . .][5]

Here identity is a territory, and it is defined first and foremost through its fixedness. Identity is thus a set of constant traits that are maintained (and would be evident) despite any variation in the subject or the community. It is often perceived as restrictive in as much as it reduces the individual or the groups to just one aspect of their identity (Grau), and its theorization does not fare well in the inevitable fluctuations of history (see Grau's example of Maalouf's inhabitant of Sarajevo). Even the "subversive" nature of the work would eventually be tied to calling this territoriality into question.

The second aspect of identity is somewhat historical or at least temporal. It places the accent on identity as singularity and difference. Whereas geography endeavors to define a stable identity, history considers it as a constantly changing process, a fluid state: not as something that one has been from the very beginning, but rather something that each one of us fabricates (or *performs*)[6] in our daily lives. Before anything else, identity immediately establishes itself in a temporal and historical context and is thus unstable and fluid. On a theoretical plane, therefore, it is no longer a matter of locating signs but of understanding how identity is produced. This is how, for example, one can understand the difference DeFrantz proposes between "the visible" and "the spirit" of Black Atlantic identity. On the one hand, it is an identity marked by the visibility of skin color and perhaps by the cultural signs of belonging to a black American community; on the other, it is an identity formed by the recognition of an experience and a history. This "historical" conception of identity could lead, I think, to a phenomenology of culture and this is, without doubt, the aim of DeFrantz's and Burt's essays, the latter of which is concentrated on the spectator's experience of the two works considered.

The question of the *oeuvre*

Rather than entering into the debate on identity itself, the first problem I would like to pose is of an epistemological order and concerns the status of the choreographic work in culturalist discourses. It has been said that, if identitarian issues and culturalist theories have, in principle, allowed one to think of dance as a social practice that goes beyond the production of works alone, the works remain an important part of the touchstone for culturalist analyses, and the three studies that follow are by no means exceptions. Identitarian theories pose the following question: "How can this or that work put the question of identity into play?" In responding to this question, however, another is unavoidable: "Under what conditions and according to what methods can works be 'made to speak'?" In other words, applied to dance (or to any other artistic form), can the theory of identity do without a specific methodology and a reflection on the medium? Laura Mulvey's seminal text on the construction of the masculine gaze and the feminine subject in Hollywood cinema (which served as a model for many choreographic analyses in the 1980s) was often readapted on the basis of the "content" of the work alone. It should be remembered, however, that Mulvey also proposed a model of formal analysis of the film medium. As Mulvey notes in Sternberg and Hitchcock, the use of framing and editing, and not only the narrative structure, organizes the masculine gaze and the objectification of the feminine figure.[7]

Choreographic works cannot be made to speak in identitarian terms or taken as the crystallization of identitarian stakes in the context of dance without a certain number of presuppositions that seem to be rather paradoxically forgotten in dance studies. It would be impossible to imagine musicology, the history of art, or the history of literature addressing their respective works without a theory of *analyse d'oeuvre*.[8] The university programs that provide training for research in these fields are rich, at least in France, in specific subject matter such as film analysis, painting analysis, and text analysis, and these sub-disciplines themselves are the object of varied theories, debates, and conflicts. Thus the question I would pose here is that of the status of choreographic works in our theoretical apparatuses and especially in culturalist discourses.

The work's identity

In the first place, it is surprising that the theoretical texts, whether they are constituted by *analyse d'oeuvre* or rely on them to illustrate a broader goal, take, as indisputable evidence and as ascertained fact, the existence of the choreographic work, a stable object containing a meaning that can simply be deciphered according to a more or less complex level of codification. A wide branch of aesthetics in the figurative arts, literature, and music is devoted to the discussion of the notion of the work of art.[9] In dance history itself, even a canonical period like Judson Church's is marked by a critique of this notion. What is a dance work and what sort of reality do identitarian or other readings claim to interpret? Above all, on what ideological basis does the notion of work and its cortege of categories (work/author, process/product, choreographer/performer) rest? Every attempt to define the dance work, which is bound to run into numerous difficulties, comes up against the same issues as the definition of identity. The choreographic work poses, first of all, a geographic problem. Where does it start and where does it end? What is its place and what are its spatial limits? What has to do with the choreography and what has to do with interpretation? Where does the process of creation end, and where does the work itself begin? There is also a historical problem. How, through different performances (because the dance work only exists in the form of successive updates), can the "contingent" variations of the work's "truth" be distinguished? Is it possible to think of a "performativity of the performance" and is it possible to think about how the work's identity is reinvented each time it is performed?

Identitarian analyses (including the three studies that precede) treat works as cultural and social micro-spaces in which identities are produced and interact with each other. The hypothesis is that of a social site that reflects the relationships and the norms of the world in general. Take, for example, the way in which the relationships and treatment of male and female performers exemplify or contradict social norms (Marquié)? Or how the relationship between a role performed by an African-American woman dancer and a group of European American dancers narrates abandonment and exclusion (DeFrantz), and so on. The way in which they are read is organized around an axis of the recognition of signs and the locating of their more or less conformist or transgressive nature with respect to the dominant norms.

"What is a work" and what effects does the question produce?

While avoiding the temptation to answer the question "what is a work," we will make an effort to trace some of the effects produced by merely introducing this problem into critical work. Pierre Bayard has shown that even in the case of the literary work, whose stable material nature and objective existence seem evident, "the work does not exist." It exists only in as far as it is reinvented by each critical text. Let me linger a bit longer on the first modality of invention Bayard has identified: the work of selection, or rather the choice of the excerpts the critic emphasizes and to which he or she confers a particular value, thereby recomposing a text that differs from that of other critics on the basis of the quotes selected.

For Bayard, it is a matter of making a difference between the *subject* and the *referent*: "Between two people discussing the work of Shakespeare the *subject* is absolutely the same provided they are using the same edition. But the *referent* of the discourse – which is to say the virtual world populated by the imaginary creatures with which they are conversing – is not equally so." And a bit further on: "The change in perspective is bound to a de-centering of the text toward the reader, who has become, to the detriment of the text, the measure and the unit."[10]

If the stability and the "reality" of the literary work can be a problem, what about that of the choreographic work, with its innumerable perennial variants? From a point of view not far from that of Susan Manning, for whom every description of a work is a reconstruction,[11] I am interested in the different ways in which the choreographic work is invented in various discourses, including that of identity. By treating the work as a cultural reality that is historically anchored but, paradoxically, transcends the moment of the representation, identitarian criticism presumes that the work contains a stable meaning, pre-codified by culture. This register of meaning is privileged through the exclusion of all others. Identitarian criticism addresses the work on the basis of its decodable aspects and an important part of this research lies in revealing these elements. (See, for example, how DeFrantz isolates the stylistic elements emphasized in African-American dance and compares them to other traits of classical ballet technique, codified by European culture, or how Marquié emphasizes the elements of the costumes and the visibility of the performer's male and female physiques; or again how Burt establishes the distortions operated in Lea Anderson's work in relationship to a certain norm of physical form.) The work is assumed to have an existence that transcends the various updates of successive performances (or occurrences). It is a carrier of a meaning that, if not univocal, is at least stable and for the most part verifiable, as it is organized on the basis of a code that goes beyond the work in itself. (By stable meaning, I mean that the relation between the work, assumed to be stable, and its interpretation, assumed to be verifiable, is stable; the possibility that the "meaning" produced is that of an identity which is fluid, mobile, and perhaps in the process of transformation is obviously not excluded.) As such, everything that has to do with the spectator's presence, interpretation, or individual "here and now" perception appears contingent. Comments on variations in interpretation, for example, are rare and are always considered peripheral or superficial in relationship to "the meaning of the work."

All of the theories of identity, at least those one encounters in the field of dance studies, rest on what Mark Franko calls the "contextualist" trend,[12] which considers dance as a product of a social and cultural context. Franko contrasts this trend (which I would risk defining dominant) to another that he identifies as "formalist," whose followers "favor movement analysis over all other critical methods."[13] This surprising shortcut has the merit of clarifying the theoretical and methodological issues that, in my opinion, implode when they are compared with *analyse d'oeuvre*. The trend of movement analysis, as it has developed in France, is above all a current of thought among dancers. What I mean by this is that it is a body of theoretical and practical knowledge developed first and foremost by and for dancers. The works of Hubert Godard, Odile Rouquet, Nathalie Schulmann, Dominique Praud, Emanuelle Lyon, and many of the other contemporary French movement analysts to which I am referring, are part of a long tradition of the theorization of movement elaborated by dancers such as Isadora Duncan, Rudolf von Laban, Doris Humphrey, Martha Graham, and many others, along with the tradition of movement studies now assembled under the name "somatics." This tradition presumes that movement *is knowledge* and not merely an object of knowledge or a passive vehicle of other fields of knowledge. This is not the place to discuss the summary introduction Franko has made on the trend of movement analysis in dance criticism – a current of which I myself am a part – but to try to reflect more profoundly on the apparent opposition he outlines between "contextualist" and "formalist."

The critical trend that Franko defines as "movement analysis," which is actually a phenomenological current that borrows its tools from movement analysis, considers the meaning of the work as bound to the dancer's and the spectator's experience *even* during the work. That is to say that it does not exclude the cultural dimension but, if necessary, includes it in the gestural praxis. One must therefore consider that there is also a "culture of feeling" and the different ways in which it appears. Vice versa, one must not assume that the gesture is impermeable or inaccessible to culture and the effects it produces. This current considers "meaning" as that which comes out of the encounter between the dancer's and the spectator's gesture in the present moment. This does not mean excluding the cultural and codified aspect, but taking into consideration, and at times giving priority to,[14] the aspect of the invention and exchange of gesture and thus of meaning here and now of the performance. In the same way, the spectator's task is considered not only as that of recognition (identification) and de-coding, but also as an individual effort in inventing and re-inventing the work, in the moment in which it is seized, and in the work of re-elaborating memory.[15]

The first current of thought (the "contextualists" according to Franko's terms) considers the work as something that has a stable existence of meaning that goes beyond its occurrences (beginning in particular from the relationships of the signifier/signified), and that refers to semiotic tools. The spectator's variations in perception, and thus in interpretation, are considered negligible, and the work, in so far as it is polysemous, is potentially *exhaustible* by critical discourse. This is the criticism Bayard qualifies as hermeneutic, in which the work of selection "is secondary with respect to the core of meaning the work already conceals and the critical approach has to know how to identify. A similar presupposition tends to unify the text and to put aside any authentic reflection of the referent."[16]

The second current of thought (the "formalists") considers the meaning as unstable, *produced* by the exchange between the dancer and spectator, which comes to modulate, or to transform, the stability of the codes otherwise put into play by the choreography. Here, the work exists solely in the variations of its occurrences and its meaning is mobile, always starting over again in the moment of the performance. Cultural codes and constant choreographic traits are no longer the only pertinent parameters but merely parameters among others. The work is considered as an ongoing process rather than a product, even in the case of what we could call "written work" or a work for which the choreography is, not necessarily notated, but fixed once and for all. "A relativist conception, based on the importance given to the referent, will not for this be foreign to all signification. It would seem however all the more de-multiplied to the extent the text is not put down once and for all as univocal and the idea itself of meaning is then profoundly transformed."[17]

Methods

The silence that separates these two points of view, these two ways of looking at the works, no longer seems insurmountable but concerns the disparity of the respective methodological tools. As previously noted, identitarian criticism draws from an ample theoretical and methodological corpus that has been developed and proved primarily outside of the field of dance. The phenomenology of dance, which takes a certain number of references from movement analysis, places the work of the dancer and the observer at the heart of its approach. What changes in the relationships made possible by these two points of view is the nature of the question posed, the status given to a certain number of parameters such as the dancer's and the observer's subjectivities (seen in one case as a negligible factor, in the other as an integral part of the work), and, of course, the methodologies employed. In other words, if the critique is an invention of the work, it is the methodological issues that make possible and visible the different modes of invention. The "work of selection" that Bayard describes for literary works is based on the selection of extracts or quotations from the work under analysis. In dance this question is even more crucial in as much as – of course – every dance work is first and foremost heterogeneous, composed of gestures, sounds, costumes, lights, and perhaps words or texts, as well as different layers. One can isolate its elements, for example, in function of the sequence (privileging certain moments of the work), or in function of the nature of the medium (gesture, music, costumes, lights, and so on), in function of aesthetic genres (assigning it to a choreographic or aesthetic style). The work can be translated into a story (see DeFrantz's analysis of Donald Byrd's *Nutcracker*). It can even be analyzed considering first and foremost its para-textual apparatus (declaration of the choreographer's intent, criticism, commentaries, programs) or intra-textual apparatus, as for example in Franko's analysis of *American Document*,[18] which rests essentially on the ballet's plot and the texts that accompany it. The question of the para-texts' status in analyzing dance works would actually merit a study of its own. Much too often, in fact, the discourses, texts, and critiques accompanying a work are taken as sufficient "proof" to justify interpretations of the work. From this point of view, Marquié's procedure, which compares the para-textual apparatus and the work, without presupposing their a priori convergence, is quite rare. Finally, the accent could be placed on the gestural dimension of the work, which is evidently the choice of movement analysis. Yet, even in this case, the way in which gesture is dissected can vary. Gesture is often described through a particular glossary: spatial figures (circles, diagonals, triangles, lines, and so forth), the names of repertoire steps (pirouette, arabesque, contraction, curve, and so on), or actions more or less effortlessly described (she lifts her hand and throws herself against him; he pushes her away, and so on). Movement analysis, on the contrary, as applied, for example, by Christine Roquet to works of dance,[19] is interested in the qualitative register of movement, with parameters such as the dynamosphere, gravitational shifts and, even more specifically, in the relationships between duet partners analyzed from the point of view of these qualitative parameters.

One understands that these variations in selection bring about important divergences in interpretation. How does the critical text organize the "identifications"; with which aspects of the work does it begin; and what criteria does it use? Can the question of masculine and feminine in a choreographic work only be grasped on the basis of conventional signs such as costumes or the relationship between the performer's and the character's gender (when there is a character)? If the analysis tries to approach the marks of "masculine" or "feminine" gesture, what norms of reference can it use? Is it possible to imagine a reading of gender based on the experience of gesture? Similarly, can the question of race or ethnicity in a work be read solely on the visible signs of skin color, for example, or by a terminology drawn from classical vocabulary, as DeFrantz proposes in analyzing Byrd's vocabulary of movement in contrast to what comes out of African-American tradition? Or, is the identity of a dancer and of a spectator (be they male or female) defined solely on the basis of traditionally delineated performer–audience territories, and is the reconfiguration of these domains enough to break down the boundaries between the two categories? The three case-studies by Burt, DeFrantz, and Marquié have a number of aspects in common. They have all chosen to interpret one or two choreographic works. They have organized their analyses on the basis of preliminary theoretical frameworks, the first two explicitly, the third more discreetly. They have also cut across, peripherally, the question of the relationships between theories of norm and theories of experience.

Norms, subversions, transgressions: what is a subversive work?

The identitarian question is always articulated around a project of political analysis: relationships of power, relationships with the norm. The question formulated for the *analyse d'oeuvre*, whatever the works may be, is always organized more or less in terms of adhesion to or subversion of these norms. Does the work comfort a certain number of patriarchal or racial stereotypes, or does it oppose them? The answer to this question presupposes two preliminary choices that are interdependent: first, the definition of the level on which these norms are considered to be expressed and legible and, second, the alleged nature of the relationship between the work and its audience.

In the culturalist hypotheses, one assumes that the audience identifies and de-codifies culturally clear signs – which does not exclude the fact that they are stratified, contradictory, and ambiguous – and that, in the end, it interprets the more or less consensual or at times subversive "message" of the work. These signs, more often than not visual or discursive, can also include an empirical aspect. This is clearly the aim of DeFrantz, who wants David Byrd's audience to recognize "black spirit" through the action, that is, the "perception of the fullness of gestural execution and the manifestation of spirit." Here, one assumes that the spectator shares something of the dancer's experience through phenomena defined as kinesthetic empathy, gravitational contagion, or trance.[20] It is not a matter of limiting the identification process to the register of the visible, but of attaching it to a culture, or to a codification, of the experience itself. While differences can be observed in the nature of the decipherable elements (which is to say in the workings of selection previously questioned), the work remains, in its relationship with the audience, a simple place of social practice. The dancers produce signs or traverse a culturally engrained experience of gravity, and the spectators decode them, all within a meta-structure of conventions. The existence of the work and the way it operates (from its production to its reception) are cultural products. Thus, the identitarian question passes first through an "identitarian making" of the work itself. To analyze the identitarian game in the choreographic work, one must first invent the work as a territorial geography implying different identities: that of gender (Marquié), that of race (DeFrantz), that of the dancer and of the spectator (Burt), or that of any of the other categories (classical/contemporary, high-brow/low-brow, child/adult, and so on). Paradoxically, therefore, the analyses of the transgressive or, on the contrary, the "conformist" nature of the work is based on the presupposition that the work is above all, if not solely, the product of these norms. The identitarian relationships will be analyzed as consensual, conflicting, transgressive, normative, and so on, but the initial and shared presupposition of these different possible interpretations is that the entire work is situated in the territorialized spaces of identities that exist independently of and beyond the work itself. The possible subversive nature of the work is thus subordinated to its inscription in the culture and in the norms of its identitarian relationships.

"This public observer conforms to a broader context; its perceptions of the work and its reactions to it are inserted into a more global logic that, in itself, has determined the conditions that led to such a work. The scheme thus seems to form a closed world, where risks are limited, a system without inner flaws in which the freedom of movement appears non-existent. In this case, it would be fairer to speak not so much of the work of art but of the show in the sense in which it was previously proposed. For, in these conditions, how could an artistic work just crop up, extract itself from an environment that predetermines it? According to this scheme, the work itself (choreographic or theatrical) conforms to the context that surrounds it."[21] In her Ph.D. dissertation on the relationships between the spatiality of choreographic work and the audience's make up, Julie Perrin demonstrates how one can think of the "community of the work" not as sociality that pre-exists and pre-determines the work, but as something constituted by the work itself. This does not mean that the work and its audience elude every norm and power relationship, but that it is not constituted solely by these norms. In other words, it is a matter of thinking of the work as a possible heterotopia, a space in which a "dis-identification" (which is to say a partial dissolution of these identitarian phenomena) can be put into play . . .

We have, therefore, on one hand, identitarian theories that only hold up under the condition that the work is considered a priori as a product of these identitarian norms and, on the other, works that are a possible place of escape from this normative world. Yet the emergence of a choreographic work cannot be totally predetermined by context, nor can it completely escape it. This tangle of the work's contextual predetermination and heterotopic nature does not pose problems from the perspective of the works themselves, but from the point of view of the theoretical formulas that attempt to possess it.

Conclusion

Examined in relationship to the contemporary context and from the perspective of *analyse d'oeuvre*, the question of identity crystallizes a theoretical issue that pervades dance studies: the status of gesture, of what is alive, and of perception in a given culture. As Burt and Franko remind us, the culturalists have rightly reproached phenomenology of universalizing experience and disregarding cultural differences. Reciprocally, it is possible to criticize a theoretical trend that fails to grasp, in the field of dance, that which clearly determines the singularity of the subject, or rather how gesture is experienced by the dancer and by whoever is watching, including the case in which the spectator is a critic. The *analyse d'oeuvre* is a privileged field of study to be taken on in a way that goes beyond this theoretical silence. Can experience be considered in cultural terms? Is there a code of feeling and how can it be analyzed? This path was initially opened by Merleau-Ponty's theory of the sensorial chiasms and furthered by Michel Bernard with the fourth chiasm, called para-sensorial, which makes every feeling contemporaneously an experience and an enunciation. Recent trends in historiography that attempt to construct history around sentiments, passions, and emotions follow this second route.[22]

This question of the relationship "from presence to presence" appropriate to every contemporary dance performance is the explicit theme of numerous works from the mid-1990s on.[23] Yet, even if it has become a *thematic* of recent works, it remains nonetheless at the core of every choreographic performance that is "modern and historical," "classical," "contemporary and neo-classical," and so on. Keeping in mind this aspect of the "presence," which is necessarily relational, unstable, and contextual, or, in other words, keeping in mind what is generally referred to as the dancers' *and* observers' interpretation (the re-writing of the instant of the work) prohibits treating choreographic works as objects, as tools, or even as illustrations of an identitarian theory or anything else. Keeping in mind the aspect of presence in dance studies (and not the "eternal present" as Franko suspects but a "cumulative" present that is also charged with history) is probably the node around which the predetermination and heterotopia of the work can be articulated or in which the identitarian geography does not prohibit historical or temporal fluidity. The aim of this sort of project is clearly one of an aesthetic order (understanding how the piece works in relationship to the audience), but it is also political, in the multiple meanings of this term as applied to dance. It is political because it imposes "an upheaval of the usual categories of thought"[24] and of perceptive organization. It is political because, for each work, as Perrin has shown, it invents a unique way of being together. But it is also political because it ceases to ignore the dancer–interpreter in his or her status of subject. Giving the work a stable meaning that transcends the different occurrences of its performances and the variations in the onlookers' perception means considering the work of the dancer–interpreter as a negligible quantity, as an instrument or vehicle, as one still often hears, of the "choreographer's thought." In short, it means basing an entire theory on the instrumentalization and the negation of the work without which the work would not be visible. This question seems indisputably political.

Notes

1 For a report on and an analysis of this project see I. Launay, 'Le don du geste', *Protée*, 2001, vol. 29, no. 2, pp. 85–98.
2 The research group of the dance department at the University of Paris VIII.
3 See for example the works of Sally Banes, Ann Daly, Ramsay Burt, Susan Foster, Susan Manning, and so on.
4 Alain Buffard quoted in H. Marquié, 'Dispositif trouble: when what is said is not what is shown', in this volume, p. 239.
5 Ibid., p. 254. There is another interpretation of this performance: see R. Huesca, 'Homme, danse et homosexualité', *Revue d'esthétique*, 2004, no. 45, pp. 139–51 [eds].
6 Reference is made here to the terminology introduced by Judith Butler. See in particular J. Butler, *Bodies That Matter. On the Discursive Limits of Sex*, London and New York: Routlege, 1993.
7 "[. . .] for [Sternberg] the pictorial space enclosed by the frame is paramount rather than the narrative or identification processes. While Hitchcock goes into the investigative side of voyeurism, Sternberg produces the ultimate fetish, taking it to the point where the powerful look of the male protagonist (characteristic of traditional narrative film) is broken in favor of the image or in direct erotic rapport with the spectator. The beauty of the woman as object and the screen space coalesce; she is no longer the bearer of guilt but a perfect product, whose body, stylized and fragmented by close-ups, is the content of the film and the direct recipient of the spectator's look. Sternberg plays down the illusion of screen depth; his screen tends to be one-dimensional, as light and shade, lace, steam, foliage, net, streamers, etc., reduce the visual field." See L. Mulvey, 'Visual Pleasure and Narrative Cinema', *Screen*, 1975, vol. 16, no. 3, p. 14.

8 The French term *analyse d'oeuvre* has been kept because it echoes its equivalents in other artistic fields. In France one talks of *analyse d'image*, *analyse de tableaux*, *analyse de film*, *analyse musicale*, *analyse littéraire*, and these sub-disciplines constitute an important basis for every theory of literature, film and visual arts.
9 See in particular the works of N. Goodman, *The Languages of Art*, Indianapolis, IN: Bobbs-Merrill, 1968; M. Guérin, *Qu'est-ce qu'une oeuvre*, Arles: Actes Sud, 1986; G. Genette, *L'œuvre de l'art. Immanence et trascendance*, Paris: Seuil, 1994; G. Genette, *L'oeuvre de l'art. La relation esthétique*, Paris: Seuil, 1997; B. Vouilloux, *Entre poétique et esthétique*, Paris: Belin, 2004. For a reflection on the status of the work in dance see F. Pouillaude, *Le désoeuvrement chorégraphique. Étude sur the notion d'oeuvre en danse*, Ph.D. dissertation, University of Lille III, 2006.
10 P. Bayard, *Enquête sur Hamlet. Le dialogue de sourds*, Paris: Éditions de Minuit, 2002, pp. 42–3.
11 See for example S. Manning, 'Introduction', in *Ecstasy and the Demon: Feminism and Nationalism in the Dances of Mary Wigman*, Berkeley, CA: University of California Press, 1993, pp. 1–14 (2nd edn *Ecstasy and the Demon: The Dances of Mary Wigman*, Minneapolis, MN: University of Minnesota Press, 2006).
12 See M. Franko, 'Dance and the Political: States of Exception', in this volume, p. 18.
13 Ibid.
14 For a rather unique example of oeuvre analysis centered on performance analyses see C. Roquet, *La scène amoureuse en danse. Codes, modes et normes de l'intercorporéité dans le duo chorégraphique*, Ph.D. dissertation, University of Paris VIII, 2002.
15 M. Bernard, *Esquisse d'une théorie de la perception du spectacle chorégraphique*, in M. Bernard, *De la création chorégraphique*, Pantin: Centre national de la danse, 2001, pp. 205–13. Suggested in some way in view of a reflection on the conditions of spectator's perception in dance. See also J. Perrin, *De l'espace corporel à l'espace public*, Ph.D. dissertation, University of Paris VIII, 2005.
16 Bayard, *Enquête sur Hamlet*, p. 43.
17 Ibid.
18 M. Franko, 'L'utopie antifasciste: American Document de Martha Graham', in C. Rousier (ed.), *Être ensemble. Figures de la communauté en danse depuis le XXème siècle*, Pantin: Centre national de la danse, 2003.
19 Roquet, *La scène amoureuse en danse.*
20 The hypothesis of kinesthetic empathy (or of John Martin's metakinesis) or of gravitational contagion (Hubert Godard), which provides the basis of numerous ideas on the workings of the relationship between dance works and the audience, is being revived today, sustained by the growing interest in phenomena of perception and sensorial chiasms in the cognitive and neuro sciences.
21 See Perrin, *De l'espace corporel à l'espace public*, p. 63.
22 See for example A. Corbin, *Le miasme et la jonquille. L'odorat et l'imaginaire social, XVIIIème et XIXème siècles*, Paris: Flammarion, 1986, or A. Vincent-Buffault, *Histoire des larmes, XVIIIème–XIXème siècles*, Paris: Rivages, 1986.
23 For an analysis of this issue see F. Pouillaude, 'Scène et contemporanéité', *Rue Descartes*, 2004, no. 44, pp. 8–20.
24 See Perrin, *De l'espace corporel à l'espace public*, p. 63.

Name index

Yes? No! Maybe . . . Seductive Ambiguity in Dance

by Emilyn Claid

Covering fifty years of British dance, from Margot Fonteyn to innovative contemporary practitioners such as Wendy Houstoun and Nigel Charnock, *Yes? No! Maybe . . .* is an innovative approach to performing and watching dance.

Emilyn Claid brings her life experience and interweaves it with academic theory and historical narrative to create a dynamic approach to dance writing.

Using the 1970s revolution of new dance as a hinge, Claid looks back to ballet and forward to British independent dance which is new dance's legacy. She explores the shifts in performer–spectator relationships, and investigates questions of subjectivity, absence and presence, identity, gender, race and desire using psychoanalytical, feminist, postmodern, post-structuralist and queer theoretical perspectives.

Artists and practitioners, professional performers, teachers, choreographers and theatre-goers will all find this book an informative and insightful read.

ISBN: 978–0–415–37156–8 (hbk)
ISBN: 978–0–415–37247–3 (pbk)